Materializing Europe

Materializing Europe

Transnational Infrastructures and the Project of Europe

Edited by

Alexander Badenoch
*Lecturer in Media and Culture Studies,
Utrecht University*

and

Andreas Fickers
*Associate Professor Comparative Media History,
Maastricht University*

palgrave
macmillan

First published 2010 by
PALGRAVE MACMILLAN

Palgrave Macmillan in the UK is an imprint of Macmillan Publishers Limited, registered in England, company number 785998, of Houndmills, Basingstoke, Hampshire RG21 6XS.

Palgrave Macmillan in the US is a division of St Martin's Press LLC, 175 Fifth Avenue, New York, NY 10010.

Palgrave Macmillan is the global academic imprint of the above companies and has companies and representatives throughout the world.

Palgrave® and Macmillan® are registered trademarks in the United States, the United Kingdom, Europe and other countries.

ISBN: 978–0–230–23289–1 hardback

This book is printed on paper suitable for recycling and made from fully managed and sustained forest sources. Logging, pulping and manufacturing processes are expected to conform to the environmental regulations of the country of origin.

A catalogue record for this book is available from the British Library.

Library of Congress Cataloging-in-Publication Data

    Materializing Europe : transnational infrastructures and the project of Europe / edited by Alexander Badenoch, Andreas Fickers.
      p. cm.
    ISBN 978–0–230–23289–1 (hardback)
    1. Infrastructure (Economics) – Europe. 2. Europe – Economic integration.
 I. Badenoch, Alexander, 1971– II. Fickers, Andreas.
HC240.9.C3M38 2010
388.094—dc22   2010012508

10 9 8 7 6 5 4 3 2 1
19 18 17 16 15 14 13 12 11 10

Printed and bound in Great Britain by
CPI Antony Rowe, Chippenham and Eastbourne

Contents

Part III   Europe between Projects and Projections

Illustrations

Tables

Figures

Acknowledgements

The chapters for this book took shape during two international workshops, one at Rolduc Abbey, Kerkrade in April 2006 and the other at Eindhoven in April 2007, both under the auspices of the Transnational Infrastructure and the Rise of Contemporary Europe (TIE) project based at the Technical University of Eindhoven. This project is supported by the Netherlands Organization for Scientific Research under the VICI scheme, awarded to Professor Johan Schot (dossier number 277-53-001). In addition to the authors here, we would like to thank participants Karin Bijsterveld, Paul Edwards, Pascal Griset, Per Högselius, Paul Josephson, Arne Kaijser, Andreas Kunz, Gijs Mom, Ekaterina Nikova, Tim Richardson, Judith Schueler and Nina Wormbs for their insights during the discussions surrounding the volume. In addition, we would like to thank Tabitha van Assem, Lidwien Hollanders, Jan Korsten, Donna Mehos, Pierre-Yves Saunier, Geert Verbong, and all of the members of the Tensations Fan Club for their support and devotion.

Contributors

Irene Anastasiadou is a postdoctoral researcher at the School of Innovation Sciences at the Technical University of Eindhoven. Her PhD thesis, *In Search of a Railway Europe: Transnational Railways Developments in Interwar Europe*, was completed as part of the TIE project in 2009.

Alexander Badenoch teaches in the Department of Media and Culture Studies at Utrecht University. He is the author of *Voices in ruins: West German radio across the 1945 divide* (Palgrave 2008) and editor of the online virtual exhibit 'Europe, Interrupted' at www.inventingeurope.eu.

Barbara Bonhage has written extensively on banking and finance infrastructures during and after the Second World War as PhD and postdoc at the Swiss Federal Institute of Technology (ETH), Zurich, Switzerland.

Cornelis Disco teaches at the Department of Philosophy of Science and Technology at the University of Twente. He has published extensively on wet infrastructures and water management and currently heads a research network on Industrial Commons in Europe.

Andreas Fickers is Associate Professor for Comparative Media History at Maastricht University. He recently edited (together with Jonathan Bignell, Reading University) *A European Television History* (Wiley-Blackwell 2008). He works on the cultural history of communication technologies in a comparative European perspective.

Christian Henrich-Franke is Akademischer Rat at the Institut für Europäische Regionalforschung at the University of Siegen.

Patrick Kammerer is a doctoral student (University of Zurich), completing his PhD on the development of mobile telephony, and currently scientific assistant at the Research Center for Social and Economic History (University of Zurich).

Eda Kranakis is Associate Professor at the University of Ottawa. She is author of *Constructing a Bridge*: *An Exploration of Engineering Culture, Design, and Research in Nineteenth-Century France and America* and is currently researching the history of European airspace as a commons with the aim of tracing the role of technology in its evolution and transnational governance.

Dirk van Laak is Professor of History at Justus-Liebig University in Giessen. He is the author of a number of books exploring infrastructures, technocracy and imperial projects, including *Weisse Elefanten. Anspruch und Scheitern* *technischer Großprojekte im 20. Jahrhundert* and *Imperiale Infrastruktur. Deutsche Planungen für eine Erschließung Afrikas 1880 bis 1960.*

Leonard Laborie completed his PhD, *La France, l'Europe et l'ordre international des communications (1865–1959) (France, Europe, and the international order of communications (1865–1959))*, in 2006 at the University of Paris IV Sorbonne (CRHI, Irice).

Vincent Lagendijk completed his PhD, *Electrifying Europe: The power of Europe in the construction of electricity networks* (2008), as part of the TIE project at the Technical University of Eindhoven, and is currently a postdoc on the ESF-Eurocores project 'Europe Goes Critical'. He has recently been awarded a three-year research grant for his project 'Transnationalizing the TVA'.

Dick van Lente is Assistant Professor for cultural history of modern societies, Erasmus Universiteit Rotterdam, and has published widely on popular perceptions of technology, most recently atomic energy.

Suzanne Lommers is completing her PhD as part of the 'Transnational Infrastructures and the Rise of Contemporary Europe (TIE)' project at the Technical University of Eindhoven on the development of European broadcasting networks before the Second World War.

Frank Schipper works as a postdoc researcher at Technical University of Eindhoven. His project 'Exploring the International Dimensions of Infrastructures: A Historical Perspective' studies the governance of cross-border electricity, railway and telegraph flows in Europe in the nineteenth and twentieth centuries as part of the Next Generation Infrastructures programme.

Johan Schot is Professor of Social History of Technology at Eindhoven University of Technology. He was leader of the National Research Program on the History of Technology in the Netherlands in the 20th century and more recently leader of the 'Transnational Infrastructures and the Rise of Contemporary Europe (TIE)' project. His research work and publications include history of technology, science and technology studies, innovation and diffusion theory, constructive technology assessment, environmental management, and policy studies.

Erik van de Vleuten is assistant professor at the School of Innovation Sciences at the Technical University of Eindhoven. He is editor, with Arne Kaijser, of *Networking Europe: transnational infrastructures and the shaping of Europe* (2006) and is currently the co-organizer of the ESF–Eurocores collaboration 'Europe goes critical' on critical infrastructures in Europe.

Waqar Zaidi teaches at the Centre for the History of Science, Technology and Medicine, Imperial College, London, where he recently completed his PhD on science and technology and liberal internationalism in France, the United States and Great Britain, 1920–45.

Introduction

Europe Materializing? Toward a Transnational History of European Infrastructures

Alexander Badenoch and Andreas Fickers

After a series of false starts, a 'Museum of Europe' recently opened in Brussels, albeit as a temporary exhibition marking fifty years since the Treaties of Rome. The museum, which is still seeking a permanent home, is dedicated to building a sense of common European identity through a narrative of European history.[1] Part of the museum's proposed permanent exhibit is devoted to a series of active maps, the last of which, representing European history after 1945, is in a room fashioned to resemble a railway waiting room. Visitors can gaze up to a moving map, which, like the flipping departures board 'in a large European railway station', shows the 'arrival' of nations in Europe. 'After the centuries of Unity through faith and the decades of Unity through the Enlightenment [represented in other maps], the Unity through the project evolves year for year, as shown by a digital counter.'[2] While this narrative of Europe's history is at best questionable, the metaphor of the train for the project of Europe is by no means inept.[3] If anything, it is too apt: while it is meant to support an optimistic story of steady modernization, the associations between Europe and material networks, particularly trains, are not so easily channelled. Observers in this waiting room might just as easily think of other trains, and darker sides of European history and modernity: the trains that never arrived, such as the pre-war Berlin–Baghdad Railway or many sections of the German-Dutch Betuwe line project, never stopped, leaving certain towns and places off the map of 'European' progress, or, like the trains in the brutal machinery of the Holocaust, never returned. Furthermore, visitors might easily feel that watching powerlessly as a mechanical process unfolds is all too emblematic of the European Union's 'democratic deficit'. Indeed, it would not be the first time that the EU was associated with a runaway train. Such symbolism, complete with all its pregnant silences and ambiguities, is so broadly resonant because it also reflects a common-sense, if ambiguous, reality: there are, and have been, human-built material links between nations and across borders in Europe which have pre-dated, accompanied and transcended the 'official' processes of political and economic integration begun after the

Second World War. The strong and varied metaphorical resonances point at once to the promise and the problems of unravelling the history of these technologies of connection and the role they have played in shaping the spaces, institutions and experiences of Europe. To put the matter simply: it seems obvious *that* technological infrastructures are related to projects of European unification, but it is far from clear *how*.

In many ways, technological infrastructures are indeed the essence of European integration. In material terms, they form the physical basis for transnational flows of people, goods and services. Already with the advent of railways and telegraphs in the nineteenth century, new networks crossed national boundaries in and beyond Europe, through which nations, empires and social groups expanded, renegotiated and transformed relations with each other. In addition to material structures, a number of institutions and regimes were formed to build and govern them. These bodies functioned beyond the national level and often at some remove from arenas of formal politics.[4] At the same time, technology formed an important part of political thought among many diplomats and politicians.[5] Many were defined as European institutions, either explicitly through their names and official remits (such as the United Nations Economic Commission for Europe) or implicitly through their actual spheres of activity, such as the International Union of Railways or the Alliance Internationale de Tourisme. To understand the way such institutions and the infrastructures they governed were constituted through expert knowledge, working practices and visions, it is important further to understand infrastructures at a discursive level. In particular, discourses and ideas of internationalism, which became increasingly interwoven with ideas of technological modernization, became a common feature of such expert communities and formed a link between them and broader movements for a united Europe. Beyond these institutional frameworks, infrastructures have also played a key role in the broader symbolic vocabulary of European integration in a number of spheres. From electricity systems in the 1920s, to coal trains in the 1950s, through to the gateways and bridges on Euro notes in the present decade, infrastructures have been mobilized repeatedly in broader spheres as symbols and metaphors for broader forms of modernization, integration and co-operation.[6] At the same time, the rhetoric of a united Europe, particularly in combination with narratives of progress, has played – and continues to play – an important part in pushing forward major infrastructural interventions. In short, material infrastructures have helped to shape a number of spaces and ways in which people have moved through, talked about and experienced 'Europe'. With this volume, we present a series of case studies that explore the material, institutional and discursive complexities involved in building and using transnational infrastructures in Europe throughout the twentieth century.

By bringing infrastructures and Europe into the same frame, this volume has three interrelated aims. First and foremost, by using material infrastructures to guide a transnational approach to European history, it reveals to historians of modern Europe underexplored dimensions of European integration. This approach allows us to explore empirically the transnational movements of things, people and ideas that lie at the heart of most projects of Europe. In so doing, we critically re-examine and fruitfully redefine 'integration' to include longer-term processes and a broader range of institutions. These chapters bring to light a number of actors, institutions and forums not normally considered in formal histories of integration, which allow us to historicize and contextualize the European Union's role as one actor in a larger and longer-term ensemble of processes that have integrated – and fragmented – societies in Europe. Opening up and exploring these processes further presses the history of technology's polemic agenda of challenging overly deterministic accounts of technology's role in shaping society. In an era when technological projects play an increasing role in the construction and governance of European spaces, simplistic stories about technology and Europe are in greater circulation than ever. Second, building on the insights of transnational history to focus on the European scale, this book productively exposes limitations in frameworks of nationalization and globalization, as well as more localized frameworks of urban history, which have dominated historical approaches to infrastructures up to now. While studies aimed at the national level have rightly stressed the role of infrastructures in projects of nation state consolidation, histories of globalization have further stressed the role of transport and communication infrastructures in capitalist expansion and imperial projects.[7] By focusing at the level of Europe, we are able to view these and other processes together and show the complex ways in which they are related. Finally, individually and collectively, the chapters assembled here offer conceptual tools, drawing on a range of disciplines, for understanding this history. But, before introducing some of these concepts, we will first locate this book within the broader landscape of literature and research in the field of European integration history, transnational history and European history of technology.

Broadening the scope of Europe and technology

The sense that Europe is related to infrastructural projects is common to both academic and lay observers alike. The increasing expansion of the European Union into various 'European' spaces and infrastructure policy arenas on the one hand, and the persistence of simple and overdetermined narratives of technology, modernization and European integration on the other, make detailed historical exploration of these topics timely, if not urgent.[8] This realization has led recently to the establishment of a research agenda based largely among historians of technology, which has sought to place such questions at the centre of scientific research.[9] Within this broader research agenda, material infrastructures and networks such as roads, railways, electricity grids, waterways and so on, long viewed as some of the most important aspects and engines of modernization processes, necessarily play an important role. The current volume is the product of a research project embedded within this framework, devoted to a long-term historical analysis of the building of transnational infrastructures in Europe in their material, institutional and discursive complexity.[10] Building on core concerns of the history of technology, this project draws on and speaks to key ideas in transnational history, European integration studies and mobility studies, among others, to open up challenging new ways of coming to grips with the historical project of Europe.

As van der Vleuten and Kaijser show in a recent review of the historiography of infrastructures and Europe, the building and use of material networks has usually been a sidelight at best in much of the grander historiography of Europe.[11] Where the role of such networks is mentioned, it is very often in terms that acknowledge their role in transforming society, but far less often to offer a detailed analysis of the complex and contested processes by which such structures came about. While studies on the processes of modernization and globalization in the social sciences have long noted the importance of such structures, analysis of the contingent processes that have gone into the construction, linking and maintenance of such networks has been of secondary concern. Concurrent developments in a number of disciplines seem poised to change this situation and open up a number of avenues of inquiry, to which the current volume will speak.

First and foremost, this volume aims to offer new perspectives on the history of European integration. As Jost Dülffer has shown in a recent historiographical essay on European integration literature, this literature is characterized by a number of prominent master narratives, reflecting the different stages or periods of scholarly debates on the aims and goals of contemporary historiography of Europe after the Second World War, which is generally seen as the crucial point of reference for the start of a new era of European integration initiatives.[12] Following Dülffer, much of European integration historiography is characterized by a master narrative that he somewhat provocatively labels the 'Christmas story' of European integration in allusion to the German tradition of lighting candles every Sunday of an advent wreath. This 'Christmas story' 'narrates the expansion of European wreath from six to nine, to twelve, fifteen and now at present twenty-seven states', reflecting a teleological master narrative which 'accepts delays, stand-stills, relaunches and – maybe – also crisis'.[13] This Christmas story of European integration, based on 'a snow ploughing after the [political] events' and dominated by sectorial studies reflecting the emergence of European institutions and agencies, has of course been challenged by authors such as Alan Milward and John Gillingham, who have developed prominent alternative narratives, stressing the persistence of national interests and criticizing the excessive bureaucratization of the political institutions. According to Dülffer, there are at least four other limitations to the 'Christmas story' approach. First, there is a neglect of institutions other than the core political institutions such as the European Coal and Steel Community (ECSC), the European Economic Union (EEU) or the actual European Union in its different constellations. Second, he detects a neglect of the role of the United States as crucial actor in the integration process. Third, he criticizes the under-representation of Eastern Europe, especially the USSR, as important players in a Cold War that formed the general political frame for the European integration process. And finally, Dülffer emphasizes the urgent need for a broader cultural approach to the European integration process under the label of 'Europeanization' as represented – for example – in the works of Hartmut Kaelble.[14]

We take Dülffer's description of the state of the art in European integration literature as an open invitation to demonstrate the various ways in which the present volume speaks to these lacunae and in which ways it offers – at least partially – new insights and perspectives in European integration history. First, the volume offers several chapters dealing with institutions or sectors largely neglected by the European integration literature. Second, several articles emphasize the role of the United States as instigator or perceived threat – or both – in such processes. Third, the volume offers – both in the introduction and in several chapters – a critical reflection of the cultural dimension of European infrastructures and institutions. Finally, all chapters are inspired by a transnational perspective on European integration, which not only stresses the integrative effects of European infrastructures, but also underlines the inherent tensions of fragmentation and de-linking – a topic not addressed at all by Dülffer.

This book opens new avenues into the study of European integration by taking a transnational approach to the study of infrastructures. The term 'transnational' itself has a long, complex and contested history, and its meanings are far from settled.[15] From these ongoing debates there are several key points we take up in this volume. First, we embrace the relatively broad definition of transnational history as that which concerns itself with flows over national borders. As Pierre-Yves Saunier argues, '[i]t means goods, it means people, it means ideas, words, capital, might, and institutions.'[16] Second, we consider this loose definition of 'going transnational' as a means of sharpening empirical focus; approaching European infrastructures as transnational problems means using them as guides to charting as precisely as possible the flows and limitations of materials, actors and discourses.[17] Third, we embrace the 'national' in the term, in so far as it allows us not only to re-contextualize the role of nation states, which are undoubtedly important actors in the period this volume charts, but also to think precisely about other categories such as the 'global' or the 'European'. A glance into the history of infrastructures quickly reveals how the circulation of things, people and knowledge has only ever been partially circumscribed by nation states. Many major networking projects, from railways to electricity to broadcasting, began as private, often international, initiatives fuelled in part by the transnational circulation of technical knowledge and capital. The establishment of state monopolies over infrastructures was either soon accompanied or even preceded by international regulatory bodies, either intergovernmental organizations, such as the International Telegraph Union (ITU, founded 1865), or non-governmental, such as the International Council on Large Electrical Systems (CIGRE, founded 1921) and the International Broadcasting Union (IBU, founded 1925).[18] Obviously nation states are relevant to the history of these processes, but taking a transnational approach allows us to see them as embedded in broader processes in which they are not necessarily the main actors, but nevertheless exercise power and agency in new ways.[19] We take the same impulse that has led to the fruitful decentring and contextualizing of the nation to develop a historiography of European integration that decentres and contextualizes the European Union and its predecessors as one entity and process among many others. Transnational infrastructures are a prime location for such an agenda because they existed prior to the formal processes of European integration. Furthermore, even after the process began, the institutions responsible for networking Europe and governing such systems long stood outside the notice of such processes. The essays in this volume by Schipper et al. and Johan Schot in particular place these institutions in the wider framework of international organizations, both intergovernmental and non-governmental, that mark one of the key fields of transnational history research.[20]

In an article laying out the initial agenda for this project, Thomas J. Misa and Johan Schot have suggested that the notion of European integration might be usefully expanded beyond the political, economic and cultural processes set formally in motion after the Second World War. Instead, they argue, we should include what they call 'hidden integration' – that is, hidden from the gaze of formal European integration studies because it points to processes that occurred partly independently of the political, economic and cultural processes officially taken up under the rubric of integration, but have nonetheless played a profound role within all these processes.[21] In opening up 'integration' to include broader processes, they suggest that we must also be alert to the processes of fragmentation, de-linking and disintegration that have also been, and will continue to be, evident, and to some extent inherent, in such projects.[22] These processes of linking and de-linking have been at the heart of the recent volume *Networking Europe*, edited by Arne Kaijser and Erik van der Vleuten.[23] In that volume, authors describe the development of a number of projects, beginning with the advent of railway and telegraph networks. The authors concentrate on the construction of systems, and mainly highlight national actors who have created, or sought to create, networks that operated across national boundaries in international, bilateral and also unilateral processes.[24] Our book is intended to build further on this agenda by placing 'Europe' more problematically at the centre of its inquiry. Where the authors of the previous volume have highlighted transnational processes *in* Europe (whilst being careful not to essentialize it), we ask what roles particular notions and spaces of Europe have played in the construction, use and/or failure of various material systems. What visions and projects of Europe have such networks and the processes of their construction made visible? How have material structures shaped practices and definitions of Europe?

Attending to these issues historically will add to the increasing scholarly attention being paid to technological infrastructures in a broad range of disciplines in the humanities and social sciences as they come to grips with the current spaces of Europe and beyond. Most specifically, this speaks to the emerging 'new mobilities paradigm' across a broad range of disciplines, which has focused attention on various systems that have mobilized – and moored – people, things and images, and how these mobilities and moorings have transformed the various spaces and times of interaction.[25] Indeed, this paradigm claims as a core research agenda 'an analysis of the relation between mobility systems and infrastructural moorings, especially as pertains to the rescaling and restructuring of spatiality under different regimes of economic regulation and state and urban governance'.[26] An important part of this emerging focus, one that is well in keeping with our agenda of understanding the processes of linking and de-linking, is the growing insistence on understanding the power dynamics of relative mobility: *who* and *what* may move in relation to which 'fixed' people and places. As the EU steps increasingly into the role of technical expert, so, too, are scholars beginning to take up the challenge of understanding the ways in which technologies are increasingly becoming part of the politics of the EU.[27] Recent work on planning at the European level has shed important light on the role of infrastructures in shaping EU policy.[28] Particularly as the notion of 'network Europe' gains currency in examining recent configurations of the European Union, a more thorough understanding of the complex processes of building and using transnational networks in Europe over a broader period of time can help to construct critical genealogies of such projects in order to capture their novelty as well as revealing strong continuities.[29] As Ginette Verstraete notes, artists are beginning to draw upon multiple alternative histories of transnational mobility to query current EU infrastructural agendas.[30] Though our tools and goals might differ, surely there is room for transnational historians to follow.

The 'Europe/technology uncertainty principle' and the question of scale

As promising a site as material infrastructures are for exploring European stories, they present a number of challenges as well. Infrastructures are, once embedded, nearly invisible but also, as Dirk van Laak notes, possess 'a signifying power of sometimes utopian quality'.[31] They are deeply political and yet often appear to follow 'neutral' technological principles. Trying to come to grips with the connections between infrastructures and Europe, one is quickly faced with what seems to be a paradox, one that came to the fore in many discussions surrounding the essays collected here, which we call, with playful allusion to Werner Heisenberg, the *Europe/technology uncertainty principle*. Put simply: the more one explores the grand aims, spatial visions and contested projects of Europe that inform the building and mediate the use of transnational systems, the more the unique material aspects of the systems fade from view. On the reverse side, the closer one comes to understanding the technologies of connection, that is, the mechanisms, standards, protocols and conventions that allow systems to connect and interoperate, the 'European' aspects soon become nebulous, if apparent at all. The questions remain as to what makes a system 'European', and what work 'Europe' actually did or does in its creation and/or operation.

Upon closer inspection, this principle is not so much a paradox as a conflation of two different, but closely linked, historical processes that intersect within infrastructures. The 'Europe' side of the principle looks to the mobilizations and appropriations of technologies for a number of projects of Europe. We argue in this book that the formal processes of economic and political integration normally understood under the term 'European integration' must be seen as one among many such projects. The 'technology' side describes the proliferation of systems, standards and practices that are part of broader processes of globalization and modernization processes more generally, but which also channel mobilities through European spaces specifically. These twin processes are also full of contradictions. Projections of Europe often cover over disjunctures of systems and spaces, as they do in tourist maps showing smooth European networks, even across the 'Iron Curtain', or in the experiences of cosmopolitan air tourists between the World Wars. In other cases, technological systems are often closely integrated in spite of sharp political or economic divisions in spheres, largely because they operate outside the notice of those spheres. The League of Nations' Organization for Communications and Transport, for example, was in many ways more effective than the body's political committees, and was able not only to achieve international co-operation but also to establish general regimes for negotiation.[32]

The dynamics of our so-called 'uncertainty principle' become most apparent when we try to understand them at macro scale, which is the particular 'transnational problem' this volume takes up. Chapter authors were given two basic guidelines: they should explore empirically the processes of building and/or using transnational infrastructures, and how these processes related to the shaping, definition, experiences and practices of Europe in the twentieth century. Furthermore, studies should not be based around national case studies but rather should focus on infrastructure developments at the European scale. The task of studying 'infrastructures at European scale' is, of course, not straightforward. Precisely because it lacks the rigid territorial boundaries and more or less centralized governing institutions of nation states, 'Europe' is what might be called a notoriously inaccurate scale for academic inquiry, particularly when studied over any sort of longer time period. Assuming that 'Europe' is – and always has been – a discursive construction, the problem begins with the very definition of Europe. As Achim Landwehr and Stefanie Stockhorst have shown, the concept of Europe has been an object of continuously negotiated meaning for various aims.[33] On all these dimensions – religious, spatial, political and historical – there are multiple definitions of where – or what – Europe is.[34] We think that Europe might best be characterized as a never-ending story, or – in the words of the German sociologist Richard Münch – as an ongoing project.[35] Like the process of western modernization, so too the process of European integration – hidden or visible, unintended or planned – was and will be a highly contested and conflict-riddled procedure.

Taking up the challenge of the uncertainty principle, we must ask in each case whether, when, for whom and to what extent 'Europe' is a matter of scaling up from national and/or regional processes, or simply a projected 'space of compensation' for processes of collective self-reassurances or a 'horizon of expectation' for transnational identity constructions.[36] The always already problematic scale of Europe is a constructive site for a more precise interrogation of other, more essentialized, scales of the 'national' and the 'global', and enable us to grasp their dynamics and problems more concretely and more precisely.[37] At the same time, a transnational approach to studying infrastructures, as we propose here, can help us to understand stories of Europe that transcend issues of scale. As Pierre-Yves Saunier reminds us, the promise of the transnational lies not in considering it as

> another scale located near the top of the nested scales, but rather a foray that cut[s] through levels and partly shatter[s] their conception as distinct entities. Accordingly, the transnational perspective allows a direct window onto the circulations and connections whose actors and structures seize these different social spheres, simultaneously or regardless of their 'nested' order.[38]

This is particularly the case in considering 'European integration'. A transnational focus on infrastructures does not merely add more threads to the already fraught weave of European integration, defined as a political process beginning after the Second World War; in fact, it challenges the very definition of that process while opening several potentially fruitful avenues for addressing that challenge. From an external perspective, studying the material spread and use of infrastructures provides one means of investigating the extent, the limits and the uses of systems that pass for European. From the point of view of network design and planning, for example, Turkey (at least as far as Istanbul) has been more closely involved in many 'European' networks than many nations whose 'European-ness' has been far less the subject of debate.[39] Moreover, as Dirk van Laak's chapter in this volume shows, the imperial logics at work in early cross-border infrastructure development argued against a notion of Europe as a natural unit of infrastructural connection. In the wake of the two World Wars, Europe came increasingly to be seen as an unruly administrative unit that could be addressed with similar technocratic projects of spatial reordering.

By looking to realms of international and transnational co-operation that are overlooked in historical accounts that focus on the nation state, the studies here thus also highlight new power dynamics between institutions, nations and individuals. Following the processes of infrastructural development can give us valuable insights into the extent to which spaces have been re-territorialized, and how. As Patrick Kammerer's essay here shows, the emergence and recognition of a protected European market space played a vital role in the struggle over standards for mobile telephony. At the same time, following the institutions and long-term plans for infrastructure building in Europe also reveals that many of the present biases toward Western Europe in the processes of formal European integration have predecessors from before the World Wars. To a certain extent, following these transnational actors has necessarily carried this geographical bias over into this book. However, this allows us to cast a precise eye on how power was exerted within these technical forums and see how apparently less powerful or 'central' nations and actors were able to use them to exert specific forms of power, often by softening their own territorial regimes to better channel infrastructural flows. Furthermore, by opening up the definition of integration, we also created the groundwork for exploring integrative processes from other regions and regimes, particularly those of Central and Eastern Europe.[40]

It is also important to recognize that infrastructures pose their own challenges of definition and scale. They are often understood, both in some academic discourse and everyday common sense, as hard-wired structures that slowly evolve, interlink and expand – and occasionally decay.[41] But they also present a far more protean face to users and academic observers alike. Their very definition proves problematic, if we accept that infrastructural systems are composed as much of institutions, routines and discursive practices as of material artefacts. Furthermore, the linkages of multiple systems, such as railways and electrical systems, or the growing links between broadcasting and road systems, make it difficult to define where a single 'infrastructure' starts and stops.[42] As Paul Edwards suggests, infrastructures are most easily defined negatively, as those systems without which modern life does not function.[43] This means that infrastructures can never be defined simply in material terms of what they *are*, but only in terms of what they *do*, and as such, they can only be understood in terms of the social structures and cultural meanings in which they function.

Edwards fruitfully argues that infrastructures can be – and indeed must be – studied at multiple scales to fully grasp their often contradictory dynamics.[44] Dramatic change at one scale often goes unnoticed at higher or lower scales. On the other hand, particularly at major nodes or linking points such as the Channel Tunnel, the Öresund bridge or the Gotthardt Tunnel, the presence of local, national, 'European' and global systems becomes visible simultaneously, in often problematic relation to each other.[45] Among urban historians, infrastructures have long provided a means of tracing the complex interconnections and power relations of the city.[46] Indeed, as Graham and Marvin have pointed out, such systems can also 'splinter' the very cities, nations or continents they appear to hold together.[47] It follows from this that, if we take 'Europe' as an actor category, the various transnational networks that crisscross, intersect and help to define it cannot be treated any differently. To suggest this does not downplay the importance, the obduracy or what Bruno Latour would call the 'agency' of material systems in shaping social relations, practices and spaces.[48] Nor does it de-emphasize the intersections between such systems and the struggles for power over and through them. On the contrary, it calls us to examine precisely these issues, but it insists that we also consider a broader range of actors (human and non-human), arenas and struggles if we are to capture the 'European' dimensions of infrastructures. The building of new technologies has often been accompanied by visions of connectivity and social transformation that went well beyond the boundaries of both nations and contemporary technological and/or economic feasibility. At the same time, many infrastructural 'networks' would not have been considered as such by engineers at all, but were disparate systems that were only 'linked' by regimes of use and representation, such as tourism.[49] Following such processes gives us insight into the way that transnational networks have been appropriated and made to signify in terms of Europe.

The goal of this volume is not to provide a 'Copenhagen interpretation' of this problem, that is, to present an overarching model for explaining the complex dynamics of infrastructures and European integration.[50] Indeed, we would argue that the shifting contexts, scales and processes we describe here would preclude such models, and that the varying approaches of our authors would rapidly undermine the effort. Instead, we seek here to highlight important sites where these complex dynamics become apparent, and show how multidisciplinary inquiry can begin to come to terms with them historically by holding them in tension with one another. With this in mind, we propose here two basic concepts for coming to terms with this challenge: *mediating interfaces* and *events*. We conceive of these as frameworks of time and space that allow us to bring the stories of technology and of Europe into the same narrative frame. In laying out these concepts, our goal is not merely to introduce the chapters assembled here, but also to make a programmatic call, together with our assembled authors, for work that will go even further in untangling the stories of technological infrastructures and Europe.

Infrastructures as mediating interfaces

Infrastructures mediate. They are structures 'in between' that allow things, people and signs to travel across space by means of more or less standardized paths and protocols for conversion or translation. Thinking of infrastructures as *mediating interfaces*, that is, as points of interaction and translation on material, institutional and discursive levels allows us to get to the heart of the dynamics we seek to capture. Points of mediation at the material level can be found in 'gateways' between systems, such as the standardized shipping container (developed in part through international organizations such as the International Union of Railways) or the variable-axle train (recently developed to solve the long-standing difference in railway gauge between French and Spanish railways), which allow incompatible systems to be linked and expanded.[51] Such gateways, as Edwards et al. remind us, cannot be seen as 'merely' material, but rather 'as combining a technical solution with a social choice, i.e. a standard, both of which must be integrated into existing users' communities of practice'.[52] In other words, such material mediation almost always requires social or institutional *mediators*, which we can understand as the institutions and individuals who work among those institutions to govern and shape infrastructural use.[53] Not all system mediators are those who build and govern systems; actors such as advertisers, educational bodies and consumer groups have often played important roles in shaping the design, meaning and use of infrastructures.[54] Finally, we may conceive of infrastructures themselves as *media* in the common-sense understanding of the word, as systems that structure relations and transmit images and signs across distances. Railways, for example, surround travellers with signs that frame travel in terms of state authority (insignias of national railways), class, national landscapes, and so on.[55] These aspects are not peripheral but central and integral to the meaning and experience of using the railways. Besides channelling and shaping such messages, infrastructures also acquire symbolic meanings of their own, as in the ambiguous symbolism of trains we pointed to at the start of this chapter.[56]

Viewing infrastructures as mediating interfaces in a number of interactions thus allows us to see how the material, institutional and discursive structures fit together. A look at broadcast infrastructures can exemplify this. On the *material level*, transmitters, networks of relay stations, cables and satellite dishes are evidence of Europe as a technically connected communication space. Because of the differing line and colour standards between Germany and France, points for signal conversion have long played a key part in such networks. On the *institutional level*, European broadcasting institutions such as the European Broadcasting Union, and telecom institutions such as the Conférence Européenne des Administrations des Postes et des Télécommunications (CEPT) and the International Telecommunication Union (ITU), have created crucial gateways for transnational interaction, on the technical and juridical level as well as on the level of intercultural communication. This institutional level stands for Europe as a social space. Combining the material and institutional approach with a discursive analysis of the transmitted and received contents of broadcast programmes means investigating the tensions between the intent of transmitting European sounds and images and their individual and creative appropriation. Sonic and visual icons of European broadcasting, like the ceremonial pomp of the Eurovision hymn, attempt to imbue the realm of technical connection with meaning as a European cultural space.

Less overtly communicative infrastructures can be approached in the same way. In Barbara Bonhage's chapter on the Eurocheque system, for example, a number of banks in Europe, fearing competition from the United States, attempted to create a system of payments that would compete technologically. They created the Eurocheque, which was a paper 'gateway' that allowed currency to be transferred between the banking and retailing systems in different countries. This defined a 'European' – or at least 'Eurocheque' – space that was at once a space of material circulation (where the cheques/funds move), a space of institutional governance and a discursive construction (a protected market or a business/tourist zone). The materiality of the system proved to be its downfall, as the volume of paper to be dealt with as the system grew more popular with increasingly mobile banking customers. At the institutional level, the Swiss banking association was able to help push for closer collaboration between banks, and indeed the development of such a system on the Western European scale helped to create a platform for developing further European mass payment systems. At the discursive level, the desire to define Europe defensively against the US in banking circles played a vital part in being able to establish the system, while the very name on the cheque helped to define the mobility of its international users as European. By tracing these varying levels of mediation carefully over time, the complicated and often contradictory dynamics of Europe and infrastructures begins to become visible.

'Eventing' European infrastructures

As we have seen, the material, institutional and discursive aspects of infrastructures 'interact' in various forms. But how can we as historians make these various processes visible at the same time? We think that this can best be done by focusing on what we call European infrastructural events. These we define as extraordinary occurrences that bring multiple elements and levels of infrastructures into view and reconfirm and/or reorganize the relations between them. Classic types of event are moments of linking, as in the building of a bridge or tunnel, or indeed moments of failure, as in the major electric system failures in 2003 and 2006. What distinguishes events from everyday experiences is the fact that they call attention to forms of mediated participation and are often highly ritualized. Preparing, organizing, staging and transmitting (live) a programme such as the 'Eurovision song contest' to millions of people in Europe and abroad means transforming a concrete historical moment into a European event, a ceremonial occasion for the affirmation of 'Europe' as a cultural space.[57] But, following the reasoning of the British anthropologist and media sociologist Nick Couldry, these phenomena of 'transnational communion' through infrastructures are privileged moments not because they are *expressions* of a Europe that really exists, but because they reveal the mythical *construction* of the mediated centre (Europe) at its most intense.[58] Our experience of Europe is of course not limited to these extravagant and rather infrequent moments of mediated participation. As sociologists have argued, our 'event society' is deeply shaped by numerous unspectacular, everyday experiences of technologies and infrastructures, often characterized by routinized and unconscious forms of action.[59] The real challenge here is how to describe or analyse these habitual interactions with technical infrastructures as 'European' without inscribing the theoretical horizon of expectation (our research question) into the materiality of the objects of study (infrastructures) or the mental disposition of their users. The Eurostar high-speed train is covered with markers of its 'European-ness', and taking it is often an 'eventful' occurrence for passengers, but does the trip under the Channel really produce a sense of 'European-ness' in passengers' minds? From personal observation, we note that encounters between travellers in the supposedly 'cosmopolitan' environment of the Eurostar train can just as well reinforce national stereotypes and prejudices. For regular travellers, by contrast, the whole process is mostly 'uneventful'. Being alert to these dynamics of eventfulness in technical encounters can help us to read them in such a way as to understand the complicated ways that infrastructures allow people to do 'European' things.

As both grand-scale events, like the song competition, and the smaller-scale example of the Eurostar journey can reveal, events are also characterized by actors within them (human or otherwise) *performing*. That is to say, they step into a recognized role that emphasizes specific aspects of their appearance. As the anthropologist Bryan Pfaffenberger has argued, we can view processes of infrastructural development as 'technological dramas':

> To emphasize the metaphor of drama, too, is to employ a richer metaphor than text. It is to emphasize the performative nature of technological 'statements' and 'counterstatements', which involve the creation of scenes

(contexts), in which actors (designers, artefacts, and users) play out their fabricated roles with regard to a set of envisioned purposes (and before an audience), and it is also to emphasize that the discourse involved is not the argumentative and academic discourse of a text but the symbolic media of myth (in which scepticism is suspended) and ritual (in which human actions are mythically patterned in controlled social spaces).[60]

During dramatic European events, actors make use of a well known pro- or anti-European rhetorical toolbox either to laud artefacts or systems as symbolic performances of European spirit and unity, or to corral European dreams into secure national or regional borders. Eve Darien-Smith has shown how, at the eventful birth of the Channel Tunnel, the EU anachronistically appropriated it as a flagship project of the Trans-European Transport Network (TEN-T), and the Thatcher government appropriated it on the national stage as an economically pragmatic internationalist, and nationally glorious, accomplishment. To many who were much less visible on the international stage, it was a blatant loss of sovereignty to an overbearing Frenchified European Union and 'the rape of Kent, the garden of England'.[61] The more specialized arenas of technical experts, such as the annual meetings of international organizations, can also be read as European events, where power is expressed through performance. Representatives of smaller or less powerful nations, in particular, have often been able to use the performances of technical expertise or European unity to position themselves more centrally on the European stage. As we argued more generally above, these often contradictory or ambiguous discourses on European technological events are not just rhetorical 'background music' to the somehow more 'real' material or political systems; instead, both the material and the discursive elements of such events play equally key parts in understanding what the technology *does*. European technological events are expressions *par excellence* of dramatic narratives, melding the fractious ingredients into a highly complex and intricate story. By looking to more visible 'eventful' moments, we begin also to gain insight into the ways in which 'normal' meanings of Europe have been constructed, internalized, reactivated and renegotiated over time.

Structure of the book

To capture the dynamic transnational stories bound up in European infrastructures, we have chosen a structure that augments the lengthier chapters addressing the building and use of transnational infrastructures with a series of short 'biographies' of things, people, ideas and symbols that have circulated through them in various ways. These biographies both illustrate the transnational trajectories of the material, social and cultural forces that work through technologies to shape them.[62] The book begins with a trio of essays that complicate common understandings of the relationships between ideas of Europe and transnational infrastructures by opening. In the first essay, Dirk van Laak explores infrastructural links between Europe and Africa to reveal the multiple ways in which projects for European network integration were entwined with imperial projects. Van Laak shows that 'Eurafrica' was either implicitly or explicitly a consistent project for network plans from the age of imperialism until well after decolonization. He suggests that much of the expertise and ideas that had gone into colonial projects before the war was turned inward into the project of European integration after the war. Alexander Badenoch's chapter analyses the important symbolic role played by infrastructures in constructing ideas of Europe. He analyses network maps as a means of creating standardized knowledge that reconciles spaces of technological circulation with ideas of territory, arguing that networks and territories mythically construct each other. Such representations not only reflect perceptions of networks in relation to Europe, but can be seen as performances where meanings of Europe and infrastructures have been constructed and contested. Johan Schot's chapter rounds out the section, exploring the links between infrastructural development and the post-Second World War processes of European integration by tracing the complex position of the transport and energy sectors in early movements toward political integration. He shows how these sectors were already governed by groups of 'technocratic internationalist' experts (a term he coined with Vincent Lagendijk[63]), who integrated these sectors while deliberately keeping them outside the formal European institutional structures. He argues that focusing on state actors as the sole force in European integration has led to a fundamental misunderstanding of the process as unidirectional and stemming from central European institutions. The focus on infrastructures allows an expanded concept of integration that takes multi-centred governance and processes of fragmentation into consideration. The section's two biographies highlight the non-material functions of infrastructures in projects of European integration. Frank Schipper's discussion of the various debates surrounding the 'capital city' of Europe shows how visions of networkedness played key roles in arguments for specific cities – and also in the construction of the polynuclear capital. Waqar Zaidi describes the role of the technology in the thoughts of early theorists of integration, David Mitrany and Ernst Haas.

In the second section, essays explore the processes of transnational mediation that have gone into constructing infrastructural networks. They pay particular attention to the mutual construction of material systems and the shaping of institutional actors and arenas. Schipper, Lagendijk and Anastasiadou describe the work of the Technical Committee for Communications and Transport (OCT) of the League of Nations. By looking at the long-ignored work of its three subcommittees, they show how 'Europe' emerged in OCT efforts as both the focus of their technical efforts and a realm in which they could be effective. In so doing, they re-evaluate the narrative of the League's 'failure' and point to the ways in which it was able to lay important groundwork for successful international co-operation in the future. Erik van der Vleuten shows how a number of existing transnational systems were linked to form a new complex network for food delivery on a European scale. He explores in particular the role of the United Nations Economic Committee in Europe's working party on perishable foodstuffs to show how they conceived of and implemented a network for the circulation of food in Europe. He shows how they used the notion of 'perishable foods' in a number of different policy arenas to attempt to build what he calls a 'second order' system. Carefully studying the results of this, he also reveals the fragmented contours of a number of different 'food Europes' that emerged in spite of the connections that were made. Both of these chapters, like Schot's chapter, reveal the power of existing European networks of experts in the infrastructural sector that limited or aided the efficacy of political actors. The biographies in this section all examine the ideas of such experts. Christian Henrich-Franke's discussion of European 'founding father' Louis Armand highlights Armand's embrace of technology as an important sphere of integration. The importance of common visions in such holding together expert networks is shown by Vincent Lagendijk's biography of Oskar Oliven's inter-war plan for a European electricity grid, which, though never built, has remained an important touchstone in engineering communities to the present day.

Two further case studies in this section look at the development of network standards. In each of these cases, the changing frameworks of European integration (intended in its broader sense) played a profound, and often unexpected, role in the rise, transformation and/or demise of the systems in question. Barbara Bonhage looks at the harmonization of payment systems among banks in Europe through the Eurocheque system. In an interesting double narrative, she shows on the one hand how the example of the United States led bankers in a number of European countries to join together to create a viable 'domestic' competitor. Patrick Kammerer tells a story of multiple expansions of the GSM standard, which took place as various national actors 'discovered' the expanded – and yet protected – market space of Europe. Colonizing this space technologically by creating a European standard, in turn, helped to define a European space in other ways – for the users of mobile phones as well as network providers – which then in turn helped the 'European' standard to 'go global'. Leonard Laborie's short biography of the French telecom pioneer Georges Valensi complements – and complicates – these two chapters together nicely, showing how Valensi's transatlantic experience marked both his national and international dealings with various standards for communication.

The papers in the third section emphasize the performances of Europe that have taken place through transnational infrastructures. In particular, they all point to the tensions and disjunctions between the material and institutional processes of linking and co-ordinating, and some of the eventful performances built upon such linkages. Andreas Fickers and Suzanne Lommers look at the creation of a number of 'European' events created through European broadcasting federations at various points in the twentieth century. They highlight the very different, and often conflicting, notions of nations and Europe that have gone into these events at the material, institutional and discursive levels, and point to how the creation of such events has shaped practices of both transmitters and receivers. Nil Disco highlights the various negotiations and performances of Europe that surrounded engineering projects on the 'natural' infrastructures of rivers. Such visions and performances of a unified Europe, he suggests, represent a key mechanism by which 'committed spectators' at specific points on a river can influence actions in arenas over which they have no formal control. Eda Kranakis finally brings together material, institutional and discursive layers of infrastructures to highlight a similar disjunction between the pragmatic, competitive and often fragmenting international politics that went into shaping the institutions and routes of early civil aviation on the one hand, and the performed narratives of a cosmopolitan European identity that informed the experience of air tourism on the other. In particular, she shows the possibilities, as well as the limits, of such newfound mobilities on a continent ruled largely by nations pursuing policies of 'hegemonic nationalism'. The final two biographies bring these ideas together to look at the ways in which imagined present and future Europes were 'materialized' into artefacts: the dream of distant travel into radio station scales in the piece by Andreas Fickers, and the 'good atom', the short-lived hope of a safe and atomically united Europe permanently inscribed on Brussels' Atomium. By learning to read such stories of Europe in technology, we can begin to unpack the complicated and fragmented stories of technology and Europe.

Notes

1. For some description of the project see the website of its present incarnation in Brussels: http://www.expo-europe.be/en/site/musee/musee-europe-bruxelles. html. Access date 21 March 2009.
2. *Museum van Europa* (Brussels: Museum of Europe 2004), p. 28.
3. For critiques of this narrative, see Jan Nederveen Pieterse, 'Fictions of Europe', *Race and Class* 32(2) (1991), pp. 3–10; Cris Shore, *Building Europe: The Cultural Politics of European Integration* (London: Routledge 2000), pp. 59–60.
4. See Akira Iriye, *Global community. The role of international organisations in the making of the contemporary world* (Berkeley: University of California Press 2002).
5. See Waqar Zaidi, *Science and Technology & Liberal Internationalism in France, the United States and Great Britain, 1920–1945* (PhD Thesis, Imperial College, London, 2009).
6. See Jo-Anne Pemberton, 'New worlds for old: the League of Nations in the age of electricity', *Review of International Relations*, 28 (2002), pp. 311–36; Shore, *Building Europe*, pp. 113–14.

7. Daniel Headrick, *The Tentacles of Progress: Technology Transfer in the Age of Imperialism, 1850–1940* (Oxford: Oxford University Press 1988); *The Tools of Empire: Technology and European Imperialism in the Nineteenth Century* (Oxford: Oxford University Press 1981). See further Dirk van Laak, *Imperiale Infrastruktur. Deutsche Planungen für eine Erschließung Afrikas 1880 bis 1960* (Paderborn: F. Schöningh 2004).

8. Ole B. Jensen and Tim Richardson, *Making European Space: Mobility, Power and Territorial Identity* (London: Routledge 2004).

9. See Tensions of Europe http://www.tensionsofeurope.eu. See also 'Tensions of Europe' Special Issue, *History and Technology* 21(1) (2005).

10. The Transnational Infrastructures and the Rise of Contemporary Europe (TIE) Project: www.tie-project.nl, led by Professor Johan Schot and supported by the Netherlands Organization for Scientific Research under the VICI scheme (dossiernummer 277-53-001). Key publications from this project to date include Vincent Lagendijk, *Electrifying Europe: The Power of Europe in the Construction of Electricity Networks* (Amsterdam: Aksant/SHT 2008); Frank Schipper, *Driving Europe. Building Europe on Roads in the Twentieth Century* (Amsterdam, Aksant/SHT 2008); Irene Anastasiadou, *In Search of a Railway Europe: International Railway Developments in Interwar Europe* (PhD thesis, Eindhoven University of Technology, 2009).

11. Vleuten and Kaijser, 'Networking Europe', *History and Technology* 21(1), pp. 26–31.

12. Jost Dülffer, 'The History of European Integration: From Integration History to the History of Integrated Europe' in Wilfried Loth (ed.) *Experiencing Europe. 50 Years of European Construction 1957–2007* (Baden-Baden: Nomos), pp. 17–32.

13. Ibid., pp. 22–3. Ben Rosamond similarly describes how the language of describing integration entrenches such notions in 'The political sciences of European integration: disciplinary history and EU studies', in Knud Erik Jørgensen, Mark A. Pollack and Ben Rosamond (eds) *Handbook of European Union Politics* (London: Sage 2007), pp. 7–30.

14. Hartmut Kaelble, *Auf dem Weg zu einer europäischen Gesellschaft. Eine Sozialgeschichte Westeuropas, 1880–1980* (München: Beck 1987).

15. Some of the richer recent discussions include Iriye, *Global community*; Akira Iriye, 'Transnational history', *Contemporary European History* 13(2) (2004), pp. 211–22; Patricia Clavin, 'Introduction: defining transnationalism', *Contemporary European History* 14(4) (2005), pp. 421–40; Pierre Yves Saunier, 'Going transnational?'; Gunilla Budde, Sebastian Conrad and Oliver Janz, *Transnationale Geschichte. Themen, Tendenzen und Theorien* (Göttingen: Vandenhoeck & Ruprecht 2006). A good overview of their meanings and uses in the history of technology specifically, see Erik van der Vleuten, 'Toward a transnational history of technology: meaning, promises, pitfalls', *Technology and Culture*, 49 (2008), pp. 974–94.

16. Pierre Yves Saunier, 'Going transnational? news from down under', *History. Transnational* 13 January 2006 (http://geschichte-transnational.clio-online.net).

17. Ibid.

18. See Lagendijk, *Electrifying*, pp. 58–9, and Fickers and Lommers in this volume.

19. Michael Mann, 'Globalization, Macro-regions and nation-states' in Budde, Conrad and Janz, *Transnationale Geschichte*, 21. For other more detailed versions of these dynamics see Alan Milward, *The European Rescue of the Nation-State* (London and New York: Routledge 2000, second edition), and a very sophisticated account of these processes in recent decades in Neil Brenner, *New State Spaces* (Oxford: OUP 2004).

20. See Iriye, *Global Community*; Patricia Clavin and Jens-Wilhelm Wessels, 'Transnationalism and the League of Nations: Understanding the Work of Its Economic and Financial Organization', *Contemporary European History* 14 (2005), pp. 465–92; as an interesting corollary, which also charts a longer history, see Hartmut Kaelble, 'The historical rise of a European public sphere?', *Journal of European Integration History* 8(2) (2002), pp. 9–22.
21. Thomas J. Misa and Johan Schot, 'Introduction: Inventing Europe: Technology and the Hidden Integration of Europe', *History and Technology* 21(1). In the years since the original publication of the article, the term has already acquired a double meaning, denoting both areas of integration that scholars have overlooked in studying European integration and engineers' and diplomats' deliberate 'hiding' of their integrative activities from the gaze of politicians and the public.
22. Misa and Schot, 'Introduction'; for narratives of fragmentation, see Andreas Fickers' work on the line standards and colour TV formats in Europe, *'Politique de la grandeur' versus 'Made in Germany'. Politische Kulturgeschichte der Technik am Beispiel der PAL/SECAM-Kontroverse* (München: Oldenbourg 2007); Andreas Fickers, 'National Barriers for an Imag(e)ined European Community: The Techno-Political Frames of Postwar Television Development in Europe' in Lennard Hojbjerg and Henrik Sondergaard (eds) *European Film and Media Culture, Northern Lights. Film and Media Studies Yearbook 2005* (Copenhagen: Museum Tusculum Press/University of Copenhagen 2006), pp. 15–36.
23. Erik van der Vleuten and Arne Kaijser (eds), *Networking Europe. Transnational Infrastructures and the Shaping of Europe 1850–2000* (Sagamore Beach: Science History Publications 2006).
24. See Helmut Maier, 'Systems Connected: IG Auschwitz, Kaprun, and the Building of European Power Grids up to 1945', in Vleuten and Kaijser, *Networking Europe*, pp. 129–60.
25. Some articulations of this focus are Nigel Thrift, *Spatial Formations* (London 1996) pp. 256–310; Mimi Sheller and John Urry, 'The new mobilities paradigm', *Environment and Planning A* 38 (2006), pp. 207–26; Kevin Hannam, Mimi Sheller and John Urry, 'Editorial: Mobilities, Immobilities and Moorings', *Mobilities* 1(1).
26. Hannam, Sheller and Urry, 'Editorial'.
27. Andrew Barry, *Political Machines: Governing a Technological Society* (London: Athlone 2001).
28. See Jensen and Richardson, *Making European Space*.
29. See the special issue on 'Rethinking European Spaces' edited by Chris Rumford, *Comparative European Politics* 4(4) (2006).
30. Ginette Verstraete, 'Timescapes: An artistic challenge to the European Union paradigm', *European Journal of Cultural Studies* 12(2) (2009), pp. 157–74.
31. Dirk van Laak, 'Infra-strukturgeschichte', *Geschichte und Gesellschaft* 27 (2001), p. 385.
32. See Schipper et al.'s chapter in this volume.
33. Achim Landwehr and Stefanie Stockhorst, *Einführung in die Europäische Kulturgeschichte* (Paderborn: UTB 2004), pp. 264ff. See also Gerard Delanty, *Inventing Europe: Idea, Identity, Reality* (London 1995); Bo Stråth (ed.) *Europe and the Other, Europe as the Other* (Brussels 2000); Anssi Paasi, 'Europe as a Social Process and Discourse. Considerations of Place, Boundaries and Identity', *European Urban and Regional Studies* 8(1) (2001), pp. 7–28.

34. See Bo Stråth and Mikael af Malmborg, 'Introduction: The National Meanings of Europe', in Bo Stråth and Mikael af Malmborg (eds) *The Meaning of Europe* (Oxford: Berg 2002), pp. 1–26.
35. See Richard Münch, *Das Projekt Europa. Zwischen Nationalstaat, regionaler Autonomie und Weltgesellschaft* (Frankfurt a.M.: Suhrkamp 1993).
36. See Alexander Schmidt-Gernig, 'Gibt es eine "europäische Identität"'? in Kaelble and Schriewer, *Diskurse und Entwicklungspfade. Der Gesellschaftsvergleich in den Geschichts- und Sozialwissenschaften* (Frankfurt: Campus 1999), pp. 163–216; David Morley has been particularly insistent on exploring the various and problematic ways in which increasingly destabilized notions of 'home' are remapped on and through changing structures of mediation. See his *Home Territories: Media Mobility and Identity* (London: Routledge 2000).
37. Michael G. Müller and Cornelius Torp indeed argue in a recent article that the polarity found in much scholarship between the global and the national 'involves the danger of neglecting space as a dimension of history altogether': 'Conceptualising transnational spaces in history', *European Review of History* 16(5) (2009), p. 611.
38. Pierre-Yves Saunier, 'Learning by Doing: Notes about the Making of the *Palgrave Dictionary of Transnational History*', *Journal of Modern European History* 6(2) (2008), pp. 173–4.
39. For an account of these forces at a local level, see also Noyan Dinçkal, ' "The Universal Mission of Civilisation and Progress". Infrastruktur, Europa und die Osmanische Stadt um 1900', in *Themenportal Europäische Geschichte* (2009): http://www.europa.clio-online.de/2009/Article=348.
40. Interesting work has already begun in this direction. See, among others, Katrin Steffen and Martin Kohlraush, 'The limits and merits of internationalism: experts, the state and the international community in Poland in the first half of the twentieth century', *European Review of History* 16 (2009), pp. 715–37; Jiři Janac, 'Europe through waterways: The European Coasts of Bohemia', *Tensions of Europe Working Papers*, 2008_8: http://www.tensionsofeurope.eu/publications/working/workingpdf/2008_8.pdf (accessed 11 July 2009).
41. This is more or less the dynamic explored by the Large Technical Systems (LTS) idea built upon the pioneering works of Thomas P. Hughes. For an overview, see Erik van der Vleuten, 'Understanding Network Societies: Two Decades of Large Technological Systems' in Vleuten and Kaijser (eds) *Networking Europe*, pp. 279–314; for a critical evaluation of both the merits and limits of the LTS approach see Bernward Joerges, 'High Variability Discourse in the History and Sociology of Large Technological Systems' in Olivier Coutard (ed.) *The Governance of Large Technological Systems* (London/New York: Routledge 1999), pp. 258–90.
42. The problem of coupling different systems was debated on several occasions during discussions surrounding this book. One way to address these problems is to focus more on the meso-level (as suggested by Schot in this book). Another possibility is discussed under the label of 'resilience'. See Hans Liljenström and Uno Svedin, 'Bridges, Connections and Interfaces – Reflections on the Meso Theme' in Liljenström and Svedin (eds) *Micro, Meso, Macro. Addressing Complex Systems Couplings* (London: World Scientific 2005), pp. 317–30.
43. Paul N. Edwards, 'Modernity and Infrastructures: Force, Time and Social Organization in the History of Sociotechnical Organizations' in Misa, Brey and Feenberg (eds) *Modernity and Technology* (Cambridge, MA: MIT Press 2003), pp. 185–226.

44. Edwards, 'Modernity and Infrastructures'.
45. See Eve Darian-Smith, *Bridging Divides: The Channel Tunnel and English Legal Identity* (Berkeley: University of California Press 1999); Per Olof Berg, Anders Linde-Laursen and Orvar Löfgren (eds), *Invoking a Transnational Metropolis* (Lund: Studentlitteratur 2000); Judith Schueler, *Materializing Identity: the co-construction of the Gotthard Railway and Swiss national identity* (Eindhoven: Aksant/SHT 2008).
46. See Maria Kaika and Erik Swyngedow, 'Fetishising the modern city: the phantasmagoria of urban technological networks', *International Journal of Urban and Regional Research* 24(1) (2000), pp. 120–38; Mikael Hård and Thomas J. Misa (eds), *Urban Machinery: Inside Modern European Cities* (Cambridge, Mass.: MIT Press 2008); Dinçkal, 'Universal Mission'.
47. Graham and Marvin, *Splintering Urbanism*. For a further discussion of the 'splintering urbanism' thesis, see Olivier Coutard, Richard Hanley and Rae Zimmerman, *Sustaining Urban Networks: the Social Diffusion of Large Technical Systems* (London: Routledge 2005).
48. Bruno Latour, *Reassembling the Social: An Introduction to Actor-Network-Theory* (Oxford: Oxford UP 2005).
49. See, for example, David Gugerli, 'The Effective Fiction of Internationality. Analyzing the Emergence of a European Railroad System in the 1950s', *Preprints zur Kulturgeschichte der Technik / 2003 / 17*: http://www.tg.ethz.ch/dokumente/pdf_Preprints/Preprint17.pdf (accessed 19 March 2007), and further Badenoch's essay in this volume.
50. For a popular explanation of the epistemological consequences or problems of modern quantum physics and on Nils Bohr's 'principle of complementarity' as an interpretation of Heisenberg's uncertainty principle see John Gribbin, *In Search of Schrödinger's Cat. Quantum Physics and Reality* (London: Bantam 1984).
51. Tineke Egyedi, 'Infrastructure Flexibility Created by Standardized Gateways: The Cases of XML and the ISO Container', *Knowledge, Technology & Policy* 14(3) (2001), 41–54.
52. Paul N. Edwards et al., 'Understanding Infrastructure: Dynamics, Tensions, Designs'. Report of a Workshop on 'History & Theory of Infrastructure: Lessons for New Scientific Cyberinfrastructures' (January 2007), p. 16. Online at: http://www.si.umich.edu/InfrastructureWorkshop/documents/Understanding-Infrastructure2007.pdf.
53. Some of these roles have been captured in the notion of the 'system-builder' in the Large Technical Systems (LTS) tradition, which looks to the actors who are able to embed technologies within social and institutional frameworks. See Erik van der Vleuten et al., 'Europe's system builders: The Contested Shaping of Europe's Road, Electricity and Rail Networks', *Contemporary European History*, 16(3) (2007) 321–47; further, van der Vleuten's chapter in this volume.
54. See Oldenziel, de la Bruheze and de Wit, 'Europe's Mediation Junction: Technology and Consumer Society in the Twentieth Century', *History and Technology* 21(1) (2005).
55. See Wolfgang Schivelbusch, *Geschichte der Eisenbahnreise. Industrialisierung von Raum und Zeit im 19. Jahrhundert* (Frankfurt: Fischer 1977).
56. Roger Silverstone and Leslie Haddon refer to this as the 'double articulation' of media as consumable objects as well as media for other products: 'Design and Domestication of Information and Communication Technologies: Technical Change and Everyday Life' in Robin Mansell and Roger Silverstone,

Communication by Design: The Politics of Information and Communication Technologies (Oxford: Oxford University Press 1996), pp. 44–74.

57. See the classical study of Elihu Katz and Daniel Dayan, *Media Events. The Live Broadcasting of History* (Cambridge, MA: Harvard University Press 1994).

58. Nick Couldry, *Media Rituals. A Critical Approach* (London/New York: Routledge 2003), p. 56.

59. Gerhard Schulze, *Die Erlebnisgesellschaft: Kultursoziologie der Gegenwart* (Frankfurt a.M.: Campus 1992).

60. Bryan Pfaffenberger, 'Technological Dramas', *Science, Technology & Human Values*, 17(3) (1992), p. 286.

61. Darien-Smith, *Bridging Divides*.

62. Such 'biographical' impulses lie at the root of seminal works on modern material culture: Arjun Appadurai (ed.), *The Social Life of Things: Commodities in cultural perspective* (Cambridge: Cambridge University Press 1986); specifically dealing with technology, see Bruno Latour's innovative biography of a never-completed network, *Aramis, or the love of technology* (Cambridge, MA: Harvard University Press 1996).

63. Johan Schot and Vincent Lagendijk, 'Technocratic internationalism in the inter-war years: building Europe on motorways and electricity networks', *Journal of Modern European History* 6(2) (2008) 196–217.

Part I

Questioning the Connections between Infrastructures and Europe

1
Detours around Africa: The Connection between Developing Colonies and Integrating Europe

Dirk van Laak

The aim of this chapter is to trace the transformation of the notion of 'Eurafrica' from the time of European imperialism up to the era of decolonization and the start of European integration. The idea that Europe and Africa should naturally be linked via expanding infrastructures was an important part of many imperial and infrastructural visions in the nineteenth century. The end of European colonial rule in Africa since the 1950s only appeared at first to be 'abandoning' the Europe-Africa connections. In fact, a belief that Europeans could offer superior technology to 'underdeveloped' countries lingered on. An almost religious belief in the ability to 'modernize' backward countries focused primarily on 'infrastructure', a term that was introduced into the political vocabulary precisely at that point in time. The term circumscribed the implementation of 'basic works' and comprised everything that was regarded as essential for 'opening up' territories and developing economies and societies alike; usually it was conceived as a public enterprise.[1]

In what follows I will argue that infrastructures form a hidden link between Europe and Africa, which in turn represent a historical link between the age of European imperialism and the age of an integrated Europe. This link was neither primarily political nor economical in nature, but rather 'technocratic'. Since the early nineteenth century, when Claude Henri de Saint-Simon, Michel Chevalier, Friedrich List and other 'technocrats' recommended the creation of a 'United States of Europe', 'infrastructure' was often meant to cut through the Gordian knot of political co-ordination by means of material accomplishments. Technocracy usually claims a primacy of rational and efficient organization as a means of approaching political, social and cultural agendas.[2] With their 'hidden' agendas, infrastructures were distinguished tools of technocratic efforts to integrate territories and societies alike. During the 1950s, institutions of European co-operation as well as late colonial development programmes were described as breeding grounds for technocracy.[3] Furthermore, it is striking how the independent nation states of Nasser, Nehru, Nkrumah, Nyerere and others applied the same high-modernist notions to map territories, people and resources and make them 'legible' for use as 'raw material' for ambitious planning and 'rational' development. The 'technocratic' goals here were to exercise control, improve revenues and coerce their young but 'backward' nations into modernity.[4]

This chapter will return to the roots of the European colonial enterprise and discuss how the confrontation with Africa helped to shape a common European identity. The focus then will shift to infrastructure as a tool to exercise colonial control, to foster colonial development and finally to retain material links between Europe and Africa. Since the late nineteenth century the idea of 'Eurafrica' reappeared time and again as a guiding theme of a common future of two complementary continents, most prominently voiced by technocrats. I will suggest that the apparently apolitical face of 'Eurafrica' both impeded its realization but, at the same time, was a prerequisite for the continuing fascination it held on both sides of the Mediterranean.

Opening up

As a political and cultural unit, 'Europe' was usually constructed in contrast to challenges from what was defined as 'non-European'. The 'oriental' Persians were faced by the 'European' Greeks, Islam by the 'Christian community' or the Turks by the combined occidental forces. European overseas expansion, starting in the fifteenth and sixteenth centuries, was marked not only by confrontations with 'the others' but by the definition of a common 'European mission' abroad. Spreading Christianity served as a strong legitimizing agency to subdue foreign societies, and Christianity was increasingly seen as synonymous with European civilization in general. Modern European colonialism was marked by its use of technological resources to conquer territories, open them up and develop an economy producing 'goods' and 'wealth'.

Within the nineteenth century Africa was subjected to European rule. At that time the technological gap between indigenous Africans and Europeans was wider than ever. Steamships allowed colonizers to infiltrate the inner territories by using the great rivers as gateways. Later on railways were built to connect different colonies and lay the foundations for economic exploitation. Because of the European technological and medical predominance, conquering foreign territories became an enterprise of little risk and relatively little investment in human and material capital.[5] Religious justifications were gradually replaced by the motive of bringing 'civilization' to indigenous peoples, which increasingly meant creating the necessary preconditions for a European concept of 'labour' and 'productivity'.[6] Consequently people in Latin America, Asia or Africa often were regarded as 'lazy' or living in a state of 'historical decline', whereas Europeans, by contrast, could boast to themselves about their material and cultural achievements.

Accordingly, imperialism entailed building infrastructures of a European economy and an administration comparable to that of the industrialized nations. Prior to the First World War all European colonial nations shifted towards a distinct policy of 'colonial development'. 'Science,' British imperial historian Robert Seeley stated in 1883, 'has given to the political organism a new circulation, which is steam, and a new nervous system, which is electricity. These new conditions make it necessary to reconsider the whole colonial problem.'[7] This was just one among countless statements characterizing a common European ideology of opening up and developing foreign territories, material and 'human' resources.[8] If it ever makes sense to name a 'religion of technology' it does so for the material 'civilizing mission' of the European colonizers.[9]

Since the late nineteenth century many Europeans considered Africa a 'natural supplement' to Europe, and a particular 'Eurafrican' affiliation was evoked for the first time.[10] In 1884/85 the Berlin Congo Conference convoked by German chancellor Otto von Bismarck marked the formal starting point for a common European endeavour to establish a geopolitically integrated Euro-African continent. The pioneering idea of a 'Free State of Congo' conceived as a zone of free trade and transport, however, was thwarted by Belgian king Leopold II's ambition to exploit this area exclusively.[11] In the age of imperialism, internationalism and chauvinistic nationalism often overlapped and came into conflict with each other, preventing the 'Eurafrican idea' from being materialized. At the same time, a great deal of co-operation actually took place among European colonizers. Institutions such as the 'Institut Colonial International' in Brussels, which grew out of the early nineteenth-century European abolition movement, became an intellectual spearhead of the movement toward a less chauvinistic and more 'rational' model of colonialism.[12]

'Us' and 'Them'

What exactly did 'European' mean in colonial contexts? The answer fundamentally depends on the level, or scale, at which one addresses the question. Usually, different 'identities' coexisted within each of the colonizers, each becoming apparent within different contexts:

1. At an *individual* level colonizers abroad were quite flexible in defining their 'identity' according to individual dispositions, situations or circumstances. At this level, 'European' was most often synonymous with the 'white race', especially with respect to the allegedly all-too-obviously backward people of Africa.

2. At the level of *national institutions and societies*, colonial enterprises never really were joint imperial adventures but appealed just to minor, however powerful and vociferous, social fractions within these societies instead. Chauvinistic as modern nationalism could be, there always were individuals or groups that emphatically argued *against* colonialism from humanitarian perspectives. After all, they increasingly succeeded in forcing colonialists to justify their efforts to the public.[13]

3. At the level of *nations* in the era of imperialism – understood less as administrative units than as cultural or even racial entities – ability to colonize was often understood as a distinct national feature. Rivalry between European colonizers was marked by competing methods of colonization. However, up to 1914 no major wars between European nations stemmed directly from colonial disputes. But the tensions built up by imperial rivalry eventually contributed to the outbreak of the First World War.

4. At the *transnational* level there was a lot of mutuality among the 'European' colonizers, especially when conflicts and opposition arose, as could be observed during the Boxer War in China in 1900/01. The more independence entered the political agenda, especially after US president Woodrow Wilson in 1918 had proclaimed peoples' right of self-determination, the more Europeans were inclined to view colonization as a common enterprise, regardless of national rivalries. Co-operative and technocratic approaches were especially suggestive.

5. Finally, European colonialism fundamentally contributed to '*globalization*'. It depends, however, on how one defines 'imperialism' whether or not one concludes that the era of imperialism really came to an end after the First World War or in the interwar years. Seen from the perspective of foreign policy, there are some good reasons to claim there was a successive termination of European colonialism. Seen from the angle of the economy, there is much less reason to do so. Seen from the perspective of infrastructural development throughout the world, this claim makes no sense at all. Following these processes, the period of decolonization can be seen as constituting an era of transition to 'globalization', but even then this can only be understood as a multilayered process of mutual influence.[14]

Trojan horses

From the early twentieth century onward, colonization understood as conquering territories and resources was increasingly – but not entirely – replaced by a form of colonization understood as developing territories and societies towards integration into world economy. This primarily meant building infrastructures for traffic and communication as well as education and health. The aim of 'Europeanizing' the rest of the world was inscribed into all 'colonial development' plans commencing after the First World War.

They did not necessarily rest upon military control, which often ended up in violence.[15] Instead, 'development' came more and more to be seen as an offer to indigenous peoples. In fact, it was increasingly demanded by them – or at least by those who were educated in a 'European' sense.[16]

Railways, the figurehead of the Industrial Revolution in Europe, were pivotal in discussions about 'colonial development'. As Davis and Wilburn argue:

> Steel rails had a capacity for transforming the societies through which they ran and for spreading imperial influence in their domestic affairs. [...They] clearly had a propensity for integrating and annexing territory, for monopolizing its resources, and for pre-empting the future of great stretches of country. All these implications, it is suggested, gave rise to a distinctive type of railway imperialism, which added a new dimension to European expansion and projected it to a higher pitch of intensity over a vastly extended range.[17]

The African railway system never came close to the Indian system built by the British colonizers. But the projected Cape-to-Cairo railway line conceived by the 'empire-builder' Cecil Rhodes and the French Trans-Saharan railway line sparked extensive discussions among imperialists.[18] The 'iron horse' was accurately viewed as a 'Trojan horse' of European influence. Creation of other infrastructures like streets, harbours, schools, medical care systems, telephone and telegraph lines, water supply and sewage systems had far-reaching effects in everyday life in European colonies as well. Building imperial infrastructures thus became a prime instrument to evoke an economy of a European archetype and to control colonial societies more efficiently.[19] Conversely, much of the wealth that was drawn from the colonies was invested into building new modern infrastructures in Europe.

Colonial development and geopolitics

The common ground of European interests in Africa had been shattered during the First World War. Germany was ousted from its African colonies, and African soldiers were involved in the fierce battles among Europeans.[20] In the long run, the war turned out to be a critical turning point of modern colonialism. Many Europeans anticipated that the European 'civil war' entailed the exposure of the European myth of superiority. Cultural interpreters already envisioned the dominance of the 'white race' being threatened by the 'coloured' people.[21] In 1914 Europe had put its power at risk and eventually lost a lot of its importance in world politics.

Between the wars, the French, Dutch, Belgian, Portuguese and British colonial administrations increasingly embarked on 'mise en valeur' or 'colonial development' programmes.[22] Their common aim was to make the colonies more profitable. The burdened European economies became increasingly dependent on future returns for their colonial investments and also on colonial resources. Long-ranging development plans were proclaimed, and colonial administrations, seeking to optimize management 'scientifically', also favoured 'technocratic' approaches to get quick revenues. Political and economic theories began to conceptualize colonies at least as 'self-supporting', if not profitable, for the metropolitan economies. At the same time, in article 22 of its constitution, the League of Nations redefined colonialism as a 'trusteeship' and viewed colonies as transient 'mandates' rather than perpetual European properties. Consequently, colonies became laboratories for 'social engineering' projects and technocratic development programmes.[23]

But once more internationalism and chauvinistic nationalism intersected and retarded the realization of plans that proposed the development of Africa as a common European enterprise. However, 'Eurafrica' still served as a strong vision to all representatives of a future European integration. Richard Count Coudenhove-Kalergi, for instance, suggested the inclusion of parts of Africa into a 'Pan-European' continent.[24] Herman Soergel, a German draughtsman, in 1928 designed an ambitious plan which comprised almost everything European 'technocrats' at this time hoped for: his 'Atlantropa' concept suggested building a large dam at the Straits of Gibraltar and letting the Mediterranean Sea evaporate gradually to a level of almost 100 metres lower. This, so Soergel reckoned, would give European engineers and architects the opportunity to connect Europe and Africa by means of land, infrastructures, economy and politics alike, and to integrate a Eurafrican continent being comparably powerful with America and Asia.[25] 'History', Soergel proclaimed, 'left Africa as a full and almost untouched savings bank for the Europeans and their technology.'[26]

Most 'Eurafrican' conceptions nourished between the wars were less ambitious – and none was equally 'technocratic' in nature. In a period of fierce nationalism, however, 'Atlantropa' was far from high on any agenda, and stood little chance of being taken up.[27] But many visionaries of European integration, and namely those proposing a French–German rapprochement, thought about redeveloping the idea of a common European engagement in Africa. The League of Nations and the International Labour Organisation with its president Albert Thomas more than once acted on this suggestion and contributed plans for 'Eurafrican' enterprises.[28]

In all these plans, the adjacent African continent was still expected to serve as an overflow space for surplus European energies. The First World War had shown how such energies became destructive and turned towards Europeans themselves. But many experts believed European vitality could be made useful again by applying it to constructive tasks beyond the scope of what isolated nation states could achieve. Consequently, Africa acted as an extension of Europe that should re-establish the balance among colonial and non-colonial powers. However, in the age of the

Great Depression and the obvious decline of the free market economy, these ideas were rivalled by spatial projects such as 'meso-regional blocks' in central Europe and building self-sufficient groups of nations that would complement each other economically and politically.[29] But these ideas of European integration were later instrumentalized for projects to establish Fascist or 'Aryan' hegemony and were additionally tainted by German and Italian geopolitical speculations in Africa during the late 1930s and the Second World War.[30]

Eurafrica

In an interview he gave in 1951 the Senegalese president Léopold Sédar Senghor refused to accept that Africa should serve as a sacrifice for a French–German rapprochement after the Second World War.[31] He argued that European integration should not make detours around Africa. Senghor added that Africa actually was a 'natural addition' to Europe. 'Eurafrica', however, should not look like the totalitarian 'Eurafrica' that Hitler had envisioned, but more like a democratic and brotherly association.[32] All early manifestations of forging a common (West) European alliance, the Pact of Brussels in 1948, the OEEC and the Hague Congress of Europe, had all indeed referred to the necessity to include the 'overseas territories' (as they were usually called now instead of 'colonies').[33] The Schuman Plan of 1950, on which Senghor was commenting, took up several initiatives of the inter-war and post-war period. In focusing on coal and steel, the plan was meant to curb the former European enemy's ability to rearm. At his presentation of the plan on 9 May 1950, the French foreign minister notably added that 'Europe then will be better equipped to pursue one of its eminent tasks: the development of the African continent.'[34]

The plan was further developed in 1952 with the Strasbourg Plan, which conceived of the Economic Commission of the Council of Europe; this addressed the British Commonwealth as well. European countries, like Italy or Germany, no longer in the colonial game would be allowed to invest in colonized territories and take part in the acquisition of capital, technology, equipment and labour in Africa.[35] The plan did not materialize; national interests were still predominant over European supra-nationalism. In partic-ular, French–British antagonism with respect to their leading role in Europe after 1945 lingered on.[36] A European Army Plan failed as well.[37] The role of the United States, however, was decisive: it successively replaced the former European colonial powers in Indochina (Vietnam) and Africa (the Congo) in order to safeguard its strategic resources in the growing Cold War, but it refused to support outright colonialism.[38] Since the proclamation of the 'Point Four' Program by President Harry S. Truman in 1948, it granted development aid instead and focused on building infrastructures for a 'take off into self-sustained growth[39]'. Backed by the United Nations and other international agencies, the US development programmes kept on spreading the high-modernist notion of sparking 'modernization' in underdeveloped countries by laying the groundwork not just for a 'Western' economy but subsequently for liberal and democratic societies as well. Here, the European 'civilizing mission' overlapped with Cold War strategies and was gradually 'Americanized' by further stressing technological imperatives.[40] The American way of development also helped to curtail the colonial appearance of European engagement in Africa.

Fuelled by various Cold War ambitions to battle an allegedly 'external' influence of political Islam, and to curb the spread of communism and separatist quests for autonomy, Europeans took up several plans for Africa already nourished in the interwar period.[41] Still the continent was claimed as a European sphere of influence. In 1945 Great Britain renewed its 'Colonial Development and Welfare Act', and installed a 'Colonial Development Corporation' in 1948. In Tanganyika, for instance, the 'Overseas Food Corporation' sought to meet the British need for fat by planting groundnuts on a large scale, but eventually failed.[42] In 1946 France established a 'Commission de Modernisation et d'Equipement des Territoires d'Outre-Mer', followed by a 'Fonds d'investissements pour le développement économique et social' (FIDES) and the 'Caisse Centrale de la France d'Outremer'. These institutions also spent their money primarily on building infrastructures. French and German experts like Erik Labonne and Johannes Semler concurrently probed plans to co-ordinate public–private partnerships for the development of Africa. During the 1950s several large-scale projects were planned, such as the construction of an industrial centre close to the Algerian city of Colomb-Béchar.[43] France and Belgium planned to dam the River Congo, creating a lake extending to Chad, and some of the largest power plants in the world in the 150 years that followed.[44] As had already become a tradition among colonial technocrats, 'greening' the Sahara desert still served as an ultimate symbol for what Europeans were presumed to achieve by their technical knowledge.[45] In all these schemes comparisons to the Tennessee Valley Authority project of the 1930s were drawn, and time and again parallels to the Marshall plan were also conjured up.[46]

With these plans and the beginning of development aid projects, many Europeans took part in a second surge of African colonization that was stimulated by the beginning of decolonization in Asia.[47] Yet, another impulse was relevant: the readiness for compensation. Wondering rhetorically in 1952 how compensation would come to Africa, a German politician suggested: 'Through new, up-to-date hygienic facilities, better roads, flats, living conditions, by more industries and an intensified development of a country and its unlimited prospects? – All this is good and important and will have to be part of a large, consistently planned and operated program for all of Africa. It is a voluminous task, so voluminous that it only can be tackled as a concerted European enterprise.'[48]

The accelerating process of decolonization turned out to be an utterly complex phenomenon, however. A range of conflicting tendencies interfered with each other and characterized the ambivalent transition zone from colonial to post-colonial times. These included late colonial ambitions, the need for resources, rising anti-colonial sentiments, Cold War strategies, the 'humanitarian' – though not too altruistic – conviction that historic economic imbalances between 'developed' and 'underdeveloped' countries could be levelled, and the aim to reconcile historical obligations. These conflicts notwithstanding, technology was unquestionably what Europeans and US Americans had to offer to the rest of the world. Technology appeared to be non-committed, matter-of-fact, appropriate and benevolent. There were no doubts that, with its help, historical evolution could be 'planned'. Moreover, this conviction was shared by indigenous African elites, who, after decolonization and the building of new nation states, often embarked on ambitious ten-, fifteen- or even twenty-year plans to quickly 'catch up' with the industrialized nations. A hegemonic 'technocratic' atmosphere not only favoured the transfer of experiences from metropolis to peripheries and vice versa. Within the new African nation states it also perpetuated the implementation of a 'welfare state' in a European sense.[49] Accordingly, the Europeans left not merely their European infrastructures in Africa, but their 'modernist' and 'Keynesian' notion of planned state interventions as well.

Winds of change

Only in the mid-1950s – after the Mau-Mau uprising in Kenya, the beginning of the war in Algeria and the Bandung Conference – did the French and the British finally realize how futile it was to further retain their imperial ambitions. The most decisive event and emblematic turning point was the Suez Crisis in 1956. Tellingly, it was sparked by quarrels over the ambitious plan to build the largest dam ever located in Africa. The Egyptian president Jamal Abdel Nasser nationalized the most outstanding of 'imperial infrastructures', the Suez canal, in order to finance the long-projected Aswan dam. In a late colonial campaign French, British and Israeli troops attacked Egypt by air. But the United States and the United Nations alike refused to endorse the action.[50] The British withdrew, the French felt betrayed – and solidarity between the two nations was severely tainted.[51]

Subsequently, the conference underway at Venice to shape a European economic co-operation was decisively pushed forward by the Egyptian incident. Only then did an integrated Europe appear as a viable alternative to the fading colonial empires. Starting with Ghana in 1957, most of Africa was quickly seized by the 'winds of change' that Harold Macmillan emblematically talked about in 1960. Louis Armand, president of the European Atomic Energy Community, in retrospect even suggested erecting a statue of Nasser as the 'federator of Europe'.[52] In this respect Africa indeed acted as a detour towards European integration. If the colonial question had retarded integration efforts up to the mid-1950s, following the crises at Suez and in Hungary it accelerated them.[53]

On 25 March 1957, the French government succeeded in extending the Treaty of Rome to the association of their 'Territoires d'Outre Mer'.[54] The Germans, the Italians and the Dutch, however reluctant to do so, eventually complied with French interests and 'greatly eased the management of decolonisation'.[55] In its articles 131 to 136, the Treaty of Rome associated major parts of French Africa with the European Economic Community and proclaimed concerted EEC development programmes, especially for building infrastructures. All initiatives were explicitly conditioned to the consent of the African or Caribbean subjects. Exemptions from customs duties were created, but at the same time – clear-sightedly – free movement of labour was constrained.

Although some (former) colonies or mandates of Belgium, Italy and the Netherlands benefited from certain privileges as well, especially in Germany it was felt that France in particular had profited from 'Eurafrican' arrangements.[56] In fact, the European Common Market was initially expected to serve as a 'substitute for empire, a new source of international prestige and influence'.[57] The French in particular sought 'to maintain special relationships with African colonies after they had attained self-government'.[58] The 'European Development Fund', to which the Germans contributed a great deal of money, did not exclusively serve Francophone ambitions, however. It also nourished the idea of continuity in developing the economic and social infrastructures of African countries. Within its first five years 581 million dollars were allocated.

In the meantime the British remained distant and observant. Since the Schuman plan in 1950, politicians such as Edward Heath had been suspicious that Germany was reinstalled into the league of colonial nations.[59] Eventually, the British were less successful than the French in bringing the rest of their Commonwealth into the European integration process, though some 'Eurafricans', such as Ernest Bevin, had been proposing to do so since 1945.[60] Shortly after almost all the African colonies became independent in 1960, Great Britain applied for integration into the EEC. But it took another twelve years to be accepted, primarily because of two consecutive vetoes by the French.[61] Spain and Portugal – the last European nations to own major colonies – entered the European Community even later, not until they finally left all imperial ambitions behind. As Peo Hansen puts it, the push towards European integration can be shown to have gained some decisive incentives from the cognizance on the part of those in power that Western Europe's global clout was on the wane.[62]

For Europeans it was still hard to leave the feeling of superiority behind. During the 1960s, however, European 'identity politics' shifted increasingly away from being shaped by 'distant mirrors' in the colonies and towards commonality among a 'multitude of cultures' instead. Cold War politics and the rivalry between eastern and western political and economic systems had powerful effects on sweeping modernization programmes on both sides. The EEC became a role model for the co-operative politics that the British in 1960 sought to copy with the transient 'European Free Trade Association' (EFTA), whereas the Eastern Bloc was often denounced as a hegemonic conception, similar to German ambitions in the Second World War. The independence of Third World countries, in contrast, was often perceived as an outburst of the nationalism that promoters of European integration sought finally to overcome.

With formal decolonization, the 'terms of trade' with almost all the twenty-five associated territories changed rapidly.[63] In the Treaty of Rome, the association had been limited to five years. The status of an association was retained until 1962, but required new negotiations thereafter. The association of overseas countries and territories was renewed between the Six and the eighteen associated African states and Madagascar (AASM) in the Treaty of Yaoundé on 20 July 1963. Here, 'Eurafrican' integration was upgraded to a co-operation that 1) demonstrated the common aim to transform colonialism into an economical, political and military correlation, 2) consolidated the resources of Europe and Africa, 3) handed at least some national sovereignty over to supranational authorities, 4) substantiated its peacekeeping and non-expansionist ambitions, 5) claimed to decolonize Africa in a self-determined way.[64] Yet the Soviet Bloc still accused the EEC of perpetuating colonialism.[65] The economic co-operation and foreign aid programmes of the later European Community and European Unity, renewed and modified in the Treaties Lomé (1975) and Cotonou (2000), presently cover seventy-seven nations in Africa, the Caribbean and the Pacific.

Future prospects

The connection between developing colonies and integrating Europe in the 1950s was an extremely complex piece of world history with many rational *and* irrational aspects and agencies. The cost–benefit analysis of colonial policy was accompanied by Cold War strategic thinking and the glacially slow abandonment of colonial attitudes. In official histories of the European Union, the close connection between decolonization and European integration is almost generally ignored. The same holds true for the material networks between European and African societies that actually had been built, and for the 'Eurafrican' notion that many technocrats nourished. In some respects African colonies acted as 'laboratories' for the Europeans.[66] They served as 'pressure-relief valves' and as overflow areas for European resources, markets and people.[67] Viewed from 'above', 'uncivilized' people in the colonies were often equalized to members of the European underclasses. Some inventions for controlling indigenous people were brought back to Europe, such as the collection of fingerprints, racial segregation, means and modes of sanitation, and even concentration camps.[68] Regarding migration, the mutual transfer between Europe and overseas territories is still highly visible today. The association of states from Africa with the EU significantly does *not* comprise a free movement of labour, because the re-migration of former colonialists and the immigration of former 'colonial subjects' to Europe after 1960 ranked among the critical consequences of the era of imperialism and is still one of the major challenges for the present European 'sphere of prosperity'. In this respect it appears that Europe once more constitutes its identity against 'non-European' 'threat'. However, the building of global infrastructures entailed that encounters between 'them' and 'us' can happen everywhere.

What is often ignored is the fact that African and overseas territories had been, and still are, part of the European Union. At the time the Treaty of Rome was signed France still included the Algerian departments, which left the European Economic Community only in 1962. Greenland, though not a Danish colony since 1953, was associated to the EU and part of the customs union. Up to now it has been the only larger territory to formally leave the European Community, which it did on 1 January 1985. The French Overseas Departments of Reunion, Guyana, Martinique and Guadeloupe continue to be part of the European Union, as do the Spanish possessions of Melilla and Ceuta – remains of the late Spanish colonial venture in Morocco after the First World War.[69] Additionally, though some territories are not part of the EU, their inhabitants nevertheless carry 'European' passports.[70] Conversely, 'Africa' and the flood of migrants coming from the southern continent mirror the magnetic wealth the European Union emanates today. Morocco, which applied for EU membership in 1986, was rejected unequivocally as non-European. The application of Turkey just one year later, however, provoked long-lasting debates on what 'European' actually circumscribes. Here, traditional conceptions of challenges from what was defined as 'non-European' also linger on.

The relationship between Europe and Africa, decolonization, the European decline in world politics and European integration involve simultaneous and complexly interwoven processes. Some inventions (and some insights) obviously made 'detours around Africa'. The establishment of 'special relationships' between Europe and Africa and the concept of 'Eurafrica' helped *both* sides to neatly translate their historic positions into a new era. The mutual transfer of knowledge, technology, goods and people – today discussed as 'globalization' – entailed a process of integration that more than ever points to a common destiny.

Notes

1. Dirk van Laak, 'Infra-Strukturgeschichte', *Geschichte und Gesellschaft* 27(3) (2001), pp. 367–93; 'Wirtschaftliche Erschliessungsprojekte als europaeische

Gemeinschaftsaufgabe? Entwicklung der Infrastruktur in Europa und Uebersee', *Wirtschaftsdienst* 35(2) (1955), pp. 63–72; 3 (1955), pp. 127–32.

2. See John G. Gunnel, 'The Technocratic Image and the Theory of Technocracy', *Technology and Culture*, 23 (1982), pp. 392–416; Stefan Willeke, *Die Technokratiebewegung in Nordamerika und Deutschland zwischen den Weltkriegen. Eine vergleichende Analyse* (Frankfurt/Main u.a.: Peter Lang 1995), p. 82.

3. Alfred Frisch, *Grossmacht Technokratie. Die Zukunft der Gesellschaft* (Frankfurt/Main: Agenor 1955). Here, the role of Josef Caillaux, Erik Labonne, Raoul Dautry, Louis Armand, Jean Monnet, Ernest Bevin, Stafford Cripps and Johannes Semler, among others, for transferring colonial knowledge back to Europe still remains to be specified. It is striking, though, that many 'founding fathers' of an integrated Europe had spent some time of their lives in colonies or had been dealing with colonial affairs prior to their European engagement. This applies to Jean Monnet, Konrad Adenauer (who served as one of the vice presidents of the 'Deutsche Kolonialgesellschaft' in the 1920s), Sicco Mansholt and Winston Churchill, among many others.

4. James C. Scott, *Seeing Like a State. How Certain Schemes to Improve the Human Condition Have Failed* (New Haven/London: Yale University Press, 1998).

5. Daniel Headrick, *The Tools of Empire: Technology and European Imperialism in the Nineteenth Century* (New York/Oxford: Oxford University Press, 1981).

6. Michael Adas, *Machines as the Measure of Men: Science, Technology, and Ideologies of Western Dominance* (Ithaca: Cornell University Press 1989); Michael Adas (ed.), *Technology and European Overseas Enterprise: Diffusion, Adaptation and Adoption* (Aldershot: Variorum 1996).

7. Robert Seeley, *The Expansion of England* (Chicago/London: University of Chicago Press 1971), p. 61.

8. Dirk van Laak, '"Auf den Hochstrassen des Weltwirtschaftsverkehrs". Zur europaeischen Ideologie der „Erschliessung" im ausgehenden 19. Jahrhundert', *Comparativ. Zeitschrift fuer Globalgeschichte und vergleichende Gesellschaftsforschung* (forthcoming in 2010).

9. David F. Noble, *The Religion of Technology. The Divinity of Man and the Spirit of Invention* (New York: Penguin 1997).

10. Max Liniger-Goumaz, *L'Eurafrique. Utopie ou réalité? Les Metamorphoses d'une Idée* (Yaoundé 1972).

11. Adam Hochschild, *King Leopold's Ghost. A Story of Greed, Terror, and Heroism in Colonial Africa* (Boston/New York: Houghton and Mifflin 1998).

12. Jan Henning Boettger, '"Bienvenue dans la capitale de l'Empire!" Die Tagung des "Institut Colonial International" in Berlin (1897) in Ulrich van der Heyden/Joachim Zeller (eds) „Macht und Anteil an der Weltherrschaft." Berlin und der deutsche Kolonialismus* (Muenster: Unrast-Verlag 2005), pp. 109–15; Janny de Jong, 'Kolonialisme op een koopje. Het Internationale Koloniale Instituut, 1894–1914', *Tijdschrift voor Geschiedenis* 109(1) (1996), pp. 45–72.

13. Maria-Theresia Schwarz, „Je weniger Afrika, desto besser". Die deutsche Kolonialkritik am Ende des 19. Jahrhunderts* (Frankfurt/Main u.a. Peter Lang 1999).

14. Campaigns like Mahatma Gandhi's to boycott European technology and economy, however, rather validate its suggestive and almost irresistible power. See also David J. Arnold, 'Europe, Technology, and Colonialism in the 20th Century', *History and Technology* 21(1) (2005), pp. 85–106.

15. Thoralf Klein/Frank Schumacher (eds), *Kolonialkriege. Militaerische Gewalt im Zeichen des Imperialismus* (Hamburg: Hamburger Edition 2006).

16. János Riesz, *Lépold Sédar Senghor und der afrikanische Aufbruch im 20. Jahrhundert* (Wuppertal: Peter Hammer 2006); Sebastian Conrad/Arif Dirlik/Andreas Eckert (eds), 'Beyond Hegemony? Europe and the Politics of Non-Western Elites, 1900–1930', *Journal of Modern European Studies* 4(2) (2006).

17. Clarence B. Davis/Kenneth E.Wilburn with Ronald E. Robinson (eds), *Railway Imperialism* (New York/Westport, Conn./London: Greenwood Press 1991), p. 3.

18. Leo Weinthal (ed.), *The Story of the Cape to Cairo Railway and River Route, from 1887 to 1922*. 5 vols (London 1923).

19. Dirk van Laak, *Imperiale Infrastruktur. Deutsche Planungen fuer eine Erschliessung Afrikas, 1880 bis 1960* (Paderborn: Ferdinand Schöningh Verlag 2004).

20. Christian Koller, *„Von Wilden aller Rassen niedergemetzelt". Die Diskussion um die Verwendung von Kolonialtruppen in Europa zwischen Rassismus, Kolonial- und Militaerpolitik (1914–1930)* (Stuttgart: Steiner 2001). In 1928, Arthur Dix also hinted at the fact that, at the same time that coloured soldiers exerted control on Germany, German members of the Foreign Legion did the same for the French in Morocco (*Schluss mit Europa! Ein Wegweiser durch Weltgeschichte und Weltpolitik*, Berlin 1928, p. 10).

21. Katiana Orluc, 'Decline or Renaissance: The Transformation of European Consciousness after the First World War' in Bo Stråth (ed.) *Europe and the Other and Europe as the Other* (Brussels: Peter Lang 2000), pp. 123–58.

22. Herward Sieberg, *Colonial Development. Die Grundlegung moderner Entwicklungspolitik durch Grossbritannien, 1919–1949* (Stuttgart: Steiner 1985).

23. Dietmar Rothermund, *Delhi, 15. August 1947. Das Ende kolonialer Herrschaft* (Muenchen: DTV 1998), p. 215; Juergen Osterhammel, *Kolonialismus. Geschichte, Formen, Folgen* (Muenchen: Beck 1995), p. 117.

24. Richard Coudenhove-Kalergi, *Paneuropa* (Wien/Leipzig 1923).

25. Herman Soergel, *Atlantropa* (Muenchen/Zuerich 1932).

26. Herman Soergel/Bruno Siegwart, 'Erschliessung Afrikas durch Binnenmeere. Saharabewaesserung durch Mittelmeerabsenkung', *Beilage zum Baumeister* 33(3) (1935), p. 39.

27. Alexander Gall, 'Atlantropa: A Technological Vision of a United Europe' in Erik van der Vleuten/Arne Kaijser (eds) *Networking Europe. Transnational Infrastructures and the Shaping of Europe, 1850–2000* (Sagamore Beach: Science History Publications 2006), pp. 99–128.

28. Oskar Karstedt, *Internationale Bekaempfung der Arbeitslosigkeit durch Erschliessung ueberseeischer Gebiete. Zugleich ein Beitrag zum Problem der Vergroesserung des Welthandelsvolumens* (Berlin 1931); Claude-Robert Ageron, 'L'idée d'Eurafrique et le dèbat colonial franco-allemand de l'entre-deux-guerres', *Revue d'Histoire moderne et contemporaine* 22 (1975), pp. 446–75; Etienne Deschamps, 'Quelle Afrique pour une Europe unie? L'idée d'Eurafrique à l'aube des années trentes' in Michel Dumoulin (ed.) *Penser l'Europe à l'aube des années trentes* (Louvain-laneuve/Bruessel: UCL 1995), pp. 95–150; Thomas Moser, *Europaeische Integration, Dekolonisation, Eurafrika. Eine historische Analyse ueber die Entstehungsbedingungen der Eurafrikanischen Gemeinschaft von der Weltwirtschaftskrise bis zum Jaunde-Vertrag, 1929–1963* (Baden-Baden: Nomos 2000), pp. 95–146.

29. Wilhelm Guerge/Wilhelm Grotkopp (eds), *Grossraumwirtschaft. Der Weg zur euro-paeischen Einheit. Ein Grundriss* (Berlin 1931).

30. Juergen Elvert, *Mitteleuropa! Deutsche Plaene zur europaeischen Neuordnung (1918–1945)* (Stuttgart: Steiner 1999); Birgit Kletzin, *Europa aus Rasse und Raum. Die nationalsozialistische Idee der Neuen Ordnung* (Muenster: LIT Verlag 2000).

For lingering fears of a German predominance in recent Europe see John Laughland, *The Tainted Source. The Undemocratic Origins of the European Idea* (London: Little, Brown 1997).

31. Arthur Rosenberg, 'Was denken die Neger von Deutschland? Afrikas Rolle im Schuman-Plan', *Die Zeit*, 9 August 1951. See also: 'Umweg ueber Afrika', *Industriekurier*, 73(Mai 16) 1950, p. 2.

32. Cited in: Juergen Bergmann, *Die assoziierten afrikanischen Gebiete in der Europaeischen Wirtschaftsgemeinschaft unter besonderer Beruecksichtigung ihrer Entwicklungsproblematik* (Cologne 1958), p. 15ff.

33. Marie-Thérèse Bitsch, 'Introduction' in Marie-Thérèse Bitsch and Gérard Bossuat (eds) *L'Europe Unie et l'Afrique. De l'Idee d'Eurafrique à la Convention de Lomé. Actes du Colloque International de Paris, 1er et 2 Avril 2004* (Bruxelles/Paris/Baden-Baden: Bruylant/LGDJ/Nomos 2005), p. 3ff.

34. Cit. in Ludolf Herbst, *Option für den Westen. Vom Marshallplan bis zum deutsch-französischen Vertrag* (Muenchen: DTV 1989), p. 211. See also Franz Obermeier, *Die Bedeutung von Franzoesisch-Afrika im Rahmen einer deutsch-franzoesischen Integration* (Muenchen 1951).

35. *Der Strassburgplan. Vorschlaege fuer die Hebung der wirtschaftlichen Beziehungen zwischen den Mitgliedstaaten des Europarates und der verfassungsmaessigen mit ihnen verbundenen ueberseeischen Laendern. Veroeffentlicht vom Generalsekretariat des Europarates* (Strassburg 1952) (German ed. Bonn, Bundesministerium fuer den Marshallplan 1953); 'Wirtschaftliche Erschliessungsprojekte als europaeische Gemeinschaftsaufgabe? Entwicklung der Infrastruktur in Europa und Uebersee', *Wirtschaftsdienst* 35(2) (1955), pp. 63–72.

36. Moser, *Europaeische Integration* (2000); Enzo R. Grilli, *The European Community and the Developing Countries* (Cambridge: Cambridge University Press 1993).

37. Jasmine Aimaq, *For Europe or Empire? French Colonial Ambitions and the European Army Plan* (Lund: Lund Univ. 1996).

38. Robert Falkner, *Auslandshilfe und* Containment. *Anfaenge amerikanischer Auslandshilfepolitik in der Dritten Welt, 1945–1952* (Muenster/Hamburg: LIT 1994); Gerhard Th. Mollin, *Die USA und der Kolonialismus. Amerika als Partner und Nachfolger der belgischen Macht in Afrika 1939–1965* (Berlin: Akademie Verlag 1996).

39. Walt W. Rostow, The *Stages of Economic Growth. A Non-Communist Manifesto*, (Cambridge: Cambridge University Press. 1960). Corinna R. Unger, 'Modernization à la Mode: West German and American Development Plans for the Third World', in: *German Historical Institute (Washington), Bulletin* No. 40 (Spring 2007), p. 143–159. *Point Four* in 1952 was accompanied by the *Mutual Security Act*, binding any aid to military assistance.

40. Michael E. Latham, *Modernization as Ideology: American Social Science and 'Nation Building' in the Kennedy Era* (Chapel Hill: UNC Press 2000); Boris Barth/Juergen Osterhammel (eds), *Zivilisierungsmissionen. Imperiale Weltverbesserung seit dem 18. Jahrhundert* (Konstanz: Uvk 2005); Michael Adas, *Dominance by Design. Technological Imperatives and America's Civilizing Mission* (Cambridge: Cambridge University Press 2006).

41. For example, Anton Zischka, *Afrika, Europas Gemeinschaftsaufgabe Nr. 1* (Oldenburg 1951); Karl Krueger, *Afrika* (Berlin 1952); Gustav-Adolf Gedat, *Europas Zukunft liegt in Afrika* (Stuttgart 1954).

42. John Iliffe, *A Modern History of Tanganyika* (Cambridge: Cambridge University Press 1979), pp. 439–42.

43. Andreas Wilkens, 'Vom Rhein bis zum Kongo. Franzoesisch-deutsche Wirtschaftsprojekte und Politik in Afrika, 1950–1959' in *Revue d'Allemagne* 31 (1999), pp. 481–96.

44. Gustav-Adolf Gedat, *Europas Zukunft liegt in Afrika* (Stuttgart 1954), p. 51.

45. Alfred Frisch, 'Zukunftshoffnungen fuer das Saharagebiet', *Wirtschaftsdienst* 34(3) (1954), pp. 156–60. For longer traditions dating back to French technocrat Henri de Saint-Simon see Michael J. Heffernan, 'Bringing the Desert to Bloom: French Ambitions in the Sahara Desert During the Late Nineteenth Century – the Strange Case of *"la mer intérieure"*' in Denis Cosgrove and Geoff Petts (eds) *Water, Engineering and Landscape. Water Control and Landscape Transformation in the Modern Period* (London/New York: Bellhaven Press 1990), pp. 94–114.

46. Johannes Semler, 'Die deutsche Wirtschaft und die Erschliessung Afrikas'. Vortrag, gehalten in Duesseldorf am 27.11.1953 im Hause des Bankvereins Westdeutschland AG, Kiel 1953, p. 22.

47. Rothermund, *Delhi, 15. August 1947.*

48. Gustav-Adolf Gedat, 'Was wird aus diesem Afrika? Wiedersehen mit einem Kontinent nach 15 JahrenStuttgart 1952), p. 49 [my translation, DvL]. At the time of publication the author was a member of the West German parliament.

49. Andreas Eckert, 'Exportschlager Wohlfahrtsstaat? Europaeische Sozialstaatlichkeit und Kolonialismus in Afrika nach dem Zweiten Weltkrieg', *Geschichte und Gesellschaft* 32 (2006), pp. 467–88.

50. Conversely, the Western bloc endorsed the former Gold Coast, now Ghana, with a dam of similar ambition: the Akosombo dam of the river Volta. Financed by the World Bank, the United States and Great Britain, it was meant to counterweigh the humiliation of Aswan and to stabilize influences on dictator Kwame Nkrumah of Ghana.

51. One of the effects was the double French veto against the British application for EEC membership in 1963 and 1966.

52. Peo Hansen, 'European Integration, European Identity and the Colonial Connection', *European Journal of Social Theory* 5(4) (2002), pp. 491–3.

53. Moser, *Europaeische Integration* (2000), p. 516.

54. For responses of decolonization for the French society see Kristin Ross, *Fast Cars, Clean Bodies. Decolonization and the Reordering of French Culture* (Cambridge, Mass: MIT 1995).

55. Roy F. Holland, *European Decolonisation 1918–1981. An Introductory Survey* (London: Macmillan 1985), p. 163.

56. Thomas Oppermann, '"Eurafrika" Idee und Wirklichkeit', *Europa-Archiv* 23 (1960), p. 700; Robert W. Heywood, 'West European Community and the Eurafrica concept in the 1950s', *Journal of European Integration* 4(2) (1981), pp. 199–211.

57. Miles Kahler, *Decolonization in Britain and France: The Domestic Consequences of International Relations* (Princeton: Princeton University Press 1984), p. 134f; William I. Zartman, 'Europe and Africa. Decolonization or Dependency?' *Foreign Affairs* 54(2) (January 1976), p. 328ff.

58. John D. Hargreaves, *Decolonization in Africa*, 2nd edn (London/New York: Longman 1996), p. 187.

59. See debate in House of Commons on the Schuman Plan on 26/27 June 1950, in *Parliamentary Debates* (Hansard Commons), series V, Vol. 476 (London 1950), p. 1963ff.

60. Anne Deighton, 'Ernest Bevin and the Idea of Euro-Africa from the Interwar to the Postwar Period' in Marie-Thérèse Bitsch and Gérard Bossuat (eds) *L'Europe Unie et l'Afrique. De l'Idee d'Eurafrique à la Convention de Lomé. Actes du Colloque International de Paris, 1er et 2 Avril 2004* (Bruxelles/Paris/Baden-Baden: Bruylant/LGDJ/Nomos 2005), pp. 97–118.

61. Gerhard Altmann, *Abschied vom Empire. Die innere Dekolonisation Grossbritanniens 1945–1985* (Goettingen 2005); Martin Lynn (ed.), *The British Empire in the 1950s. Retreat or Revival?* (Basingstoke: Palgrave 2006).

62. Hansen, 'European Integration', p. 490.

63. Robert Lemaignen, 'Die Assoziierung der ueberseeischen Laender mit der Europaeischen Wirtschaftsgemeinschaft', *Bulletin der Europaeischen Wirtschaftsgemeinschaft* 8/9 (1960), pp. 5–14.

64. Moser, *Europaeische Integration* (2000), p. 143.

65. Werner Ungerer, 'Die Assoziierung afrikanischer Staaten und Madagaskars mit der EWG im Lichte antieuropaeischer Kritik' in *Europa-Archiv* 20(8) (1965), pp. 308–14.

66. Dirk van Laak, 'Kolonien als "Laboratorien der Moderne"?' in Sebastian Conrad and Juergen Osterhammel (eds) *Das Kaiserreich transnational. Deutschland in der Welt 1871–1914* (Goettingen: Vandenhoeck & Ruprecht 2004), pp. 257–79.

67. See, for instance, Gabrielle Hecht, *The Radiance of France. Nuclear Power and National Identity after World War II* (Cambridge, Mass./London: MIT 1998), and the 'Colonialism, Decolonization, and Development' section of the 'Tensions of Europe' programme, www.tensionsofeurope.eu.

68. See, for instance, Wolfgang Uwe Eckart, *Medizin und Kolonialimperialismus. Deutschland 1884–1945* (Paderborn: Ferdinand Schoningh 1997). Presently, there are even disputes about the causal connection between genocidal wars in Africa and the Holocaust; see, for instance, the conference on 'Genocide and Colonialism' held at the University of Sydney, 18–20 July 2003; Juergen Zimmerer, *Von Windhuk nach Auschwitz. Beitraege zum Verhaeltnis von Kolonialismus und Holocaust* (Muenster: LIT 2007).

69. Peter Gold, *Europe or Africa? A Contemporary Study of the Spanish North African Enclaves of Ceuta and Melilla* (Liverpool: Liverpool University Press 2000).

70. Hansen, 'European Integration', p. 489.

Biography 1: An Electrifying Legacy: The Long Life of the Oliven Plan

Vincent Lagendijk

Although Oskar Oliven (born 1870, Breslau) died in 1939, he continues to live on in several ways. For one, he is immortalized in the Dr Oskar Oliven Memorial Scholarship, established in 2003 by his son Gerald and his wife Hedy at the Weizmann Institute of Science in Tel Aviv, Israel. For another, his name repeatedly surfaces in processes of building a European electricity network throughout the twentieth century. That latter legacy dates back to November 1930, when he unveiled a plan for a European electricity system. His ideas were not only about increasing system efficiency. A European system was also connected to peace and prosperity under the aegis of European cooperation. While his plan is relatively well known among historians, the memory of Oliven and his plan has also been frequently invoked by engineers of successive generations, nearly always at moments of important changes in the European electricity network.

In 1930 Oliven, Director of the *Gesellschaft für Elektrische Unternehmungen* (GESFÜREL), gave a General Address to the World Power Conference. Whereas most engineers had thought in terms of local, regional and sometimes national networks, Oliven presented a bold scheme for the electrification of Europe. He envisaged a network of approximately 9.750 km, consisting of five main lines. Technologically, Oliven did not see insurmountable problems. He pointed out that new 200 kV lines were built to operate eventually at 400 kV. However, he expected that 'personal and political motives' would be potential barriers. Such motives had prevented otherwise sound interconnections of plants and systems on smaller scales earlier, and prevailed over economic–technical logic. Importantly, Oliven did not see his grand vision as likely to be completed for generations to come. He recognized a growing number of interconnections between emerging national systems, and regarded these as 'a very good interim solution for the period until the time when the difficulties standing in the way of a common European high voltage system are removed by international agreements'. The first practical step towards a rational electricity supply in Europe was to create a European electricity network.

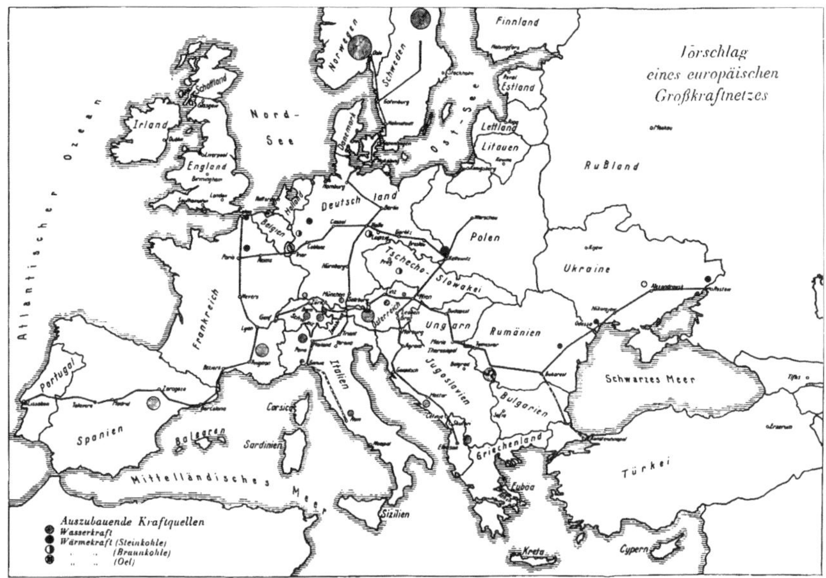

Figure B1.1   Oliven's plan for a European system

Source: Oskar Oliven, 'European super power lines: Proposal for a European super power system' (General address presented at the World Power Conference, Berlin, 1930). Used by permission of the World Energy Council, London.

Subsequent steps were taken to study the possibilities of forging a European electricity system in the following years. The League of Nations' Organisation for Communications and Transit, the International Labour Office under the guidance of Albert Thomas, and also the well-connected engineer Dannie Heineman all participated in this activity. During the Interbellum, Oliven's name almost became a synonym for any idea on a European electricity system. Yet his plan fell from its pedestal once Hitler rose to power, and peaceful international relations were stymied. In those turbulent years Oliven was also personally affected. The 'aryanization' of GESFÜREL in 1934 deprived him of his position, and he went into exile in Zurich, Switzerland, where he died three years later.

His legacy lived on, however. Immediately after the Second World War, engineers met in a spirit of mutual trust and of hope, wishing to rebuild Europe. Italian engineer Amilcare Berni reminded his colleagues of Oliven's plan and his unfavourable timing. In the reigning atmosphere of collaboration between European nations, new hope arose of studying this issue, according to Berni. His Swiss colleague René Hochreutiner similarly referred to Oliven's plan as an example of the ambitions of engineers to eventually create a high voltage European system. Rather than building new interconnections at 400 kV, Hochreutiner proposed first to use existing transmission lines to their full extent, and then to gradually expand the number of interconnections and forge an interconnection system.

By 1961 a well-integrated system was in place in Western Europe. On the eve of a meeting of electrical engineers, chairman Strahringer of the *Vereinigung Deutscher Elektrizitätswerke* placed this development into a historical context, under the title *The future is rooted in the past*: 'Today, when very high voltage lines pass through all our countries, when the island kingdom of Great Britain is being connected to the French mainland by a cable through the Channel, and the connection of the Scandinavian energy potential to the German supply system is planned in the North, we are reminded of the Oliven Plan.' He stressed how terms like *co-ordination* and *co-operation* were taken into daily use after the Second World War, and the drive towards efficiency and rationalization bore its fruits. But Strahringer underlined also how efforts for European co-operation à la Oliven 'help us towards our goal and promote welfare and peace among the nations'.

Plans for new interconnections certainly proceeded. With well-developed regional interconnections, engineers clearly started to consider cross-regional cooperation. In that process, a momentous event took place in 1995, when the systems of four Central and Eastern European countries were connected to the Western European system. This not only ended a decades-long struggle to build interconnections across the Iron Curtain, it also gave rise to new ideas on the future of the European system. Such was the topic of an article by engineers Brumshagen and Schwarz. They discussed the current weaknesses of the system – the recent reconciled German system, the Balkanization of the former Yugoslav system – and potential new reinforcements, such as a ring structure connecting countries around the Baltic sea and a very high voltage direct current line from Russia to Germany. Although mainly dealing with the future, the authors also drew on the past. They highlighted how Oskar Oliven envisioned an 'all-European' interconnected electricity system in 1930. 'In those days the ideas of Oliven were considered a vision', they explained, 'but today such ideas have become realistic.'

Literature

Vincent Lagendijk, *Electrifying Europe: The Power of Europe in the Construction of Electricity Networks* (Amsterdam: Aksant 2008).

Helmut Maier, *Erwin Marx (1893–1980), Ingenieurwissenschaftler in Braunschweig, und die Forschung und Entwicklung auf dem Gebiet der elektrischen Energieübertragung auf weite Entfernungen zwischen 1918 und 1950* (Verlag für Geschichte der Naturwissenschaften und der Technik 1993).

Harald Brumshagen and Jürgen Schwarz, 'The European power systems on the threshold of a new East-West co-operation,' *IEEE Transactions on energy conversion* 11, no. 2 (1996): pp. 462–474.

2
Myths of the European Network: Constructions of Cohesion in Infrastructure Maps

Alexander Badenoch

Figure 2.1 Title page, *Länderkarten des Europäischen Fernsprechdienstes*, Berlin, 1928. This image shows an idealized network: it does not correspond to any of those portrayed in the book

> Here's Europe wrinkled with new boundaries. But never you mind that … here Europe is.
>
> Thomas Cook & Son, 1924[1]

> The concept of a European road network is an old one … … and it had complex infrastructure too.
>
> European Roundtable of Industrialists, 1989[2]

Introduction: An interruption

At the start of the 1970s, the energy committee of the United Nations Economic Commission for Europe (UNECE) set out to create an 'International Map of Gas Transmission Networks in Europe'. As is common practice in assembling such maps, the committee asked every member nation to submit a map of its own gas network, conforming to certain specifications of representation and scale. Turkey duly supplied a map for the second edition that detailed its gas 'network': a single pipeline, 10 cm in diameter, stretching 130 km between three cities on the 'European' side of the Bosporus (see Figure 2.2). The accompanying letter acknowledged that this 'network' might not merit inclusion in such a lofty project, stating drily: '[i]t is up to you to decide whether to include it in the revision work being undertaken.'[3]

From the map, it is hard to interpret the actual intent of its makers. Was it only an honest report, submitted in the spirit of international participation and co-operation? Was it meant to deflect international interest away from Turkey's resources or conversely to attract attention to it as an 'empty' place worthy of 'development' and assistance? Was it the result of a misunderstanding of what was meant by 'Europe', only showing pipelines on the 'European' side of the Bosporus? Whatever its intent, the map can certainly be read as an interruption of the entire project of mapping the European network. Not only is its 'network' not connected to 'Europe', but it seems to lack any relation to the territory in which it is situated: it neither connects major cities nor fills the space provided. It seemed *out of place* in the project and raised the question of whether it should be included at all.

To an extent, this map reveals the difficulties that have plagued mapping projects since the so-called 'cartographic revolution' of the sixteenth century: namely the problem of bringing together a series of local knowledges into an apparently universal framework. As David Turnbull argues, maps have been one of the key instruments by which

> the motley of scientific practice, its situated messiness, is given a spatial coherence through the social labour of creating equivalences and connections. Such knowledge spaces acquire their taken for granted air and seemingly unchallengeable naturalness through the suppression and denial of the work involved in their construction.[4]

In this particular map, bringing Turkey into the harmonized knowledge space of the map (by fitting local data to the prescribed scale and map specifications) has not suppressed but rather revealed other forms of 'messiness': a disconnection between network practice and territorial practice that shows the contingent nature of both.

By attempting to reconcile their conceptual tensions, network maps act as important mediators within and between the material, institutional and discursive frames of European infrastructures.[5] On the material level, maps are media that represent material structures in a widely legible code, asserting a series of relations beyond those immediately visible from any specific point. They form a key means by which human actors within a system or territory co-ordinate and harmonize system activities in time and space.

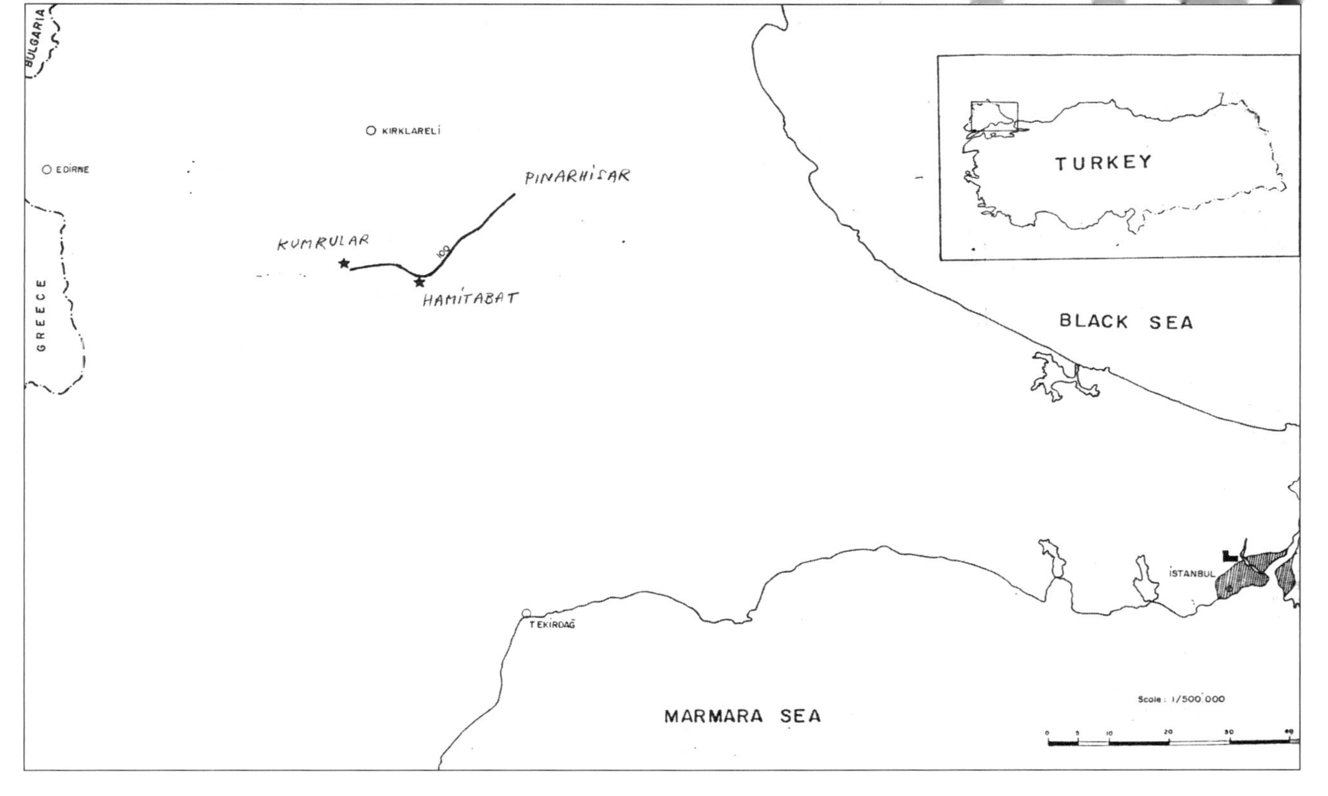

Figure 2.2   Turkey's submission for the UN ECE's International Map of Gas Transmission Systems in Europe, 1980
Source: UN archives.

In this way maps also mediate between the material and the institutional. Maps are used to circulate standardized knowledge within institutions such as the UNECE, as well as to mark off the boundaries of institutional power and knowledge to both internal and external viewers. Finally, within and beyond these frameworks, maps are components of discourses, shaped by and shaping the series of practices and beliefs surrounding the spaces and networks they represent.[6] Maps are, as I will show, one means by which institutions, networks and/or nations perform European-ness and also a means by which disparate national and/or local regimes and structures perform as a unified network.

In what follows, I use maps of European networks to explore historically the relationships between technological infrastructures, national territories and ideas and experiences of Europe.[7] My goal is neither to provide a thorough history of European network cartography nor to elaborate on spatial theory. Instead, acknowledging the long-standing and widespread tensions that have existed between notions of European space and beliefs about technological networks, I want to present a set of important texts and analytical tools to show the recurring strategies for addressing or reconciling those tensions. To remain in spatial metaphors: this essay is not meant to be a map, but rather an orientation and initial landscape survey. I will present some useful lenses for observation, train them on significant points in the landscape and make suggestions for how we might travel between them meaningfully and usefully.

The assumption that infrastructures and territories are more or less naturally linked has remained one of the dominating ideologies in the Western world. As Graham and Marvin point out, infrastructures 'are believed to bind cities, regions and nations into functioning geographical or political wholes. Traditionally, they have been seen to be systems that require public regulation so that they somehow *add cohesion* to territory, often in the name of some "public interest"'.[8] In the nineteenth and early twentieth centuries, the consolidation of statewide monopolies over energy, transportation and communication networks operated under this assumption and set out to 'energize' national territories by integrating them more thoroughly into networks.[9] To this day, cohesion of national territory is an argument for infrastructural development that needs little further elaboration.[10] However, as Andrew Barry notes, 'i]f the territorial boundaries of states are generally fixed, zones of technological circulation are not.'[11] Transport and communication technologies have circulated transnationally via engineering communities, not to mention material links between nations, since the initial embedding of these systems in societies. Similarly, the idea that infrastructures will bind territories together has not been limited to the national arenas, but has also been powerful in movements for European integration and unification. The Enlightenment view of transport and communication networks as the circulatory systems of a body is a particularly persuasive expression of this sort of 'oneness' of infrastructure and territory. Besides the material connections between people and nations that they have created, lines of roads, rails and electricity wires crossing borders have served as powerful metaphors and visual symbols of international co-operation and European identity. The logic at work in much of the drive to build European infrastructures has been summed up neatly by J. Peter Burgess in his analysis of Robert Schuman's discussions of the European Coal and Steel Community: 'An empirical unity – a *de facto* – unity is necessary to preserve, defend, and cultivate a spiritual one, and, inversely, it is the *de facto* unity, the assembly of empirical realities proper to the nations and ethnic groups of Europe that gives rise to the spiritual unity so *idealistically* evoked by Schuman.'[12]

By always defining one in terms of the other, such chicken-and-egg logic of European unity acknowledges yet talks around the ways in which neither Europe nor its various infrastructural networks have ever been terribly cohesive. Defining Europe, whether materially, spatially or spiritually, has been a matter of constant ideological struggle and shifting boundaries.[13] The process of building networks in Europe has been particularly diffuse and contested, involving a wide range of national and international actors, often with varying and conflicting visions of the networks they are building. As Latour insists, a network is also 'local at all points'.[14] Even when transnational links between networks have been built, such as in the recent cases of the Channel Tunnel and the Öresund Bridge, but also in older cases such as the Gotthard Tunnel in Switzerland, their meaning as local projects, bilateral links or European network nodes has been unstable and contested.[15] Many of the networks that supposedly unite Europe also transcend any cohesive geographical notion of Europe and uneven access within those spaces results in internal 'splintering' of localities.[16] As the internal boundaries between EU member states have gradually become more porous through the rise of a 'network Europe' characterized by instantaneous flows of people, goods and capital, more attention is being paid toward the hardening and networked proliferation of 'external' boundaries and (re)assertions of territorial space.[17]

These problems of space return us to the problems of maps, and in particular of those maps that have sought to portray the large and fragmentary constructions of Europe and infrastructures in the same frame. In spite of what EU officials would occasionally have one believe, various material infrastructures have purported in one way or another to be 'the European network' long before the process described as European integration began.[18] The role and power of maps in shaping ideas of nations as well as ideas of Europe has been well documented.[19] Similarly, as noted, the connection between the growth of transport and communication infrastructures in strengthening ties both within and between nations in Europe has been frequently asserted. Maps of networks, particularly transport and communication networks, thus form an important, and largely underexplored, site where the ideologies and tensions surrounding European networks become visible.[20] Maps' two-dimensional representational framework presents an enduring code of representation that requires strategic simplifications and silences in order to reconcile the complex relations they seek to describe.[21] These representational devices, in turn, guide and shape network practices.

To make these processes visible I will proceed in two parts here. In the first part, drawing on analytical tools from recent critical engagements with maps specifically, and space in general, I will point to various ways in which the cohesion of infrastructures and the cohesion of 'European' space have been co-constructed through maps. This will be based on observations drawn from a broad survey of maps collected over the course of research on a number of different networks.[22] In the second part, I will look at two cases of how cartographic myths of the European network have been employed in specific contexts and at different levels. One highlights the role of maps in the planning and partial execution of a single road-building project in the interwar period to show how a number of spatial visions of European networks flowed into and out of the processes of construction; the second examines maps of European road and rail networks made for tourists during the Cold War to show how enduring visions and material links were embedded within the divided geopolitical framework.

European networks as myths

In recent years, critical engagement with maps, particularly following on from the work of J.B. Harley, has led to a general understanding of them not as disinterested reporting of facts, but as 'representations of belief and ideology – rooted in particular cultures and institutions'.[23] Much of this critical understanding has been based around the semiological analysis of maps' functioning as myths, defined by Roland Barthes as 'second-order signifiers' that mobilize representations of historically contingent circumstances and events as forms that signify them as universal, natural and/or disinterested fact.[24] Maps not only represent the physical relations of objects in space, they also select them, frame them, bound them, name them and assert the co-presence of their various disparate elements as natural and significant.[25] As Harley has pointed out, the expert knowledge of cartography, much like that of engineers, makes 'black boxes' out of many maps that mask their ideological agendas by appearing to be purely products of neutral technical practices and standards.[26] At the same time, maps assert power over space, not least through their linkages to notions of territory.[27] By exploring a map's various silences, ambiguities and margins, analysts seek to denaturalize its various elements to see the various ideologies at work through them.

While I will draw on such semiotic tools to analyse the maps in question, I also agree with post-structuralist critiques of such approaches, which stress that they are often so focused on 'de-mythologizing' maps in a 'search for conspiracies' by the mapmakers that they overlook maps' intertextual and ambiguous natures.[28] In seeking to account for the ways in which meanings of places and spaces are generated and practised, Rob Shields looks to a more dynamic model of the way specific places and spaces acquire mythical meaning through the accumulation of 'place-images' and 'space-images'.[29] These are partial, and often exaggerated, but through practice '[a] set of core images forms a widely disseminated and commonly held set of images of a place or space. These form a relatively stable group of ideas in currency, reinforced by their communication value as conventions circulating in a discursive economy.'[30] Maps act as place and space images by ordering representations of various places and spaces in relation to each other with regard to a number of binary oppositions such as central or peripheral, connected or disconnected, natural or civilized, or, indeed, European or non-European. The truth value of maps, which includes their mythical persuasions, grants them particular currency in reinforcing or transforming the myths of the various places they represent. At the same time, being alert to the disjunctures and ambiguities between place and space myths can draw attention to various realms for resistant identity formation. Such insights help us to understand maps as integral parts of changing material, institutional and discursive assemblages that are structured according to evolving regimes of practice.

To be clear: in stressing these additional layers of maps' meaning, my point is not about how or whether maps 'lie' or misrepresent material realities, or that they operate in a symbolic sphere somehow divorced from material or spatial practices.[31] Quite the contrary, my argument is that maps offer a means of understanding the complex material, institutional and discursive assemblages of European networks because they are *part of* the 'reality' of infrastructures. Highlighting the ideological and symbolic dimensions that structure infrastructures' design and use sheds important light on how such systems have been embedded and contested over time. Bearing this in mind, I will sketch here briefly some of the most frequently recurring mythologies and point to some of their ambiguities and rhetorical uses.

Europe is where the network is. One of the most noted aspects of maps is their power to name.[32] Unlike nation states, the absence of a precise hegemonic definition of European space affords network maps greater persuasive power in claiming to be 'the European network', particularly when the network seems to be their primary object. This is visible, for example, in a map of 'Europe's Autobahn Network' from a German book on roads from 1959 (Figure 2.3).[33] While showing a space that is mostly filled by Germany – notably with its pre-Second World War borders – the map claims to be of 'Europe's' network. Few readers of the map would consider the space described as all of Europe, but by claiming that the network is 'European' it claims definitively that the space it shows is central to it. The rest is off the map, unimportant, *less European*. An overview of collected system maps

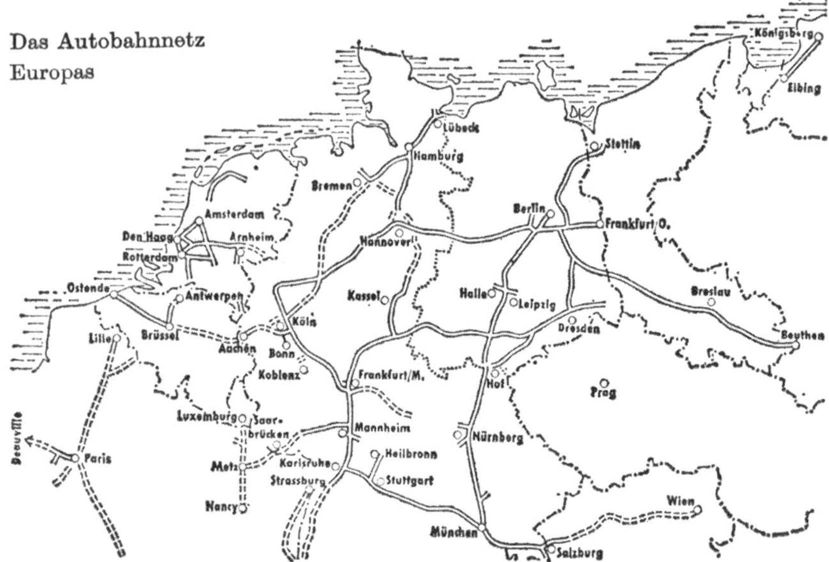

Figure 2.3   'The European Motorway Network' from Herman Schreiber, *Sinfonie der Strasse*, 1959

shows that the spatial definition of Europe as expressed through maps of its infrastructure reflects strongly the many competing notions of where Europe is. The much-problematized Eastern boundary of Europe is defined differently from map to map, with maps sometimes including and naming Russia and showing Moscow as included in the network; sometimes all of Turkey is present, most often half or merely its west coast, sometimes including only Istanbul. The same is also true in the other cardinal directions: Northern Scandinavia, the Iberian Peninsula, Southern Italy and North Africa are routinely out of frame. Notably, this range of framings of European networks, both in the maps of planners and in maps produced by external organizations such as the tourist maps below, seems to change little over time. To be sure, the national boundaries, when they are shown, usually (but not always) change with the changes in politics, but in matters of framing, presence or absence of national boundaries, or portrayal of natural features, there are no readily identifiable periodic shifts. As I will show, even during the sharp divisions of the Cold War, both visions and practices of cross-'Curtain' networks persisted.[34]

Networkedness. Lines on a map suggest connection and even flow between all points.[35] As Barry points out, networks have not only become a commonplace entity within society; they also function as metaphors for it.[36] Maps can powerfully emphasize such images, as in the classic example of Henry

Beck's London tube map, which did away with scale and incorporated the London suburbs into an image of a compact, well-connected city (I am surely not alone in having cursed the name of Henry Beck whilst hurriedly trying to get between trains at a neat-appearing 'node' on his map).[37] At the European level, many such maps of networks were not normally produced by the system administrators, but by third parties with a vested interest in portraying the various systems as a transnational network. In the mid-nineteenth century, British mapmaker Bradshaw and later tour operator Thomas Cook (among others) began producing railway maps and timetables for 'the Continent' to help travellers to cope with what was often perceived as the 'chaos' of a continent served by numerous different private companies.[38] Several decades later, while plans to build a European motor-road network were still being debated, the Swiss firm Hallwag was producing a motor-touring atlas that already presented Europe's roads as a transcontinental network, ordered hierarchically and appearing as a coherent whole that did not relate to national boundaries (Figure 2.4).[39] Maier usefully highlights the importance of networks in constructions of twentieth-century territoriality, in which he argues that 'identity space' and 'decision space' until

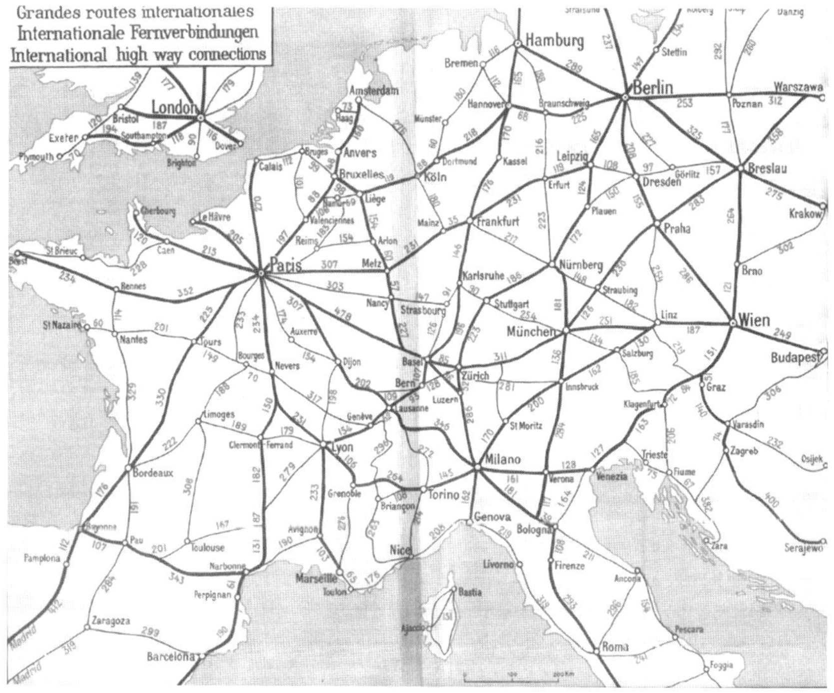

Figure 2.4   The European road network, *Europa Touring*, Hallwag, 1929

around 1970 'coexisted like magnetic fields and electrical fields, orthogonal but overlaid, movement through one generating energy in the other'.[40] On a rhetorical level, maps can also emphasize *imbalances* as a means of justifying intervention. The European Roundtable of Industrialists, for example, called for infrastructure intervention by invoking international connections as a larger network, reframing several points as 'missing links' or 'bottlenecks' in a larger network.[41]

Obduracy refers to the sense of things portrayed in maps as fixed, durable and long-standing. Obsolescence is the greatest threat to a map.[42] Most maps therefore 'exist in the present, or, if they can possibly get away with it, the aorist: no time at all'.[43] This temporal assumption about maps reinforces assumptions that both (national) territories and infrastructures are static or slowly changing. As Barthes has argued about myths, maps function by holding the histories of spaces and places at a distance but in reserve, at once acknowledging their presence and not allowing them into the narrative.[44] But obduracy does not apply equally to all elements in a map. As Denis Wood argues, 'every sign system is potentially figure and every sign system is potentially ground.'[45] The hierarchies of obduracy in a map are seldom unambiguous, and even subtle shifts in relative density of lines, colours and so forth can powerfully emphasize or alter a map's argument. In general, networks are assumed to be the more dynamic element in a system. This becomes apparent when maps do state a specific time, which draws attention to what could change; it asks questions about the relation of the network to the areas beyond, and can dramatize the map's boundaries and frames as spaces that are potentially to be networked.

Naturalness. Naturalizing relations is a key function of myths generally. On European network maps, 'nature', in its colloquial sense, plays an important role in such strategies. Inserting natural features, usually to the exclusion of all other signs of habitation, can assert the naturalness of a space, in which a network (particularly one fitted to its contours) then seems a 'natural' addition. Such features are also useful in positing national borders as 'unnatural' objects. Would-be network-builders, from Hermann Sörgel's overly-ambitious Atlantropa project in the 1930s to Marshall Plan proponents in the 1950s and the European Union in recent years, have all mobilized natural-looking relief maps of Europe as arguments for integrated European-scale technological networks.[46]

Neutrality is a common cartographic myth that pervades European network maps in a variety of particular ways. Both the technology of map-making itself (and the authority behind it) as well as the technical networks portrayed on maps appear as neutral or disinterested. Similarly, the disinterested nature of the nation as 'imagined community' carries over into representations of national territories and justifies their being filled with national networks.[47] Transnational system-builders, by contrast, have often been at pains to portray their networks as existing without any interest in – or effect on – national territories whatsoever, as part of an agenda of 'hiding' their integration work.[48] Maps drawn up by international bodies such as the UNECE contain disclaimers, stating that they make no statement 'concerning the legal status of any country or territory or of its authorities, or concerning the delimitation of the frontiers of any country or territory'. By freeing map-makers of involvement in international tensions, such statements further suggest that the networks on the map are somehow disinterested, serving their own harmless or benevolent purpose. Even maps that are used for clearly interested purposes, such as those embedded in tourist advertisements, often seem to act as neutral testimonials 'quoted' by the interested institution, or as evidence of their knowledge or competence over the network and space portrayed.

Invoking the European network: The transcontinental motorway[49]

The period after the First World War saw a rapid, if uneven, rise of automobility in Europe, spurred on in various ways by the war, as well as by the new demands of peace.[50] Increased desire for cars brought increased pressure to build roads better adapted to them. At the same time as plans for building national motor-road networks also came many proposals to build transnational roads in Europe. Several different plans to build a European network of motor-roads, all of which were more or less unsuccessful, were proposed through a number of different international bodies throughout the 1930s.[51] The demand for transnational roads was part and parcel of the understanding of the uses of cars in their earliest incarnation as leisure vehicles for the rich, namely racing and touring.

One such plan was proposed in 1930 by the British Automobile Association to the Alliance Internationale de Tourisme (AIT), a confederation of mostly European national motoring clubs to build a road from London to Istanbul. The AIT did not have the funds to build roads, but they did have the ability, individually and collectively, to lobby governments. At a time when many plans for large-scale road-building in Europe were being proposed, the AIT plan was quite modest, and as such made it relatively easy for state governments to support. The plan was not to build a new road but to improve existing roads along a specific route to a minimum standard, and to produce numerous materials that would guide motorists along the route. It would be up to each individual nation through which the road passed to design and build its own section along the route prescribed. In short, the AIT used existing structures to invoke ideas of a European network in order to shape practices in a number of settings and contexts.[52]

Many maps of the road show it proceeding in straight lines from capital to capital, making it implicitly a link between nations. Though seldom referred to explicitly, the focus on directness and speed in planning the road reflected an overall view prevalent at the time that increased rationality and efficiency would necessarily bring greater prosperity where it was built.[53] Indeed, the maps that were produced of the route closely resemble many maps for European networks, both extant and planned, that were in circulation at the time. One standard for the road was adhered to as strictly as possible: 'In principle, the route of the road between the large centres which have been marked out should be as direct as possible.'[54]

Although the idea as initially proposed by the AA was only to build a road to Istanbul, the plans soon were expanded to include the British colonial outlook, with extensions going on from Istanbul to Cape Town and Calcutta (see Figure 2.5). The map of the route that the AA produced to support this route, which was published in various places, expresses several spatial visions. Through the use of the large title inset over the bulk of Asia and a distortion in the size of Europe, the map bears some semblance to medieval T-O maps that show Europe, Asia and Africa as three equally balanced parts of the world, with Jerusalem (almost) as the middle point.[55] Whereas the medieval maps expressed a balanced world, however, the tipped axis of the road in the AA map, and the list of distances counted from London, make it clear where the road's physical and ideological origins lie.

For the nations through which the road passed, the road's inscription on the map was an invitation not so much to create a road, but to *join a reality*. The road's first inspection survey in 1933, in which a well-known British motoring journalist drove the proposed route, is what first constructed the road as a single, uniform entity, out of the disparate national roads it was laid over. Within two years of that survey, all the member governments through whose territories the road passed had adopted it into their national road-building schemes, and many gave the road highest priority. While the road was portrayed as a single line, it was meant also to invoke by its very presence a European network. A stated aim of the project was to form 'the first channel to conduct road traffic to and from Europe, and from and to the Continents of Africa and Asia', envisioning that traffic would 'flow into and out of the Route at hundreds of points'.[56] Many nations that were not part of the proposed route saw the plan as an opportunity to 'get on the map' in Europe.[57] The Dutch added their own colonial visions to the project with an extension onward from India, hoping the road would improve tourism to their colonies in Indonesia.[58] The Touring Club of Norway sought to put their own nation on the map by proposing a route that would come down all the way from Kirkenes to Hamburg.[59] By connecting to the London-Istanbul route, and so to Cape Town, the road would thus create a complete North-South Axis, spanning from the 'Northern Cape' to the 'Southern Cape'.[60] The map of the road was not merely an invitation to join in cartographic fantasy, however. Its presence and coming-into-being also provided the AIT (via its members in national touring clubs) with a powerful

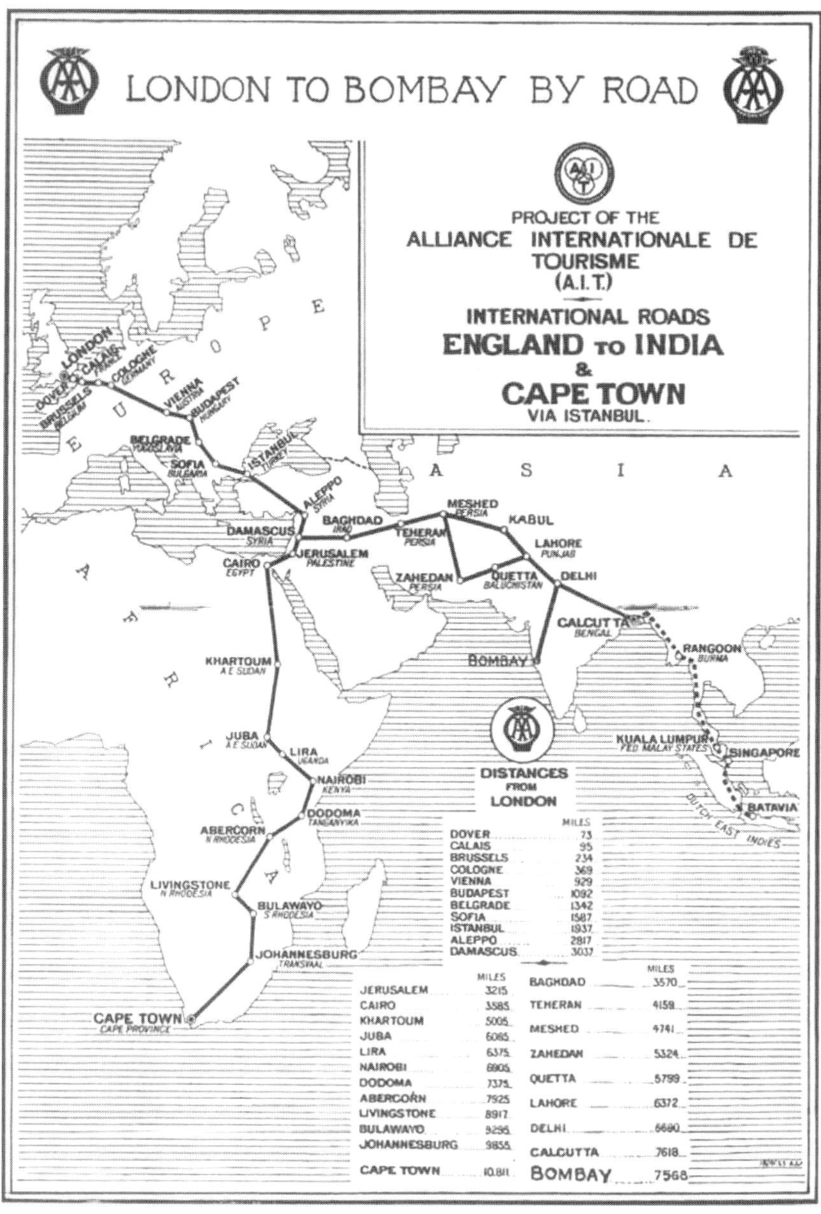

Figure 2.5 'London to Bombay by Road' from the Western India Automobile Association, 1935

Source: Image courtesy of the Automobile Association.

argument for lobbying their governments to adopt uniform standards for road design, border crossings and customs activities.

The vision of the road as the first part of a complete rational network, offering apparently equal links and access between all cities on the route, while playing an important role in the representation and acceptance of the road, also stood in tension with existing place-myths of the places it was joining up. Although the road also travelled a great distance from north to south, it was 'read' by its makers almost exclusively in terms of its east-west axis. Such views were reflected in the map of the route produced by the AA in 1935 (Figure 2.6). While also resembling maps of transnational auto races, with their emphasis on the route rather than the outlines of larger geographical spaces, this particular map actually shifted the map by several degrees. Europe appears not so much dis-oriented as *hyper*-oriented, entirely concerned with its route to the East. The planned road resembles nothing so much as a river flowing across the continent. Indeed, this particular map was to show the intersections of the road with the natural feature of the Danube, and the existing Orient Express rail line.

The vision of the road as a 'natural' link between East and West was expressed during the first meeting of the route's permanent committee. Paul Duchaine, president of the Belgian touring club as well as long-time secretary general of the AIT, stated majestically:

> It is not the AIT, it is geography, it is the sun, which has chosen the path of the road that unites London and Stamboul. This path was once the route of warlike invasion, the route of the peoples of Asia, coming to invade Europe. From henceforth, it will be the great artery of commerce and industry, the beautiful road of the future, joining Europe peacefully to Asia.[61]

Though speaking of London and Istanbul being united by the 'natural' path between them, Duchaine actually points to the mental difference. The creation of peace between the two continents is about *reversing the flow* along the path, bringing Western wealth and enlightenment to the East. The choice of Budapest as a host of the meeting was praised by many of the speakers as being the centre-point between West and East, while all made equally clear that this 'centre' was also in the East, praising its 'oriental' nature. When his turn came to address the meeting, Rechid Safvet Atabinen of Turkey also spoke of Budapest in similar terms, though with markedly different emphasis:

> The Turks, who traditionally have experience of Hungarian hospitality, thus consider that our meeting in this city has much to recommend it. It is not merely situated at the geographical centre of the route, but the path of the Asiatic invasions which brought the Huns, the Magyars and

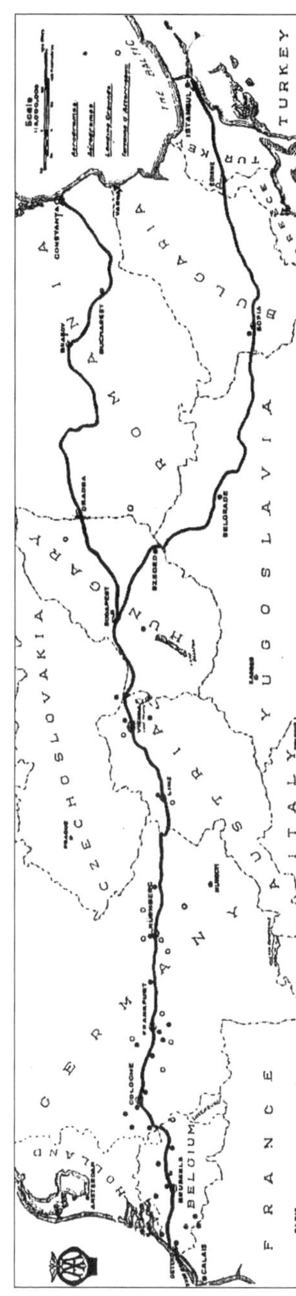

Figure 2.6 Europe, oriented: The London to Istanbul road from a 1933 planning map

Source: Image courtesy of the Automobile Association.

the Kumans to this region, will henceforth be a route of interpenetration of the interests and cultures of Europe and Asia.[62]

Both speakers invoked the same history with regard to the road and the city of Budapest, as well as its symbolic and physical position just east of the centre of Europe. While Duchaine spoke of *reversing* the flow of the road toward the East, Atabinen recalled the former Ottoman possession of much of the Danube basin, presenting the road as following a 'natural' course of *interpenetration* between Europe and Asia. From the time it was proposed, the transcontinental road followed much more the vision expressed by Duchaine, clearly being 'read' in one direction, from West to East. Quite apart from the routine way of referring to the road as 'London to Istanbul' (or 'London to India', or 'London to Cape Town'), the recitation of the road's journey from West to East was even written into the planning practice for the road. The permanent committee's rotating presidency, as well as the order of reports presented to it, followed 'the geographical order of the road' passed on from West to East. In this light, Atabinen's flowery speech becomes intelligible as strongly worded resistance to a number of practices and myths surrounding the road. He does not only draw on the myth of networkedness to assert the *historical* relations of Turkey to the nations further west, but uses the road to put a modern, *contemporaneous* Turkey on the map.

The road's already well-entrenched position in physical and symbolic space had the effect of making its position in time a great deal less certain. Some accounts referred to it unproblematically in the present tense as a road that could be driven straight away, others still in the future tense. When the Second World War finally drew a halt to the construction work, the position still remained uncertain, and this uncertainty continued into the 1950s. A British film reel from 1944 showed both maps, one after another, and mentioned the road as an extant thing.[63] At a meeting of the AIT in 1949, the Turkish delegate explained that the Turkish section of the road was nearly complete, and advocated that, once the road was finished, the headquarters of the permanent committee be moved to Istanbul so that road-building could then be concentrated more on Asia.[64] A British touring guide from 1950 mentions the road, with reference to the segment of it in Belgium as a road still in progress, as does a film advertising for the Marshall Plan in 1951, and the 1952 edition of *Europa Touring* mentioned it in the sections on Hungary and Bulgaria, but nowhere else.[65] It is noteworthy that the mentions in the latter touring guides referred specifically to *national* road networks, where the myth of the European network served as evidence of those nations' modernity and integration long after the actual road had been bypassed in the European road network building.[66]

The supposedly 'organic' planning path of the road was smoothed considerably by invoking specific visions of European space. Imperial powers read it as a way of inscribing their colonial controls and ambitions on and beyond the map of Europe, while many of the smaller states were able to place themselves on the map as modern European nations. For the Balkans and Turkey it was about becoming modern nations; for the countries in the West it was at least in part about looking at their own past in the East. While unifying Europe was one of the purposes that were stated for the road, ultimately the process actually worked the other way around: on maps and in practice, 'Europe' unified the road.

The European network as ghost: Addressing the 'Iron Curtain'

The Second World War did not completely interrupt networking activity in Europe. If anything, military logistics and Nazi plans for large-scale economy (*Großraumwirtschaft*) in the lands they conquered resulted in the proliferation and circulation of ideas and visions for uniting the continent technologically.[67] As the resurrection of the London-Istanbul road in the closing days of the war also indicated, these visions and plans had a momentum of their own that echoed forward past the war. On the material side, the post-Second World War division of Europe did not create a sudden, clean or even steady division of Europe's existing transport networks, although the blocking of cross-border networks became one of the most dramatic, and in many cases traumatic, phenomena of the post-war division of Europe.[68] On the other hand, the perceived mutual threat meant that both sides had an interest in keeping the border in place and obvious.[69] Turning away from the divide, however, both the Americans and the Soviets also had a vested interest in seeing the nations in each respective bloc integrated, both for economic reasons and to bind the countries together for mutual defence. Marshall Plan propaganda specifically targeted national boundaries across roads and railways as 'unnatural' hindrances to the freedom of roads and railways.[70] One major impetus for the reconstruction of transport networks, as well as the lowering of national restrictions on travel, particularly in Western Europe, was to once more get revenue flowing from the 'hidden export' of tourism, particularly for Americans.[71] Movement between countries was to become as free as possible, not only for Europeans, but also for Americans, who tended to see Europe as a single place, and wanted to see multiple countries on their tours.

At the same time, there were also efforts at bridging the divide through networks.[72] The most notable of these was the UNECE, mentioned at the start of this paper. Established in 1947, the UNECE set out explicitly to link all of Europe through the building of material systems. Initially, at least, they were particularly successful in the realm of road-planning. By the beginning of the 1950s, a proposal for a Europe-wide network of roads, the E-road system, was drafted.[73] Working in much the same way as the London to Istanbul Road had worked before, the E-road network was conceived of not as specific roads but as a series of itineraries, which were laid out across the Cold War divide. Each nation was able to designate which routes would make up the network, and improve them in the way that they were best able. Perhaps paradoxically, one of the main drivers behind the creation of the E-road network was the International Road Federation, a body made up largely of Western (including US) oil, rubber and auto industries, which were primarily interested in promoting automobility in the West, where they would be able to sell their products. Maps of transport networks were caught between these two important tensions: the need to acknowledge the geopolitical division of the continent, but also to present visions of connectivity and mobility.

These tensions are very visible in the 1952 edition of the Swiss-based auto guide *Europa Touring.* The dramatic language of division was written into the book's 'key', which told readers that 'the countries at present behind the "Iron Curtain" [...] are grouped at the end of the book,'[74] and indeed on the following page those countries are shown, out of the alphabetical order in which the other countries are arranged, separated from them by a line of 'x's that call to mind nothing so much as a row of barbed wire. The following page provides a political map of Europe showing all the nations portrayed in the book as a key to the breakdown of maps in the rest of the book. The 'Iron Curtain' runs as the heaviest line across the map (Figure 2.7). Apart from this spatial removal, however, the tourist information is nearly as thorough as for many of the other countries portrayed, complete with driving instructions and list of attractive sights to see, without any mention of border crossings. The individual maps of these countries are presented as smaller, generally one country per page in contrast to those of Western nations. At the back of the book, however, the route-planning map shows the network in full (Figure 2.8). All the nations of Europe, including Russia (but not, notably, going as far back as Moscow), are visible, with each of the countries pictured (with the exception of the Maghreb, and Turkey beyond Istanbul) pictured with its national auto-symbol. The map of the network here is shown as crossing boundaries to the East with the same ease as in the West. The reverse side of the map shows touring information only for the countries in the West, laid out in a convenient table.

A more dramatic approach to Europe and its borders is the Esso 'Road Map and Pictorial Guide to Western Europe and Adjacent North Africa.'[75] On one side of the map appears the 'Esso guide to happy motoring' (Figure 2.9), designed to give the reader an idea of what is worth seeing. Small iconic figures fill the map on the Western side, portraying the West as a fecund place, filled with historical places, natives in traditional costumes, and modern leisure pursuits. Pictures of women in swimsuits beckon the presumably heterosexual male driver to beaches. Set against this abundance, on the other side of the divide there is merely empty yellow space, and a small sign announcing 'travel is restricted in areas shown in yellow (September 1950).' The rigid date attached to the travel restriction is at once a citation of

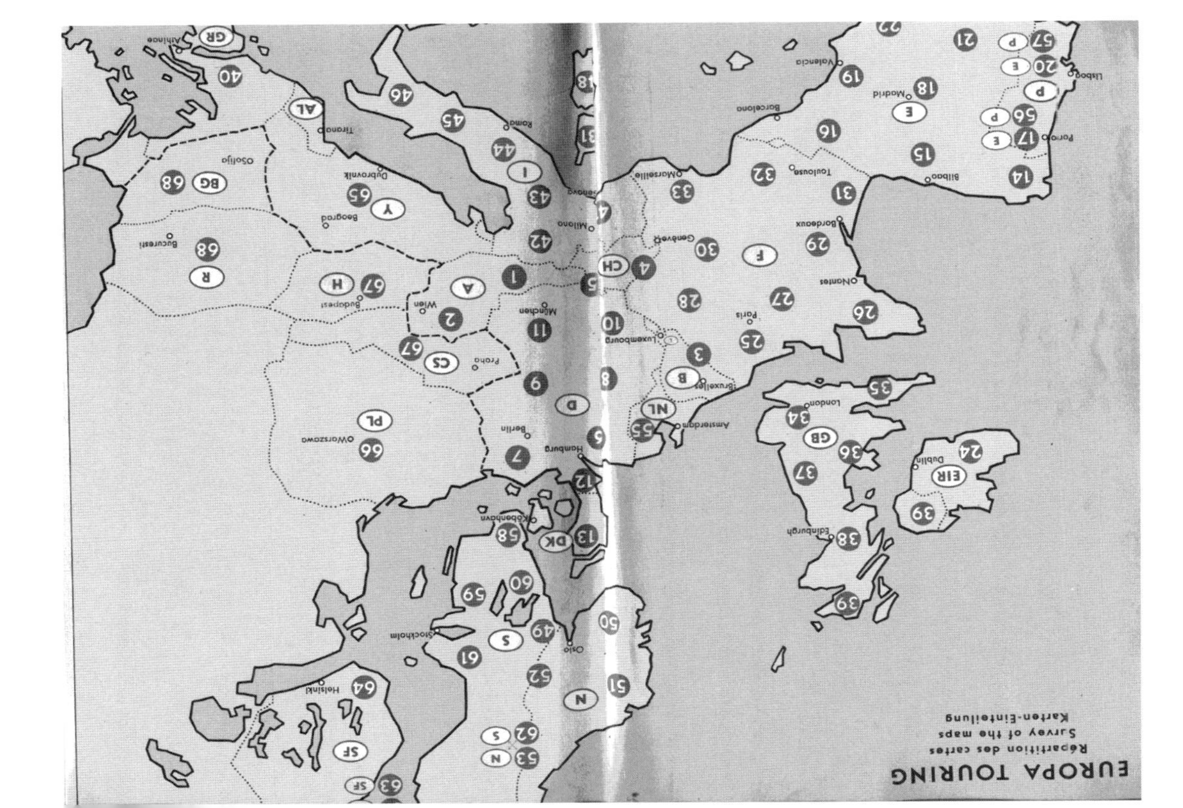

Figures 2.7   Front map from *Europa Touring*, 1952

Source: The front 'territorial' map draws attention to the Cold War divide. Used by permission of Hallwag.

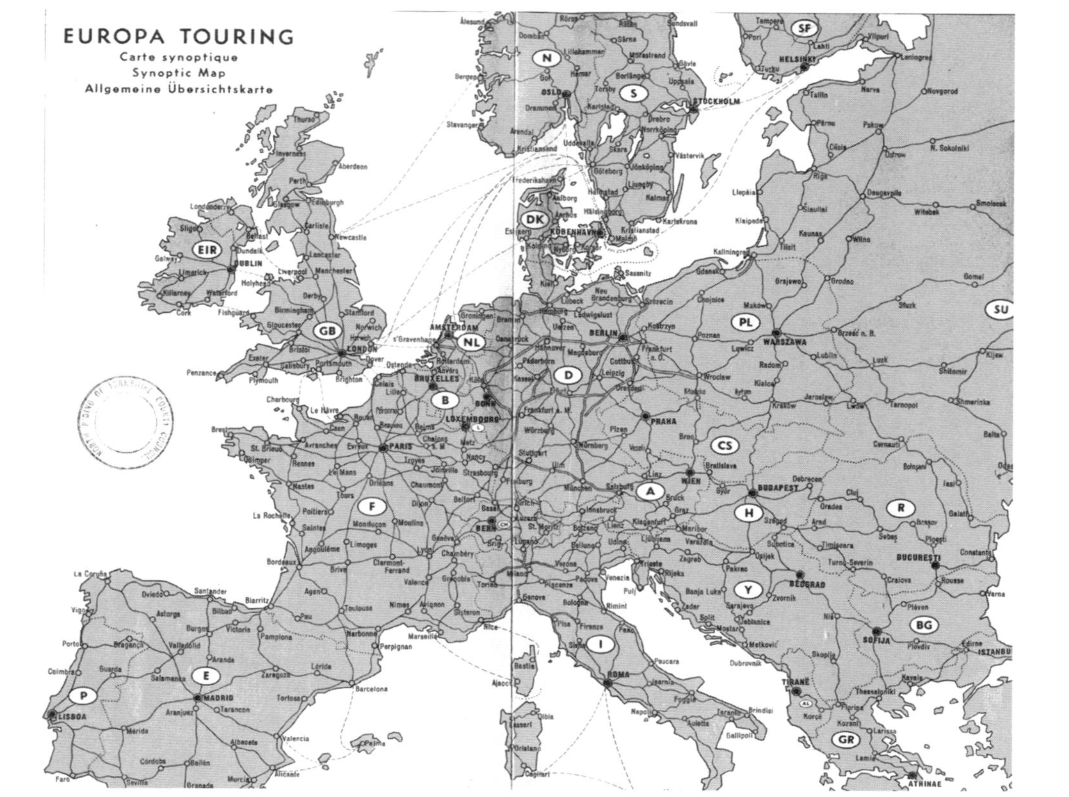

Figure 2.8 Back map from *Europa Touring*, 1952

Source: The network map in the back ignores it entirely. Used by permission of Hallwag.

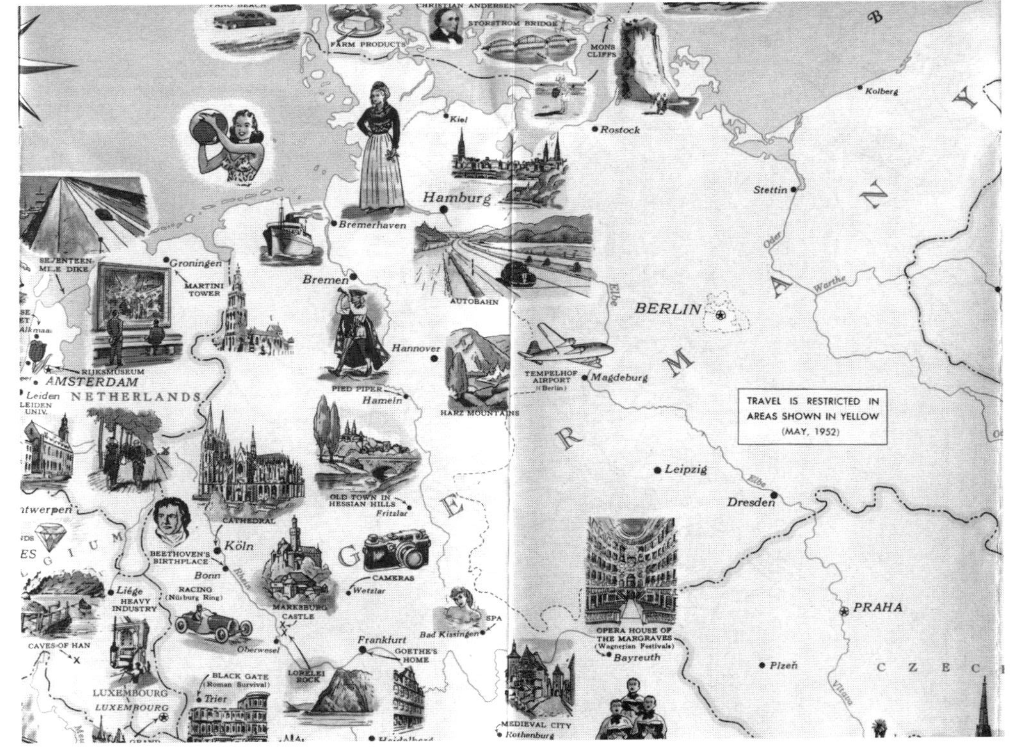

Figure 2.9 Road Map with Pictorial Guide' 1955

Source: Detail from the 'Pictorial guide to Happy Motoring' on the 'Esso Map of Western Europe and Adjacent North Africa – Copyright American Map Corporation – used with permission.

unnamed authority and a gesture that freezes the Eastern side in time. The note's temporal message is all the more evocative – and ambiguous – given that it sits inside an outline of the German borders from 1937, within which the cities all bear their German names (this was not unusual for German maps through the 1970s). The unease visible in the assertion of the 1937 eastern border is mirrored in the unease surrounding the disputed internal border, which is here partly obscured by images of transport infrastructure, the 'Autobahn' (clean and modern, with a lone car) and 'Tempelhof Airport (Berlin)', not placed over Berlin, but instead obliterating the borderline.

The reverse side of the map then portrays the road network, laid out over a map rendered to the same scale as the 'Happy Motoring' guide. Although the division of Europe is designated with a thick but pale pink line, the actual road network is portrayed as crossing the lines as part of a complete network, with the distances between Krakow and Budapest given just as those between Bonn and Luxembourg. At a basic level, the road network follows a separate logic from the political boundaries that are represented on the map. An apparently unified network is laid over a territory that is strongly divided politically. Though in not quite such dramatic fashion, the Shell map of Europe follows a similar pattern.[76] The front side of the map shows a Europe expanding quite far to the East, covered with a full European road network. The E-road network is marked with little green signs, along which one can follow trajectories, on paper at least, through to Russia. The only acknowledgement of the 'Iron Curtain' is the addition of checkpoints over the border. The reverse side is filled with information for the tourist, all of which advertises tourism in Europe as an abundant land of plenty: visa and customs regulations (symbolized by the cartoon of a fat man smoking a giant cigar, riding a liquor bottle on wheels), a calendar of 'events in Europe', almost exclusively composed of folk festivals, lists of the various national auto-stickers, all for the Western nations in Europe – not to mention the full range of Shell auto products.

Both Esso and Shell, like other Western petrol companies, had a vested interest not only in getting people into cars in Europe, but also in keeping them in places where they sold petrol. As an advert for Shell maps of Europe in the mid-1960s reminded readers, 'Wherever you go in Western Europe – except in Spain and Yugoslavia – Shell service stations are always near at hand.'[77] For the driver in the West, to whom the maps are addressed, the appearance of the broader network could potentially appear as a statement of the 'natural' freedom of roads. If you have a car, you can go anywhere there is a road, if only political divisions do not get in the way. However, juxtaposed with the 'Happy motoring guide' or the bright colourful information on the back of the Shell map, the 'freedom' of the road network in the East also appears somewhat more sinister when the network crosses the border. Whereas in the West the road will take you through lands filled with extraordinary sights and pleasures, the East, by contrast, appears as a place that is *merely* rational. Filled neither with natural landscapes and natives in costumes, nor with modern sites for play, the Eastern countries are represented as being without past or future, but as stuck in the everyday, that is, just slightly behind.[78] On that side of the map, the network is a ghost: a visible but intangible relic, haunting a place from an indeterminate point in the past.

A railway network map for tourists in 1955 by the CICE, the information branch of the Union Internationale de Chemins de Fer (UIC), the international railway union, seems to take the opposite approach to the Cold War divide by ignoring it outright. The railway network in this map is shown laid out over a topographic map of Europe, depicting Europe as a natural whole, with no national boundaries and no 'Iron Curtain' at all. The network stretches out in gently curving lines, connecting capital cities, which are specially highlighted on the map. The flags that surround the map highlight the internationality of the network. The blurb above the map portrays the network as a unified system, kept running smoothly by expert international co-operation.

> While the passengers speed forth at 120 km per hour, thousands of well-trained and specialized men are looking out for their security in the stations, on the lines and on the telephones. Everywhere, at the signal houses and command posts, the railwaymen of Europe are working hand in hand to ensure you a good journey.[79]

This tone is continued throughout the brochure in blurbs that explain that the train is fast, convenient, modern, and 'lets you see the landscape'. Throughout these blurbs, variations on the theme of 'the European railway' are repeated almost like a mantra, ensuring the reader that the railway network in Europe functions smoothly, like one large machine. This is significant: for all that the map of Europe stands at the centre of the brochure, the rest of the brochure has very little to say about what Europe actually contains, other than railways. The most important feature of Europe to be seen is a uniform, cohesive railway network.

One has to look past the map to notice that the brochure is actually only about railways in the West. On the map itself, the inset showing the modern trains of the German, Danish and British railways handily covers over the Soviet Union (which quit the UIC after the war) and moves the capitals of the cities in East Central Europe to the apparent edge of the map. Indeed, they are shown as linked only to the centre and not to each other, as outposts, and, in the case of Warsaw, as terminus of the network that is centred in West Central Europe. The flags that surround the map are also only of nations in the West, so, while at first glance they appear to uphold the image of a Europe made up of nation states, only those in the West are actually legitimated. As one reads further into the brochure, the small pictures are all accompanied by the insignias of Western railways, and a list of travel times from Dutch cities cites destinations of Paris, Brussels, Hamburg and Luxembourg. The map of a large, unified Europe appears to be there entirely to signify the apparently free and frictionless movement of the traveller through the network, and to appropriate the designation of Europe for the networks in the West. In other words, while apparently taking precisely the opposite approach to the Iron Curtain from the roadmaps cited above, the overall effect is very similar, in that it attempts to get the traveller to *look away* from the division that would restrict movement.

To highlight the ambivalence of such networks, I will point to one more road map, this one from Poland's state cartographic publisher in 1985.[80] The opening pages of the Polish atlas present the reader with three maps of Europe, which, particularly seen in rapid succession, seem to make evocative statements about the unity of Europe. The first page offers a route planning map with all the major roads in Europe. Although they are not labelled as such, this is the E-road network. The map itself is a very broad map of the continent, stretching well beyond Moscow, containing almost all of Turkey and the northern tip of Scandinavia, as well as Iceland in an upper corner. This map is framed with the flags of all the nations portrayed (except those in North Africa), presenting the reader with a vision of a Europe united under a road regime governed by individual sovereign states. The next pages give an overview map showing the breakdown of individual maps to be found in the atlas. Here an even larger version of Europe is shown, this time with national boundaries and no roads, but instead with the major rivers, presenting Europe as a natural whole. Lest the reader miss the point, the next pages provide the exact same breakdown of maps again, but this time superimposed over a full relief map of Europe.

Particularly taken together, these three maps bear a strong resemblance to the 1955 railway map discussed above. Both provide a view of Europe as a large, natural space, gently filled with a network. But, whereas the former mostly used the space of Europe to mark the many other aspects of the railway network as European, here the roads appear as one of three expressions of belonging to a broader Europe. These maps are particularly interesting given the revival of the discourse of Europe, and in particular Central Europe, that was taking place on both sides of the map during much of the 1980s.[81] These maps are also intriguing because they describe a range of mobility that was still simply not available to the majority of people in the countries where they were produced. After 1989, many countries formerly in the Soviet bloc or Soviet Union created new 'cartographies of independence' to show proudly their position in Europe.[82] Motoring maps of the frame and style shown here played an important role in these new persuasive geographies.[83] The cartographic obduracy of the network became the proof that (at least some parts of) 'the East' had always been *central* to Europe, and formed one building block in the rhetoric that eventually moved many of the nations in the 'middle' to the 'West'.[84]

Disconnecting network from territory: Another interruption in place of a conclusion

The mapping processes I have described have shown in most cases how maps of European networks have been used, alternately or together, to call into being a networked place called Europe. In the case of the London to Istanbul road, while myths of a rational, straight road through empty space were superimposed on the map, specific place-myths of Europe were repeatedly called upon to make the road seem like a 'natural' occurrence and expression of places that already existed. In the case of the Cold War maps, the network appeared as a ghost: something visible and indelibly tied to a place, but intangible and unstuck in time.

I will close by considering one further map, produced by A SEED Europe, one group that has actively opposed the various transport networks of the EU on an EU-wide basis.[85] As the map claims:

> This is what Europe looks like. For a large part a busy, densely populated and ever-building small-size continent. Unfortunately, the green lines on this map aren't showing valuable forests or nature areas but the extensive infrastructure that is planned for Europe – East, North South and West. The EU driven projects TENs and TINA corridor links (Transport Infrastructure Needs Assessment) are mega-billion projects that should make Europe 'a coherent, easily-accessible continent'. [...] Take a close look! It's quite 'green' isn't it?[86]

This map attempts to hijack the myth of Europe as a networked space and turn it into a map of local resistance, showing widespread dissatisfaction and 'friction' against the coming of infrastructures. At first glance, it appears to be a very familiar map. It lists priority European projects in red (and hard-to-read) numbers, and has a series of alternate nodes in yellow flags, each one a listing for an organization working to oppose the projects, and visually outnumbering the red dots.

Unlike the other maps discussed here, where the network has appeared as more or less naturally integrated into the territory portrayed, this map posits the continent of Europe as a natural space *against* the network. The yellow flags make specific appeals to places, asserting their historicity and locality against the 'flows' of the network. In so doing, however, whether deliberately or not, the map also makes an appeal to an apparently naturally and nationally based European territory. The Maghreb and the Asian part of Turkey appear in white (which the legend lists as 'other continents'), while, interestingly, the European side of Turkey is coloured in, and an

Istanbul-based resistance group is listed. Ironically, it reproduces a similar cartographic confusion to that in the map with which I began this chapter. Above all, the map highlights the as-yet-limited spatial rhetoric of resistance to network projects at the European level, both in terms of the points at which resistance can be exercised and also in terms of the alternate visions available in current discourse.[87] It suggests that, like EU planning processes themselves, resistance may ultimately be best expressed 'off the map'.[88]

Notes

Many thanks to the staff at the ANWB archive in The Hague, and the cartographic collection at Utrecht University for their kind assistance. I would like to thank Paul Edwards in particular for his insightful commentary on drafts of this paper, as well as Gijs Mom, John Walton and the anonymous JTH reviewers for their comments on the L–I road section.

1. Inscription over Europe in Thomas Cook & Son world map: 'Mr Kennedy North's entirely accurate map of the world…' in Piers Brendon, *Thomas Cook. 150 years of Popular Tourism* (London: Secker & Warburg 1991), endpapers.
2. Roundtable of European Industrialists, Need for Renewing Transport Infrastructure in Europe – Proposals for Improving the Decisionmaking Process (Brussels: ERT 1989), p. 11. The caption refers to a map of the Roman road network.
3. Ismail Sakarya to George Koranyi, 28 January 1980. Archive of the United Nations, UN ECE Economic – Coal – Gas – International Map of Gas Transmission Systems in Europe GX 11/13/40 box 2044.
4. David Turnbull, *Masons, Tricksters and Cartographers: Comparative Studies in the Sociology of Scientific and Indigenous Knowledge* (London: Routledge 2000), p. 8. See further Michel de Certeau, *The Practice of Everyday Life* (Berkeley: University of California Press 1984), p. 121.
5. See Andreas Fickers' and my introduction to this volume.
6. Ole B. Jensen and Tim Richardson, *Making European Space: Mobility, Power and Territorial Identity* (London: Routledge 2004), pp. 41–50.
7. On the promise of spatial artefacts as historical instruments, see Karl Schlögel, *Im Raume lesen wir die Zeit. Über Zivilisationsgeschichte und Geopolitik* (Munich: Carl Hanser Verlag 2003).
8. Steven Graham and Simon Marvin, *Splintering Urbanism: Networked Infrastructures, Technological Mobilities and the Urban Condition* (London: Routledge 2001), p. 12, emphasis in original.
9. See Erik van der Vleuten, 'In search of the networked nation. Transforming technology, society and nature in the Netherlands in the 20th century', *European Review of History*, 10 (2003), pp. 59–78; Charles S. Maier, 'Transformations of Territoriality 1600–2000' in Gunilla Budde, Sebastian Conrad and Oliver Janz, *Transnationale Geschichte. Themen, Tendenzen und Theorien* (Göttingen: Vandenhoeck & Ruprecht 2006), pp. 32–55.
10. See a recent op-ed piece on the railway network of Wales by George Monbiot, 'Dr Beeching turned the country I have come to love into an outpost of empire', *The Guardian*, 30 December 2008, p. 28.
11. Andrew Barry, *Political Machines: Governing a Technological Society* (London: Athlone 2001), p. 25.

12. J. Peter Burgess, 'Coal steel and spirit: the double reading of European unity (1948–1951)' in Bo Strath (ed.) *Europe and the Other and Europe as the Other* (Brussels: Peter Lang 2000), p. 433, emphasis in original. See also Cris Shore, *Building Europe: The Cultural Politics of European Integration* (London: Routledge 2000) pp. 113–14.

13. See Gerald Delanty, *Inventing Europe: Idea, Identity, Reality* (London 1995); Larry Wolff, *Inventing Eastern Europe: The Map of Civilization on the Mind of the Enlightenment* (Stanford: Stanford University Press 1994).

14. Bruno Latour, *We have never been modern* (Cambridge, Mass: Harvard University Press 1993), p. 117.

15. See Per Olof Berg, Orvar Löfgren and Anders Linde-Laursen (eds), *Invoking a Transnational Metropolis: The Making of the Øresund Region* (Lund: Studentenlitteratur 2000); Eve Darian-Smith, *Bridging Divides. The Channel Tunnel and English Legal Identity in the New Europe* (Berkeley: University of California Press 1999); Judith Schueler, *Materializing Identity: the co-construction of the Gotthard Railway and Swiss national identity* (Eindhoven: Aksant 2008); Vincent Lagendijk and Alexander Badenoch, 'Myths of Kaprun: Material visions of Europe and Austria', paper presented to European Identity and the Second World War conference, Amsterdam, 10–11 December 2007.

16. Graham and Marvin, *Splintering Urbanism*.

17. For a succinct overview of these issues see Chris Rumford, 'Rethinking European Spaces: Territory, Borders, Governance', *Comparative European Politics*, 4(2/3) (2006), pp. 127–40.

18. European Commissioner for Transport and Energy Loyola del Palacio comments that the 1993 Trans-European Transport Network (TEN-T) proposals marked 'the first time since the Roman era that Europe had started to think about transport systems going beyond national frontiers', in CEC, *Trans-European Transport Networks TEN-T Priority Projects* (2002), p. 3.

19. See Wolff, *Inventing*; Michael Wintle, 'Renaissance maps and the construction of the idea of Europe', *Journal of Historical Geography* 25(2) (1999), pp. 137–65.

20. James R. Akerman, 'Introduction', in James R. Akerman (ed.) *Cartographies of Travel and Navigation* (Chicago: University of Chicago Press 2006), pp. 1–15. A recent conference on 'Cartography as a Historiographical Argument in the Writing of Overlapping National Histories in Europe' highlights the growing interest in maps as historical tools, but also an ongoing neglect of network maps. See http://hsozkult.geschichte.hu-berlin.de/tagungsberichte/id=1923&count=1905&recno=20&sort=datum&order=down.

21. See John Gerard Ruggie, 'Territoriality and Beyond: Problematizing Modernity in International Relations', *International Organization* 47(1) (1993), pp. 139–74; William Walters, 'Rethinking Borders Beyond the State', *Comparative European Politics* 4(2/3) (2006), pp. 141–59.

22. In addition to those collected through my own research, particularly in the map collection at the University of Utrecht, I am very grateful to my colleagues Irene Anastasiadou, Vincent Lagendijk, Suzanne Lommers, Frank Schipper, Johan Schot and Erik van der Vleuten for sharing maps they have found in their research. I claim exclusive credit for any errors or stupidity in presenting and interpreting material they have provided.

23. J.B. Harley and David Woodward, *History of Cartography. Volume I: Cartography in Prehistoric, Ancient, and Medieval Europe and the Mediterranean* (Chicago: University of Chicago Press 1987), p. 3. See also: J.B. Harley, 'Deconstructing

the map' in Trevor Barnes and James G. Duncan (eds) *Writing Worlds: Discourse, Text and Metaphor in the Representation of. Landscape* (London: Routledge 1992), pp. 231–47; Jeremy Black, *Maps and History: Constructing Images of the Past* (New Haven: Yale University Press 2000); Denis Wood, *The Power of Maps* (New York: Guilford Press 1992); Wintle, 'Renaissance maps'.

24. Roland Barthes, *Mythologies* (New York: Hill and Wang 1972), pp. 111–16 and passim.
25. See Wood, *Power of Maps*, chapter 7 for a taxonomy of these various 'codes of extrasignification'.
26. Harley, 'Deconstructing', p. 235.
27. David Gugerli and Daniel Speich show how the initial publication of Dufour's topographic map of Switzerland met with considerable resistance because it was interpreted as the assertion of a central authority that did not yet exist. *Topographien der Nation: Politik, kartographische Ordnung und Landschaft im 19. Jahrhundert* (Zürich: Chronos Verlag 2002). Similarly, a recent article in *Der Spiegel* highlights the threat of European gas dependency with an image of the control room of the Russian gas company Gazprom where they gaze on a map of European pipelines. Erich Follath and Matthias Schepp, 'Der Konzern des Zaren', *Der Spiegel,* 5 March 2007, p. 122. *Not* producing a map can also be a means of asserting control over space. Jensen and Richardson show how, in order to keep nation states from competing over which projects to put on the map, the EU reduced or eliminated their use during phases of the TENs projects (Jensen and Richardson, *Making European Space*, pp. 107–11).
28. Jeremy Black, *Maps and Politics* (Chicago: University of Chicago Press 2000) p. 22; Vincent Del Casino Jr and Stephen P. Hanna, 'Representations and identities in tourism map spaces', *Progress in Human Geography* 24(1) (2000), pp. 23–46, here 28.
29. A 'place' is understood as a space that can be circumscribed and bounded, such as a city, region or nation; a space denotes something broader and more inchoate, but no less real, such as The North or The East.
30. Rob Shields, *Places on the Margin: Alternative Geographies of Modernity* (London: Routledge 1991), p. 60.
31. On the former point, see Mark Monmonier's seminal and humorous *How to lie with maps* (Chicago: University of Chicago Press 1991).
32. Gugerli and Speich, *Topographien*, p. 76ff.
33. H. Schreiber, *Sinfonie der Strasse: Der Mensch und seine Wege von den Karawanenpfaden bis zum Super-Highway* (Düsseldorf: Econ-Verlag 1959).
34. See, for example, Vincent Lagendijk, 'High voltages, lower tensions. The interconnections of Eastern and Western European electricity networks in the 1970s and 1980s' in Éric Bussière, Sylvian Schirrmann and Michel Dumoulin (eds) *Milieux économiques et intégration européenne au XXe siècle. La crise des années 1970 de la conférence de La Haye à la veille de la relance des années 1980* (Brussels: Peter Lang 2006), pp. 135–67; Frank Schipper, 'Was the road to Europe paved with good intentions? Building highways in the Balkans' (2007), TIE working document 18; Per Högselius, 'Connecting East and West? Electricity systems in the Baltic Regions' in Erik van der Vleuten and Arne Kaijser (eds) *Networking Europe: Transnational Infrastructures and the Shaping of Europe (1850–2000)* (Sagamore Beach: Science History Publications 2006), pp. 245–78.
35. Mark Monmonier, *How to lie with maps* (Chicago: University of Chicago Press 1991).

36. Barry, *Political Machines*, pp. 14–15; Latour, *We have never*, p. 117.
37. Schlögel, *Im Raume*, p. 102ff.
38. James Buzard, *The Beaten Track: European Tourism, Literature, and the Ways to 'Culture' 1800–1918* (Oxford: Clarendon 1993), pp. 77–9; Akerman, 'Introduction'.
39. *Europa Touring – Guide automobile d'Europe* (Berne: Hallwag 1929).
40. Maier, 'Transformations', p. 48.
41. Jensen and Richardson, *Making European Space*, p. 75.
42. Schlögel, *Im Raume*, p. 81ff.
43. Wood, *Power*, p. 112.
44. Barthes, *Mythologies*; James G. Duncan and Nancy Duncan, 'Ideology and Bliss: Roland Barthes and the Secret Histories of Landscape' in Trevor Barnes and James G. Duncan (eds) *Writing Worlds: Discourse, Text and Metaphor in the Representation of Landscape* (London: Routledge 1992), pp. 18–37.
45. Wood, *Power of Maps*, p. 140.
46. Alexander Gall, 'Atlantropa: a technical vision of a united Europe' in Erik van der Vleuten and Arne Kaijser (eds) *Networking Europe: Transnational Infrastructures and the Shaping of Europe (1850–2000)* (Sagamore Beach: Science History Publications 2006), pp. 99–128, here 114. Both the Marshall Plan film *Clearing the Lines*, Kay Mander (Wessex Films, 1951) and the EU promotional film, *Europe of Railways* (2003), available on the website of the European Commission, use a relief map of Europe as a key part of their argument that nation states present 'unnatural' barriers to European transport networks. For the latter, see http://ec.europa.eu/dgs/energy_transport/video/rail/2003_rail_en.mpg (accessed 2 March 2007).
47. Benedict Anderson, *Imagined Communities: Reflection on the Origins and Spread of Nationalism* (London: Verso 1991), p. 144; Gabrielle Hecht, *The Radiance of France: Nuclear Power and National Identity after WWII* (Cambridge, Mass: MIT 1998), p. 13.
48. Erik van der Vleuten and Arne Kaijser, 'Networking Europe', *History and Technology* 21(1) (2005), pp. 23–4, and see Johan Schot's contribution in this volume.
49. This section draws on a more thorough account in my article 'Touring Between War and Peace: Imagining the "Transcontinental Motorway" 1930–1950', *Journal of Transport History* 28(2) (2007), pp. 192–210.
50. See Kurt Möser, 'World War I and the Creation of Desire for Automobiles in Germany' in Susan Strasser (ed.) *Getting and Spending: American and European Consumer Society in the Twentieth Century* (Cambridge 1998), pp. 195–222; Stephen L. Harp, *Marketing Michelin, Advertising and Cultural Identity in Twentieth-Century France* (Baltimore 2001), chapters 3, 6.
51. See Gijs Mom, 'Roads without rails: European highway network-building and the desire for long-range mobility', *Technology and Culture* 46(4) (2005), pp. 745–73; Lando Bortolotti, 'Les Premières Propositions d'un Système Européen d'Autoroutes, 1926–1937' in Albert Carreras, Andrea Giuntini and Michèle Merger (eds) *European Networks, 19th–20th Centuries: New Approaches to the Formation of a Transnational Transport and Communications System*, B8 Proceedings 11th International Economic Congress, Milan, September 1994 (Milan 1994), pp. 47–59; Frank Schipper, *Driving Europe: Building Europe on roads in the twentieth century* (Eindhoven: SHT/Aksant 2008), pp. 83–158.
52. I borrow the term 'invoke' from Berg, Löfgren and Linde-Laursen, *Invoking*.
53. Jo-Anne Pemberton, 'New worlds for old: the League of Nations in the age of electricity', *Review of International Relations* 28 (2002), pp. 311–36.
54. *Proces-Verbale de la Conference International Route Londres-Stamboul, Budapest, 10 au 15 Septembre* (1935), p. 96.

55. See Wintle, 'Renaissance maps', p. 143; Harley and Woodward, *History of Cartography*, p. 296ff.

56. *Proces-Verbale de la Conference International Route Londres-Stamboul, Budapest, 10 au 15 Septembre* (1935), p. 118.

57. In some ways, this can be seen as a rehearsal of the process described around the EU spatial planning in Jensen and Richardson, *European Space*, esp. pp. 107–8.

58. *Procés-Verbaux de l'Assemblée générale de l'AIT et de l'Assemblee générale extraordinaire*, Rome, 25–30 September 1933, p. 42.

59. *Procès-verbeaux de l'Assemble générale de l'Alliance Internationale de Tourisme* (London, 1934), p. 50.

60. See 'Kaapstad-Kirkenes en London-Batavia per Auto!' *Het Vaderland*, 2 May 1935.

61. In *Proces-Verbale de la Conference International Route Londres-Stamboul, Budapest, 10 au 15 Septembre* (1935), p. 11.

62. *Proces-Verbale de la Conference International Route Londres-Stamboul, Budapest, 10 au 15 Septembre* (1935) pp. 11, 16.

63. *I Travel the Road*, Pathé film reel, 12 June 1944.

64. *Minutes of the AIT General Assembly* (1949), p. 54.

65. *Sunday Times Travel and Holiday Guide to the Continent of Europe* (London 1951), p. 440. While mentioning the road, this book does not so much as mention the existence of Hungary, Romania or Bulgaria, where the road theoretically would have passed; *Clearing the Lines*, Kay Mander (Wessex Films 1951); *Europa Touring* (Berne: Hallwag 1952) pp. 296, 303. Notably, both sections list Paris, and not London, as the road's western terminus. The route furthermore appears as a traceable solid line, though not labelled, on the 'synoptic map' in the back of the book.

66. Much of the road was absorbed into the E-road network as the route E-5, although its path changed to go through Greece rather than Bulgaria. As larger motorways were built, however, this particular route was literally bypassed and can no longer be spoken of as a single road – if it ever really could have been. On the other hand, a Belgian acquaintance recently told me that his grandparents still refer to the Ostend-Brussels motorway as 'the road to Istanbul'.

67. On technical networks, see Helmut Maier, 'Systems connected: IG Auschwitz, Kaprun and the building of European power grids' in Erik van der Vleuten and Arne Kaijser (eds) *Networking Europe: Transnational Infrastructures and the Shaping of Europe (1850–2000)* (Sagamore Beach: Science History Publications 2006), pp. 129–60. The overall connection between Nazi visions and European ideas is stressed by John Laughland, *The tainted source: the undemocratic origins of the European idea* (London: Little, Brown and Company 1997), although particularly approaching this history from a technical perspective leads to a much more nuanced reading than Laughland's.

68. The sudden closing of the Friedrichstrasse train station in the middle of Berlin caused hysteria in a number of residents. See Joe Moran, 'November in Berlin: The End of the Everyday', *History Workshop Journal* 57 (2004), p. 217.

69. See the tenth anniversary poster put out by NATO in 1959, which shows a wall composed of the flags of the member states of NATO, protecting a mother and child from an unseen threat. See http://www.nato.int/education/images/posters/otan-01.pdf.

70. See *Clearing the Lines*, Kay Mander (Wessex Films 1951).

71. See Ernest W. Wimble, *European Recovery and the Tourist Industry* (Report prepared for the International Union of Official Travel Organisations) (London 1948); Valene Smith, 'War and Tourism: An American Ethnography', *Annals of Tourism Research* 25(1) (1998), pp. 202–27; Christopher Endy, *Cold War Holidays: American Tourism in France* (Chapel Hill: UNC Press 2004).
72. See Erik van der Vleuten and Arne Kaijser, 'Networking Europe', *History and Technology* 21(1), pp. 42–4; see also Vleuten's chapter in this volume.
73. See Mom, 'Roads' and Pär Blomqvist, 'Roads for Peace' in Vleuten and Kaijser, *Networking Europe*; Schipper, *Driving Europe*, p. 159ff
74. *Europa Touring* (Berne: Hallwag 1952).
75. 'Road Map and Pictorial Guide to Western Europe and Adjacent North Africa' (New York: General Drafting Co. 1960).
76. 'Shell Europa' (1969).
77. 'Plan a European Tour with Shell Maps – they're free', advert in *World Travel* 56 (Dec 62–Feb 63), p. 36.
78. As Joe Moran reminds us, drawing on Lefebvre, the everyday always fails to keep up entirely with modernity: 'November in Berlin', p. 227.
79. 'Neem de Trein op Reis door Europa. Kaart van het Europese Spoorwegnet' (Union Internationale de Chemins de Fer (UIC) 1955).
80. *Europa – Atlas Samochodowy* (Warsaw: Panstwowe Przedsiebiorstwo Wydawnictw Kartograficznych 1985).
81. See, for example, Susan Gal, 'Bartok's Funeral: Representations of Europe in Hungarian Political Rhetoric', *American Ethnologist* 16(3) (1991), pp. 440–58.
82. D.J. Zeigler, 'Post-communist Eastern Europe and the cartography of independence', *Political Geography* 21 (2002), pp. 671–86.
83. Ibid., pp. 681–2.
84. J. Hagen, 'Redrawing the imagined map of Europe: the rise and fall of the "center"', *Political Geography* 22(4) (2003), pp. 489–517.
85. Jensen and Richardson, *Making European Space*, p. 75.
86. A SEED Europe, 'MATE (Map of Activities on Transport in Europe)', Amsterdam, March 2000.
87. Jensen and Richardson, *Making European Space*, pp. 75, 250ff.
88. Ginette Verstraete, 'Timescapes: An artistic challenge to the European Union paradigm', *European Journal of Cultural Studies* 12(2) (2009), pp. 157–74.

Biography 2: David Mitrany and Ernst Haas: Theorizing a United Europe

Waqar Zaidi

The relationship between the theory and practice of European integration is not always clear. Proponents of functionalist and neo-functionalist theories of international relations argued that the pragmatic tackling of technical and economic problems in the international sphere, rather than comprehensive plans for international federation, was the most fruitful method of achieving some measure of international integration and thereby tackling what David Mitrany called 'the baffling division between the peoples of the world'. Many of these theorists drew inspiration from the work of the early post-Second World War proponents of European integration, and indeed these proponents themselves have now come to represent historical embodiments of the political theories of these theorists – the likes of Alberto Spinelli, Jean Monnet and Robert Schuman were all, claims the literature on European integration, either functionalists or neo-functionalists. But if the historical actors have come to embody functionalist theory, what do we know about the theorists as historical actors? It is noteworthy that the two leading theorists, David Mitrany and Ernst Haas, were themselves products of transnational circulation of experts.

David Mitrany was born in Bucharest, Romania in 1888, and moved to London to study sociology and economics at the LSE in 1912. He quickly became known as an expert on European affairs – eventually undertaking intelligence work for the Foreign and Colonial Office, writing for the *Manchester Guardian*, and editing publications for the Carnegie Endowment for International Peace. After completing his PhD in 1929 and DSc in economics in 1931 he moved into academia, and in 1943 produced a pamphlet that expressed in detail, for the first time, his functionalist approach to international organization: *A Working Peace System: An Argument for the Functional Development of International Organization*. It is this approach, developed through further articles, for which he is now best remembered.

Concerned, like many other intellectuals at that time, with the problem of reconciling national sovereignty with international peace, the internationalist Mitrany argued that national sovereignty needed to be curtailed in order for international peace and prosperity to come about. This, he argued, could not happen through a constitutional approach to international organization or world government, but rather through what he termed a functional approach.

Drawing inspiration from many areas, particularly the American TVA project and the various specialized United Nations organizations (particularly the Food and Agricultural Organization), he argued that the most successful trans-border organizations were those pragmatically set up to tackle specific trans-border problems – those whose powers were limited to specific areas sufficient to fulfil their limited functions. Apolitical technocrats would ensure the success of such international organizations, and convince nation states to further empower them to deal with other technical areas. As the number and functions of these organizations increased, he argued, national sovereignty, and eventually the nation state itself, would gradually wither away. Technical international organizations would also help in the prevention of war; '…a joint European transport organisation such as the new European Central Inland Transport Organisation,' he argued in 'The Growth of World Organisation' (*Common Wealth Review,* June 1946), 'should be able to plan the railways and canals of Europe with a view to improving civilian communications and facilitating trade, but prevent the construction of railways and roads primarily for strategic purposes.'

Fuelled by early expectations of the United Nations experience, the functional approach came to be celebrated amongst international relations and government policy circles through to the early 1950s. By that time, however, it had become clear that the UN, even in its supposedly functional organs, had become bogged down in political wrangling. International relations theorists began to rethink Mitrany's functionalist approach within a regional context – foremost amongst them was the German émigré Ernst Haas.

Born in Frankfurt in 1924, Ernst Haas immigrated with his family to the United States in 1938. After completing a PhD in public law and government in 1952 from Columbia University, he began his academic career in 1951 at the University of California at Berkeley, where he remained until his death in 2003. From early on in his career, he took a strong interest in the phenomena of nationalism, and his 'neo-functionalist' theory of international relations looked to move beyond Mitrany's functionalism and explain what he saw as being one of the most important aspects of international relations at that time: the integration of Europe. In his early works, particularly *The Uniting of Europe* and *Beyond the Nation State*, he argued that Mitrany's functionalist understanding of international integration could not adequately explain the actual development of transnational technical organizations.

The *Uniting of Europe* was first published in 1958, and soon became inextricably linked with the European project itself. Haas argued that a modified functionalist theory of international integration could explain the advent and success of the European Coal and Steel Community better than Mitrany's functionalist theory. Haas agreed with Mitrany on the need for a gradual approach to international integration, and argued that, as long as certain initial conditions were satisfied, a specialized technical international organization could expand its functions through what he termed 'spill-over'. As Haas put it:

> From the initially merged sectors, a demonstrable process of expanding group expectations among industrialists, dealers, and trade unions emerges. A spill-over into as yet unintegrated economic areas and a concern over political techniques appropriate for the control of new and larger problems is manifest.

This process, he believed, would eventually lead to the decline of the nation state and international integration. The crucial differences between the two theories arose with regard to the fundamental driving force behind the increased influence and scope of the international organizations. The success of such organizations within Haas' 'neo-functionalist' theory was predicated on the self-interestedness of national politicians and institutions, and their consequent commitment to international organizations and associated technocrats. Their success within Mitrany's functionalist theory, on the other hand, was predicated on the apolitical activity of internationally minded technocrats. Although such technocrats were recognized and celebrated by Haas as well, spill-over was ultimately about national actors and institutions accommodating themselves to the existence of supranational organizations.

The initial conditions that Haas postulated as being required for spill-over limited his theory to one of regional integration: unlike Mitrany, Haas believed that functional integration could only occur amongst highly industrialized pluralistic democracies. His initial conditions included the presence of functioning parliamentary democracies in the participating states, as well as scope for expansion with regard to the functions of the original international organization. These conditions, he argued, were to be uniquely found in Western Europe in the late 1940s, leading to some measure of European integration by 1958.

Although neo-functionalist theory was immensely influential in academic circles, a perceived slowdown in European integration in the 1960s led most in the field of international relations, including Haas himself, to argue that the theory in its original form no longer applied to European integration. It failed to take into account several crucial factors, the argument went: most prominently the rise of de Gaulle and his highly nationalistic politics.

Interest in both functionalist and neo-functionalist theories continued to decline until the mid-1980s, when the relatively easy passage of the Single European Act led to a resurgence of interest in these theories within European Studies circles. International relations theorists and proponents of European integration, taking their cue from the writings of the post-war European integrationists and Haas himself, have once again come to focus on the connection between these theories and the period of European institution-building from the late 1940s to the 1960s.

Literature

David Mitrany, 'A Working Peace System' in idem. *The Functional Theory of Politics* (London: London School of Economics and Political Science 1975).
Ernst B. Haas, *The Uniting of Europe: Political, Social and Economic Forces 1950–1957* (Stanford: Stanford University Press 1968).

3
Transnational Infrastructures and the Origins of European Integration

Johan Schot

Ideas for integrating energy and transport infrastructures were intensively discussed in the post-Second World War era, and such discussions eventually led to the establishment of the European Union's predecessors: the *European Coal and Steel Community* (ECSC) and the *European Economic Community* (EEC). In the 1960s and 1970s, however, integration in these sectors was widely seen as a huge failure, and as a consequence general European integration histories often ignore both sectors.[1] This chapter will do exactly the opposite. It will delve into this past to explain why the European Economic Community was unsuccessful in taking up infrastructural integration in transport and energy, and explore the implications of this explanation for the history of European integration. The argument is based on both a theoretical and an empirical exploration. My theoretical exploration takes its cue from the neo-functionalist interpretation of the origins of European integration, in particular the work of Ernst Haas.[2] Neo-functionalism is a good point of departure, not only because it is treated in many textbooks and theoretical overviews as the starting point for integration theory, but also because, contrary to other theories, it puts infrastructural integration at the centre of its theoretical analysis.[3] Although neo-functionalists did not use the notion of infrastructure but instead talked about sectors such as transport, energy or communication, their notion of 'sector' essentially equals the notion of infrastructure used in this chapter. I use the term here in a broad sense, including not only the material networks built for facilitating movement of people, information, goods and services, but also the standards, policies and regulations needed to use the networks.[4]

European integration is a problematical category, not only because it inherently assumes a certain direction towards integration, and so easily provokes writing a history of fulfilment, but also because the definition of what counts as an integration process is highly contested, both by the historical actors and in the historiography.[5] At this point I refrain from providing a definition of the term, as redefining it is a key goal of the analysis that follows. In the final section I argue that integration history should decentre the EU and its direct predecessors and portray integration as fragmented, both spatially and functionally. By doing so, we can avoid the teleology embedded in the most current notions of 'integration'. Such a history would not only be one possible response to the volume editors' call for clarification on how infrastructures relate to European unification, but also contribute to an emerging new transnational history of European integration.[6] The central thesis of this chapter is that emphasizing the importance of non-governmental actors and institutions allows us to re-evaluate Alan Milward's interpretation of European integration history as rescue of the nation state. In highlighting the role of technical experts in various transnational committees and organizations related to the sectors of energy and transport, I argue that post-war efforts in sectoral integration were at least partly the result of an influential technocratic internationalism. This technocratic internationalism, which originated in the interwar years, deeply influenced the design and implementation of transnational infrastructures shaped by technical experts, and challenged the political initiatives to foster European integration through supranational bodies and authorities.

Although never advertised as such, it could be argued that neo-functionalist integration theory already pointed to the importance of transnational history. In order to demonstrate this, we will start our chapter with an outline of neo-functionalist theory, followed by a critical assessment of this theory in the light of new approaches to European integration history in the field of the history of technology. I will show the validity of such re-evaluation by presenting exemplary case studies of several sectors, offering both a chronological and a thematic exploration of the European integration process through the lens of transnational infrastructures. Finally, in concluding remarks I will discuss both the merits and the shortcomings of neo-functionalist theory as explanandum of a sectoral integration process in Europe and reflect on the complex and sometimes hidden logics of infrastructural integration and fragmentation in the post-war European history.

The neo-functionalist ideas on European integration

From the late 1950s until the late 1960s, neo-functionalist theory developed by political scientists (rather than historians) dominated the historical understanding of European integration. The seminal work is *The Uniting of Europe* by Ernst B. Haas, in which he analyses the establishment of the ECSC and its effects. From there, Haas and others developed their ideas further over the next decade.[7] The central idea was that integration, and hence the creation of a long-term system of peace in Europe, could be engineered by creating sector-specific international organizations that perform certain functions such as coal and steel production, transport, communication, healthcare, defence and so on. According to Haas, once started in one sector, the integration process would give rise to an expansive integration logic. In neo-functionalism, the term 'spill-over' is used to describe this logic. There are three types of spill-over effects: functional, political and cultivated spill-over.[8] A functional spill-over is a process in which integration in one sector encourages other sectors to integrate as well. The main idea is that starting integration in, for instance, the coal and steel industries will soon give rise to integration in the entire energy sector, and will also put pressure on the transport sector because of the need to integrate the transport of coal and steel. Political spill-over refers to the emergence of a new political community (an elite of civil servants, politicians, managers and union leaders), which would no longer have loyalties toward the nation states involved because it would recognize that the integration process was better able to generate welfare and satisfy needs than the individual nation states. Cultivated spill-over refers to the role of the central institution: the High Authority in the case of the ECSC and the Commission in the case of the EEC. In neo-functionalist theory an important precondition for integration was that such institutions should be supranational, since this would allow the leading civil servants to upgrade common interest and thus encourage the other two processes of spill-over to happen.

Neo-functionalists developed a very eloquent and elaborate theory, to which I cannot do justice here. Instead I would like to stress two features of this interpretation that are important to my argument. First, for Haas and neo-functionalist theories, integration meant the emergence of a new federal European state. Second, it is important to recognize that, although Haas argued that integration would have an expansive and unfolding dynamic, he also acknowledged in later work that such dynamic would still require agency.[9] This would come not only from the supranational institution but also from a new political community of experts, managers and civil servants, who would be able to interfere in the power play of nation states. This elite would acquire room to manoeuvre because nation states are by definition pluralist and thus have no control over the actions of all the different elites representing the nation state.

Neo-functionalists seemed to have got it right with the ratification of the Rome Treaty in 1957 and the establishment of the European Economic Community and a *European Atomic Energy Community* (Euratom). They argued that these two organizations were the outcome of the spill-over process which had begun with the creation of the ECSC, and they anticipated next steps that would eventually lead to a federal state.[10] But let us first re-investigate the history of the first twelve years of post-war integration efforts, with a focus on attempts to integrate energy and transport infrastructures. Unavoidably this leads to a rehash of some known textbook integration histories, yet coming into this history from the point of infrastructure allows me to weave some new threads, and show the centrality of infrastructure to the integration process.

European integration born out of reconstruction

In March 1947, the *United Nations Economic Commission for Europe* (UNECE) was set up to facilitate concerted action for the economic reconstruction of Europe, including transport and energy.[11] Not only the USA and all eighteen European members of the UN, including Russia and many Western and Eastern European countries, but also European non-members of the UN participated. It was thus a genuinely pan-European organization that aimed explicitly to integrate Europe economically, though this was not part of its official mission. It was led by the Swedish economist and politician Gunnar Myrdal, whose vision was that European integration should include Eastern Europe. From the beginning the ECE worked mainly through specialized technical committees staffed with experts, including committees for inland transport and electricity. This was an explicit part of the ECE organizational philosophy. As Myrdal explained later on:

> the committees and all their suborgans met in private and the documentation was not made public…this greatly contributed to unhampered and effective discussion of practical problems. Stress was from the beginning laid on the technical and non-political character of the work. Issues were never put to vote…Practical results of cooperation between governments are reached when several of them – not necessarily all or even a majority – agree on something.[12]

In the year of the ECE's establishment, American officials came to the conclusion that their strategies for promoting stable recovery in Europe were not working and that the way to achieve growth was through boosting output and productivity. This could only happen in Europe, they believed, through market expansion. Consequently it was argued that Europe needed to integrate economically, by means such as establishing a customs union to reduce restrictions on trade and movement of production factors. The Americans sought not only to reconstruct Europe economically, however, but also politically. Economic integration would not work without replacing the old European state system, which had nurtured economic nationalism during the interwar years and would do so again. Its replacement could take the form of US-style federalism, but in any case American policymakers saw a strong need for a supranational solution that would include central institutions of co-ordination and control.[13]

One important channel through which America's politicians and policymakers could apply pressure for a United States of Europe was its reconstruction and aid effort. Integration became a condition for Marshall Plan aid. With this initiative the USA abandoned piecemeal aid policies in favour of a comprehensive recovery plan that was to be agreed by the Europeans themselves and used to support the unification of Europe. When the ideas behind the Marshall plan were first discussed, the UNECE seemed to be in a good position to run the program. Yet eventually the USA did not want to work through the UNECE because of Soviet participation – the Cold War had begun. Accordingly, on the insistence of the USA, sixteen European countries created a new organization in 1948: the *Organization for European Economic Cooperation* (OEEC). It became focused on creating closer economic co-operation, and worked on issues such as trade liberalization, productivity, and currency convertibility. It did not became the supranational planning body envisaged by the Americans, but an intergovernmental body in which technical committees, for transport and energy among others, were to play an important role. For the French and British foreign offices, the OEEC had to represent an apolitical and technical organization in order to avoid too much US political interference.[14] Consequently, in 1948 two organizations existed side by side, the OEEC and the ECE, both of which heavily relied on experts and had similar committee structures. American experts were present in meetings of both organizations. While this working method was the result of an explicit strategy for the ECE, for the OEEC it was the default effect of a strategy to prevent Europe's refashioning according to American standards. The overlapping mandates set the stage for some competition between both organizations, but also for co-ordination and division of labour, not least because the same experts often worked in the committees of both organizations, and shared a similar perspective on integration. Both organizations worked on a wide range of topics. By looking at the attempts to integrate the transport and energy sectors, this chapter will show how their relationship worked in practice.

Transport integration

Between 1947 and 1950 the ECE Transport Committee developed a Declaration on the Construction of Main European International Traffic Arteries.[15] The aim was to integrate Europe's roads in a network of E-Roads. The declaration identified main arteries, numbered E1 to E22, and feeder roads, numbered E31 to E92. The road system had a clear pan-European flavour, including Southern and Eastern Europe. By signing the declaration, states promised to build or rebuild the selected national roads according to European standards, which were specified in technical annexes.[16] The working method was based on a consensus among road planners and engineers that such a European network could not be built top-down, as American experts would have preferred. Instead it would connect national networks and Europeanize them. This preference was the outcome of interwar discussions among international road organizations and engineers on how to build a European motorway network.[17] This approach identified European roads that should ideally be important not only for international but also for national traffic, since this would enhance the chances that national countries would finance the upgrading of their own E-road stretches. In the period up to 1975, when a major revision was done, the network grew, becoming denser and more up-to-standard. While the traffic on it exploded, the standards became more stringent (since the level of application was related to traffic density).

The UNECE not only designed the E-road network, it also developed an elaborate legal framework for cross-border road traffic in collaboration with international non-governmental organizations such as the International Chamber of Commerce and the International Road Transport Union.[18] The most important achievement was a multilateral agreement for freight transport, which had failed to emerge during the interwar years. After the war, cross-border truck traffic was not always allowed, and sometimes goods even had to be unloaded and reloaded at the border. Under American pressure the Transport Committee of UNECE managed to develop an agreement that liberalized transit traffic for six months starting on 6 December 1947. All Western European countries, as well as Hungary and Czechoslovakia, signed the agreement. These agreements were extended several times, but in the 1950s countries began to develop barriers for international transport of goods, in particular quotas (using a licence system) and tariffs. Since the UNECE Transport Committee anticipated that the days of liberalization would soon pass, it worked to create a regime for international road transport which would ease the crossing of borders. For example, it arranged a mutual recognition of driving licences and helped abolish the pre-war system in which private vehicles used for tourism had to be imported when crossing a border. It also introduced the so-called TIR (*Transport Internationaux Routieres*) scheme that abolished all customs duties for transit road freight transport (and a similar TIT schema for rail transit). For perishable food it helped to develop special refrigerated railway wagons, schemes for icing stations along transport routes, and standards for packaging of fresh fruits and vegetables, up to establishment of a new international rail and road organization that would run a complete cooling chain. As a result, in 1955 'Transfrigoroute Europe' was founded.[19] This was an association of the most prominent refrigerated road carriers of nine countries. In March 1951, a multilateral scheme was negotiated granting licences to international bus services. These bus services were also provided by railway companies. Under the brand name 'Europabus', the *Union des Services Routiers des Chemins de Fer Européens* (URF) started offering services already in April 1951, while other private companies, such as Viking Continentbus and Trans-European Buslines, also served the fast-growing demand. In 1956 Europabus had more than 100 lines and circular tours covering 40,000 km in seventeen countries.

In the 1960s cross-border traffic of tourism and goods transport exploded in Europe. This mobility explosion cannot be directly linked to the establishment of the European E-road network and the series of agreements, standards and conventions for the management of the traffic flows discussed here. But it is our hypothesis that without these accomplishments growth would have been more difficult.

Energy integration

Transport was a sector in which the UNECE was most active via its Inland Transport Committee, and where it turned out to be a more important actor than the OEEC Transport Committee. In the case of energy, the situation was a bit different. Here the OEEC Electric Committee took the lead.[20] The 'US European Cooperation Act' that called the Europe Recovery Plan ERP into being had explicitly mentioned the need to boost power production. Subsequently a separate electricity programme was developed. This programme would assist in building new electric facilities, not only located in the various nation states, but also ones that would be internationally financed and owned in order to share the electricity generated. For G.W. Perkins, who was overseeing the programme on behalf of the USA, the internationally owned and financed facilities were the most important part of the electricity programme. Yet these failed to materialize. Western European utilities and their experts who were sitting on the OEEC Electric Committee did not propose any project that would meet the American criteria for an international project. The committee was in favour of internationalization, but they opposed plans for international ownership of power plants or even transmission lines. As became clear in a report based on a study trip of twenty-five electrical engineers to the USA – much to the chagrin of the American OEEC officials – engineers and utilities favoured regional groupings that would gradually interconnect national systems. As in the case of transport, they preferred to build on a consensus on how to internationalize electricity production that had emerged in the interwar period. This solution was based on voluntary exchange of electricity across borders whenever utilities saw a need. The network managers trusted that they would serve each other's needs whenever required, because they had developed a spirit of mutual trust in each other.[21] The main barriers they saw to this voluntary exchange were political ones, such as electricity companies' obligation to ask permission from national governments to transmit electricity over the border. Accordingly, they expressed a need to lift this obligation. The Americans had hoped for the development of an international programme that would place final authority in the hands of a newly established organization. Instead of such a supranational solution, the European engineers proposed an international electricity power pool to be controlled by joint operation of utilities. The exchanges would be arranged bilaterally and on a voluntary basis, in line with common practice.[22]

For the Americans this meant that their international programme initiative had failed. Yet the idea for a power pool was endorsed by the OEEC Council in March 1950 and led to the creation of a co-ordinating body, the

Union for the Coordination and Transport of Electricity (UCPTE), by representatives of utilities from eight European countries in May 1951.[23] Following UCPTE, the basis for electricity exchange should be voluntary. It should work independently of other international organizations, so it was not linked to either the OEEC or the UNECE, although members of the UCPTE staffed the electric committees of both organizations. The informal nature of the Union was reflected in the first article of its statute, which stipulated that, although the members were delegates of public administrations or private utilities, the Union was made up of people, not of organizations.[24] In the following years the UCPTE managed, among other things, to create an integrated standardized network operating at 50 Hz, which was controlled by national or regional utilities. Subsequently, while national production grew steeply, the ratio of electricity exports relative to national production improved for many years after 1956. Integration, measured in terms of growth of traffic, economic dependence and a set of agreed arrangements among state and non-state actors, certainly did happen.

Yet the work of OEEC's and UNECE's technical committees on transport and energy integration is largely invisible in integration historiography. As Gillingham argues, 'real progress in fitting the unification puzzle together began only with the Schuman Plan', since it heralded integration upon accepting the creation of a new supranational institution.[25] Let us thus now turn to this plan, which is a key to the history of integration from an infrastructural perspective. It did not only involve the integration of one important energy carrier, coal, but also contained an element of transport integration, as we will see. More importantly, it became the example to emulate, as well as to avoid, for a number of other attempts at energy and transport integration.

The European Coal and Steel experiment

On 9 May 1950 the French Foreign Minister Robert Schuman announced that the coal and steel industries of France, Germany and other willing nations would be integrated. In April 1951 six countries signed the ECSC treaty, and it was ratified in spring 1952.[26] The newly appointed president of the so-called High Authority of the ECSC, Jean Monnet, believed that 'the United States [had] begun'.[27] Monnet's positive mood in Spring 1952 was induced not only by the creation of the ECSC, but also by other developments, such as attempts to create a European Defence Community (EDC), which seemed to prove him right that the ECSC was only a start.[28]

The reasons why coal and steel were the starting points have been abundantly analysed in the literature.[29] First, it was assumed coal would remain a main source of energy for the future, and thus a crucial asset for the needed modernization of European economies. Second, and more directly practically, France simply wanted to ensure continuing supplies of cokes from

German coal for one of their strategic industries: steel production. The Schuman plan was thus an extension of the modernization of French industry. For Jean Monnet, one of the architects of the French modernization plan and author of the Schuman Plan, and his American allies, who had put pressure on governments to sign the Treaty, there was more at stake.[30] Coal and steel were just starting points. Their ultimate aim was not merely to protect French interests, but to create a new European sector of industry that would serve as a first step towards the emergence of a new federal state. To his mind, it could only work if there were a powerful central directorate, the High Authority, that would get a mandate to push for integration. Monnet had not been the first to argue for coal and steel integration. During the interwar years German coal and steel producers had developed successful forms of co-operation with foreign partners. The formation of the International Steel Cartel in 1926 had been one of the first steps in this process, which continued well into the 1930s, and led to the establishment of several other cartels. However, Monnet did not push for cartels any more, but for competition organized by a High Authority.[31]

The six nations that finally signed the Treaty agreed to accept the emergence of a supranational institution, and thus gave up their own rights to make policies in this area. Even more, this central body gained powers to set prices and influence production that were not previously exercised by national governments.[32] In the plan as proposed by Monnet there was only one central institution, the 'High Authority' (HA). During the negotiations a 'Council of Ministers' and a 'European Parliamentary Assembly' were added. This reflected the concern of national governments for creating a check on the powers of the HA. Although Monnet wanted the ECSC to regulate the market and to encourage modernization, the big difference with the interwar period was that he aimed for *public dirigisme*. He strongly pressed for the organization of the common goods market and for the breaking up of private cartels, following the strong American antitrust policies. Modernization should be accomplished through 'organized competition' supervised by the High Authority. The HA had the mandate to protect the market from anticompetitive mergers, cartels, national governmental pricing policies, subsidies and other distortions. Yet it would be a guided competition, since the HA was charged with the task of softening the social consequences of the liberalization of the market. In addition, it could set prices to stabilize the market and impose production quotas in times of overproduction.[33]

It is clear that the ECSC and EDC embodied a different vision on integration from the OEEC or UNECE. Promoters of the sectoral integration approach aimed at political integration, while for the OEEC and UNECE economic integration was more important, albeit some would argue that such integration needed a political complement. For Jean Monnet, the OEEC was a byword for futility since it had no supranational element.[34] Another important difference was that the members of the HA had to exercise their functions in complete independence. In the ECSC treaty text (article 9) it was stipulated that none of them could represent a national government or could be connected to the coal or steel industry.[35] This is a striking difference from the OEEC and UNECE. The Transport and Electric Committees were manned with experts who sought to represent their national ministries, agencies, administrations, utilities and other international organizations active in the field precisely because this national representation would put them in a position to contribute to the implementation of the agreed measures within their own national frameworks.

Monnet's public dirigisme and preference for supranationalism were not favoured by his own colleagues, and were strongly resisted by industry.[36] Still, in its first years the High Authority did manage to remove national tariff barriers and quantitative restrictions. But it was less successful in removing discriminatory and distorting practices, such as unequal national freight railway rates, which varied greatly due to government policies and subsidies and made up a substantial part of the price of coal and steel. Yet it did succeed in ending the system of breaking up freight transport charges into separate sections, one for each country of transit, which meant that transport companies paid two or more so-called fictive terminal fees for loading and unloading at the border. By 1956 it also managed to bring about the abolition of directly discriminatory rates, that is, the charging of higher rate for goods crossing national frontiers. One might argue that this was the beginning of the sought-after functional spill-over effect on transport.[37] However, for Monnet the effects were too little and they came too late. After the French voted down the EDC in the summer of 1954 he decided to leave the ECSC to be in a better position to work on sectoral integration projects for transport and energy. However, he ignored the fact that sectoral integration in transport had been debated a lot and with concrete results – albeit in other institutional and organizational frameworks than the ones he imagined. As we will see, these debates had started in the Council of Europe three months after Schuman had given his famous speech on coal and steel integration. These initiatives clearly influenced the relaunch of sectoral integration initiatives staged by Monnet and others in 1954/1955.

More integration by sector?

The Bonnefous initiative: A supranational transport authority

On 16 August 1950, Edouard Bonnefous proposed that the *Consultative Assembly of the Council of Europe* explore sectoral integration for transport.[38] The Council of Europe was the institutional outcome of the Congress of Europe held in May 1948 in The Hague, organized by various streams of organizations pushing for some kind of federal Europe. Its statute was signed as the 'Treaty of Westminster' by representatives of ten states.[39]

Notwithstanding the unhappiness of several foreign ministries, in particular the British, about its establishment, the pressure to form the Council of Europe was too strong to be resisted. Many supporters of European integration came to consider the outcome as unsatisfactory, since the established European Parliament, called 'Consultative Assembly', could debate and discuss policies and offer recommendations to a Committee of (Foreign) Ministers without being able to bind them in any way. The opportunity for debate was seized, however. The Assembly gathered some of the most ardent supporters for a European federal state. They developed a range of proposals for European federation from its first session, in 1949, when Paul-Henri Spaak became president. Although the discussions were not taken up by the Committee of Ministers, they did contribute to the creation of a constituency that was receptive to ideas on European unification. The lack of success of direct federation, together with the enthusiasm created by the Schuman plan, led the Assembly to focus more on plans for sectoral integration in the autumn of 1950, discussed under the heading of 'specialized authorities'. For example, in August 1950, the Assembly not only discussed a proposal by Bonnefous for a European transport authority, but they also passed on to the Committee of Ministers a recommendation for setting up a European organization in agriculture, building on a number of earlier plans.[40]

Bonnefous was a member of French Parliament, a delegate of the Assembly and an ardent supporter of European unification. According to him, transport was an area where 'it is easiest to advance and rapidly obtain tangible results'.[41] Bonnefous proposed a supranational European transport organization that would, firstly, co-ordinate the modes of transport, including civil aviation, railroads, roads, and coastal and inland navigation at the European level. Secondly, it would build a common transport network, and should therefore be given the mandate to decide on large-scale investment programmes. Finally, this supranational transport organization could co-ordinate the activities of other international transport organizations. The proposed 'European Transport Authority' could best be attached to the Council of Europe since it had a large enough geographical scope (not limited to the six countries involved in ECSC negotiations), and it would have a structure similar to that of the future ECSC, including an Executive Committee comparable to the High Authority proposed in the Schuman Plan.

While the initiative was heavily criticized for its supranational characteristics by the British and Scandinavian members of the Assembly, other members preferred to wait and see what would happen with the ECSC before embarking on this new adventure. The history of this initiative within the Council of Europe is quite complex, and this is not the place to go into details.[42] The main point I would like to stress in the context of this chapter is that the national ministries of transport and international transport organizations, although not involved in the CoE in any way, used the negotiations within the committee to criticize the supranational aspect. They disapproved of a form of political integration that would weaken the existing network of international organizations that already existed in the transport field, and argued against an authority that would leave decisions in the hands of a body not staffed by technical experts. The final proposal that became accepted by the Assembly was prepared by the Frenchman Maurice Lemaire. Lemaire was chairman of the important *International Railway Organization* (UIC), which represented the voice of various transport organizations and transport ministries. In September 1952 he proposed a European Council for Transport that would be purely advisory and would bring together representatives of transport ministers of governments, international organizations, members of the Council of Europe, the ECSC and the international Chamber of Commerce. It should focus on studying problems and produce proposals for all actors involved. Ironically, in his explanatory memorandum Lemaire stressed the importance of the proposed Council for checking the ambitions of the ECSC in the area of transport.[43] What had started as an adjunct to the ECSC and a co-promotion of political unification was now designed as a counterforce and even competitor of the ECSC.

The Bonnefous legacy: An expert-driven European transport organization

After the acceptance of the final proposal by the CoE's Assembly, two initiatives were taken that aimed to take the proposal in a different direction. Both the British and French governments decided to organize a conference as a follow-up. The French prime minister pushed his transport minister to include not only the six countries involved in the ECSC initiative, but also Austria and Switzerland, since they seemed central for transport co-ordination.[44] The original intent of the French prime minister's government was to discuss again a High Authority for transport, as originally proposed by Bonnefous. But for strategic reasons it was decided not to push this agenda, since the French foreign office considered negotiations on a new European Defence Community more important.[45] Subsequently other issues dominated the agenda, such as ongoing UNECE, UIC and OEEC initiatives in the area of the planning of a European road network, or issues of standardization. A main output of the conference was the decision to enlarge an existing agreement between German and French railway organizations on the mutual use of wagons. The next step was to standardize these wagons following common technical norms. This plan was developed by Louis Armand, who gave it the name of EUROP Pool to signify its broader intentions not only to cover more countries in the future, but also to serve as a stepping stone in the process of European integration.[46] At the conference it was also decided to complement the pooling and standardization of wagons with the establishment of a new company for jointly financing new wagons under the name of 'Eurofima'.[47]

While the French originally intended to use the Paris conference to discuss a supranational solution for transport integration, the British government acted on the CoE proposal for the opposite reason. Since the proposed organization was only of consultative character, this fitted their overall foreign policy objectives to establish a practical alternative model for the supranational ECSC (and EDC). This foreign policy objective of avoiding a supranational solution synchronized with the objectives of transport ministries in Europe, including those in Germany and France. They feared that the sectoral approach would lead to the establishment of a supranational transport authority headed by non-experts and become subject to outside intervention into their realm, crowded with many international organizations controlled by transport experts. They favoured strengthening co-operation by means of multilateral agreements on separate aspects of European transport using the existing expert channels. The fear of outside intervention was alleviated by the ongoing discussion within the ECSC subcommittee on transport, which had begun to urge the High Authority to develop an overall transport policy. The British foreign office invited the OEEC's inland transport committee to act on the CoE proposal. The committee accepted the British proposal and embarked on the organization of a series of conferences. Following the logic of the OEEC's organizational set-up, the conferences were dominated by experts and transport ministries. Although the German and French transport ministries agreed to work with the British foreign ministry, they did not like the liberal British approach, also favoured by the OEEC, towards integration. But at least using the OEEC as a platform would preclude the supranational option from appearing on the agenda.[48]

Transport ministries were not in favour of a liberal approach, since that would treat transport as just another sector of the economy, and focus on taking away all distortions for a free market. This would include encouraging competition between modes of transport. The transport ministries and transport experts felt transport was a sector with distinctive characteristics. It was seen as an instrument of public policy to secure a wide range of economic goals (modernization of the economy) as well as social welfare goals (universal access at a reasonable price). Wasteful competition among various modes should therefore be avoided. The task of any transport organization should be to allow each mode to do what it can do best. In particular, competition between road haulage and railway transport should be avoided.[49]

The series of conferences organized by the OEEC finally led to the establishment of a new transport organization. On 17 October 1953, sixteen countries decided to found the *European Conference of Ministers of Transport* (ECMT). It was to be an independent organization working with national transport experts, focusing on technical issues, and collaborating with other international organizations. Decisions were to be taken by a council of transport ministries which met once a year and provided recommendations adopted by majority vote. Transport ministries succeeded in creating an organization that pursued their own integration approach, and this against the will of the Foreign Offices of the governments of Britain,

Sweden and Denmark, who pushed for a link with the OEEC. As a compromise, the ECMT administrative secretariat was finally integrated into that of the OEEC, but the precise relationship with the OEEC remained unclear. Furthermore, the ECMT was ordered to report annually to the CoE Consultative Assembly, although this body did not welcome the ECMT. On the contrary, it expressed disapproval, since it lacked any supranational element and hence would never have any political significance.[50]

Demise and relaunch of sectoral integration

With the French National Assembly's rejection of the EDC in August 1954, the possibilities of further political integration of Europe seemed rather limited, and Monnet and his adjutants had to re-examine their options. As a result, they decided to push for sectoral integration in conventional energy and transport, and for atomic power.[51] They wanted to focus on sectors that were perceived as politically less sensitive, and which would easily accept centralized planning. Energy and transport seemed to be the perfect candidates, since they were highly regulated industries. To some degree, the concentration on transport and energy meant a return to the original scenario, as transport and energy always had been mentioned as the next sectors to integrate after coal and steel. Only political circumstances had forced Monnet to move towards the field of defence. But Monnet did not consider the fact that the situation in these sectors had changed. Partly due to the creation of the ECSC, experts in the transport and energy sector had developed a strong aversion to any supranational solution.

Monnet was convinced that atomic energy was the best option on which to concentrate his efforts. Nuclear energy promised to be the most important energy source for the future, which could diminish Europe's dependency on oil and American imports of coal. The dependency issue had already led to long debates within the OEEC, and the drafting of an expert report under the leadership of the influential French engineer Louis Armand, who was highly involved in developing the French nuclear industry. The report introduced the idea of European nuclear energy production. It was Armand who suggested to Monnet to focus on nuclear energy as the next step toward political integration. For Armand, the main fuel for Europe should not be oil, which would unavoidably bring external dependencies, but atomic energy.[52]

From August 1954 onward, Monnet was in frequent and close contact with Paul-Henri Spaak in order to seek ways to get European integration going again. As the president of the Council of Europe, Spaak had been an alert spectator of the transport discussions in the Assembly. Sectoral integration was an important option for him. When he looked at ways to implement it using his restored position as foreign minister for Belgium, his hopes also centred on the idea of a common transport or energy policy governed by another High Authority, or by the ECSC. But, after his contacts with Monnet, Spaak became convinced of the spectacular possibilities for European integration in the nuclear field. In April 1955, he sent a set of proposals he had agreed with Monnet to the ECSC foreign ministers. The proposals called for a general conference of the Six to discuss the creation of new High Authority for energy, atomic energy or transport. Two days after the invitation by Spaak, the Dutch foreign minister J.W. Beyen proposed to the Benelux foreign ministers a plan for economic integration of Europe, while he argued against further integration by sector. This plan did not come out of the blue. Trade liberalization had been discussed almost continuously since 1948 in the OEEC context, but also as part of a range of plans for custom unions. The OEEC's liberalization programme proved to be fragile, and in the early 1950s new protectionist barriers were raised, threatening the further growth of the Dutch open economy. Future access to major trading partners seemed insecure. The Beyen plan had been designed to provide a mechanism which would limit trading partners' ability to raise new trade barriers. It sought automatic reductions of internal tariffs and a common external tariff in various stages to be negotiated. Beyen was also a proponent of a supranational mechanism to prevent what had happened in the interwar period, when a relative dynamic growth in the twenties was aborted by a trade war in the 1930s.[53]

Subsequently, the Benelux foreign ministers, Beyen, Spaak and Bech of Luxembourg, decided to join forces and combine the Spaak–Monnet and Beyen proposals. If the ambitious plans for an economic community were to fail, the fallback option of sectoral integration could still work. Spaak expected that protectionist France would never accept such a proposal. The three men shared a commitment to some form of supranationality, and had already worked together very closely in London during the war on the creation on the Benelux. They formulated the so-called Benelux memorandum, which was sent to the other foreign ECSC ministers, who met in June 1955 in Messina. The memorandum requested a conference for drafting new treaties. At the meeting, as anticipated, the French were not inclined to create such a conference. They did agree, however, to study the issues through an ad hoc intergovernmental committee chaired by Spaak. The committee was instructed to: 1) pursue joint development plans for European transport; 2) consider an overall policy for conventional forms of energy; 3) investigate the possibility of setting up a common organization for ensuring peaceful development of atomic energy; and 4) create a common market to remove obstacles to trade and harmonize economic policies and social regulations. It was decided that the committee would be assisted by experts from existing European organizations such as the ECSC, OEEC, Council of Europe and the ECMT. The committee established four commissions of experts to examine the general common market, conventional energy, atomic energy, and transport respectively. The transport committee established separate subcommittees for communication and air transport.

The discussions on transport and conventional energy turned out to be difficult, since the invited transport and energy experts argued that the development of a common market, such as the ECSC had established for coal and steel, was not possible.[54] Transport had to fulfil public obligations, which differed strongly in each country, and competition between various transport modes had to be avoided. Finally, the area covered by the six did not make sense from a transport point of view; at a minimum, Austria and Switzerland must be added. Another issue raised was that a new organization was not needed, since the ECMT already existed. The transport ministers were afraid that their independent international role would be restricted by a new institution staffed by the foreign affairs and economic ministries. The experts in the conventional energy committee also argued that the manufacture, transport and distribution of gas and electricity differed enough from traffic of manufactured goods that they could not be integrated in a common market. The industry was made up of a range of small monopolies that could not be easily broken, so competition would never work. They focused on technical issues, such as how to meet peak demand and to assess future benefits of investments, which were considered of minor importance by Spaak. Although Spaak tried to force the experts to come up with results, no concrete proposals for sectoral integration emerged, while the deadline set for a final report in the Messina Resolution in October 1955 passed. Consequently, Spaak took the decision to take matters out of the hands of the experts. This had three results that are important to my story. First, the common energy policy was dropped. This was not only a result of visions on integration by experts, but also because Spaak (and Monnet) had come to believe that the rapid formation and growth of a European nuclear industry they sought would create a transition of the whole economy from a coal to a nuclear base. Hence, the importance of the conventional forms of energy would diminish strongly. Second, a separate community would be established for European Atomic Agency (Euratom), and finally, transport would be integrated in the common market policy.

From the start, the negotiations on Euratom were difficult, and here national foreign policies were vital. The treaty text made it possible for France and Germany to pursue their own national nuclear policies, and thus Euratom never became an effective co-ordination mechanism, except for certain minor areas. Although, in this case, national foreign policies can explain why Euratom was stillborn, it needs to be researched whether technocratic internationalism also played a role. The incorporation of transport into a common policy also proved to be difficult. Transport experts protested vigorously against the idea that the sector would become subordinate to common market imperatives, and negotiators could not reconcile the conflicting positions. Hence the decision was to leave the text on transport vague and open-ended.[55] Conflicting issues should be solved later on. The transport section in the treaty opens with a statement that transport should be subject to common market principles; that is, a common transport policy should strive for the abolition of obstacles to freedom of movement for persons, services and capital as well as ensuring that competition in the common market is not distorted. However, the second article dilutes this by stating that the implementation should take into account the distinctive features of transport. In the first decades of the common transport policy the built-in conflict of these two different positions prevented any effective EEC common transport policy from emerging. After several ambitious but failed attempts to create such a policy, the action of the Commission tended to be more piecemeal, generally limited to technical issues (standardization of emission standards, axle sizes etc.) and social concerns (lorry drivers' hours), focused on separate policies for each mode of transport, and based on collaboration with other actors in the field. In these limited areas the CTP was successful as an adjunct to the work of the ECMT, UIC and other actors.[56]

Technocratic internationalism and European integration

If we interpret the notion of integration as the creation of a policy environment that was conducive to new integration proposals, the UNECE, OEEC, ECSC and CoE initiatives and their outcomes can be seen as a proof for an expansive integration logic as theorized by the neo-functionalists.[57] Functional spill-overs happened, but the nature of the outcome was different from that desired or promoted by the supporters of sectoral integration, since the supranational element was lacking. For this reason neo-functionalists (and subsequently much of the integration history) paid no attention to the various organizations discussed here. They were condemned as ineffective before they started, not only by many of the supporters of European unification at the time, but also by the theorists and historians of European integration. This did not bother the experts, who were put in a position to control the new European organizations in various sectors, and happily took up the offer to articulate and implement their own views on integration.

These views were characterized by three ideas. First, network-building serves public aims. It should be used to induce economic growth, modernization, social equality, and peace. This idea was based on what might be called the myth of networks.[58] They believed that networks create economic interdependencies which would automatically generate growth, unify people and lead to a better mutual understanding between nations and peace. Second, networks can be built by connecting national networks, which also require development and form the basis of internationalization. This obviates the need to dichotomize national and international or

European solutions as many of the promoters of European unification did. Instead, both developments should be co-ordinated. Third, the best method for international collaboration is to create consensus among experts, who would find the optimal solution by applying their scientific thinking. Experts preferred to stay away from what they defined as power politics and the petty nationalism of many diplomats. They asked governments to give them a broad mandate and limit political interference as much as possible. This could be accomplished by underlining the technical and non-political nature of the questions they addressed and avoiding all publicity. For the engineers and experts involved, depoliticization and voluntary agreements did not signify weakness, but rather embodied the belief in their ability to harmonize European and national interests through gradual processes of mutual orientation.

Together these ideas form a specific technocratic internationalist perspective on European integration, which is largely invisible in the integration historiography. Already in the interwar years these ideas became a distinctive mode of thinking on how to unify networks, and they were carried over into the post-war era.[59] However, there is nothing in technocratic internationalism that specifies a preference for a preconceived notion of Europe, and in the expert view the ultimate goal should be global reach anyway. The spatial spread of the networks should be arranged to be as efficient and effective as possible. So it should be determined by the technical characteristics of the networks and the possibilities for innovation. From this perspective, for example, experts saw it as highly artificial to limit transport integration to the six countries that signed the ECSC Treaty. Yet already during the interwar years technocratic internationalism became infused with European integration initiatives. Due to the ongoing initiatives and discussions, experts and their international organizations working on internationalization aligned themselves firmly with a European unification agenda (sometimes upon invitation and sometimes actively promoted by experts themselves), which resulted in a host of specific European organizations, each with its own spatial reach, and each imbued with a specific understanding of Europe. The OEEC integration efforts focused on Western Europe, while the UNECE sustained their efforts to include Eastern European countries. The notions of political spill-over and cultivated spill-over advanced by Haas seem to capture this process very well, but, as is the case with functional spill-over, we need to redefine their content. Political spill-over can be adapted to refer to the formation of cross-border networks of actors that began to operate outside and beyond the level of interstate relations towards forms of European integration. This understanding matches very well the emphasis in recent historical integration historiography on what is called transnational network formation. These transnational networks contributed not only to the integration process (e.g. understood as building of the EEC) but also to the formation of specific international societies that used the notion of Europe as a boundary object.[60] Cultivated spill-over should refer not only to the work of supranational institutions, but to all international organizations and networks dedicated towards building a particular European society. This work includes the articulation, accumulation, comparison and transformation of local and national experiences into European ideologies, practices, standards and regulations, and subsequently the promotion and monitoring of its implementation.

Post-war European infrastructural integration happened at the junction of two forces: technocratic internationalism on the one side, and political initiatives for European integration on the other side. The latter initiatives came in various strands: from sectoral integration to economic integration and immediate political integration. Technocratic internationalism shared nothing with the last strand, except perhaps the belief in the myth of networks. With the promoters of sectoral integration it shared the vision that the path towards integration should be hidden and engineered by independent experts. Finally the adherents of technocratic internationalism agreed with the proponents of economic integration that such integration was far more fundamental and important than political integration, since it would directly help to create economic growth and welfare. The power of the network idea also easily gelled with a view that focused on economic integration, but the emphasis on the importance of establishing a free market did not match experts' preference for public planning. While both parties believed in the necessity of central planning, each sought a very different outcome: a new European federal state versus the creation of well-operating networks. Technocratic internationalism is a diffuse set of ideas, elements of which were articulated and mobilized by experts in the various interwar and post-war discussions on infrastructural integration. It never became the explicit focus of a political movement, but this would also not fit its ambitions. It aimed at what might perhaps best be called a hidden integration process.[61] Europe would become a community of circulating people, goods and information using networks imagined and constructed by engineers.

Fragmented European integration

In the course of the 1960s neo-functionalists found out that, despite a promising start, prospects for further integration were few and far between. Disintegration appeared more likely. Haas tried to adapt his theory by introducing concepts such as disintegration and integration plateau, but ultimately he himself conceded that neo-functionalist theory was no longer adequate.[62] In the 1980s a new interpretation of the integration process emerged within political science and European integration studies. It was labelled as the intergovernmental perspective.[63] Their work was reinforced by perhaps the most influential historian of European integration history, Alan Milward. For Milward and the intergovernmentalists in political science, national governments were uniquely powerful actors in the process of European integration. They controlled the nature and pace of the integration, guided by their concern to protect and promote national interests. Nation states do contain plural elites, but they never allow these elites to enter the space of international relations before having agreed nationally on the position to be taken. Accordingly, the activities of men such as Monnet and Spaak are nothing but footnotes in history. No transnational elites or organizations managed to manipulate the interests of the nation states. After the Second World War ended, all the elites of the nation states wanted to re-establish their own supremacy and legitimacy. They understood that this would be possible only if they brought about affluence and employment for the entire population. European integration was an important element in this national strategy. Consequently, Milward coined the notion of European integration as the rescue of the nation state.[64] Milward's view prevails among historians, and resulted, ironically, in the burying of the subject in diplomatic history.[65] According to this view, European integration had such a troubled history because nation state leaders needed it for certain purposes, but never wanted it to flourish. But should this be the conclusion?

From the story of infrastructural integration it can be inferred that Milward is overstating his argument. Although it is clear that foreign offices and nation state policies deeply influenced the pace and direction of the sectoral integration process, this should not lead to the conclusion that the impact of networks of experts or other societal actors can be neglected.[66] For the case of transport and energy integration, experts were able to divert from foreign policies pushed by their own government. They clearly had their own views and agenda on integration, which tend to be neglected in histories of European integration. Ironically, we might argue that this is what the experts wanted themselves: they strove for a hidden integration of Europe outside the spotlights of diplomatic and political arenas.

This chapter argues that the hidden integration project was far from marginal to integration discussions, and that many different visions and projects on why and how to unify proliferated. Sectoral integration, political integration and economic integration were inarticulate and imprecise visions that needed tailoring to rapidly changing circumstances. This is equally true for the hidden integration project fuelled by technocratic internationalist thinking. Nobody knew what integration meant. The first twelve post-war years of European discussion on infrastructural integration can perhaps best be seen as an experimental and learning process in which the actors found out what was desirable and possible and what was not. They did this in a context heavily overdetermined by the decolonization process and the development of the Cold War. The process should therefore not be pictured as 'the road to Rome', since there were many roads and not all of them led to the signing of the Treaty of Rome. This becomes particularly visible when trying to write an integration history from the perspective of transnational infrastructures. An exclusive focus on the EU and its predecessors is therefore more than problematic. Many different organizations were created in this process, with overlapping mandates and visions. While the political impact of some of these organizations or committees is limited to the 1950s, others continued to play important roles in the 1960s and beyond. Some of these organizations are included in the standard literature about European integration history, but generally on a very marginal level (for example the *United Nation Economic Commission for Europe*). Others are completely neglected, particularly those created to arrange infrastructural integration (EUROP-Pool (1950), the *Union for the Coordination and Transport of Electricity* (UCPTE), and the *European Conference of Ministers of Transport* (ECMT)). Many of them are discussed in this volume: for example, the *Technical Committee for Communications and Transport of the League of Nations,*[67] the *International Broadcasting Union* (IBU), the *European Broadcasting Union* (EBU), the *Organisation Internationale de Radiodiffusion et Télévision* (OIRT)[68] and the *International Air Traffic Association* (IATA).[69]

As a consequence, the integration process was fragmented, both spatially and functionally. It was functionally fragmented since a range of separate organizations, set up in the nineteenth century or interwar years as well as newly created in the post-Second World War period, dealt with different issues, covering the set-up of an entire network or standards for specific items such as railway wagons or perishable foods. It was partially fragmented by the range of different open-ended spaces each organization covered. Each organization had its own signatories, but expansion was anticipated. Conventions were often not signed by all, while their impact often radiated outside the space covered by the founding organizations, since countries that had not (yet) joined implemented the agreed standards. Accordingly, multiple European integration processes proliferated, mostly without sharp geographic borders. The European impulse often simply ran in certain directions, depending on the reach of the standards and rules generated by the various organizations and the carrying expert communities.

These conclusions lead me to the central issue of this article, which is to explain why transport and energy infrastructure policy initiatives of the European Economic Community were mostly unsuccessful. It is because the work was claimed by experts who created their own organizations and were able to implement (partly) their hidden integration project, sometimes helped by nation state foreign policies that wanted to prevent the supranational option from gaining strength. The hidden integration project embraced a mode of thinking that believed in the unifying power of networks, and a technical apolitical road to integration. The project competed with other integration projects, but also allowed collaboration with promoters of economic integration in particular.

The story of infrastructural integration suggests that writing European integration history should focus less on states and the debate over whether it led to a federal state or supranational institutions. We are better off using concepts introduced in political science during the 1980s – in particular the governance concept. The governance concept highlights the set of various formal and informal rules constituting specific regimes. In addition to public actors, private actors are closely involved in drafting and enforcing these regulations. They often work together in policy networks, and when they are expert-driven we might speak of epistemic communities.[70] These have recognized expertise and competence in a particular domain and subsequently hold an authoritative claim to policy-relevant knowledge. Accordingly they are put in position to help nation states and other social actors to identify and frame their interest and propose and implement specific policies. Regimes must be understood as something more than temporary arrangements that change easily. Infrastructural regimes are institutions that govern specific stakeholders and actors. This does not mean that actors will always comply with the terms of the regime. There were deviations, yet the existence of infrastructural regimes resulted in the widespread adoption and legitimacy of particular European ways of constructing and using infrastructures.[71] It follows that regimes should not be viewed as external to actors; rather, they have constitutive effects since they regulate behaviour and contribute to the definition of the identity of actors. Consequently we have found a third source of fragmentation: participation in a range of different regimes led to a fragmented process of European identity formation for designers and users of infrastructures alike. Designing and using various infrastructures implied participating in many different Europes simultaneously, which perhaps is one of the explanations why Europe is so elusive. These considerations suggest a definition of European integration that focuses less on the emergence of state-like structures, and more on the emergence of a wide range of transnational regimes carried by a range of policy networks and guided by a set of different integration ideals. Needless to say, the scope and influence of these regimes might differ. This definition implies that in the twentieth century the essence of the European integration process has been fragmentation.

In 2004, just before his death, Haas himself declared that his earlier declaration, that neo-functionalism was obsolete, had been wrong after all. He explained that new directions in the neo-functionalist theory that focus on governance and agency did indeed save much of what is valuable in neo-functionalism.[72] The story of infrastructural integration grants him at least the benefit of the doubt.

Notes

This chapter is part of ongoing work within the research programme Transnational Infrastructures and the Rise of Contemporary Europe (TIE), supported by the Netherlands Organization for Scientific Research under the VICI scheme (dossiernummer 277-53-001). See www.tie-project.nl. I would like to thank in particular

Alec Badenoch, Paul Edwards, Andreas Fickers, Christian Franke, Wolfram Kaiser and Waqar Zaidi for comments on an earlier draft and Kiran Patel for ongoing exchanges on a transnational history of European integration, as well as all the participants of the first international TIE workshop and the members of the TIE group in Eindhoven: Irene Anastasiadou, Alec Badenoch, Vincent Lagendijk, Suzanne Lommers, Frank Schipper and Erik van der Vleuten.

1. For transport see, for example, Handley Stevens, *Transport Policy in the European Union* (Houndsmills/New York: Palgrave MacMillan 2004) and Michel Dumoulin, *The European Commission, 1958–72. History and Memories* (Luxembourg: European Communities 2007), chapter 22. For energy see, for example, Stephen George, *Politics and Policy in the European Union* (Oxford: Oxford University Press 1996), chapter 8, and N.J.D. Lukas, *Energy and the European Communities* (London: Europa Publications 1977).

2. His seminal work is Ernst B. Haas, *The Uniting of Europe. Political, Social and Economic Forces 1950–1957* (Notre Dame, Indiana 2004, 3rd edn (1st edn 1958)). Other works are mentioned in other footnotes below.

3. This chapter can thus also be read as a contribution to attempts to reactivate some elements of neo-functionalist thinking, which had fallen out of fashion in the 1970s.

4. For a discussion on the origins of the infrastructure concept see Dirk van Laak, 'Infra-Strukturgeschichte', *Geschichte und Gesellschaft* 27(3) (2001), pp. 367–93. My treatment of infrastructures resembles the way they are defined in the large technical systems literatures. For an overview see Erik Van der Vleuten, 'Understanding Network Societies. Two Decades of Large Technical System Studies' in Erik van der Vleuten and Arne Kaijser (eds) *Networking Europe. Transnational Infrastructures and the Shaping of Europe 1850–2000* (Sagamore Beach: Science History Publications 2006), pp. 279–314.

5. For a discussion see Ben Rosamond, *Theories of European Integration* (Houndsmills: Palgrave MacMillan 2000), pp. 9–14.

6. Wolfram Kaiser, 'From State to Society? The Historiography of European Integration' in Michelle Cini and Angela K. Bourne (eds) *European Union Studies* (Houndsmills: Palgrave MacMillan 2006), pp. 190–208. For an insightful overview of transnational history and a call to apply it to European integration history, see Kiran K. Patel, 'Überlegungen zu einer transnationalen Geschichte', *Zeitschrift für Geschichtswissenschaft* 52 (2004), pp. 626–45. The transnational approach is also promoted for writing a history of Europe and European integration by the Tensions of Europe Network. This project is discussed for its exploration of a transnational approach by Pierre-Yves Saunier, 'Learning by Doing: Notes about the Making of the Palgrave Dictionary of Transnational History', *Journal of Modern European History* 6(2) (2008), pp. 159–80, p. 178, and E. van der Vleuten, 'Technological History and the Transnational Challenge: Meanings, Promises, Pitfalls', *Technology and Culture* 49 (2008), pp. 974–94.

7. See Ernst B. Haas, *The uniting of Europe*, especially new prefaces to 1968 and 2004 editions. See also Leon Lindberg, *The political dynamics of European Economic integration* (Stanford 1963), Ernst B. Haas, *Beyond the Nation-State* (Stanford: Stanford University Press 1964) and Leon Lindberg and Stuart A. Scheingold, *Europe's Would-Be Polity* (Prentice-Hall 1970). For the best summary of their ideas and their development see Ben Rosamond, *Theories of European Integration*, chapter 3.

8. This distinction is introduced by Tranholm-Mikkelsen in his analysis of neo-functionalism, 'Neofunctionalism: Obstinate or Obsolete?' *Millennium: Journal of International Studies* 20(1) (1991), pp. 1–22.
9. See the new introduction by Haas to the third edition of his *Uniting in Europe*, published in 2004.
10. Haas, *Uniting of Europe*, pp. 299–317.
11. The United Nations Charter (article 52) signed on 26 June 1945 encouraged the possibility of regional groupings. The origin of the ECE lies in the investigations in Europe of the UN Temporary Sub-Commission on the Economic Recovery of Devastated Areas. On the history of UNECE see among others Jean Siotis, *ECE in the Emerging European System* (New York: Carnegie Endowment for International Peace 1967).
12. Gunnar Myrdal, 'Twenty Years of Economic Commission for Europe', *International Organization* 22(3) (1968), pp. 617–28.
13. The best source for the origins of the Marshall Plan is Michael J. Hogan, *The Marshall Plan. America, Britain, and the reconstruction of Western Europe, 1947–1952* (Cambridge: Cambridge University Press 1987).
14. See Alan Milward, *The Reconstruction of Western Europe 1945–51* (London: Routledge), chapters 2, 3 and 5, particularly chapter 6; on the OEEC see also Richard Griffiths (ed.), *Explorations in OEEC History* (Paris: OECD 1997).
15. On E-road network see F. Schipper, *Driving Europe. Building Europe on Roads in the Twentieth Century*, PhD thesis, Eindhoven University of Technology (Amsterdam, Aksant/SHT 2008), and Pår Blomkvist, 'Roads for Flow-Roads for Peace: Lobbying for a European Highway System' in Van der Vleuten and Kaijser, *Networking Europe*, pp. 161–86.
16. Signed by five states in 1950: Belgium, France, Luxembourg, the Netherlands, and the United Kingdom. Others would follow later: Austria in 1951, Greece and Sweden in 1952, Norway in 1953, Portugal and Turkey in 1954, and Germany and Italy in 1957. Other states signed in the 1960s, including Bulgaria and Hungary in 1962, Finland and Romania in 1965, Denmark in 1966, Ireland in 1968 and Czechoslovakia in 1973.
17. On this interwar discussion see Schipper, *Driving Europe*, chapter 3; see also Johan Schot and Vincent Lagendijk, 'Technocratic Internationalism in Interwar Years. Building Europe on Motorways and Electricity Networks', *Journal of Modern European History* (2008) 2.
18. This summary of the work of UNECE is mainly based on Schipper, *Driving Europe*, chapters 5 and 7. See also Paul J. Kapteyn, *Europa sucht eine gemeinsame Verkehrspolitik* (De Tempel, Brugge 1968), part one, chapter 2.
19. For the UNECE work on perishable food see Erik van der Vleuten, 'Feeding the Peoples of Europe. Transnational Food Transport Infrastructures in the early Cold War, 1947–1960', this volume.
20. This section is based on Vincent Lagendijk, *Electrifying Europe. The power of Europe in the construction of electricity network*, PhD thesis, Eindhoven University of Technology (Amsterdam, Aksant/SHT 2008), chapter 4.
21. See various reports of engineers presented at the first post-war conference of the Union Internationale des Producteurs et Distribution d' Énergie Électrique (UNIPEDE), published as *Compte rendu des travaux du huitième congrès international tenu à Bruxelles en septembre 1949, vol 2, Rapports des Comités d'Études IV*

à IX (Paris: Imprimerie Cahix 1949), and extensively discussed in Lagendijk, *Electrifying Europe*, pp. 137–42.

22. Ibid.

23. Belgium, Germany, France, Italy, Luxembourg, the Netherlands, Austria and Switzerland.

24. UCPTE, *Rapport Annuel 1951–1952* (Paris: UCPTE 1952) p. 5, cited in Lagendijk, *Electrifying Europe*, 148.

25. John Gillingham, *Coal, Steel and the Rebirth of Europe 1945–1955* (Cambridge: Cambridge University Press 1991), p. 366.

26. For history of ECSC we refer to Haas, *Uniting of Europe*, Gillingham, *Coal and Steel* and W. Diebold Jr, *The Schuman Plan: A Study in Economic Cooperation: 1950–1959* (New York: Praeger 1962).

27. His first address to the ECSC Assembly is cited in Mark Gilbert, *Surpassing Realism. The Politics of European Integration since 1945* (Lanham: Rowman & Littlefield Publishers 2003), p. 49.

28. I will not discuss the EDC initiative any further in this paper. It was proposed by the French Prime Minister René Pleven on 24 October 1950, but devised by Jean Monnet. The EDC would create a European army and would have a similar institutional structure to the ECSC. See E. Fursdon, *The European Defense Community. A History* (London: Macmillan 1980).

29. See footnote 27, and in addition D. Spierenburg and R. Poidevin, *The History of the High Authority of the European Coal and Steel Community: Supranationality in Action* (London: Weidenfeld 1994).

30. Monnet was part of an informal transatlantic policy network; for the network of Monnet see Brigitte Leucht, 'Transatlantic policy networks in the creation of the first European anti-trust law' in Wolfram Kaiser, Brigitte Leucht and Morton Rasmussen, *The History of the European Union. Origins of a trans-and supranational polity* 1950–1972 (London: Routledge 2009), pp. 56–73.

31. For an analysis of the notion of competition and its role in the process of European integration see Matthias Kipping, 'Les tôles avant les casseroles. La compétitivité de l' industrie Française et les origines de la construction européenne', *Enterprises et Histoire* 5 (1994), pp. 73–93.

32. Conclusion of Diebold, *The Schuman Plan* (1959), pp. 78–9.

33. On the HA see literature mentioned in footnotes 27 and 29.

34. Robert Marjolin, *Memoirs 1911–1986. Architect of European Unity* (London: Weidenfeld & Nicolson 1989), p. 270.

35. For treaty see http://europa.eu/scadplus/treaties, accessed 25 March 2009

36. See Alan Milward, *The European Rescue of the Nation-State* (London and New York: Routledge 2000, 2nd edn), p. 206. Monnet's attempts to turn the High Authority into a strong centre of decision-making had made him, as well as the High Authority, disliked.

37. For the work of the ECSC on transport issues see Diebold, *The Schuman Plan*, chapter 8 and see Kapteyn, *Europa Sucht*, part I, chapter 4.

38. On the history of the Bonnefous transport initiative, and the subsequent discussions that led to the establishment of the ECMT, see Christian Henrich-Franke, 'Mobility and European Integration. Politicians, professionals and the foundation of the ECMT', *Journal of Transport History* 29(1) (2008), pp. 64–82. In addition see Kapteyn, *Europa Sucht*, part I, chapter 3. Bonnefous had been active in the French resistance and became a French politician for the Union démocratique et socialiste de la Résistance. He was an ardent supporter of European integration but not driven by any special interest in transport.

39. Belgium, Denmark, France, Britain, Ireland, Italy, the Netherlands, Luxembourg, Norway and Sweden. On the history of the Council of Europe see Derek Urwin, *The Community of Europe. A History of European Integration since 1945* (London/ New York: Longman, 2nd edn 1995), chapter 3.

40. This episode often only gets minimal attention in the European integration literature; see for example Derek W. Urwin, *The Community of Europe. A History of European Integration since 1945* (London and New York: Longman 1995, 2nd edn), pp. 58–60. See also the published *Working Papers of the Consultative Assembly of the Council of Europe*, vol. 1, document 13, pp. 267–85, present in the European Document Centre of the European University Institute in Florence.

41. See Edouard Bonnefous, 'L'organisation européenne des transports', *Notre Europe* 2 (1951), pp. 45–6, cited from the European Navigator: www.ena.lu

42. See Henrich-Franke, 'Mobility and European Integration'.

43. See Jan Brabers, 'The Failure of European Transport Integration (1945–1955)' in Gilbert Trausch (ed.) *Die Europäische Integration vom Schuman-Plan zu den Römischen Verträgen* (Baden-Baden 1993), pp. 57–73, here pp. 67–8.

44. See Brabers, 'The Failure of European Transport Integration', p. 68.

45. Franke, 'Mobility and European Integration', p. 74.

46. See Henrich-Franke on Armand, this volume; on EUROP-Pool, see Friedich Walther, 'Die Europäische Güterwagengesellschaft', *Die Bundesbahn* 13 (1953), pp. 604–16.

47. M. de Vos, 'Eurofima- Société Européene pour le finacement de matériel ferroviaire', in special edition of *Zeitschrift Europa-Verkehr* (Darmstadt: Otto Elsner Verlagsgesellschaft 1957), pp. 48–50.

48. On the various discussions and bilateral exchanges between Ministries see Franke, 'Mobility and European Integration', pp. 74–7.

49. For a discussion and contemporary views on competition in transport see Kapteyn, *Europa sucht.*

50. See European Documentation Centre, Florence, European University Institute, Documents Consultative Assembly of the Council of Europe, Fifth Ordinary Session, 21 September 1953, Document 196, pp. 1053–4.

51. The best general overview of the negotiations and the work of the Spaakcommittee is Hanns Jürgen Küsters, *Die Gründung der Europäischen Wirtschaftgemeinschaft* (Nomos 1982).

52. On this episode see Francois Duchêne, *Jean Monnet, The First Statesman of Interdependence* (New York/London: Norton 1994), pp. 269–79. See also John Gillingham, *European Integration 1950–2003. Superstate or New Market Economy* (Cambridge: Cambridge University Press 2003), pp. 43–4, and Andrew Moravcsik, *The Choice for Europe* (New York: Cornell University Press 1998), pp. 139–42.

53. On the Beyen Plan and its background see R.T. Griffiths, 'The Beyen Plan' in R.T. Griffiths (ed.) *The Netherlands and the Integration of Europe 1945–1957* (Amsterdam NEHA 1990), pp. 165–82.

54. On these negotiations on transport see Carlo degli Abbati, *Transport and European Integration* (Brussels 1987), pp. 29–42; Christian Henrich-Franke, 'Europäische Verkehrsintegration im 19. und in der zweiten Hälfte des 20. Jahrhundert' in C. Heinrich-Franke, C. Neutsch and G. Thiemeyer (Hrsg.) *Internationalismus und Europäische Integration im Vergleich* (Nomos 2007), pp. 133–76, in particular pp. 164–72. For energy see Lukas, *Energy and the Communities*, pp. 11–29.

55. For this reason, the ECSC transport committee concluded already during the treaty negotiations that the proposal would fill the wastepaper basket of the transport ministries, and for that reason prepared its own proposal (the so-called

Kapteyn report), which was transferred to the transport committee of the newly established EC General Assembly. See Kapteyn, *Europa Sucht*, p. 32.
56. For an overview of the achievements see Abbati, *Transport and European Integration*.
57. For a discussion on neo-functionalist definitions see Rosamond, *Theories of European Integration*, pp. 59–65.
58. The importance of visions for infrastructural development is argued for by Cornelis Disco, 'From Sea to Shining Sea. Making Ends Meet on the Rhine and the Rhone', this volume. On the broader circulation of network myths in and out of policy circles, see Alexander Badenoch' essay 'Myths of the European network' in this volume.
59. See Schot and Lagendijk, 'Technocratic Internationalism in Interwar Years'. For the connection between technocracy, infrastructures, colonization and decolonization see Dirk van Laak, 'Detours around Afrika. The Connection between Developing Countries and Integrating Europe', this volume. Technocratic internationalism was based on similar assumptions and concerns as scientific internationalism, which was also present in the interwar period and blossomed in the post-war period in high-energy physicists, but also attracted mathematicians, chemists, biologists, medical researchers and geologists. One important difference is that technocratic internationalism never sought or attracted such publicity. On scientific internationalism see Joseph Manzione, ' "Amusing and Amazing": The Legacy of Scientific Internationalism in American Foreign Policy, 1945–1963', Diplomatic History 24(1) (2000), pp. 21–55; Geert Somsen, 'A History of Universalism: Conceptions of the Internationality of Science, 1750–1950', Minerva 46 (2008), 361–79.
60. See Wolfram Kaiser, 'Transnational networks in European governance' in Kaiser, Leucht, and Rasmussen, *The History of the European Union*, pp. 12–33.
61. For this notion see Thomas J. Misa and Johan Schot, 'Inventing Europe: Technology and the Hidden Integration of Europe', *History and Technology* 21(1) (2005), pp. 1–20, and Johan Schot, 'Building Europe on Infrastructures', *The Journal of Transport History*, 28(2) (2007), pp. 167–71.
62. Ernst B. Haas, *The Obsolescence of Regional Integration Theory* (Berkeley: University of California 1975).
63. See Rosamond, 'Theories of European Integration', chapter 4 for an introduction. The most important reference is Andrew Moravcsik, *The Choice for Europe: Social Progress and State Power from Messina to Maastricht* (Ithaca/New York: Cornell University Press 1998).
64. Alan Milward, *The European Rescue of the Nation-State*.
65. Milward saw his history writing as economic history, and would agree that the process of integration had been a central aspect of national history. Many diplomatic historians would probably disagree with his economist explanation. Yet, his state-centred emphasis somehow reinforced the image that European integration history is a history of negotiations between foreign offices. Wolfram Kaiser, personal communication.
66. For example, Wolfram Kaiser argued that transnational networks of Christian Democrats co-shaped the integration process; see his *Christian Democracy and the Origins of European Union* (Cambridge University Press 2007).
67. See Frank Schipper, Vincent Lagendijk and Irene Anastadiadou, 'New Connections for an Old Continent. Rail, Road and Electricity in the League of Nations' Organisation for Communications and Transit', this volume.

68. See Andreas Fickers and Suzanne Lommers, 'Eventing Europe: Broadcasting and the Mediated Performances of Europe', this volume.
69. Eda Kranakis, 'European Civil Aviation in an Era of Hegemonic Nationalism: Infrastructure, Air Mobility, and European Identity Formation, 1919–1933', this volume.
70. For an introduction to various theories see Antje Wiener and Thomas Diez, *European Integration Theory* (Oxford: Oxford University Press 2004), in particular part II on European governance. For the notion of epistemic communities see Peter M. Haas, 'Epistemic Communities and International Policy Coordination', *International Organization* 46(1) (1992), pp. 1–35. For the notion of regime in international relations see V. Rittberger (ed.), *Regime Theory and International Relations* (Oxford: Clarendon Press 1993).
71. The emergence of a regime could also be perceived as a process of institutionalization, considering that institutions are systems of rules. This notion of institutionalization fits very well into current European integration theory; see, among others, Alec Stone Sweet, Wayne Sandholz and Neil Fligstein (eds), *The Institutionalization of Europe* (Oxford University Press 2001).
72. Haas, *Uniting Europe*, second preface, 2004.

Part II

Mediating Europe: Moving Things, Building Systems

4
New Connections for an Old Continent: Rail, Road and Electricity in the League of Nations Organisation for Communications and Transit

Frank Schipper, Vincent Lagendijk and Irene Anastasiadou

During the Second World War, former League of Nations official John E. Wheeler contemplated what international organizations would look like after the war's end. At that time he was authoring a study for the prestigious London-based Royal Institute of International Affairs on pre-First World War and interwar organizations with a strong focus on infrastructures.[1] Wheeler argued that 'there is no official European body whose field of activity extends to all branches of transport and communications, but the League of Nations Transit Organisation, [...], has concerned itself very largely with Europe'.[2] The 'Transit Organisation' to which Wheeler referred was the Organisation for Communications and Transit (OCT), a body not originally founded with a European scope, but as part of the universal League of Nations (1919).[3] Wheeler's suggestion that the OCT might have been an effective body in dealing with European affairs raises two important and, as we will argue, closely related issues about the League of Nations: its 'European' focus and its overall success (or rather failure) as an organization. Both these issues are central to the way in which historical scholarship has framed the League up to now. By taking the OCT's activities in the field of infrastructure as central rather than peripheral aspects of the League's method and mission, we look here to revise these narratives. In so doing, we point to the ways in which technology, and in particular technological expertise, formed a central plank in efforts to integrate and unify Europe before the Second World War. Furthermore, we will show here how the structures and operating procedures of the OCT were carried over into post-war institutions that took up the same cause.

The League was an unprecedented experiment in its time.[4] Its creators intended to provide new forms of interstate relations for the future while breaking the ways of the past. It is hard to underestimate the singular importance of the American president Woodrow Wilson in shaping the League. As Wilson's brainchild, the organization bubbled with worldwide ambitions. Despite these intentions, the League became a deeply Eurocentric body from the start.[5] Wheeler acknowledged that the work of the OCT mainly concerned European affairs.[6] This notion of the League as a mostly European body has been widely shared by contemporaries and historians alike.

A similar consensus holds that the League was an organization plagued by failure, its incapacity to maintain peace often being equated with a dreary performance overall. In the face of fascist expansionism it became a mere bystander in the maelstrom leading up to the outbreak of war in 1939. For Zara Steiner, the League became an *adjunct* rather than an *alternative* to the great power politics it wanted to break. Its members anxiously clung to their sovereignty, making genuine co-operation hard to achieve. She echoes the earlier position of E.H. Carr, an influential critic of the League. In 1939 he claimed that national interests always lay hidden behind the lofty rhetoric so often heard in Geneva.[7] A recent book on the peace treaty negotiations concisely sums up this stance by claiming:

> [o]nly a handful of eccentric historians still bother to study the League of Nations. Its archives, with their wealth of materials are largely unvisited. Its very name evokes images of earnest bureaucrats, fuzzy liberal supporters, futile resolutions, unproductive fact-finding missions and, above all, failure.[8]

We maintain that this narrative of failure should be nuanced. We agree that the League's most visible work with regard to international politics did not meet with many successes. The organization did indeed fail in its self-described primary task: to guarantee world peace.[9] But its less visible 'technical' work has hardly been scrutinized at all.[10] In the course of the interwar years the League developed into an unmistakeable focal point for international collaboration on a whole range of down-to-earth matters. To someone like Wheeler it was evident that the League's failure in international politics contrasted with its relative success as a technical organization – to such an extent that he thought any post-war organization in the field of transport and communications should build upon its legacy.[11] But, instead of giving rise to genuine global co-operation in line with its general purpose, the League became the *de facto* central arena for European integration in the interwar period. As such it pertained to a set of international organizations that we have elsewhere identified as 'Europe's system builders'.[12] These are a range of organizations made up largely of engineers and other technical experts that began to proliferate at the end of the nineteenth century. Often operating outside the sphere of formal politics, these bodies were responsible for building – or at least planning – many of the cross-border infrastructures in Europe.

Infrastructures provide an appealing subject for investigation in this context for several reasons. First, the operation of infrastructure networks was among the first issues the League took on after it had been established. Second, infrastructures constitute the material underpinning for flows of trade and people across borders. Much international cooperation was concerned with how best to enable and stimulate such flows. Indeed, the League's inspiration came from the notion that strong nationalist sentiments were reactionary and primitive in the light of scientific and technological developments that supported all kinds of cross-border flows and made the borders themselves seem obsolete. In the conception of the prominent South African politician Jan Smuts, British representative at the Peace Conference in Paris, transport and communications were 'bursting through the national bounds and [...] clamouring for international solution'.[13] On the basis of such convictions the League sought to found a 'new order of things'.[14] The League's technical committees were the main institutions that embodied this new order, forming its main 'instrument of cooperation'.[15] The key player for infrastructures and their cross-border operation was the OCT, whose work on railway transport, electrical questions and road traffic we highlight in this chapter.

We concur broadly with the historical consensus that the League was a Eurocentric organization. This claim is probably illustrated best by the League's absorption of Aristide Briand's famous project for European unification in the early 1930s. But ultimately it is not surprising that Briand's project for continental federation was European in character. A more challenging puzzle is why the European character of the League also permeated subjects for which it was not obvious that the geographic range of its activities should be restricted. We intend to demonstrate how European countries and their interests often dominated the OCT's agenda, and specify the circumstances under which this happened. In doing so, this chapter explores the extent to which the OCT should be viewed as a key institutional mediator for shaping specific European types of transnational interaction. This undertaking serves the subsidiary purpose of putting the work of one of the main technical committees of the League on display and examining it critically against the dominant view of the League's failure. We will suggest that, at least with regard to the OCT, the question of the League's 'success' or 'failure' is one of scale: the OCT's limited spatial scope in fact helped to cement a lasting institutional infrastructure on a transnational scale in Europe, which in turn shaped the building and governance of material infrastructures for many decades to come. In what follows we examine the outcome for the League's work on infrastructure networks and their operation across borders. After a concise elaboration on the Eurocentrism embedded in the League machinery, there follows a general introduction to the OCT. The chapter subsequently zooms in on railway, electricity and road networks to reveal in each case how the League became a focal point for European network-building in the interwar period.

The league, Europe and the organisation for communications and transit

The League's – and the OCT's – Eurocentrism can be attributed to a combination of political, procedural and technical factors. Wilson's aspiration to establish a global organization suffered a major blow when the United States Senate voted down American membership of the League of Nations.[16] Combined with the Soviet Union's non-membership, this implied that the largest upcoming political powers remained outside the institution that was supposed to provide the ultimate forum for global understanding. As a result, European countries dominated the Council, the highest decision-making body in the League.[17] Substantial rapprochement between European victors and former aggressors in the course of the 1920s further reinforced the European character of the League. The restructuring of German reparations in the 1924 Dawes Plan and the fixation of the Franco-German border in the 1925 Pact of Locarno settled two major issues. This allowed détente to set in and a kind of regional European policy to emerge.[18] The renewed optimism specifically stimulated collaboration among Western European powers, who now settled matters behind closed doors in what Sally Marks has labelled the 'Locarno tea parties'.[19] 'Locarno' paved the way for German admission to the League in 1926, and it immediately became a permanent member of the Council.[20]

Yet membership can only partly explain why Eurocentrism became so prominent in the League. Over half of the original thirty-two members were non-European. Although European members certainly formed a plurality and grew in relative weight in the course of the interwar years (Figure 4.1),[21] the organization remained more inclusive than anything that had existed prior to it.[22] One factor that clearly mattered was the League's seat in Geneva. The Swiss city was within easy reach for European representatives at a time when intercontinental travel was difficult and expensive.[23] Permanent representatives could partly solve this problem, but Guatemala or Siam could hardly hire a team the size of France's or Italy's. Non-European governments often refrained from assigning experts and nominated plenipotentiaries from countries around Geneva as representatives. These were often regular diplomats who lacked the in-depth knowledge of the technical issues the League's technical organizations dealt with.

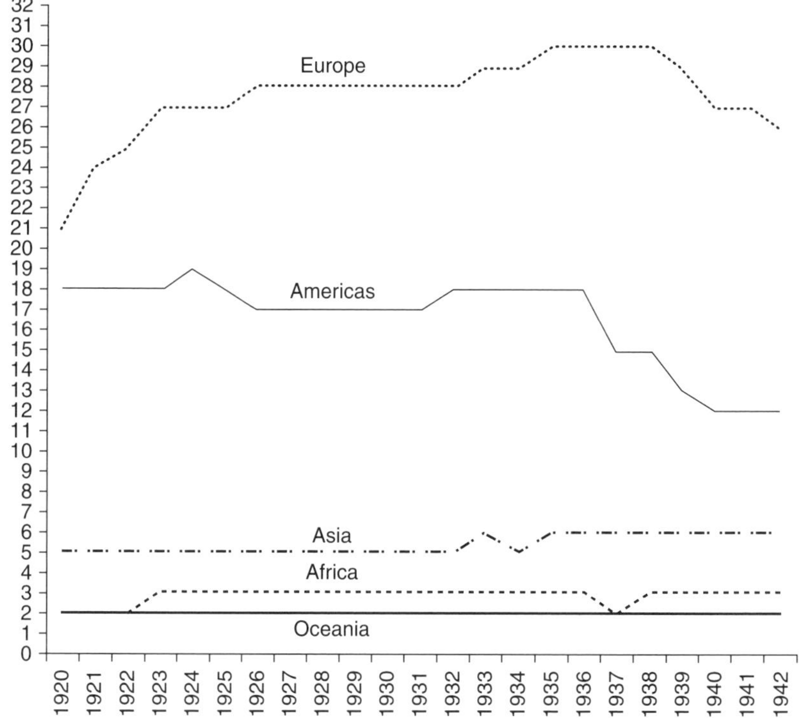

Figure 4.1   League of Nations Membership, 1920–41

Source: adapted from http://www.indiana.edu/~league/nationalmember.htm.

Geneva also became a centre stage for several 'projects for Europe', which sometimes clashed with the universal principles on which the League was built.[24] In 1927 the League organized the World Economic Conference (WEC). Despite the 'world' in its name, the Conference was in fact inspired by the ideas of Louis Loucheur, who promoted an economically united Europe based on industrial co-operation.[25] Building efficiency and co-operation at the scale of Europe appeared key to helping the rest of the global economy.[26] The better-known initiative of French Minister of Foreign Affairs Aristide Briand for a full-fledged European federation invoked Article 21 of the Covenant, which had left a door open for initiatives on the regional plane within the League.[27] Some feared that a European subsystem within the League would absorb the best people available at the Secretariat and thus hollow out its universal tasks.[28] Nevertheless, no European state wanted to be left out, and all supported the creation of the Commission for Enquiry on European Unity (CEEU), although it made little headway.[29] According to Antoine Fleury, this was mainly due to the ailing political activities of the League, aggravated by political and economic crises, and not so much due to the underlying idea of European cooperation as such.[30]

The prominence of European issues in the general work of the League also permeated the OCT's activities. The general opinion was that international co-ordination of maritime, rail and river transport required immediate attention for two reasons. First, the Paris Peace Treaties of 1919 had substantially shifted the borders of existing states and created new ones – especially in Europe. The multiplication of borders threatened to disrupt prior trade patterns, for example in the territories that had formerly belonged to the now defunct Austro-Hungarian Empire. Second, building on the conviction that the scale of these forms of transport and communication transcended national boundaries, was the idea that such systems could bring greater economic prosperity through more efficient organization.[31] Institutionally, the OCT also built upon forms of co-operation remaining from the First World War, when Inter-Allied Councils (1918) had rationed and controlled food, shipping, coal and munitions.[32] Good experience with this machinery gave rise to the idea that the League could similarly foster economic co-operation.[33] At the Paris Peace Conference this resulted in the creation of a Commission of the International Regime of Ports, Waterways and Railways. The first Secretary-General of the League, Sir Eric Drummond, envisioned this body as an advisor to the League and an example of how to establish a permanent organization within the League machinery.[34] A section on communications and transit was therefore formed within the Secretariat, headed by the Italian Bernardo Attolico.[35] Simultaneously the French government joined representatives from the Allies, their associates and neutral states in an ad hoc Commission of Enquiry on Freedom of Communications and Transit in September 1919.

These two initiatives merged in December 1919, when the secretary-general of the French ad hoc Commission, Robert Haas, joined the Secretariat.[36] His main task was to establish a permanent communications and transit organization. On 13 February 1920 the Council of the League of Nations invited the French commission to submit proposals for the formation of a permanent organization under the aegis of the League.[37] It was decided to organize a general conference to discuss, inter alia, how the clauses from the Peace Treaties should be enshrined in general international conventions.[38] Most importantly the conference should provide a guarantee for the freedom of communications and transit. According to Haas, the OCT presented an alternative to diplomatic negotiations, which had until recently presented the 'only method available [...] to obtain freedom of communications by peaceful arrangements and by international co-operation'.[39] That freedom was necessary as 'most of the European countries depend on imports and exports for their existence'. Instead, he argued, the OCT created direct contact between people of various countries who were handling these issues, and thus relied upon technical experts.[40] The OCT's overtly technocratic focus was thus directly related to the European scale of its operations.

A Council Resolution of 19 May 1920 invited member states to send representatives to the General Conference on the Freedom of Communications and Transit in Barcelona.[41] The Barcelona Conference established the rules of procedure for subsequent general conferences and created a permanent committee that would act as a consultative and technical body to propose and consider all measures that could help ensure the freedom of communications and transit.[42] The OCT had four main elements: a permanent Committee for Communications and Transit, a number of temporary and permanent committees addressing more specific matters, a permanent secretariat provided by the League's Secretary-General, and periodic conferences that were convened to conclude and revise international conventions.[43] Just as with the other technical organizations, the OCT's agendas, jurisdictions, recommendations, and correspondence with national governments required Council approval, while the Assembly approved its budget. In most cases, however, the Council merely rubber-stamped OCT proposals, as 'foreign ministers and diplomats on the Council had limited knowledge, interest, and time' to study the proposals properly.[44]

In its three general conferences after Barcelona (see Table 4.1)[45] as well as in the work of its subcommittees, the OCT gave rise to thinking about international regimes specifying the rules for international operation of different infrastructures. It reflected the awareness of the important role of relatively new means of communication and transport on the international economy.[46] On the whole, the OCT started out as a body with a universal approach, though with a European bias. Towards the end of the 1920s, however, the European element had become more firmly entrenched in the OCT's work. This becomes particularly apparent when looking at the actions at the subcommittee level on railway transport, electricity and road traffic (Figure 4.2), to which we now turn.

Table 4.1 General conferences of communications and transit (1921–31)

Dates	States	Main issue
1921 (10 March – 20 April)	44	Freedom of Transit
1923 (15 November – 9 December)	42	Conventions for Railways, Maritime Ports and Electricity
1927 (23 August – 2 September)	41	Revision Statutes OCT
1931 (12–24 October)	39	Various issues

Source: Pierre le Marec (1938), *L'Organisation des Communications et du Transit*, Rennes: PhD Thesis, pp. 128–30.

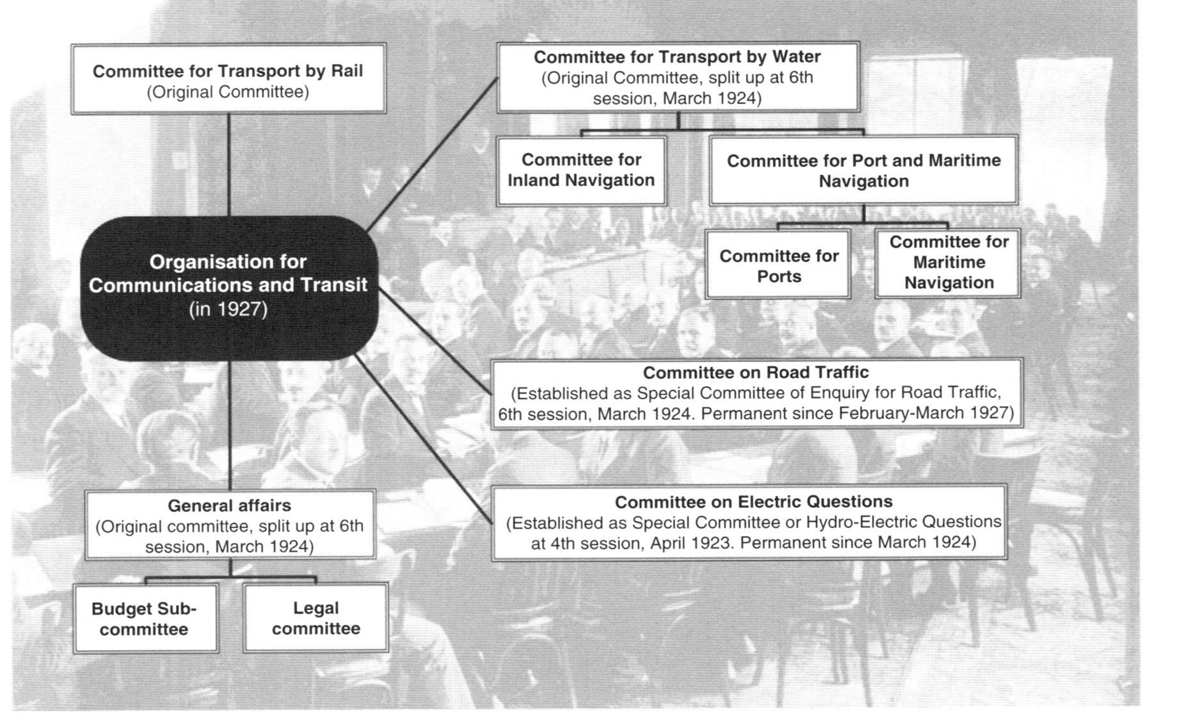

Figure 4.2   Structure of the Organisation for Communications and Transit (1927)

Source: Minutes of CCT sessions.
The original caption of the picture in the background reads 'The Geneva Transit Conference', referring to the 1923 General Conference on Communications and Transit, see League of Nations, *Illustrated Album of the League of Nations* (Geneva: Atar 1926). Available at the League of Nations Photo Archive (www.indiana.edu/~league) http://bl-libg-doghill.ads.iu.edu/league-web/book/p60.html, accessed 14 December 2009.

Transport by rail[47]

The OCT engaged with railway issues from the start. Railways were a 'mature' infrastructure in Western and Central Europe, and European powers had built railway networks to their colonies to strengthen their rule.[48] Eastern and Southern European railways had expanded before the war, but at a slower pace. International railway co-operation between governments and railway administrations was well developed across Europe.[49] In a League study on the general transport situation (1921), Professor Filippo Tajani of the Royal Polytechnic College in Milan wrote:

> the railways of continental Europe, and, more especially those of central and western States, had arrived at an almost perfect system of internationalism, thanks to certain agreements concluded between the parties concerned, either on technical questions, or on the commercial relations established by the development of the railways.[50]

The issues facing the committee were thus not about creating international co-operation, but rather re-establishing and co-ordinating it to address a new series of problems. European railway networks had been heavily damaged during the First World War. The greatest challenge was to re-establish international railway traffic in Central and Eastern Europe. The redrawn borders of the new states created ownership problems for certain lines and abruptly disrupted existing cross-border flows. Borders became obstacles to international traffic, a situation that remained unchanged throughout the interwar period.[51] The circulation of rolling stock in new states was a particularly thorny problem. Here, too, disagreement over ownership delayed necessary repairs, since states refused to repair wagons they might not own. Wagon exchange at borders took place on a wagon-by-wagon basis.[52] A series of conferences slowly re-established European transport to pre-war levels and the numerous international organizations concerned with international railway traffic, mainly in Europe, gradually resumed their activities.[53]

The OCT took over some activities of the Communications Section of the Supreme Economic Council established at the Paris peace conference. During its first years the OCT devoted most of its attention to placing railways in the service of creating the new international community the authors of the Peace Treaties envisioned. The Commission of Enquiry for Freedom of Communications and Transit (1919) was the first body to prepare a *General Convention on Railways*.[54] The draft worked on the principle that, to ensure freedom of communications and transit, the convention should specify general technical conditions for use on all railway lines.[55] The Barcelona Conference, however, rejected the draft convention. Discussions underlined the regional character of railway technology, which had developed in close relation to geographical features and socio-political conditions and formed an obstacle to a worldwide convention. States were also unwilling to subordinate national interests to international ideals. A Brazilian delegate observed:

> The situation of the countries of South America as regards railways, and particularly that of Brazil, is very different from the European situation or from that of North America. [...] Brazil is still passing through a period of construction – a difficult period for us. [...] You will understand then how difficult it would have been for us to agree to any Convention which is not restricted to generalities.[56]

Even European delegates found it hard enough to agree among themselves. Article 3 of the draft stipulated reciprocal use and exchange of rolling stock. The Spanish, Finnish and Portuguese delegations objected to the article because their railway gauge differed and its modification would entail high costs.[57] A British representative argued against loading-gauges diverging from the British one, while other delegations argued about other technical characteristics in which national railway networks could differ.[58] Consequently, a convention harmonizing technical and administrative conditions, establishing a certain homogeneity and ensuring freedom of transit and equitable treatment of commerce, proved impossible to achieve.

Undeterred by the difficulties in Barcelona, the OCT's rail sub-committee started drafting a new convention, compiling a questionnaire for League members and non-members alike on their adherence to existing railway agreements, their opinion on the gaps therein, and whether they regarded a worldwide railway convention as useful. Many governments contested the value and feasibility of the sub-committee's venture to draw up a global convention, but welcomed a European one.

Nevertheless, the sub-committee did not abandon its initial global pretensions.[59] It modified the character of the convention into a code of international rail traffic obligations, which the committee mainly based on European experience.[60] In addition, the convention specified basic principles for future agreements of a regional scope.[61] The Second General Conference on Communications and Transit (1923) approved the draft, a move hailed as the League's most important railway achievement.[62] Most European countries ratified it, while no non-European state with a large railway network did, apart from India and Japan.[63] The 1923 convention illustrates the difficulties that co-operation in railway traffic posed to the League's ideal of universality and the way it contributed to the 'regionalization' of the organization. In contrast to aviation or shipping, railways developed as a regional means of transportation influenced by geographical conditions and socio-political circumstances.

The rail committee continued to work on facilitating the operation of railways throughout the remainder of the interwar period. It worked hard to introduce a system of uniform time for rail transport, improve the negotiability of railway transport documents, unify transport statistics, and compile a uniform nomenclature of goods for establishing international railway tariffs. In these endeavours it worked closely with the International Chamber of Commerce (ICC, founded 1919) and the International Union of Railways (UIC, founded 1922). Its preferred method of work was to undertake studies among governments and then try to co-ordinate their actions on specific topics. Furthermore, throughout the interwar years, the OCT acted as an arbitrator in disputes concerning international railway traffic, as an alternative to the judicial procedures of the Permanent Court of International Justice.[64] Simplifying frontier formalities presented an obvious way to improve the efficiency of railway operation across borders. The war had greatly complicated border crossings. In collaboration with the ICC, it distributed a questionnaire to governments in 1927, inquiring about the conditions of crossing borders. These debates partly concerned so-called 'mixed issues' important not only for railways, but also for other transport modes. Passports are a prime example. Many saw the period before the war as the ideal situation, when one could travel without a passport in most cases. Although abolishing passports altogether was no longer possible, reducing time loss due to border controls was. Thus the second passport conference in Geneva (May 1926) stipulated that issuing of entry or transit visas and passports control should in general be handled on board the train. Where this was impossible, trains were to stop in only one of the two frontier stations, where controls would take place on behalf of both states simultaneously.[65]

Following the difficulties of the 1923 convention, whenever issues of a technical nature arose, the League addressed them to the UIC, with mixed results. One such case was the question of establishing a standard automatic coupling on European railways, an issue that was brought forward by the International Labour Office (ILO). Coupling wagons manually was dangerous work, involving people between heavy moving railway wagons, and railway workers were regularly killed in the process. After the First World War, workers' organizations called increasingly for the use of safe automatic couplers on all European railways. While the ILO and the OCT pressed the UIC towards achieving an international agreement, the UIC was unable to find a technical standard it deemed worthy of implementation on all railways, and thus it delayed taking action. No international agreement was reached before the Second World War.[66]

On balance, it is clear that the League dealt with a wide range of issues in relation to rail transport, with the 1923 Convention as its main result. Notably, throughout OCT attempts to draft a worldwide railway convention, the negotiations underlined the importance of supplementary regional conventions. Technological limitations, and especially many differing but well-established standards, prohibited any sudden leap towards universality for railways. Continental or subcontinental solutions seemed more feasible as an intermediary step. Through this venture the OCT clearly articulated the importance of concentrating the efforts towards regional, European collaboration in the field of railways.

Electric questions[67]

The transmission of electric power was a newcomer vis-à-vis rail and road transport. Unlike railways, electricity networks certainly did not cover large parts of Europe. The technology for long-distance transmission had only been developed relatively recently. Nevertheless, the OCT concluded that the 'growing international aspect of the transmission of electric power necessitated the intervention of the League', since '[e]lectric power nowadays was transported just as persons and goods'.[68] But, although the OCT recognized electricity networks as an important topic, it did not give them the same attention it paid to railways. First, electricity transmission was not part of its anticipated activities, and second, the eventual OCT committee working on electricity transmission met infrequently. However, the nature of its activities substantially changed over time, from a universalistic yet European-inspired to an explicitly European approach.

The first discussions on the international transmission of electric power arose during the 1921 Barcelona Conference in discussions concerning the international railway regime. Several members of the Barcelona Conference envisioned the electrification of international railway lines. In that case overhead lines would follow rails across borders. This led to a discussion on which country was responsible for the electricity on the overhead rail lines. According to the Italian delegation – which brought forward the issue – it was 'obvious' for the country with the largest supply of hydroelectricity to be responsible for the traction. Although the Italian suggestion did not prevail, several delegates nevertheless thought the issue interesting enough for further study and established a special subcommittee.[69] They focused on drafting conventions for two issues emerging from the Barcelona Conference. The first concerned the *Convention on the Transmission in Transit of Electric Power,* an attempt to settle 'all matters connected with' the transmission of electricity from one country to another, over the territory of a third country. The second, the *Convention relating to the Development of Hydraulic Power on Watercourses forming Part of a Basin Situated in the Territory of Several States,* sought to arrange possible difficulties arising from the utilization of hydro-power in international waterways.[70]

Although both conventions were intended to have universal impact, they also responded to concrete problems in the European realm. The *Convention on Transmission in Transit of Electricity* related to two interrelated developments. One was the introduction of higher voltages in the first two decades of the twentieth century. This enabled long-distance transmission of electricity, also across borders. In the 1920s, such transmission lines existed in the border regions between Germany, France and Switzerland (around the Rhine), and Italy, as well as between Denmark and Sweden. At the same time, however, national authorities increasingly intervened in the electricity sector, and often hampered the international exchange of electricity. On the one hand, authorities stimulated national network expansion in order to make electricity available to as many citizens as possible. On the other hand, this related to the general climate in which European nation states sought to protect domestic economic interests.[71] Therefore, according to many electrical engineers at the time, cross-border transmission was restricted for political and economic reasons, despite being technologically feasible.[72]

Practical issues also inspired the second convention. A prominent example originated from the Franco-German border region.[73] While the Versailles Treaty returned Alsace-Lorraine to France, it also gave the French exclusive rights to exploit the Rhine – now the border with Germany – for irrigation and electricity generation. While Germany had to contribute to the necessary costs, France needed to repay half of the value actually produced, and needed approval of the Rhine Commission for its plans.[74] France immediately pursued the construction of a parallel canal between Strasbourg and Basel, which aroused strong criticism from Germany, but also from Switzerland. They feared French competition in electricity as well as for the navigability of the Rhine.[75] An agreement was eventually reached in 1922. The *Convention relating to the Development of Hydraulic Power on Watercourses* should lay down the basic stipulations on how to deal with such cases.

Both draft conventions were accepted in 1923, but few nations ratified them: only four in the case of the *Convention on the Transmission in Transit of Electric Power*, and five in the case of the exploitation of hydraulic power.[76] This did not come as a surprise. Already when presenting the conventions, the chair confessed to having had difficulty drafting them and excused himself to the OCT for providing rather 'general and very elastic terms'.[77] They were intended as general governing principles, and the sub-committee expected that in practice more detailed arrangements between states would be needed.[78] According to an observing Belgian official, many countries simply did not feel a need for such conventions, and in particular not such crude ones.[79] In addition, the texts contained political pitfalls, even though both conventions stressed that 'technical considerations' should prevail over political interests and national frontiers. Yet all solutions should fit within the 'limits of national laws'.[80] Germany, for example, opposed the reference made to the Versailles Treaty in the conventions, but was thwarted by France.[81]

Despite the general character of the conventions and the absence of electrical engineers in drafting the conventions, the work of the OCT attracted the interest of the emerging international electrotechnical community.[82] The International Electrotechnical Commission (IEC, 1906) already existed, but the *Conférence Internationale des Grands Réseaux de Transport d'Énergie Électriques à Tres Haute Tension* (CIGRE, 1921), the World Power Conference (WPC, 1924) and the *Union Internationale des Producteurs et Distributeurs d'Énergie Électriques* (UNIPEDE, 1925) were all founded within a decade of the OCT. These organizations brought together engineers and electricity entrepreneurs, primarily from European countries.[83] The OCT, on the other hand, decided in 1924 that the sub-committee would be continued on a permanent basis, renamed as Committee on Electric Questions. Electrical engineers and other specialists increasingly staffed the committee.[84] To strengthen ties with the international community, the Secretariat established liaisons with WPC, CIGRE, UNIPEDE and IEC, in the form of representation on the committee. But these developments did not imply that the committee's impact increased. For one thing, the committee barely met after 1924. For another, no new conventions or regulations came under discussion. One other aspect was membership: whereas the special sub-committee had always had either a Brazilian or a Venezuelan member in its midst, after 1924 the permanent committee had European members only (Figure 4.3).[85]

In December 1930 a new initiative reactivated the committee's work. In the light of the work done by CEEU, the Belgian government proposed to study the organization of the electricity supply on the *European* level. Regretting the disappointing result of the first attempt to come to a general convention, it suspected that a European approach would have immediate effects and thereby continue the work started by the League in this area.[86] The proposal contained two specific topics to study: the creation of a more liberal regime of international electricity exchanges and a European high-voltage electricity network. These proposals also reflected a tendency within the international electrotechnical community, where, since 1929, a number of engineers had presented schemes envisioning an electricity system on a European scale.[87] As the OCT took the Belgian proposal under consideration, relevant international organizations again showed their interest in the League's work. UNIPEDE expressed its interest in both plans, and offered its services where needed, as did the WPC, which supplied the OCT with documentation on legislation across Europe.[88]

Yet the initiative was short-lived. After almost three years of collecting information on the electricity structure of European countries, the OCT

Figure 4.3 Membership of the Electricity Committee

Source: OCT, minutes of sessions.

concluded in 1933 that the Belgian proposals could not be brought into practice due to the depression and heightened international tensions. At the same time, the OCT pointed out that the development of electricity systems was limited to national frameworks.[89] Two years later, the OCT added that the growing international political tensions had 'entirely transformed the regime of the international exchange of electric power'.[90]

Within a decade after its foundation, the Committee on Electric Questions had shifted its attention from drafting universal conventions aiming to regulate electricity transmission and production in international waters to studying a single European grid and a European electricity exchange regime. Nevertheless, the conventions saw few ratifications, and the European studies never went beyond collecting data. As one engineer put it, 'European countries today are not yet mentally and economically mature enough for the mutual exchange of electricity.'[91]

In the short run, the OCT's activities had failed to achieve immediate results. In the long run, however, its work helped to fix engineers on Europe as a unit for organizing electricity exchanges. This line of thought would be taken over after the Second World War. Eventually, in the 1950s and 1960s, Western European countries loosened their restrictions on electricity exchange.

Road traffic[92]

Like electricity, road traffic was absent from the initial workload of the League. This is unsurprising, as automobiles in Europe were still uncommon. The subject reached OCT's agenda at its second session in March 1922 through a letter from Harold Butler, deputy director of the ILO, who requested the OCT to discuss the introduction of an international driving licence on behalf of the International Federation of Transport Workers.[93] The OCT decided to broaden the Federation's concern to a wholesale debate on the desirability of a revision of the existing *Convention on Motor Traffic* (1909). It was the first international convention on road traffic and had introduced a predecessor to the international driving licence.[94]

To investigate the issue, the OCT instituted a Committee of Enquiry for Road Traffic and appointed Belgian railway inspector Dr A. Stiévenard as its chair. The Chilean legal expert F. Amunátegui and the French Edmond Chaix, spokesperson for the *Association Internationale des Automobile-Clubs Reconnus* (AIACR), joined him as members. As vice-president of the influential *Automobile-Club de France* and a prominent administrator of the *Touring Club de France*, Chaix was a key figure in the international road lobby and one of the first whom the Secretariat contacted to hear the views from the field on the issue.[95] Further positions in the committee were reserved for representatives from Denmark, Germany, Italy, the Netherlands, Switzerland and the United Kingdom. The Dutch civil

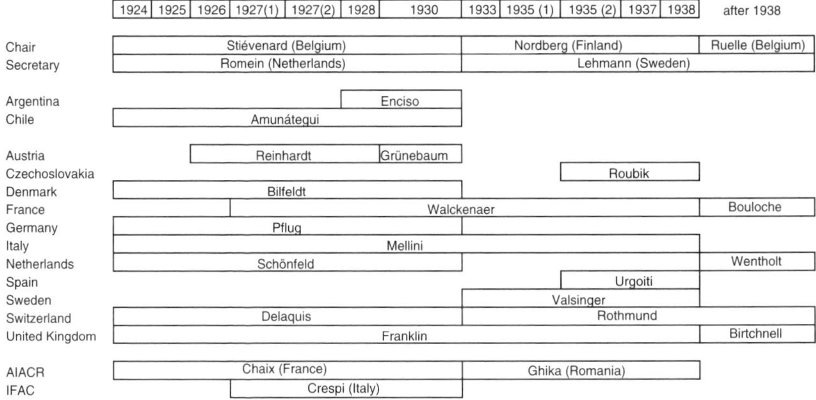

Figure 4.4   Membership of the Committee on Road Traffic

Source: CCT, minutes of sessions. The Road Committee did not meet after April 1938, but nevertheless the OCT appointed several new members at its twenty-first and twenty-second meetings (column 'after 1938'). IFAC = International Federation of Automobile Clubs.

engineer and Secretariat official Romein served as the committee's secretary (Figure 4.4).[96]

The committee devoted itself to drafting a revised convention to replace that from 1909. The latter had instituted an international road certificate that could only be used for a single journey and applied simultaneously to an automobile, its owner, and his mechanic (if any). At an earlier OCT session Chaix had already made a vigorous plea on behalf of the automobilized elite to split up the single document into a separate certificate for the vehicle and a licence for the driver, and to extend the validity of these documents beyond just a single journey. Several governments declared themselves in favour of the proposal.[97]

The 1909 Convention had been concluded at a conference in Paris under the auspices and on invitation of the French government. The follow-up revision conference therefore also took place in the French capital.[98] The resulting 1926 conference led to bitter competition and resentment between the French government and the OCT. The committee had invested much time and energy in preparing a draft convention. The French government had promised to distribute it, but instead unexpectedly presented a draft of its own, which included a section on the rules of the road as desired by Chaix and the AIACR, without circulating the committee's draft to all participants. The rules of the road, in particular, contained stipulations (such as driving on the right) that not all nations felt compelled to adopt. The issue was resolved by splitting the rules of the road from the draft convention, creating two legal instruments signed on 24 April 1926 that could be ratified (or not) separately: an *International Convention relating to Road Traffic* codifying the rules of the road, and an *International Convention relative to Motor Traffic* containing all administrative, customs and fiscal regulations for motorized non-commercial traffic.[99]

Their lone Chilean member notwithstanding, the goal of the committee never was to come up with universal arrangements. As the preparations for Paris were drawing to a close, Delaquis and Mellini testified they were convinced of the need for a central body that would collect documentation and co-ordinate the work of other organizations dealing with road traffic in specifically European ways. They recommended that after the conference 'the Special Committee should be instructed to continue [...] its investigations into the unification of all regulations concerning road traffic [...] in view of the unification of the system of traffic in all countries in Europe'.[100]

Soon thereafter the committee became a permanent OCT committee. In total it held twelve meetings between October 1924 and April 1938, each lasting for several days. Meetings in the 1920s took place at different locations, while in the 1930s they were typically organized in Geneva. Committee membership was overwhelmingly European (Figure 4.4). This explains in part why the call by Delaquis and Mellini eventually came to reflect actual practice in the committee.

The committee convened a European Conference on Motor Traffic in Geneva in March 1931, which formed the apex of the League's interwar work in this respect. The most notable characteristic of the event was that participation was restricted to Europe. The conference discussed four instruments, namely an agreement concerning lost or undischarged triptyques (see below) and three draft conventions on taxation of foreign motor vehicles, signs and signals for road traffic and international commercial road traffic.[101] The subjects reflected the work of the committee between 1926 and 1931 and also the preoccupations of international non-governmental organizations, which now co-operated much more closely with the committee than had hitherto been the case. The *Alliance International de Tourisme* and particularly the International Chamber of Commerce (ICC) joined the automobile clubs and transport workers that were already more deeply involved in the committee's deliberations.

Without doubt the economic aspects of road traffic formed the most important subject of the conference. The aim was to put international road traffic on an equal footing with other transport modes. So far the principle of freedom of transit had not applied to road traffic.[102] At the ICC conference in Amsterdam two years earlier, Romein had ascribed road traffic's exclusion in this respect to the fact that the tremendous development of road traffic had not been foreseen when the Statute on Freedom of Transit was drafted. By 1929, he claimed, it was clear that the freedom of transit should also cover road traffic.[103] Yet divergent opinions on the position of commercial road traffic in the overall transport system impeded agreement. The assembled delegates suspended the work on commercial motor transport and called for further investigation, advising dissatisfied states to resort to bilateral agreements.[104]

In contrast, tourists travelling across European borders benefited more from the results of the conference. The *Agreement between Customs Authorities in order to facilitate the Procedure in the Case of Undischarged or Lost Triptyques* complemented the existing triptyque system. A triptyque was a customs document for tourists by which an automobile or touring club guaranteed that the vehicle for which it was issued would not be imported permanently into the country visited, but would be re-exported within a certain lapse of time. The *Convention on the Taxation of Foreign Motor Vehicles* exempted tourist vehicles from taxes for ninety days. But perhaps the most tangible outcome of the conference was the *Convention on the Unification of Road Signals*. Stiévenard considered any contribution of the committee to the harmonization of the rules of the road in continental Europe as an OCT contribution to European unification.[105] Neighbouring states that had not signed the convention nevertheless started to employ its signs (Figure 4.5). Signs were divided into three categories, each with an exclusive shape. Triangular signs warned of danger, circular signs entailed an obligation for road users, while rectangular signs gave indications. In terms of colour use, red should predominate in prohibition signs. Though signs certainly did not become uniform all across Europe, a short glance at the existing variety of signs gives a hint of the tremendous reduction of international divergence.[106]

In the remainder of the 1930s the committee remained more active than its counterparts and continued to work on a broad array of topics.[107] Apart from the attempt to secure the legacy of the 1931 conference, the facilitation of motorized tourist traffic across borders and road safety issues remained important topics. Yet many of these had to wait until after the Second World War before they could be brought to a definite conclusion. More importantly, the non-European world continued to play a marginal role in the discussions. It was only after Uruguayan representative De Castro remarked in 1938 that unifying the direction of traffic on the right or the left was a universal problem that the committee received instructions from OCT at its twelfth session to broaden its discussion beyond Europe.[108] By then it was too late; the committee would not convene again.

Conclusion

When the League of Nations emerged from the ruins of the First World War with clear universal ambitions, its work on infrastructures with their

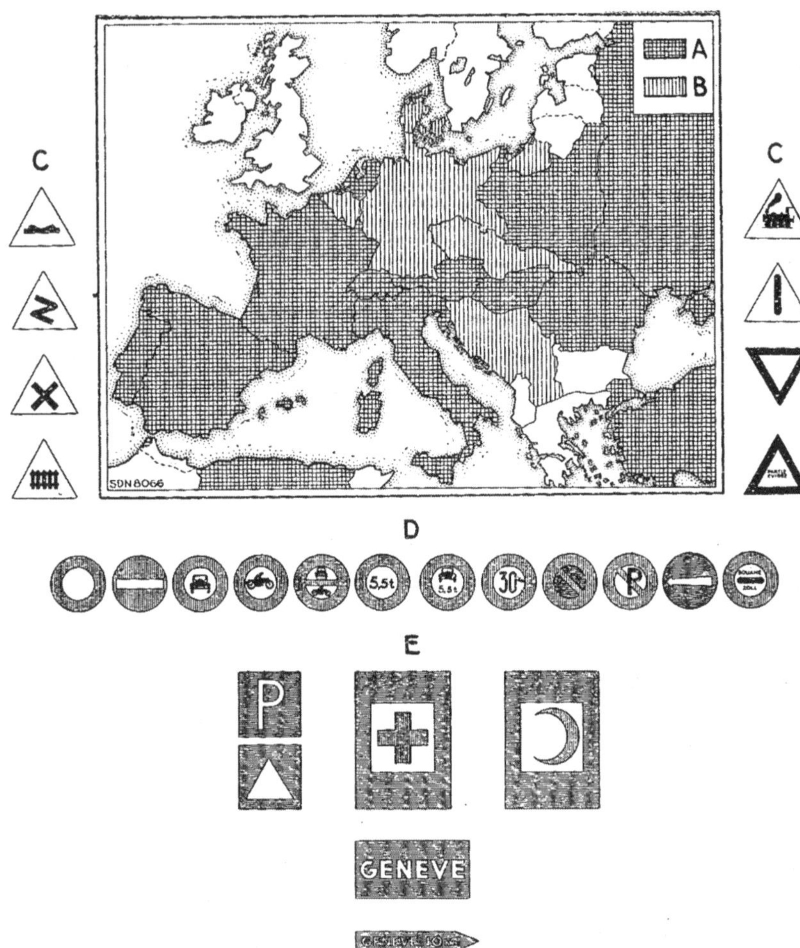

CONVENTION ON THE UNIFICATION OF ROAD
SIGNALS. (Geneva, 30. III. 31.)

A.—Countries which have ratified or acceded to the Convention.   B.—Other
countries utilising the system of road signals laid down in the Convention.   C.—Danger signals.   D.—Signals giving definite instructions.   E.—Signals merely providing information.

|||| = red   ≡ = blue

Figure 4.5   Convention on the Unification of Road Signals (1931)

Source: LoN, *Essential Facts about the League of Nations* (Geneva: Information Section, Secretariat
of the League of Nations 1938), p. 240.

supposedly universal technical principles appeared to be an ideal way to meet those ambitions. The accounts of the work on railways, electricity and road traffic presented in this chapter suggest otherwise. Rather than fortifying the League's global outlook, the results the League harvested for these three infrastructures hint at its character as a central locus for the construction of Europe prior to the Second World War rather than a global agent. In fact, the League's universalist technical operating principles turned out to be tools that operated most effectively as an institutional mediator on a European scale.

Within the specialized machinery of the League, the OCT provided the key platform for shaping the regulatory regimes for making infrastructures work across national borders. In focusing on the OCT, this chapter has sought to rectify the academic neglect of the League's technical committees. Arguably, infrastructures were among the key themes taken up in the international scene even before the end of the First World War. The OCT displayed its First World War roots by continuing forms of wartime co-operation, while at the same time rejuvenating the regulatory regimes governing pre-war communications and transport routes. In doing so, the OCT gradually transformed itself into the institutional core steering the League's mediations with regard to mitigating the Europe/technology uncertainty principle alluded to in the introduction of this book.

The OCT established separate committees for each infrastructural realm, providing specialized settings to discuss infrastructure-specific issues relating to their transnational character. Each committee had its own track record. In the 1930s, the debate on the material networks themselves entered the Committee on Electric Questions, while its rail and road equivalents solely discussed rules and regulations governing trans-border traffic. The European focus also varied per committee and over time, but it was strongly present in each of them throughout. Europe became embodied in the League's infrastructure work in different ways.

First, experiences from Europe and finding solutions to specifically European problems often informed the work of the committees. These were dictated in part by material structures and conditions. For one, devastation after the First World War, which was the immediate concern of the committees, was mostly restricted to the European 'peninsula'. Furthermore, the OCT's implicit European focus stemmed in part from the fact that Europe was a continent dense in both infrastructures and national borders that potentially hindered their use. Simply put, Europe was a place where problems relating to the transnational use of infrastructures came most obviously and often to the fore. While the technical issues they addressed were abstractly universal, they were practically European. Second, in addition to the endemic clashes between the existing and emerging material structures and shifting national institutions on the European peninsula, there was also an emerging institutional infrastructure on mostly

European scale. European states had a century-long history of mitigating problems resulting from cross-border infrastructure use in such settings as, for example, the Central Commission for Navigation on the Rhine and various railway bodies. In the era of the League, this international community expanded. The OCT proved most effective when they were able to co-ordinate and/or lead the efforts of existing communities of bodies of experts, many of which shared a similarly implicit or explicit European focus. In other cases, such as the UIC's stalling on automatic coupling, or the AIACR's insistence on competence over rules of the road, the OCT was not able to assert its influence over an existing set of international protocols. One way or another, Europe was the space in which the OCT needed to focus in order to be effective at all. While committee membership and the effective sphere of influence were overwhelmingly European, we would suggest that the resulting Eurocentrism was of a different type than often suggested in the available literature. Most accounts focus on the political and maintain that the League was somehow a continuation of the Concert of Europe dominated by large states like Germany, France and the United Kingdom. Yet, where the non-European world remained largely excluded from the League's work on electricity, roads and, somewhat less, rails, Europe's smaller states had an influential role in all. Denmark, Portugal, Sweden and Switzerland were strongly represented on the Electricity Committee. Transit countries from the Benelux or the Alps as well as Scandinavian representatives played their part alongside larger states in the Rail and Road Committees. Nations in Eastern Europe remained more aloof, but it is clear that 'Europe' cannot simply be equated with the small number of powerful European states.

The existing institutional frameworks were not the only limitation to the OCT's efficacy outside European contexts. The legal instruments that should be considered a main outcome of the work of the League obtained a European outlook in the course of their ratification process. Agreeing on a convention is far cry from seeing the effects on the ground. Implementation did not always happen smoothly, to put it mildly, and their content often fell short of expectations. Nevertheless, the available evidence suggests that they cannot be considered as completely inconsequential either. The impact of these measures was usually restricted to the League's European members. European states dominated the ratification of the 1923 Convention, the most important fruit of the Rail Committee's work. Countries such as Brazil preferred not to be bound by a convention that was clearly inspired by the presence of a well-developed railway network with ample interaction across borders. Similar considerations can be seen at work in the electricity and road cases.[109] The lasting impact of the OCT reached beyond the Interbellum. During the Second World War, allied organizations were established once again to steer war logistics among the allies and prepare for the post-war situation. The European Central Inland Transport Organization considered rail and road issues, while the Emergency Economic Committee for Europe had a Public Utilities Panel dealing with electricity. Both thus tied Europe and infrastructures together. The League's successor, the United Nations, reserved a prominent place for technical work. In contrast to the League, the UN did become a truly global endeavour, but the League's *de facto* European character lingered on in the Economic Commission for Europe (ECE), one of the UN regional commissions resorting under the Economic and Social Council.[110] In the same *Palais des Nations* where the League had taken up its residence in 1936, the ECE's Electricity and Inland Transport Committees continued where the OCT had been forced to halt. As Wheeler had noted in 1942, although the OCT might not have formally been a European organization, it surely acted like one.

Notes

1. Sir Osborne Mance and J.E. Wheeler, *International Telecommunications* (Oxford: Oxford University Press 1943); Sir Osborne Mance, *International Road Transport, Postal, Electricity and Miscellaneous Questions* (Oxford: Oxford University Press 1946); Sir Osborne Mance, *Frontiers, Peace Treaties, and International Organization* (Oxford: Oxford University Press 1946); Sir Osborne Mance and Ralph Wedgwood and Wheeler, *International Rail Transport* (Oxford: Oxford University Press 1946).
2. J.E. Wheeler, 'The International Machinery of European Transport and Communications', paper presented at the Research Conference on International Agencies for Economic Reconstruction, London, 16–17 October 1942, copy attached to Wheeler to Lukač, 6 October 1942, box R-4264, 9A/41447/39706, Archive of the League of Nations (hereafter: LoN).
3. In League terminology 'communications' referred not only to what we would today call 'telecommunications' but also to 'transport'. The former in fact constituted only a tiny part of the League's workload. 'Transit' referred to the passage of flows through countries not being the origin or destination of those flows.
4. The notion of experiment is invoked in Robert Cecil, *A Great Experiment: An Autobiography by Viscount Cecil* (London: Jonathan Cape 1941).
5. Steiner, *The Lights that Failed: European International History 1919–1933* (Oxford: Oxford University Press 2005), p. 350.
6. Wheeler, 'The International Machinery', pp. 29–30.
7. Steiner, *The Lights*, p. 349; Carr, *The Twenty Years' Crisis, 1919–1939: An Introduction to the Study of International Relations* (London: Macmillan 1939).
8. Margaret MacMillan, *Peacemakers: The Paris Conference of 1919 and Its Attempt to End War* (London: John Murray 2001), p. 92.
9. Steiner, *The Lights*, p. 350.
10. 'Technical' in League terminology covered the work of its technical committees, including anything from public health and education to maritime buoys or the unification of statistics. In many ways the word was used as an antonym of 'political': see Pitman B. Potter, 'Note on the Distinction between Political and

Technical Questions', in *Political Science Quarterly* 50(2) (1935), pp. 264–71. For a recent review of studies on the League of Nations, see Susan Pedersen, 'Back to the League of Nations (review essay)', *The American Historical Review* 112(4) (2007), pp. 1091–117. She also underlines the lack of a study on the OCT.

11. A similar opinion is expressed by F.P. Walters, the author of *A History of the League of Nations* (London: Oxford University Press 1960, reprinted from 1952 as one volume), p. 180.

12. Erik van der Vleuten, Irene Anastasiadou, Frank Schipper and Vincent Lagendijk, 'Europe's system builders: The Contested Shaping of Europe's Road, Electricity and Rail Networks', *Contemporary European History* 16(3) (2007), pp. 321–47. Particularly after the Second World War there were manifold contenders for fostering European co-operation, such as the United Nations Economic Commission for Europe, the Organisation for European Economic Cooperation, the Council of Europe and the European Economic Community.

13. J.C. Smuts, *The League of Nations: A Practical Suggestion* (London: Hodder and Stoughton 1918), p. 43. Jan Smuts' pamphlet is considered among the most influential inputs for the set-up of the League; see MacMillan, *Peacemakers*, pp. 97–9. Jan Smuts became South Africa's prime minister in September 1919.

14. Jo-Anne Pemberton, 'New Worlds for Old: The League of Nations in the Age of Electricity', *Review of International Studies* 28 (2002), pp. 311–36, at pp. 312, 314.

15. Pierre Gerbet, Marie-Renée Mouton and Victor-Yves Ghébali, *Le Rêve d'un Ordre Mondiale de la SDN à l'ONU* (Paris: Imprimerie Nationale 1986), p. 42.

16. For a well-informed account of why the United States did not join the League of Nations, based on an analysis of domestic American politics, see John M. Cooper, *Breaking the Heart of the World: Woodrow Wilson and the Fight for the League of Nations* (Cambridge: Cambridge University Press 2001).

17. The permanent members of the League were France, Germany (1926–33/4), Italy (until 1937), Japan (until 1933), the Soviet Union (1933/4–9) and the United Kingdom. In addition there were between four and eleven elected members; see Patricia Clavin and Jens-Wilhelm Wessels, 'Transnationalism and the League of Nations: Understanding the Work of its Economic and Financial Organisation', *Contemporary European History* 14(4) (2005), pp. 465–92, note 43.

18. Éric Bussière, *La France, la Belgique et l'Organisation Économique de l'Europe, 1918–1935* (Paris: Comité pour l'histoire économique et financière de la France 1992), pp. 301–13, and Patrick O. Cohrs, 'The First "Real" Peace Settlements after the First World War: Britain, the United States and the Accords of London and Locarno, 1923–1925', *Contemporary European History* 12(1) (2003), pp. 1–31.

19. See Sally Marks, *The Illusion of Peace: International Relations in Europe, 1918–1933* (London: Macmillan 1976).

20. This move infuriated Brazil, which had been denied a permanent seat, and it promptly left the League. Spain left temporarily, while a Polish walkout was prevented. During the next decade more Latin American countries renounced their membership. On the problems caused by German membership see Georges Scelle, *Une Crise de la Société des Nations: La Réforme du Conseil et l'Entrée de l'Allemagne à Genève (Mars-Septembre 1926)* (Paris: Presses Universitaires de France 1927).

21. 'Europe' as defined here includes Austria, Bulgaria, Finland, Luxembourg, Albania, Yugoslavia, Belgium, Czechoslovakia, France, Italy, Poland, Spain,

Greece, Denmark, Switzerland, The Netherlands, Norway, Sweden, the British Empire, Roumania, Estonia, Latvia, Hungary, the Irish Free State, Germany, Turkey and the USSR.

22. Akira Iriye, *Global Community: The Role of International Organizations in the Making of the Contemporary World* (Berkeley: University of California Press, 2002), p. 22.
23. Patricia Clavin, 'Europe and the League of Nations', in Robert Gerwarth (ed.) *Twisted Paths: Europe 1914–1945* (Oxford: Oxford University Press 2007), pp. 325–54, at p. 325.
24. For the notion 'projects for Europe', see Peter Bugge, 'The Nation Supreme: The Idea of Europe 1914–1945' in Kevin Wilson and Jan van der Dussen (eds) *The History of the Idea of Europe* (London: Routledge 1995), pp. 83–149.
25. Veronique Pradier, 'L'Europe de Louis Loucheur: Le Projet d'un Homme d'Affaires en Politique', *Études et Documents* V (1993), pp. 293–306, at p. 295. Also see Eric Bussière, 'L'Organisation Économique de la SDN et la Naissance du Régionalisme Économique', *Relations Internationales* 75 (1993), pp. 301–13, at p. 304.
26. This was reflected in the WEC's closing resolution, stressing how 'the Conference has fully carried out its task of setting forth the principles and recommendations best fitted to contribute to an improvement of the economic situation of the world and in particular to that of Europe, thus contributing at the same time to the strengthening of peaceful relations among nations', LoN, *World Economic Conference: Discussion and Declarations on the Report of the Conference of the Council of the League of Nations on June 16th 1927* (Geneva: LoN 1927), p. 14.
27. 'Nothing in this Covenant shall be deemed to affect the validity of international engagements, such as treaties of arbitration or regional understandings like the Monroe doctrine, for securing the maintenance of peace'. http://avalon.law.yale.edu/20th_century/leagcov.asp#art21 (accessed 14 December 2009). The Avalon Project at Yale Law School published the full Covenant online.
28. Arthur Salter, *The United States of Europe and Other Papers* (London: George Allen and Unwin 1933), Chapter 7, 'The French Memorandum on a European Federal Union', 20 May 1930, pp. 105–24.
29. The CEEU has been described elsewhere; see for example Antoine Fleury, 'Une Évalution des Travaux de la Commission d'Étude pour l'Union Européenne 1930–1937', in Sylvain Schirmann (ed.) *Organisations Internationales et Architectures Européennes 1929–1939. Actes du Colloque de Metz 31 mai – 1er juin 2001. En Hommage à Raymond Poidevin* (Metz: Centre de Recherche Histoire et Civilisation de l'Université de Metz, 2003), pp. 35–53, and Fleury and Lubor Jílek, *Le Plan Briand d'Union Fédérale Européenne: Perspectives Nationales et Transnationales, Avec Documents* (Bern: Peter Lang 1998).
30. Fleury, 'Avant-Propos', in: Ibid., p. xv.
31. See Irene Anastasiadou, *In Search of a Railway Europe: International Railway Developments in Interwar Europe* (PhD thesis, Eindhoven University of Technology 2009), Chapter 4.
32. See for example J.A. Salter, *Allied Shipping Control: An Experiment in International Administration* (London: Clarendon Press 1921).
33. Lord Hankey, *Diplomacy by Conference: Studies in Public Affairs* (London: Ernest Benn 1946); J. Salter, *Allied Shipping Control*; and Smuts, *The League*, p. 7.
34. Martin David Dubin, 'Transgovernmental Process in the League of Nations', *International Organization* 37(3) (1983), pp. 469–93, at p. 484.

35. During the First World War the Italian professor Attolico worked as an economist on the Allied Maritime Control Council.
36. Haas (1891–935) had worked for the Communications section of the French army, and served as the deputy secretary-general of the Committee on Ports, Waterways and Railways during the Peace Conference. 'Deaths of M.Haas and M.Watier, Directors of the Transit Section: League of Nations Information Section', 5 November 1935, box R-4259, 9A/20727/30397, LoN.
37. Mance, *Frontiers*, p. 60.
38. LoN Document, 20/31/58, 'First General Conference on Freedom of Communications and Transit, preparatory documents (May 1920)', p. 13.
39. R. Haas, 'World Transit and Communications' in *Problems of Peace: Lectures Delivered at the Geneva Institute of International Relations* (London 1927), pp. 212–13.
40. A recent article that focuses on the role of experts in international organizations such as the LoN is Johan Schot and Vincent Lagendijk, 'Technocratic Internationalism in the Interwar Years: Building Europe on Motorways and Electricity Networks', *Journal of Modern European History* 6(2) (2008), pp. 196–217.
41. The agenda included the freedom of communications and transit and General Conventions on the international regime of transit, ports, waterways and railways as referred to in Articles 338 and 379 of the Treaty of Versailles.
42. For an account of all technical committees, see H.R.G. Greaves, *The League Committees and World Order: A Study of the Permanent Committees of the League of Nations as an Instrument of International Government* (London: Humphrey Milford 1931).
43. Mance, *Frontiers*, pp. 175–6.
44. Dubin, 'Transgovernmental Process', p. 490.
45. A fifth conference scheduled for 1935 was first postponed to 1936 and then cancelled for budgetary reasons and due to the worsening political climate. See '5ème Conférence Générale des Communications et du Transit', box R-4275, 9A/13666/13666, LoN.
46. The OCT also served as an arbiter settling disputes with regard to communications and transit that, if unsuccessful, could be referred to the Permanent Court of International Justice (Mance, *Frontiers*, p. 28).
47. For a more extensive treatment of the League's work on railway issues, see Anastasiadou, *In Search*, Chapter 3.
48. Alice L. Conklin, *A Mission to Civilize, The Republican Idea of Empire in France and West Africa, 1895–1930* (Stanford: Stanford University Press 1997); Jonathan S. McMurray, *Distant Ties; Germany, the Ottoman Empire and the Construction of the Baghdad Railway* (London: Praeger 2001); Daniel R. Headrick, *The Tentacles of Progress; Technology Transfer in the Age of Imperialism, 1850–1940* (Oxford: Oxford University Press 1988), pp. 180–203; C.B. Davis, K.E. Wilburn Jr. and R.E. Robinson (eds), *Railway Imperialism* (London: Greenwood Press 1991).
49. Norman J.G. Pounds, *An Historical Geography of Europe 1800–1914* (Cambridge: Cambridge University Press, 1985), pp. 1–36, 449–61. On international railway co-operation before the outbreak of the war, see Wedgwood and Wheeler, *International Rail Transport*, pp. 1–7.
50. LoN, 'General Transport Situation in 1921; Statements Submitted by the States which took part in the First General Conference on Communications and Transit, held in March-April 1921' (Geneva: LoN 1922), p. xi.

51. Elemèr Hantos, 'Une Nouvelle Organisation des Transports en Europe Central', *Revue Economique Internationale* 23 (1931), pp. 271–2.
52. 'Les Difficultés des Chemins de Fer de l`Europe Centrale', in *Revue Generale des Chemins de Fer* 41(1922), p. 250.
53. Wedgwood and Wheeler, *International Rail Transport*, pp. 8–32.
54. LoN Document, 20/31/58), pp. 13–15.
55. 'Freedom of transit would be meaningless if, after having been afforded legal guarantees on those railways over which the various States exercise any degree of control or action, could not be effectively exercised owing to the general conditions of working and utilisation of these lines.' League of Nations, Barcelona Conference, *Verbatim Records and Text of the Recommendations Relative to the International Regime of Railways and of the Recommendations Relative to Ports placed under an International Regime*, Annex to Section IV, Report on the Draft Convention on the International Regime of Railways, p. 208.
56. LoN, Barcelona Conference, p. 15.
57. The Spanish delegate proposed the following amendment: 'without this implying any obligation to alter the tracks of two neighbouring countries when these tracks are of essentially different type', LoN, Barcelona Conference, p. 43.
58. LoN, Barcelona Conference, p. 44.
59. LoN Documents, 19707, 23342, 9108, 23512, Box R-1122, LoN.
60. LoN Document, C.C.T./V.F./4, 'Advisory and Technical Committee for Communications and Transit, Rail Sub-Committee, *Papers*'.
61. In their memorandum to the CCT, the railway sub-committee observed that 'the general convention would assure the form of a compendious international code of recognised international obligations with regard to transport by rail', LoN Document, C.C.T./V.F./4, p. 2.
62. Mance, *Frontiers*, pp. 0–71. It co-operated closely with the International Union of Railways (UIC, 1922) and the International Chamber of Commerce (ICC, 1919) in promoting the unification of transport statistics, and the revision of the Berne Convention on the Transport of Goods by Rail (*Convention Internationale Merchandises* CIM, 1890). Laurent Tissot, 'Naissance d' une Europe Ferroviaire: La Convention Internationale de Berne (1890)', in Michèle Merger and Dominique Barjot (eds) *Les Entreprises et Leurs Réseaux: Hommes, Capitaux, Techniques et Pouvoirs XIXe-XXe Siècles: Mélanges en honneur de Francois Caron* (Paris: Presses de l'Université de Paris-Sorbonne 1998), pp. 283–95.
63. Exceptions were Bulgaria, Czechoslovakia, Luxemburg, Portugal, and the Soviet Union. By September 1, 1938, 25 Governments had adopted the Convention, while Australia, Canada, China, South Africa, the whole of South America, the United States and the U.S.S.R. never adopted it. Hostie, *The Organisation of Transit and Communications of the League of Nations*, typewritten manuscript, Library LoN, p.84.
64. Osborne H. Mance, 'Recent Developments in International Railway Questions', *Proceedings of the Great Western Railway (London) Lecture and Debating Society* 1929–30(236) (1929), p. 7. The Permanent Committee for Transport by Rail met only once in the years 1931–45 (in 1935). Hostie reports that, owing to the primarily regional character of railway problems and the dominant position of the *Reichsbahn* in Europe, Germany's withdrawal from OCT was a paralyzing factor in the field of both railways and navigable waterways. Hostie, *The Organisation*, p. 255.

65. Mance, 'Recent Developments', p. 6; *Les Problèmes de Transport Résultant de la Guerre de 1914 – 1918 et l' Oeuvre de Reconstitution Entreprise dans ce Domaine par la Sociètè des Nations* (Geneva: LoN 1945), pp. 38–9.
66. See Anastasiadou, *In Search*, chapter 4.
67. See further Lagendijk, *Electrifying*, pp. 61–6, 86ff.
68. LoN, 'Convention relating to the Transmission in Transit of Electric Power. Convention relating to the Development of Hydraulic Power affecting more than one State. Records and texts', 1924, p. 7, box R-1122, 14/20588/36472, LoN.
69. LoN Document, C.212.M.116.1922.VIII, 'Advisory and Technical Committee for Communications and Transit. Procès-verbal of the second session, held at Geneva March 29th–31st 1922', pp. 8–9, and Annex 7: 'Report by M. Bignami to the Advisory and Technical Committee for Communications and Transit on the advisability of the League of Nations taking action for facilitating the Cession by one Country to another of Electric Power for the Operation of Railways of International Concern', pp. 29–31. The members were Mr Holck-Colding (Denmark; chair), Paolo Bignami (Italy), Mr P. Charguéraud-Hartmann (France), Robert Hérold (Switzerland) and Mr E. Montarroyos (Brazil).
70. LoN Document, C.378.M.171.1923.VIII, 'Second General Conference on Communications and Transit. Preparatory documents: III – Electric Questions: Report concerning the draft Conventions and Statutes relating to the transmission in transit of electric power and the development of hydraulic power on watercourses forming part of a basin situated in the territory of several states', pp. 3–4.
71. This point was explicitly made by German engineer Werner Kittler, who wrote that 'Das Bestreben, die eigene Wirtschaft ausländischen Einflüssen gegenüber möglichst abzuschließen, was besonders heute wieder in den zollpolitischen Maßnahmen einzelner Länder sehr stark zu Ausdruck kommt, macht sich auch in der Elektrizitätsgesetzgebung gelten.' See his *Der Internationale Elektrische Energieverkehr in Europa* (Munich: Oldenbourg 1933).
72. Lagendijk, *Electrifying*, pp. 59–60.
73. Examples like this one were never explicitly mentioned in discussions on the conventions.
74. Treaty of Versailles, 2 June 1918, Article 358b. Also see Nil Disco's chapter in this book.
75. A. Desaunais, 'Le Bief de Kembs, Premier Tronçon du Grand Canal d'Alsace', *Les Études rhodaniennes* 9(2) (1933), pp. 143–8, at p. 146.
76. LoN Document, C.486.M.202.1923, pp. 9–11. The draft Conventions are found in the document's Annexes. By 1938 this number had increased to, respectively, 11 (Czechoslovakia, Danzig, Denmark, Egypt, Great Britain, Iraq, Greece, New Zealand, Panama, Spain and Western Samoa) and 10 (Danzig, Denmark, Great Britain, Iraq, Greece, Hungary, New Zealand, Panama, Siam, and Western Samoa). See Mance, *International Road Transport*, pp. 148–50.
77. LoN Document, CCT/E.E/13, 'Sub-Committee for Hydro-Electric Questions. Minutes of the meeting held at Geneva, on March 22st, 1923', p. 3, Box R-1120, 14/18088/19965, LoN.
78. LoN Document, C.486.M.202.1923.VIII, 'Advisory and Technical Committee for the Communications and Transit. Minutes of the Fourth meeting: Report of the Sub-Committee for Hydro-electric questions', p. 9.

79. Map: '1921–1926'- C.194 Communications, Letter Pierrard (Director-General of the Marine) to Belgian Minister of Foreign Affairs, 23 December 1923, File 11440: Commission Consultative des Communication et Transit, Diplomatic Archive of Belgium (hereafter: Diplobel).
80. LoN Document, C.378.M.171.1923.VIII, pp. 3–5.
81. Letter Pierrard to Minister of Foreign Affairs, Diplobel.
82. This can be read by the fact that two publications on the European electricity sector both reprinted the Convention; see Kittler, *Der Internationale*, p. 21ff, and Joseph Legge, *Grundsätzliches und Tatsächliches zu den Elektrizitätswirtschaften in Europa* (Gebrüder Lensing 1931), p. 191ff.
83. UNIPEDE was initially established by the electricity industry from Belgium, France and Italy, but other European nations joined soon after. The IEC consisted of European countries only, with the exception of the United States and Japan. The WPC, notwithstanding its name, was composed of mainly European countries as well as their (former) colonies. Here, too, the United States was a member. See Lagendijk, *Electrifying*, p. 57ff.
84. New members were the director of the Elektrobank, J. Chuard, the Swede and Director-General of Hydraulic Power and Canals, F.W. Hansen, and the Frenchman G. Arbelot, who held the position of Director of Hydraulic Power and Electricity Distribution in the Ministry of Public Works. LoN Document, C.196.M.61.1924.VIII, 'Advisory and Technical Committee for the Communications and Transit. Minutes of the Sixth meeting' (1924), pp. 4, 6.
85. Ibidem, p. 6. The members came from Denmark, Greece, France, Sweden, Switzerland, Spain and Lithuania. The last member was from Venezuela, but he, however, still had 'to be assigned' even at the time of the printing of the minutes, suggesting a completely European Committee.
86. LoN Document, C.706.M.298.1930.VII / C.E.U.E.3, 'Commission of Enquiry for European Union, LoN Library archive. Proposals put forward by the Belgian government for the agenda of the commission for European Union, communicated to the members of the Commission and the Members of the League, Geneva, 19 December 1930'.
87. Lagendijk, *Electrifying*, p.76 ff. A vital link between the industry and politics was Dannie Heineman, a friend of Belgian Minister of Foreign Affairs and Europeanist Paul Hymans, who proposed the study to the CEEU. See letter dated 19 January 1931, Collection Hymans, #11440 I, Diplobel. Heineman chaired the Brussels-based *Société Financière de Transport et d'Entreprises Industrielles* (SOFINA) and was a close friend and associate of one of the drafters of a general plan for the electrification of Europe, Oskar Oliven. See Oliven, 'Europas Großkraftlinien. Vorschlag eines europäischen Höchtspannungsnetzes', *Zeitschrift des Vereines Deutscher Ingenieure* 74(25) (21 June 1930), pp. 875–9. For relations between Heineman and Oliven see Liane Ranieri, *Dannie Heineman, Patron de la SOFINA: Un Destin Singulier, 1872–1962* (Brussels: Éditions Racine 2005).
88. President UNIPEDE to Stoppani, 16 February 1932, Box R-2572, 9E/1668/1668; Letter from D. Dunlop to R. Haas, 6 July 1931, box R-2572, 9E/11978/1668, LoN.
89. LoN Document, C.98.M.33.1934.VIII, 'Memorandum of the Secretary-General of the Committee on Transport and Transit of Electric Power and the Regime of International Exchange of Electric Power in Europe. Geneva, November 2nd, 1933', p. 97.

90. LoN Document, C.266.M.159.1938.VIII, 'Records of the work of the Twenty-first session. Held at Geneva from August 1st to 4th, 1938', p. 13.

91. Robert Haas, 'Austausch Elektrischer Energie zwischen verscheidenen Ländern', in *Transactions of the World Power Conference, Basle sectional meeting 1926, volume I*, pp. 987–99, at p. 987.

92. For a more extensive treatment of the League's work on issues related to cross-border road traffic, see Schipper, *Driving Europe*, Chapter 4.

93. LoN Document, C.212.M.116.1922.VIII, 'Advisory and Technical Committee for Communications and Transit, Procès-Verbal of the 2nd session, annex 12, Butler to Secretary-General League of Nations, letter on the institution of an international driving license, 18 March 1922', p. 45.

94. LoN Document, C.667.M.267.1923.VIII, 'Advisory and Technical Committee for Communications and Transit, Minutes of the Fifth Session (29 August–1 September 1923)'.

95. LoN Document, C.196.M.61.1924.VIII, 'Advisory and Technical Committee for Communications and Transit, Minutes of the Sixth Session (12–14 March 1924)', p. 5, sub 4, p. 6.

96. O. Bilfeldt, F. Pflug, Enrico Mellini, J.F. Schönfeld, Ernest Delaquis and P.C. Franklin, respectively, filled these vacancies; LoN Document, C.72.M.36.1925. VIII, 'Advisory and Technical Committee for Communications and Transit, Minutes of the Seventh Session (26–29 November 1924)', p. 3.

97. Belgium, Switzerland and the United Kingdom sent in favourable replies (LoN Document, C.196.M.61.1924.VIII, p. 3).

98. LoN Document, C.621.M.203.1925.VIII, 'Advisory and Technical Committee for Communications and Transit, Minutes of the Eighth Session (24–30 July 1925)', p. 18.

99. For more details on this episode, see Schipper, *Driving Europe*, pp. 136–41.

100. LoN Document, C.237.M.86.1926.VIII, 'Road Committee, Minutes Third Session (1–3 March 1926)', p. 12.

101. For the draft texts, see LoN Document, Conf/CR/1, European Conference on Road Traffic – Preparatory Documents, 30 September 1930.

102. le Marec, *L'Organisation*, p. 90.

103. ICC, *Proceedings of the Congress, Amsterdam, July 1929*, Supplement 2 to *World Trade* (Paris: ICC) (October 1929), p. 69.

104. LoN Document, C.234.M.102.1931.VIII, 'Final Act, European Conference on Road Traffic (Geneva, March 16th–30th, 1931), 10 April 1931', pp. 8–9.

105. As a first step Stiévenard suggested translation of the road regulations in the possession of the Secretariat. Stiévenard to Haas, 20 March 1925, box R-1130, 14/43574/19600, LoN.

106. LoN Document, CCT/CR/024(1), 'Road Committee, Minutes Fourth Session (25–28 April 1927)', p. 4; LoN Document, C.234.M.102.1931.VIII, p. 9. For a more elaborate discussion on road signs, see Frank Schipper, 'Unravelling Hieroglyphs: Urban traffic signs and the League of Nations', *Métropoles* 6 (2009), pp. 65–100.

107. Hostie, *The Organisation*, pp. 244, 260.

108. LoN Document, C.380.M.256.1937.VIII, 'Advisory and Technical Committee for Communications and Transit, Minutes of the Twentieth Session (31 August–4 September 1937)'; LoN Document, CCT/CR/137(1), 'Road Committee, Minutes Twelfth Session (25–30 April 1938)', p. 8.

109. Precisely for the geographic reasons cited here, it is possible that matters were very different for the OCT's maritime committee. Further study would be needed to establish this.
110. Other regional economic commissions were established for Africa (ECA), Asia and the Pacific (ESCAP), Latin America and the Caribbean (ECLAC), and Western Asia (ESCWA).

Biography 3: Louis Armand – Between United Atoms and Common Railways

Christian Henrich-Franke

> To solve the contemporary problems we have to pay attention to the legislation of the technical era: the legislation of dimension and change.
>
> Louis Armand and Michel Drancourt, Le pari Européen, 1968

Few men have survived in public memory as 'founding fathers' of European integration. Jean Monnet, Paul-Henri Spaak, Robert Schuman, Alcide de Gasperi and Konrad Adenauer are probably the most prominent. Some experts even mention Louis Armand, the first president of the European Atomic Energy Community (Euratom). However, few are aware of the name Louis Armand being connected with an additional good number of far-sighted projects of European integration – especially in the railway sector.

Across Europe, Louis Armand came to fame for his involvement in the 'European Reliance' as founding father of Euratom. In a report prepared in 1953 for the Organisation of European Economic Cooperation (OEEC) on the future of energy supply in Europe, he already drew the conclusion that nuclear power was necessary for Europe's industrial future. Indeed, the costs inherent in developing atomic energy would have exceeded the European nation states' financial capacity. Hence atomic energy had to be developed on the European level. When the Benelux countries raised the issue of the European Reliance in 1955, Armand formed a working alliance with Jean Monnet, though he felt bemused by the latter's focus on political objectives. He considered such a-technical aims the 'slightly superficial side of Monnet's thinking'. Nevertheless, both combined their respective expertise and in the end made their common idea a success: EURATOM became part of the Treaties of Rome in 1957.

In the railway sector Armand's main concern was increasing the railways' economic efficiency by lowering the high cost structures the railway companies suffered under in the growing transport competition. He was convinced that railways could only regain competitiveness if they pooled their resources on the European level. He thus launched a series of plans for the material or institutional networking of Europe.

In 1950 Armand proposed a pool for shared use of freight wagons between Western Germany and France, upon which both administrations agreed in 1951. This pool replaced a system in which wagons had to be sent directly back to their home company. Armand even made the Germans agree to label it EUROP-Pool to reflect his vision of its covering all of Europe. After becoming International Union of Railways (UIC) president, he successfully launched the plan within the UIC, and by 1953 seven other railway administrations joined the pool.

For Armand EUROP-pool was only a first step. The next was a 1951 plan to create a European financing system for railway rolling stock. Armand intended to break into highly protected national markets for railway equipment and force the industry to exploit economies of scale. This plan met with stiff opposition from national industries, which feared a European demand monopoly. Nevertheless, this plan finally resulted in the founding of the European Company for the Financing of Railroad Rolling Stock (Eurofima, 1955). His third step, getting European governments to agree on a common standard for the electrification of railways, failed primarily because the technology to use his chosen standard of 50 kHz was not fully developed in the early 1950s.

Similar projects bearing Armand's name included the UIC's Office for Research and Experiments (ORE), established in 1950, and the Trans-Europ-Express (TEE), which was the first genuine European railway service network. Last but not least, he intensively lobbied for the Channel Tunnel. In 1957 he played a leading role in establishing the Channel Tunnel Study Group, which contributed a great deal to the project that eventually emerged.

In all his activities Armand was motivated by a vision of the *'technical era'*. He believed technological innovations would confront human society with a new reality within which the spatio-temporal perception of the world would be completely changed. Communication and transport technology would turn all people into neighbours, and automation would revolutionize the industrial mode of production. Eventually technological and scientific development would call into question political institutions and mentalities around the globe. Armand's guiding vision was based on a technological enthusiasm that was very popular among engineers at that time.

Armand was not a supporter of too strong political or cultural unification of Europe. On the contrary: he saw Europe as a technical necessity: European nation states could only avoid marginalization by pooling their resources. As his interest was more in a strong European economy than politics, he felt free to use the contemporary concepts of European integration rather eclectically. On the one hand he fell in with Monnet on the supranational construction of Euratom, while promoting non-governmental forms

Figure B3.1 Louis Armand, before a collage portraying his various European activities

Source: Josette Buzaré, *Louis Armand, le savoyard du siècle* (2000).
Reproduced with kind permission of La Salévienne.

of co-operation between the railway companies on the other. Putting his personal approach in political terms, Armand ultimately aimed at a federal '*Europe à la carte*'.

The federal '*Europe à la carte*' should be based on a new 'spirit of co-operation'. Such a spirit seemed only attainable within the 'ideologically neutral domain of science and technology'. In that point he shows the typical (and ultimately mythical) image of the apolitical technical expert. To Armand, however, experts, who were not bound by governmental rules, could best contribute to common transnational aims and objectives. Expert committees on the European level, which fulfilled their duties for the public benefit, were thus the sole institutional solution for the political and economic organization of European societies. Politics had to become technified and negotiations had to be kept outside the public sphere. Even on that point he could fall in with Monnet, who preferred technocratic governance.

Armand was equipped with a multitude of talents, which he used to get his ideas put into practice. One of these was his gift of rhetoric. When Euratom threatened to fail in the French parliament in 1956, Armand was invited to speak as an expert witness. It is said that he electrified the parliamentarians with a brilliant speech and swayed the debate Euratom's way. Jean Monnet characterized that speech as a 'tour de force of illumination and clarification'. A second talent was his target-oriented exploitation of personal networks. As senior alumnus of the French state's oldest school for mandarins, the Polytechnique, he was dean of a tight-knit informal network that permeated the French government. According to Jacob Meunier Armand was said to 'possess a progressive management style and considerable economic savvy'. In spite of his apolitical rhetoric, Armand quite often promoted French interests as the best solutions for Europe. This sometimes caused controversial disputes, for example on the involvement of French banks in Eurofima. Actually, Armand did not want to bypass the other Europeans; he simply took it for granted that France had to guide Europe into the 'technical era'.

Just recently Louis Armand's visions regained topicality: in his 1963 statement that if 'trains could survive the twentieth century, their success in the new millennium would be assured', he predicted one of the EU's top issues of today's transport policy: the revitalization of the railways.

Literature

Louis Armand and Michel Drancourt, *Le pari Européen* (Paris: Fayard 1968).
H.T. Du Cros, *Louis Armand. Visionnaire de la modernité* (Paris: Éditions Odile Jacob 1987).
Jacob Meunier, *On the Fast Track. French Railway Modernization and the Origins of the TGV, 1944–1983* (London: Greenwood 2002).

5

'Feeding the peoples of Europe': Transnational Food Transport Infrastructure in the Early Cold War, 1947–1960

Erik van der Vleuten

> Human nutrition is becoming more and more a problem of balance… What is most harmful is not occasional fasting, but prolonged and unremedied malnutrition, which eventually slows down the activity of a whole nation. Endemic malnutrition is, therefore, the enemy, but victory lies not only in increasing production, though this is of course necessary, but also, and perhaps to a greater extent, in a more even distribution of the foodstuffs produced, a sphere in which transport plays a technical role of the first importance.[1]
>
> Secretariat of the United Nations Economic Commission
> for Europe, 1949

Introduction

The quote above points to one of the major problems in Europe after the Second World War: the poor state of food supply. During and immediately after the war, outright food shortages occurred regularly, mainly due to the collapse of grain production and imports, and many of Europe's inhabitants had considerable difficulty reaching sufficient daily calorie intakes. However, such *under*nutrition is not what the quote is about. Instead it is about *mal*nutrition: by 1949 endemic hunger was nearly ended in Europe, but malnutrition persisted. It was caused by overly monotonous diets based on grains and potatoes; the challenge, then, was to increase the intakes of foods providing a wider variety of nutrients. Such foods were often labelled 'perishable foodstuffs', the most important of which were meat, fish, eggs, dairy products, and fruits and vegetables.

The quote does more than spotlight the lack of perishable foods as Europe's new post-war enemy. It also asserts that improving the intakes of such foods crucially depended on transport. In other words, it connects the feeding and health of Europe's individuals and nations to transport infrastructures, in particular those transport infrastructures that were already then known as the 'refrigerated chain' or the 'cooling chain'. These had to be either radically improved or, in the case of the deep freezing chain, built from scratch before they could start 'feeding the peoples of Europe'.[2]

Finally, although the notion of 'Europe' is not explicitly mentioned in the selected opening quote, it looms heavily in the background. It is important to note where the quote is from: a report by the secretariat of the United Nations' first regional body, the Economic Commission for Europe (UN ECE, 1947), which – among many other initiatives – inspired an enduring effort to build Europe-wide transport systems for perishable foods. This effort reflected the UN ECE's mission statements and its particular vision of what Europe could, and should, become: a Europe of nations jointly solving their food problems, as well as other economic problems, by means of international co-operation and division of labour; in short, by building a pan-continental economic system. For the UN ECE secretariat, the stakes were huge: they argued that pan-European co-operation and interdependency would not only foster economic recovery, but also prevent a return to national autarchy and nationalism and a deepening cleavage between the emerging Eastern and Western blocks that might eventually cause a Third World War.[3] The UN ECE thus was a post-war successor of the interwar League of Nations' functional organizations, working for European economic, social and infrastructural integration at a time when the initiative that would ultimately become the European Union had scarcely been born, and would involve only a handful of countries for decades to come.[4]

This junction of food, transport and European integration – and its corollary, fragmentation – is the subject of this chapter. The lead question is whether any 'Europe' was produced in the sphere of (perishable) food infrastructure building, and what this 'food Europe' looked like. I shall try to disentangle several material, institutional, discursive and statistical aspects of this theme in the 1940s and 1950s, when Europe's endemic malnutrition was attacked and supposedly overcome. To do so, I take relevant UN ECE efforts and archives as a privileged research entry. This organization provides a promising research site because it initiated, monitored and hosted negotiations on international food transport infrastructures with the explicit purpose of building an integrated Europe. As a veritable 'food system builder', it proceeded by identifying problems and bottlenecks, thus bringing into view integration efforts, but also failure and fragmentation on a pan-continental scale. In short, it was a first row witness to the dynamics and tensions of pan-European food infrastructure development.[5]

This perspective allows us to inquire into the shaping of 'food Europe' – or, in the terms of this book, mediations between 'infrastructure' and 'Europe' in the food domain – in several dimensions. Section 3 examines the ideological or *discursive* dimension, here represented by the cited UN ECE vision promoting a particular understanding of post-war Europe by a rhetorical linkage to such issues as malnutrition, perishable foods, and transport infrastructure. Section 4 investigates how this vision was translated into a programme for actually *building* international perishable food chains. It tracks the wide range of actions, in both the material and institutional spheres, intended jointly to produce a pan-European food economy. Section 5 spotlights the *negotiated* character of this effort, which produced – like any infrastructure project – inclusion and exclusion, those connected and those passed by, and thus a particular fragmentation in European food collaboration. Section 6, finally, exploits UN ECE efforts to statistically monitor food production and trade on an aggregate level to evaluate what 'food Europe' looked like by the 1960s in terms of actual food circulation. Before proceeding, however, I will briefly discuss the research theme in the light of existing literatures on European food history and infrastructure history.

Toward a transnational European food history

There is a large and growing scholarship on European food history, witnessed by an impressive number of books featuring 'food' and 'Europe' in their titles and the establishment of European food history associations.[6] Remarkably, the relationship between food history and European integration has been barely investigated in this booming field. The same is true for the infrastructural dimension of food supply. On one hand, this literature clearly delineates the main event in *European* food history, the food supply 'revolution' of the last century and a half, and *mentions* the pivotal importance of infrastructure contributing to this revolution. Century-old dreams of the 'Land of Plenty' were actually fulfilled during this period of time. At least in Europe, food became abundant, varied and cheap.[7] Others speak of a 'nutritional transition' or the emergence and diffusion of a 'modern food culture.'[8] This transition to abundance and variety can be further specified as a rise in the daily per capita energy intake from around 2,000 to 3,000 kilocalories, and the replacement of a monotonous diet of starchy staples (cereals, potatoes) by a varied diet including meat, fish, fruits, vegetables, and processed foods such as sugar and butter, thus overcoming both undernutrition (lack of calories) and malnutrition (lack of essential nutrients). This transition coincided with a dramatic rise in life expectancy for the populations involved, although the precise role of food vis-à-vis other factors is still under debate.[9]

Among the drivers of this important historical process, transport infrastructure is generally mentioned as a crucial element, next to increasing agricultural productivity and rising real incomes, that enabled consumers to buy more expensive foodstuffs and diversify their diets. The assumption is that infrastructures such as transport networks and associated techniques of conservation (cooling and freezing, pasteurization, packaging) enabled long distance food trade, thereby loosening the traditional ties between food and territory. Hence, failing harvests and seasonal shortages could be overcome by acquiring foods produced elsewhere: food supply was 'delocalized.'[10] Of course there always had been trade in foodstuffs, but foreign foods had remained a privilege of the wealthy few until the nineteenth-century industrial and transport revolutions.

On the other hand, this literature remains vague about *how* transport infrastructure was involved in this transition, and what exactly was 'European' about it. 'Europe' is predominantly taken as a self-evident category, tacitly equated with the cumulated experience of national food histories. This nation-centred framework of analysis, which goes under the banner of comparative history, is clearly reproduced in published European food histories, which nearly always juxtapose (sub)national case studies.[11] The very term 'Europe', if used at all, tends to stand for an abstracted development pattern from a limited number of individual countries.[12] A transnational perspective that may, for instance, place national food developments in the context of international circulation of foods, spotlight transfers *between* countries and other mechanisms connecting (or separating) national food histories, and inquire into the importance of national borders vis-à-vis other borders, seems to be missing so far.[13] Yet such a perspective is needed in order to inquire how 'food Europe' was integrated and fragmented. Focusing upon transnational food infrastructures, this chapter explores one possible avenue to investigate this theme.

A similar argument goes for the relationship between food history and transport infrastructure. Food historians acknowledge the pivotal role of transport; they have also embraced infrastructure-like concepts such as 'food chains' or 'food systems', though on a national scale. Such concepts invite study of the entire food cycle from production to consumption, and draw together (often isolated) research fields such as agricultural history, retail history and diet history.[14] Incidentally, the food chain concept was originally developed in the context of perishable foods in the early twentieth (perhaps late nineteenth) century, then denoting uninterrupted refrigeration of the successive stages of production, transport, storage, retail, and consumption of perishables.[15]

Yet the role of transport in these 'chains' or 'systems'– and thereby in the modern food transitions at large – is scarcely investigated. Like 'Europe', transport infrastructures are generally taken for granted. Food historians tend to focus on junctions in the food chain – agricultural fields, food processing factories, retail shops, and consumption sites such as kitchens and restaurants, neglecting the transport links that connect them. As a result, the (selectively) connecting, territorial element of food chains so important to the research questions of this book is largely overlooked. Only a few studies relating food transport to nation-building processes suggest the importance of transport for studying integration/fragmentation issues.[16]

From a perspective of transnational infrastructure, the relationship between transport, food chains and European integration can be further specified. In this volume, food chains are interpreted as a form of infrastructure. Their development processes, however, may differ substantially from familiar 'first order infrastructures' such as railway, road, electric power, or telecom systems. Instead food chains can be interpreted as 'second order' infrastructure, built on top of first order ones by a new set of actors outside the familiar network industries – in this case related to the food sector.[17] These actors *mobilized and used* road, rail and waterway infrastructure to hook up food sector nodes (farms, fields, factories, warehouses, shops, kitchens) into a new infrastructure functionally dedicated to food supply, that is, food chains. To do so they deployed, as we shall see below, a variety of strategies, including the development of refrigerated wagons, trucks and containers serving as interfaces between transport and food supply infrastructure. Studying food supply as a sectoral or institutional use of transport infrastructure for building food chains brings into view the territorial aspects of food supply and, hopefully, features of European integration and fragmentation.[18] This chapter delves into the choices made in such processes and searches for the 'Europe of perishable foods' that they helped produce.

In so doing, this chapter aims for a transnational history that is more than cross-border studies. Rather, it inquires into connections and fragmentations in European food chain building, whether they run across or within national borders. I therefore use the term 'international' for the cross-border food chains that the UN ECE wished to construct, as opposed to self-reliant 'national' food systems it sought to break open. The term 'transnational' food chains refers to the overall configuration comprising cross-border as well as national food chains. It is in this overall configuration that we may find the relative success or failure of UN ECE efforts, which connections and fragmentations characterized Europe's food supply, and thus what kind of 'Europe' was constituted in the food domain.[19]

A vision of 'food Europe'

In February 1948, the UN ECE's Inland Transport Committee decided to set up a Working Party on Transport of Perishable Foodstuffs. The idea was to 'determine whether there are any transport bottlenecks in the way of moving the food available, and if so, develop the necessary arrangements for eliminating those bottlenecks'.[20] The Working Party obtained a mandate to 'take any immediate action which might improve or facilitate the transport of perishable foodstuffs'.[21] Unless international law was involved, it could do so without prior consent of the UN ECE's highest organ, the Commission, an annual assembly of national government representatives. This state of affairs was typical for UN ECE work. Since its political prestige and financial capacity were severely limited, not least after it had lost the bid for distributing the Marshall funds to a rival organization (the Organization for European Economic Cooperation, 1948), the annual Commission meetings allegedly had degenerated into 'merely another cockpit for waging the cold war'.[22] By contrast, at the level of day-to-day activities a spirited and active secretariat headed by executive secretary Gunnar Myrdal, much praised for its data-gathering and processing abilities, worked with a large subsystem of committees and working parties on a range of economic issues, from inland transport and energy infrastructures to agriculture, trade, housing and steel.[23] Now, perishable food was added to the list.

By way of preparation, Myrdal and his secretariat contacted all UN ECE member state governments requesting information on the state of perishable food transport.[24] On the basis of the replies, the secretariat drafted a report of the European food situation after the war, identifying bottlenecks demanding immediate attention and proposing a number of measures. The study articulated what perishable foods were, why they were so terribly important for Europe, how this 'Europe' should be conceived, and what role transport played in all this. In short, it presented a vision for building 'Europe' in the domain of perishable foods.

The starting point in this discursive constellation, as noted, was that malnutrition had become endemic in many parts of post-war Europe. During and immediately after the war there had also been quantitative undernourishment in some regions. In Germany, for instance, the wartime daily per capita energy intake of 2,800 kilocalories fell to 1,500 in several periods of 1946/47.[25] Qualitative nutritional deficits causing malnutrition, however, were much more widespread. Europe's endemic food problem, the secretariat concluded, was not starvation but malnutrition, 'which eventually slows down the activity of a whole nation'. In short: 'endemic malnutrition…is the enemy'.[26]

How to beat this new post-war enemy? Here, the concept of perishable foodstuffs came in as supplier of the missing nutrients, needed 'for the maintenance of human life itself and man's energy requirements for the performance of various functions'.[27] Already during the war, new insights in nutritional science had given perishable foods a key role in food rationing. According to Dr J.M. Latsky, a nutrition expert of the United Nations' Food and Agricultural Organization (FAO, 1945), 'it is unfortunate that the most nutritious, and therefore the most expensive, foods should be so highly perishable.'[28] In the Secretariat's vision this was translated to 'the foodstuffs most necessary to man are unfortunately those which are normally the most perishable and the most dearest.'[29] Thus supplies of fresh milk and cheese, meat, fish and eggs needed to be increased in order to secure protein intakes. Offal (the organs of slaughtered animals), today considered either waste or a delicacy, was also included as a vital protein supplier. An

increase in fresh cream and butter consumption should increase the intake
of fats and fat-soluble vitamins. Increasing supplies of vegetables and fresh
fruits, finally, were badly needed to improve the intake of mineral salts,
water-soluble vitamins (A, B and C), and cellulose.

The problem behind Europe's malnutrition, then, was the reduced intakes
of perishable foods during the recent war. According to FAO data, annual
per capita meat intakes had only remained relatively stable at 50–60 kilo-
grams (kg) in countries specializing in animal husbandry, such as Ireland
and France. In other countries meat intake sharply declined: in the United
Kingdom it had dropped from 60 kg in the period 1934–8 to 48 kg in
1947–8. Others fared far worse: Austrians experienced a decline from 54
to 25 kg, Germans from 51 to 12–16 kg (depending on occupation zone),
and Italians from 20 to 14 kg. In Eastern Europe, low pre-war meat intakes
had further declined: in Bulgaria from 22 to 18 kg, in Hungary from 36
to 23 kg, in Poland from 26 to 17 kg, and in Rumania from 18 to 14 kg.
Similar discrepancies and declines were observed for fresh fish, eggs, and
dairy products.[30]

How, then, to increase the availability of perishable foods? In the vision of
the UN ECE secretariat, the answer was international co-operation:

> The time is now past when nations could, separately and independently,
> solve the problem of balancing production and consumption. The solu-
> tion must be based on a rational system of exchanges between countries
> with a production surplus and those with a deficit. Perishable foodstuffs
> remain a vital element in these exchanges. In the case of Europe in par-
> ticular, FAO surveys have shown that improved distribution of the fol-
> lowing foodstuffs was essential: fresh fruit and vegetables, meat, fish,
> eggs, milk and dairy products.[31]

The issues of malnutrition and perishable foods were thus connected to a
particular meaning of 'Europe': an interconnected Europe, in which 'nations'
collaborated in an international division of labour. As noted above, this
conception of Europe was part and parcel of the UN ECE sense of mission.
The very (and initially controversial) idea of a 'regional' organization in the
'universal' United Nations framework was that Europe's common history
and geographical scattering of resources made treatment as a single development region desirable.[32] Once established, the secretariat further added to
this mission statement by stressing that binding Europe's nations together
in economic co-operation and interdependency would not only secure
common prosperity, but also prevent future rivalry and war.[33] When the
ECE was evaluated and made permanent in 1951, the UN General Assembly
accepted the ECE argument that all-European economic co-operation was
essential to economic growth as well as world peace.

For the case of perishable foods, the secretariat suggested – without documentation – that large-scale intra-European trade had once existed. However, already in the 1930s this trade had allegedly been greatly reduced due to the Great Depression and associated protectionist policies. The Second World War, poor harvests in 1946 (Eastern Europe) and 1947 (Western Europe), and post-war protectionist trade policies further caused record low levels of trade in perishable foods in 1947 (see Table 5.1). In order of volume, fruits, meat, vegetables, fish, dairy products and eggs were the most dominant perishables traded. However, in the eighteen countries for which data were available, total exchanges had fallen significantly – from an annual nine million tons in the pre-war period to under seven million tons in 1947. Trade in vegetables had recovered by then, and trade in fish had slightly inclined. Yet trade in eggs and dairy products had collapsed, while trade in fruits, and to a lesser degree meat, had been reduced significantly.[34] 'Europe', it seemed, was increasingly becoming a Europe of autonomous states rather than an interdependent region. In the UN ECE vision, this certainly did not help in beating Europe's malnutrition enemy.

Finally, this vision for 'feeding the peoples of Europe' connected the previous concepts of malnutrition, perishable foods, and an integrated pan-Europe to the issue of cross-border transport and transit. If perishable food intakes were to be increased, increasing food production and dietary awareness of consumers were important, but transport infrastructure

Table 5.1   Annual imports/exports of perishable foods in eighteen European countries* for which data were available in 1947

Most traded perishable foods	1934–8		1947	
	Exports × 1,000 tons	Imports × 1,000 tons	Exports × 1,000 tons	Imports × 1,000 tons
Fruits	628	2,940	510	1,763
Meat	327	1,255	98	1,125
Vegetables	573	611	588	637
Fish	433	397	458	538
Butter and cheese	410	718	133	493
Eggs	204	257	55	112
All perishable foods:**	2,737	6,517	1,951	4,969

* Belgium, Czechoslovakia, Denmark, Finland, France, Germany, Greece, Iceland, Ireland, Italy, Luxembourg, Netherlands, Norway, Poland, Portugal, Sweden, Switzerland, United Kingdom.
** Adding poultry, milk, beer, fruit juices, yeast, and flowers and bulbs.

Source: ECE, Survey, chapter III, p. 2. (Compare figures for individual countries in ECE Secretariat, 'Survey on transport of perishable foodstuffs', annex 3.)

constituted the major bottleneck to international trade. Here, the problem was twofold.

First, common European standards for product quality and quality control were badly needed, for 'the conveyance of perishable foodstuffs by international transport cannot yield satisfactory results unless the foodstuffs carried are of good quality and are suitably selected and packed.'[35] Such standards should be developed by experts and preferably be agreed in the legal instrument of International Conventions.[36] Second, the challenges to transport itself were speed and good travel conditions. As for speed, little attention was given to building new rails or roads, although it was noted that constructing a Channel Tunnel and other tunnels and bridges would greatly speed up transports and eliminate transhipment. Instead, most problems concerned better use of existing rail and road infrastructure. Rail transport greatly dominated perishable food transports by land, but crossing borders was slow, and international rail tariffs lacking even on some major routes. Road transport by motor lorries was promising because it enabled door-to-door delivery, but was poorly developed (nearly exclusively serving Dutch and Danish exports) and highly irregular. Inland waterway and air transport of perishable foodstuffs was negligible. Intermodal freight transport by containers was promising, but containers were not yet equipped to store perishable foods. Besides, international tariffs for combined transport were lacking almost completely.

As for travel conditions, the most pressing problem perhaps was the 'more or less general inadequacy' of the so-called refrigerator chain.[37] The promise of this refrigerator chain was wonderful:

> Even the most perishable foodstuffs can be stored in their natural state at production centres, transported over long distances, and warehoused near the consumption centres where they will finally be sold, always providing that all these operations be carried out at a practically uniform low temperature. This need for an unbroken sequence of refrigeration facilities suggested the metaphor of links in one single 'refrigerator chain.'[38]

The report further compared the situation in 'Europe' with that in the United States, and concluded that Europe fell far behind in building such chains. For instance, European railway companies in fifteen countries for which data was available jointly owned about 16,500 wagons with temperature-controlling facilities: one wagon per 12,000 inhabitants. In the US the ratio was 1 per 1,000 inhabitants, but, since US wagons had three times the payload of European ones, the correct comparative figure was 1 per 330. A further problem highlighted by comparison with the US was that Europe's large export countries, Italy, France and Germany, owned over 80% of the European wagon park, but used wagons mainly for domestic transport. Importing and transit countries hardly owned any rolling stock with temperature control equipment. The situation in other transport modes was worse, and immediate action necessary.

To complete the circle in this discursive journey, it is noteworthy that the secretariat regarded the transport issue as so pressing that it was inscribed into the very definition of perishable foods, as opposed to foods like wheat or wine that did not pose challenges to transport in European trade. It developed a concise and pragmatic working definition: perishable foodstuffs were 'foodstuffs which, by reason of their fragility or their susceptibility to rapid change when fresh, require special precautions in transport: speed at which conveyed, use of refrigeration, ventilation in transit, etc'.[39] By defining perishable foodstuffs as precious foods requiring a specific mode of mobility, the Working Party mobilized the concept for a European cold chain-building programme.

Building the cold chain, 1949–60

The visions described above were relevant not only as a discursive mediation between 'Europe' and 'infrastructure', or as an effort to keep alive and promote the idea of a continentally integrated Europe in severely adverse times.[40] As Tom Hughes has argued, the intellectual effort of critical problem articulation also serves to suggest solutions inviting specific actions crucial to overall system development.[41] When the Working Party first convened in June 1949, it adopted not only the secretariat's sense of urgency and mission, but also its identification of bottlenecks to the 'feeding of the peoples of Europe' in the realm of international transport.[42] In response, the Working Party developed an impressive array of actions to address these problems. This section explores the *variety* of actions taken to remove 'bottlenecks' in order to mobilize transport infrastructures for international perishable food distribution.

Notably, the Working Party was not alone in this effort. Rather, it was a self-appointed spider in a rapidly growing web of actors formed around the theme of international perishable food supply. Next to national delegates and experts, the Working Party associated a host of international organizations adding specific expertise and competences to the task at hand, as we shall see below. One of its key activities, therefore, was social network-building. Among these collaborations, the United Nations global food agency – the Food and Agricultural Organization – deserves particular mention. The FAO had already worked on European fisheries trade and transport problems in 1947.[43] But, when the UN ECE Working Party was established, a division of labour was agreed: the UN ECE would be responsible for food transport issues, while the FAO would focus on food production and consumption issues. This latter work would, for instance, include setting global nutrition standards (with the World Health Organization and UNESCO), and lobbying with member governments for the establishment of national food authorities to further promote these standards on national and local levels. While this crucial strategy for increasing perishable food intakes awaits further research, this section examines initiatives concerning perishable food transport infrastructure only.

Socio-technical system-building: A wide range of activities

The Working Party started by emphasizing two factors pivotal to trade in perishable foods over which it had virtually no influence: national production and trade policies. Then it focused upon what it could do in the international arena. In the resulting list of activities we find an insight into the transdisciplinary nature of refrigerated food system-building.[44] For instance, the 1951 work programme contained thirty-three items.[45] From the point of view of mobilizing transport systems for international circulation of perishables, we may group these problem-solving activities into four major categories.

A first set of tasks centred on designing appropriate transport vehicles for perishable foodstuffs; we might call these 'gateways' between existing transport systems and emerging perishable food distribution systems. Thus the International Railway Union and the International Institute of Refrigeration were asked to design insulated, refrigerated and mechanically refrigerated railway wagons as well as so-called 'fruit and vegetable wagons' (requiring, for instance, shock absorption and ventilation). Already by 1950 this work had resulted in specifications for insulated and refrigerated wagons of SS-class, that is, allowing speeds of up to 120 km/h. Next to complete wagon designs, these organizations researched specific elements such as inside wagon walls (of stainless steel or aluminium alloys to withstand frequent chemical cleaning after fish or fruit transport); shock-absorbing devices; ways of securing loads on wagons; standards for air-tightness of vehicles; sealable passages in wagons allowing insertion of a thermometer from the outside; and so on. Similar work went on for lorries and for containers, now involving the International Road Transport Union, the European Union of Coachbuilders, and the International Container Bureau. Next to such technical research, these actors worked on auxiliary infrastructures such as icing and re-icing facilities. For ice-cooled transport, an entire infrastructure of ice factories, ice bunkers, and re-icing stations along transport routes was needed. This infrastructure needed to be mapped and possibly reorganized; for instance, re-icing stations should preferably be placed at compulsory stopping points such as customs, frontiers, and locomotive changing points.

A second realm of activity was not concerned with gateway designs, but with organizational and legal measures to speed up the flows of perishables. By the early 1950s they had identified major asymmetries in European perishable transport. For example, in 1951 the journey Hamburg–Prague took two days, while Rotterdam–Prague, a shorter distance, allegedly took six to eight days.[46] In response, the Working Party worked with the International

Freight Train Time Table Conference to attempt to rebalance transport by further reducing transport times for perishable transports. It also tried to persuade the International Rail Transport Committee (CIT), an association of national railway administrations working on international legal issues, to decrease the maximum time limits allowed for perishable transports. Furthermore, the International Chamber of Commerce should design international transport documents, while national governments were requested to support special fares for perishable transit traffic.

Much work was done to reduce delays at frontiers, much of which was inscribed in international law. Sometimes the Working Party secured the interests of perishable foods in legal work done by other UN ECE bodies. Most of its recommendations on railway traffic were implemented in an *International Convention to Facilitate the Crossing of Frontiers for Goods carried by Rail* (1952), arranging for customs clearance in the interior of states instead of at borders; simplified procedures for clearance of goods in transit; recognition of the national seals of other states; placing customs offices of neighbouring countries at the same location so that control could be exercised simultaneously; and harmonizing customs opening hours. Also, perishable goods transit traffic should be given priority at border crossings. Maximum delay times were not specified, but referred to bilateral agreement.[47] For road transport, the draft *Customs Convention on the International Transport of Goods by Road* (June 1949) addressed similar issues. It introduced the so-called TIR (*Transports Internationaux Routieres*) carnet, which deserves special mention: cargos were sealed and only checked at the country of origin and destination, not in transit countries. The 1949 draft convention was later succeeded by the *TIR convention* (1959, revised 1975), which still today counts as one of the UN ECE's most important contributions to international freight traffic. In 1952 just over 3,000 TIR Carnets were issued for individual transports; the number increased to 100,000 in 1960, 800,000 in 1970, and 2.7 million (representing 34,000 companies) in 2001.[48] Finally, for intermodal transport a *Customs Convention on Containers* (1956) was negotiated.

A third set of actions was to develop European standards for perishables and their transportation, which again were inscribed in international law. These included quality standards for perishable foods prior to transport, which greatly affected their preservation *en route*. As such standards primarily involved producers and exporters, the Working Party sought co-operation with the UN ECE Committee on Agricultural Problems, where these groups were represented. This Committee set up its own Working Party on standardization of perishable foodstuffs in intra-European trade.[49] By 1958 general provisions for all fruit and vegetables were defined in a Protocol (a less heavy legal instrument than a Convention, but still legally binding) accepted by most countries. By the mid-1960s recommendations were issued for standards in size, colour and classification of twenty individual perishables. From the early 1960s these standards were called 'European standards'.[50]

In addition, the Working Party on Transport of Perishable Foodstuffs negotiated standards concerning transport conditions. The International Chamber of Commerce, national governments, rail, road, aviation, and containers transport organizations, and the International Standards Organization helped to produce standards for packaging fresh fruits and vegetables, eggs in shell, and other produce in draft recommendations available by the early 1950s. Packaging in international transport should henceforward be new; non-returnable; parallelepiped in shape (no baskets etc); tested for sturdiness, load stability and ventilation; provided with devices for interlocking; designed for use with or without lids; conforming to standard dimensions; and marked by an official control stamp. For instance, saw-wood fruit boxes could be of five sizes with specified weights.[51] Work on transport standards also included handling operations; the mechanization of handling operations, reducing damage to perishables, involved standardized pallets, fork lift trucks and cleaning procedures.

Much work, finally, went into defining standards on the meaning and testing of perishable foods transport itself, including standards for terms such as 'insulated', 'refrigerated', 'mechanically refrigerated' and 'heated', and procedures for their verification. As we shall see below, negotiations were difficult. Such standards were first proposed in an annex on perishables to the *General Agreement on Economic Regulations for Road Transport* (1954) and an *Agreement on Special Equipment for the Transport of Perishable Foodstuffs and on the Use of such Equipment for the International Transport of some of those Foodstuffs* (1962). Both were used by a limited number of countries only. The breakthrough was the *Agreement on the International Carriage of Perishable Foodstuffs and on the Special Equipment to be Used for such Carriage* (*ATP*, 1970). This is the best-known product of the Working Party today. It currently has forty-two member states and specifies classes of refrigeration equipment, testing procedures and maximum transport temperatures for a range of foods. Thus frozen fish was to be transported at max –18 °C, frozen butter at –10 °C, non-frozen poultry at +4 °C, and non-frozen fish 'must always be carried in melting ice'.[52]

A fourth problem area that needed to be addressed, finally, concerned the actual construction and operation of cooling chains once wagon designs, customs procedures, quality standards and so on were in place. The 1949 Secretariat report had suggested a solution: new international rail and road organizations could plan, build and operate cold chains, taking the idea out of laboratories and meeting rooms and into practice. The wish for a railway company dedicated to temperature-controlled transport was immediately served. At the first Working Party session in 1949, the Belgian and French representatives proudly reported that the International Railway Company for Refrigerated Transport had been created. *Interfrigo* began as a body studying refrigerated transport problems, but was currently drafting statutes for commercial operation. The company would create a European park of refrigerated rolling stock; importing countries would share in its costs. Membership was open to all European railway administrations (see below).[53] In 1993 *Interfrigo* merged with *Intercontainer* (1967) into *Intercontainer-Interfrigo* (ICF). *Interfrigo* did not have a monopoly, though; it was one of a number of companies providing refrigerated services.

Regarding road transport, the Working Party pushed for a similar initiative. At its ninth session in July 1952, the International Road Transport Union IRU was officially asked to establish an international body to assist the development of intra-European road transport facilities for perishable foods. Rather than an official international body, it should be an association strengthening the international bonds between road transport enterprises.[54] *Transfrigoroute Europe* was formally founded in 1955 as an association of the most prominent refrigerated road carriers of nine countries. It was headquartered in Basel (later Bern), Switzerland, and IRU president (and refrigerated transport entrepreneur) Paul Schweizer became its first president. *Transfrigoroute Europe* members had to comply with formal refrigerated transport standards; in return they obtained the *Transfrigoroute* identity card and carried the *Transfrigoroute* sign, which should give them priority at borders and other privileges.

Already by the late 1950s, *Transfrigoroute* adverts claimed that it had 'created the unbroken cooling chain on roads'.[55] Its 'rolling refrigerators' allegedly allowed door-to-door transport of perishables, from ships to cold storage, ship to importer, cold storage to ship, or producer to consumer (Figure 5.1). By 1976 it had 1,175 valid ID cards registered. Renamed *Transfrigoroute International* in 1982, it presently serves the interests of the temperature-controlled road sector divided into twenty-five national member associations in Europe and North Africa. In 2005 it claimed to associate about 1,700 firms and organizations, covering some 80% of the perishable food road transport market.[56]

Whose 'food Europe'?

By 1960, then, international cold chains seemed well under way. We saw that this effort was achieved by many actors in perpetual co-operation and negotiation on a number of issues. However, such negotiation might also involve disagreement, even conflict, and refusal to cooperate. It is in the contested features of food transport system-building that we may find important clues as to which 'Europe' was under construction in the domain of perishable food chains.[57] In search of territorially selective aspects of food chains, I shall focus here on the participation or absence of states in this impressive international collaboration. Such inclusion or exclusion can be found on several levels.

First, as noted above, the UN ECE's overall sense of mission stipulated that 'Europe' should be as inclusive a category as possible.[58] In the context of the early Cold War this translated into a focus on East–West cooperation and

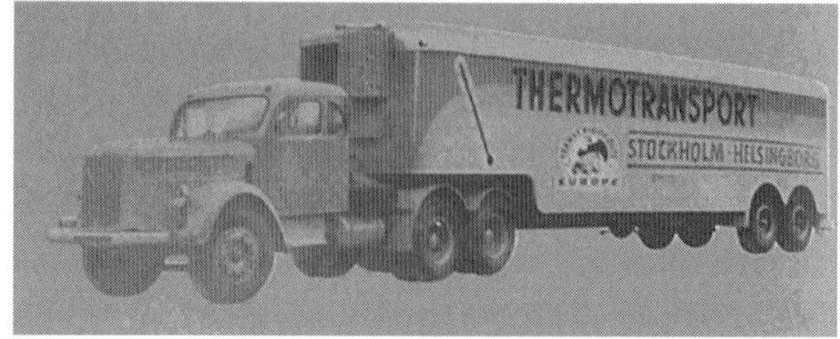

Figure 5.1   Transfrigoroute lorries in the late 1950s

Note: Transfrigoroute lorries identified by the Transfrigoroute logo. They served (inter)national routes connecting major harbours and consumption centres (Stockholm–Helsingborg in Sweden, Marseille–Lyon–Paris in France, Barcelona–Madrid–Gerona in Spain and Amsterdam, the Netherlands–Düsseldorf, Germany–Frankfurt–Munich–Vienna, Austria).

Source: *Transfrigoroute Brochure*.

perpetual attempts to involve (Central) Eastern European states and Soviet republics as formal ECE members. The imbalances the Working Party noted above between Western ports and Prague were thus not grabbed from thin air. Also, non-UN countries (Albania, Austria, Bulgaria, Finland, Hungary, Ireland, Italy, Portugal and Roumania until 1955; Switzerland until 2002), which could not be *de jure* included in the Commission, were invited to participate informally in the committees and working parties from the start.[59]

These attempts at East–West co-operation encountered problems, especially in the early years. Although the UN ECE had been founded by eighteen states, notably including such Soviet republics as the Byelorussian and Ukrainian SSRs, escalating Cold War tensions caused a massive walk-out of (Central) Eastern European members. Until these tensions eased in 1953/4, the organization was predominantly a 'Western' one – save for Poland's participation in the Coal Committee. From 1953 many Eastern European delegates returned, and the Soviet Union started to participate in all UN ECE committees. Even East Germany, which was not recognized by most Western countries and was barred from international organizations, participated in practical work from 1953 (it only gained *de jure* membership in 1973). Finally, the UN ECE seems to have respected the 1946 UN embargo against the last remaining 'Axis power', General Franco's Spain, until 1955.

Second, this push for all-European co-operation did not necessarily materialize in the concrete work on perishable foods. When the Working Party gathered for its first session, it associated representatives of fourteen governments under the chairmanship of F. Martin and O. Schoenewald from Italy and the Netherlands, respectively: two countries with major export interests in perishables. In the following decade, national representation was clearly skewed towards North-Western and Central Europe (including Austria, Belgium, Denmark, France, the Netherlands, Norway, Sweden, Switzerland, the United Kingdom, and Western Germany from 1950). The United States were also present.[60] By contrast, Southern Europe was poorly represented throughout the 1950s. Italy was the exception, taking a leading role throughout the period under investigation. Spain only joined in 1956, after the UN boycott had been lifted. Portugal and Albania remained absent, and Greece and Yugoslavia participated only once or twice. As for what was increasingly called Eastern Europe, only Czechoslovakia, Hungary and Poland participated at the first session, but by its third session in June 1950 no Eastern country participated. The Working Party, too, had become a 'Western' body. When the Cold War tensions eased, Bulgaria, Czechoslovakia, Hungary, Poland, Rumania, the USSR and the Eastern zone of Germany became regular guests. By then, participation suggested more East–West co-operation than North–South co-operation.

A third level of inclusion and exclusion is visible in reviewing which countries adopted the results of Working Party efforts, most notably the international treaties discussed above.[61] Regarding border crossings, for instance, the *International Convention to Facilitate the Crossing of Frontiers for Goods carried by Rail* (1952) with special provisions for perishable foods was signed only by the Benelux countries, France, Italy, Norway, Sweden and Switzerland. While Austria, Spain and Portugal followed within a decade, Eastern and South-Eastern European states were absent and remain so today (though Albania joined in 2004). The corresponding Convention for containers (1956), signed when Cold War tensions had eased, added to the previous list Germany and the UK, but also Hungary and Poland among its original signers. (Former) Soviet republics never joined, though. For road traffic, the *TIR convention* (1959) was originally signed by nine usual suspects (Austria, the Benelux countries, West Germany, France, Italy, Switzerland and the UK), but within two years Southern (Greece, Spain and soon Portugal) and

Eastern European (Bulgaria, Czechoslovakia, Hungary, Poland and soon Rumania) participation was achieved. Turkey soon joined, but the USSR followed only in 1974 and exempted a few articles of the Convention, such as the passage allowing states to extend the provisions to their colonies (the USSR categorically condemned colonialism). By then over thirty countries had joined, including Canada, Iran, Israel, Japan and Jordan.

As in the Working Party representation, one may discern in these treaties a group of front-runners constituted by Northern, Western and Central European states and Italy. Southern and (Central) Eastern European states joined incidentally, mostly later, and often not at all. This pattern was repeated in the difficult treaty negotiations on standards for refrigerated transports. Most governments of Working Party members refused to sign the *General Agreement on Economic Regulations for Road Transport* (1954) annex C.1 on perishable food transports, which as a result never formally entered into force.[62] After much debate the annex was signed only by Belgium, France, Luxembourg and the Netherlands, which desired to move ahead as quickly as possible. This schism continued when the Working Party tried to negotiate a new treaty valid for all transport forms, but proved unable to agree. Some members then proposed to weaken the standards of the 1954 annex, but here the front-runners protested because, in the words of the French delegates, this would entail a step backward rather than forward.[63] The story continued eight years later when the follow-up treaty *Agreement on Special Equipment for the Transport of Perishable Foodstuffs* (1962) was soon signed by five usual suspects plus Bulgaria, Poland and Spain. However, it never entered into force since it was never ratified by at least five countries, as specified in the conditions. Finally, the successful *ATP Agreement* (1970) was rapidly accepted by seven usual suspects plus Portugal and the USSR. Although the number of contracting parties rose to forty-two today, except for Bulgaria (1978), Eastern European countries acceded with some delay.[64] Fourth and finally, the cooling chains as organized in practice by rail company *Interfrigo* and road carrier association *Transfrigoroute Europe* also show clear geographical selectiveness. Pending further research into these organizations, a few observations can already be made here.

The establishment of *Interfrigo*, as noted above, was proudly announced at the first Working Party session in 1949. Founding *Interfrigo* members were the railway administrations of the front-runner countries Belgium, France, Italy, the Netherlands, Switzerland and the United Kingdom. Membership was supposedly open to all European railway administrations, but most did not join. The opposition was articulated in reply to the Swiss delegate suggesting explicit Working Party approval of this initiative: a private company should not receive a near-monopoly position. For the US representative, Working Party support of *Interfrigo* would imply 'a recommendation that the virtual monopoly control of refrigerated transport in Europe should be invested in what was apparently a private concern'.[65] Supporters of *Interfrigo* replied that the company was a 'quasi inter-governmental' body since the majority of members was state-owned, but to the US representative 'to regard such undertaking as an intergovernmental body was stretching the definition rather far.'[66] The Czechoslovakian and Polish representatives supported this critical stance. The Polish delegate went even further and articulated an Eastern European standpoint disapproving of the idea of an international company in the first place, instead placing the responsibility for building and controlling cold chains with national governments. The deadlock persisted and the Working Party decided not to mention *Interfrigo* explicitly in its session reports. The company was deliberately ignored until the mid-1950s, when it was finally acknowledged as an important ally in the construction of cross-border food chains. It remained a Western body, though.

Transfrigoroute Europe, too, started out as a Western European gathering. Its founding members were road carriers from Austria, Belgium, West Germany, France, the Netherlands, Spain and Switzerland. Almost immediately Italian, Danish and Swedish members joined. This geographical focus was reproduced in the envisioned *Transfrigoroute* distribution (compare Figure 5.1). It also showed in its lobby activities, for instance when requesting priority treatment at selected custom offices: a 1956 list focused entirely on border crossings in the West.[67]

The case of *Transfrigoroute* also reveals another type of friction, namely between international food chains and national authorities, which were frequently mentioned as obstructive and uncooperative. One concern was the slow procedure for obtaining national transport permits, which allegedly 'jeopardized' the objectives of the association.[68] Another obstacle was the new ban on Sunday and holiday travel introduced in Germany in 1956, followed by Austria, some Swiss cantons, and others, which also 'constituted a serious threat to the European refrigerator chain'.[69] Persistent complaints and lobbying, however, soon exempted perishables from these bans. A third source of complaint was delays at customs offices. Thus, fresh strawberry and vegetable traffic from Brittany (France) to the Netherlands 'at present time usually takes three days…as carriers are too often compelled to wait at the French, Belgian and Netherlands frontiers until the customs offices open. But this journey should, on the face of it, take less than 48 hours'.[70] Myrdal and the UN ECE secretariat contacted national governments to discuss such problems and some of these were solved, but in the perception of road carriers tensions between international transport and national authority persisted.[71]

'Food Europe' around 1960

As noted earlier, this chapter aims for a transnational history of European food supply that looks at connections as well as fragmentations running across, along or within national borders. One advantage of studying 'food Europe' through the eyes of the UN ECE is that it provides a research focus upon this privileged observer's identification of bottlenecks, initiation of solutions, witnessing of negotiations and fragmentations, and also monitoring the entire process on an aggregate level. Such monitoring included collection and interpretation of food production and trade statistics, in close co-operation with the UN Food and Agriculture Organization. The UN ECE secretariat's agriculture division published its first analysis of this kind in 1962, focusing upon nine important foods representing over two-thirds of Europe's trade in so-called temperate agricultural products, meaning foods that were (also) produced in Europe.[72] These foods, the report suggested, could in theory form the basis of an integrated European food system: wheat, barley, maize, sugar, meat, butter, cheese, eggs and fresh fruit. Thus, thirteen years after the 1949 report calling for international perishable foods infrastructures to build a European food economy, the secretariat now presented data evaluating the circulation of the most important starchy staples and perishable foods, except, unfortunately, fish and vegetables. What kind of 'food Europe' did these figures show?

For the secretariat, they must have caused mixed feelings. On one hand, the domestic production of perishable foods as well as grains had greatly increased, implying rapid reduction of malnutrition and undernutrition (Table 5.2). As for wheat, by far the most important food in terms of weight, production had increased from about 91 million tons in the early 1950s to 125 million tons by 1960. Egg production rose from 3 to 5.7 million tons, butter production from 2 to 3 million tons, and the value of meat production (in Western Europe only) from under 8 to over 11 billion US dollars. The malnutrition enemy was being beaten.

On the other hand, in spite of the existence and continued growth of integrated transport networks for food supply, an integrated European food system clearly had not emerged. 'Agricultural products have become the

Table 5.2 Average annual production of selected foods 1951–60 in 1,000 metric tons (millions of US dollars in the case of meat)

	Wheat		Meat		Eggs		Butter		Cheese	
	1951–3	1960	1951–3	1957–9	1951–3	1960	1951–3	1960	1951	1960
Western Europe	39,448	48,211	7,835	11,141	2,427	3,364	1,355	1,760	1,444	2,009
Eastern Europe and USSR	51,798	76,566	–	–	1,622*	2,326	876*	1,293	–	–

* Figures for 1954–56.

Source: ECE, *Ten years of agricultural trade in Europe*, tables I-8, IV-7, VII-6, V-7 and VI-5.

Table 5.3 National self-sufficiency for selected foods: domestic production as % of available supply (production + net imports) in weight% (value% in the case of meat)

	Wheat (%)		Meat (%)		Eggs (%)		Butter (%)		Cheese (%)	
	1951–3	1960	1951–3	1957–9	1951–3	1960	1951–3	1960	1951	1960
Belgium–Lux	44	70	99	98	100	114	80	107	32	37
France	102	114	100	100	98	98	95	102	102	104
West Germany	58	80	95	89	74	61	96	95	85	77
Italy	85	96	94	87	95	81	83	71	100	96
Netherlands	25	36	151	161	237	226	288	166	213	216
EEC total	**80**	**94**	**100**	**97**	**97**	**91**	**99**	**100**	**101**	**99**
Austria	53	77	99	102	93	86	98	115	98	110
Denmark	88	71	267	321	350	259	485	342	277	301
Finland	47	72	100	101	100	127	98	138	181	221
Ireland	53	78	275	300	131	101	91	113	125	116
Norway	10	7	100	99	106	105	124	145	105	134
Sweden	90	103	98	101	111	111	121	116	100	93
Switzerland	42	46	91	86	70	56	82	99	145	154
United Kingdom	34	39	55	60	82	95	6	9	29	46
Other NW Europe total	**42**	**50**	**86**	**89**	**99**	**103**	**76**	**70**	**81**	**99**

Continued

Table 5.3 Continued

	Wheat (%)		Meat (%)		Eggs (%)		Butter (%)		Cheese (%)	
	1951–3	1960	1951–3	1957–9	1951–3	1960	1951–3	1960	1951	1960
Greece	74	97	84	86	95	99	98	98	94	100
Portugal	81	80	100	99	100	100	114	115	106	107
Spain	94	98	97	96	98	99	82	85	100	98
Turkey	105	99	101	100	120	102	100	101	–	–
Yugoslavia	81	100	105	111	100	115	88	100	101	101
Southern Europe total	**94**	**98**	**100**	**101**	**101**	**103**	**97**	**101**	**99**	**100**
Western Europe TOTAL	**76**	**86**	**96**	**95**	**98**	**96**	**90**	**88**	**95**	**99**
Bulgaria	102	96	–	–	164*	158	100*	130	–	112
Czechoslovakia	68	51	–	–	97*	102	80*	80	–	101
East Germany	80	49	–	–	91*	98	81*	80	67*	65
Hungary	110	86	–	–	113*	106	147*	129	–	146
Poland	93	58	–	–	110*	123	102*	120	100*	–
Rumania	103	98	–	–	100*	105	98*	108	–	–
Eastern Europe	**93**	**71**	**–**	**–**	**105***	**112**	**91***	**95**	**–**	**–**
USSR	103*	110	–	–	99*	100	103*	104	–	–

* 1954–6 (data lacking for 1951–3).
Numbers over 100% signify net exports.

Source: ECE, *Ten years of agricultural trade in Europe*, tables I-8, IV-7, VII-6, V-7 and VI-5. Regional groupings adopted from the original.

problem child of international trade,' read the opening sentence of the 1962 report.[73] Indeed, production and trade figures first of all revealed that 'food Europe' to a large degree was a 'Europe of individual states' which were overwhelmingly self-sufficient in terms of foods (Table 5.3).

With few notable exceptions, the majority of countries were approaching self-sufficiency by 1951; that is, domestic production largely made up total domestic supply (production + net imports). By 1960 the degree of self-sufficiency had often increased rather than decreased; there was little evidence of an emerging system of international specialization and trade replacing the primary organization of food supply within individual countries. By 1960, domestic production of individual countries in Western Europe made up 86% of their total wheat supplies, 95% of meat supplies, 96% of egg supplies, 88% of butter supplies and 99% of cheese supplies. For countries in Eastern Europe the corresponding figures were 71% for wheat, 112% for eggs (figures over 100% denote a modest net export) and 95% for butter; for the Soviet Union 110%, 10% and 104% respectively. Although individual export-oriented countries (e.g. Denmark and the Netherlands) or import-dependent ones (notably the UK) might deviate significantly from the pattern, the main conclusion is that Europe's post-war malnutrition enemy was beaten primarily by national food supply systems rather than by international ones.

The 1962 report was quite explicit about explanations for this strong national dimension in European food supply. Unlike in the 1949 report, transport and quality control issues no longer figured as prominent bottlenecks to international specialization and co-operation. Neither did world market prices, company behaviour, or food production problems – after all, food *had* become abundant in Europe. In the final analysis, the explanation was of a political nature. In all countries in Europe, as the secretariat and the Working Party had already feared back in 1949, national governments had heavily intervened in the agricultural sector. Their agricultural policies were committed to supporting domestic farming sectors by means of financial, technical and educational support, and the creation and protection of domestic food markets. Thus, while international food transports did increase vastly in absolute terms (see below), they were outgrown by even faster increasing food production and distribution within national boundaries.

As for trade that did occur, this massive state interference allegedly made the agricultural sector the most regulated in world trade. Indeed, the 1962 report characterized European trading countries by either 'more or less regulated and protected trade in agricultural products' or by 'outright state trading', categories roughly corresponding to West and East of the Iron Curtain.[74] In the West, national governments supported their domestic agriculture by means of import barriers and export subsidies. In the East, world market prices played an even smaller role as national governments centrally planned their foreign trade (volume, distribution and composition). Nevertheless, the report observed, the absolute volume of trade was expanding, probably even faster than the rise of incomes. The volume of Western European agricultural imports increased by 50% between 1951 and 1960; in Eastern Europe it also grew rapidly, though exact figures were missing.[75]

Who, then, traded with whom? In terms of mesoregional groupings, the report first of all addressed the East–West cleavage, and its conclusions were rather negative. Indeed, one may discern a 'Cold War Europe' in food trade (Table 5.4). In the late 1950s the OEEC countries (a category then over-lapping with some 90% of the category 'Western Europe') acquired some 27% of its imports from the OEEC area, a mere 3% from Eastern Europe, and no less than 70% from outside Europe. The report lacked comparable data for Eastern Europe, but estimated that most agricultural trade took place within that region, followed by trade with the rest of the world and, finally, Western Europe. East–West trade, then, was marginal. The pattern, of course, did not fit all countries and commodities; for instance, 82% of Poland's meat exports, 77% of its butter exports and 94% of its egg exports went to Western Europe.[76]

Three more conclusions were drawn from the table. First, intra-regional trade in both Eastern and Western Europe was substantial for all perisha-bles. In Eastern Europe, this was also the case for wheat. Second, especially for Western Europe, imports from the 'rest of the world' were substan-tial. Wheat, predominantly imported from the United States and Canada,

Table 5.4   Imports in Western and Eastern Europe by origin 1957–60

	Western European imports from (dollar%)			Eastern European imports from (weight%)		
	Western Europe	Eastern Europe	Rest of the world	Western Europe	Eastern Europe	Rest of the world
Wheat	10.4	8.3	81.3	0.8	82.1	17.1
Meat	51.8	8.2	40.0			
Butter	44.7	3.7	51.6	17.3	75.0	7.7
Cheese	67.2	0.6	32.2			
Eggs	71.1	11.9	17.0	5.8	36.6	57.6
Fruits	43.2	0.8	56.0			
All agricultural products*	28.7*	2.3*	70.5*			

* Figures for the OEEC area, then comprising over 90% of the category 'Western Europe'.

Source: ECE, *Ten years*, tables 3, 4 and 5.

dominated the aggregate figure. As for perishables, the significance of overseas trade fluctuated. The figure for meat imports, for instance, is misleading because it was largely made up by British imports (some 70–80% of this figure); much meat (particularly Irish, Danish, Yugoslavian, Austrian and French) was traded within the region. Fruits, by contrast, were predominantly imported from overseas. The most traded commodity, citrus fruits, arrived from North and South Africa, Latin America, Israel and the US, in addition to regional suppliers such as Spain, Italy and Greece. Ninety % of all bananas, the second biggest group, came from overseas (and 10% from Spain's Canary Islands). Transatlantic and post-colonial food relationships, too, heavily characterized the 'food Europe' of 1960.

Third and finally, the 1962 report found the impact on food supply of organizations such as the Council of Mutual Economic Assistance CMEA (1949) and the European Economic Community EEC (1957), forerunner to the European Union (1992), quite limited so far. The 1960s might produce a turning point: the 1962 CMEA congress in Moscow promised a change from bilateral to multilateral co-ordination of food supply in Eastern Europe. In the same year the six EEC members agreed on a Common Agricultural Policy. The UN ECE report, however, was sceptical on both initiatives, and expected a food Europe of relatively autonomous states to endure for some time to come. Either way the EEC certainly was not responsible for beating Europe's malnutrition enemy in the 1950s, though today EU proponents regularly claim the credit for bringing peace and prosperity to the subcontinent.

Conclusion

Conventional wisdom, cited in the introduction to this chapter, holds that the nutritional transition in Europe was brought about by the mobility of food enabled by global transport and communication revolutions. This chapter has shown, however, that mediations between 'food', 'transnational infrastructure' and 'Europe' were much more complicated. We may conclude, especially from the 1962 statistical survey on European agricultural trade, that Europe's post-Second World War malnutrition enemy was beaten not by the new international cold chains constructed in the 1950s, but by national ones – although international food chains certainly gained in prominence later on. By 1960 national cold chains still constituted the gravity points in Europe's transnational cold chains, while linkages between them were relatively weak. We may also conclude that, if international infrastructure did not initially create European diets of variety and abundance, the reverse relationship can be documented: visions of a healthy European diet inspired and helped shape cross-border European food infrastructure, in particular the construction of an international cold chain.

This chapter took a particular organization – the UN ECE – as a privileged research entry. If historiography is about drawing conclusions from well-defined sources, the present study demonstrated that investigating this organization as a food system-builder brings into view a number of food–infrastructure–Europe mediations on a pan-continental scale. For instance, at the discursive level the UN ECE incessantly promoted the notion of 'all of Europe', in this case by posing a pan-continentally integrated food economy as the solution to the endemic malnutrition problem of the late 1940s. According to several UN historians, keeping this broad notion of Europe alive in severely adverse times of nationalism and Cold War tensions, when 'Europe' was increasingly equated with states in Western Europe, may have been a major contribution to the course of contemporary European history.[77] Furthermore, at a practical level this research strategy made visible how an array of international organizations collaborated on international cold chains. The role of international organizations in food supply has regularly been criticized for overlap and redundancy, poor exploitation of complementarities, bureaucracy, and lack of power and impact.[78] Yet it was precisely the overlapping effort of multiple organizations that produced the context in which international cold chain-building was possible, rather than a single strong organization such as the EEC. Third, this research strategy provided at least some insights into the negotiated and uneven character of this system-building effort. As a weak yet centrally positioned agency, the UN ECE monitored and articulated who was in and who was out. It observed a group of front-runners, including major food exporting countries from North-Western Europe plus Italy, which stood to gain economically from increased food trade. Southern and Eastern European countries joined later, if at all. Fourth and finally, UN ECE data gathering and analysis allowed us to find 'Europe' in food flows by 1960, revealing a transnational configuration of cold chains with gravity points in national food systems, clear Cold War features, and notable impacts of transatlantic and post-colonial relations.

Other features of Europe's emerging transnational food system were not found in the selected sources. Though a qualified pan-European observer, the UN ECE typically missed those voices not represented in the organization, such as nations without a state (Catalonia or Cold War Slovakia) or social groups with low political representation. A transnational European history of food and infrastructure should certainly be aware of such categories, which merit further investigation. Still, this chapter demonstrated how a research focus on pan-European organizations such as the UN ECE can bring into view a much broader picture of European food infrastructure integration and fragmentation than has hitherto been the case in existing national comparative studies.

Notes

1. Secretariat of the Economic Commission for Europe, 'Survey on transport of perishable foodstuffs' (2 May 1949, restricted document E/ECE/TRANS/WP.11/1), annex 2, p. 2. UNECE archives (Geneva), G.IX 13/5/1/7 Box 1338 Index 6567.
2. Ibid., chapter VIII, p. 1 and annex 8.

3. For a vivid articulation see Gunnar Myrdal, 'Twenty years of Economic Commission for Europe', *International Organization* 22(3) (1968): 617–28. For a recent UNECE history and further references see Yves Berthelot and Paul Rayment, 'The ECE: a bridge between east and West', in Yves Berthelot (ed) *Unity and diversity in development ideas. Perspectives from the UN regional commissions* (Bloomington: Indiana University Press 2004), pp. 51–131.

4. See Schipper et al., in this volume

5. For this approach see Erik van der Vleuten, Irene Anastasiadou, Frank Schipper and Vincent Lagendijk, 'Europe's system builders', *Contemporary European history* 16 (2007), pp. 321–47. It builds on Thomas Hughes, *Networks of power. Electrification in Western society 1880–1930* (Baltimore: Johns Hopkins University Press 1983).

6. For example, the *International Commission for Research into European Food History* (1989); see www.vub.ac.be/SGES/ICREFH.html (accessed 25 February 2009).

7. For a masterful narrative see Massimo Montanari, *The culture of food* (Blackwell 1996; Italian orig. 1993), published in Jacques le Goff's *The making of Europe* series.

8. David Grigg, 'The nutritional transition in Western Europe', *Journal of historical geography* 22(1) (1995), pp. 247–61; Grigg, 'The changing geography of world food consumption in the second half of the twentieth century', *The geographical journal* 165 (1999), pp. 1–11; Derek Oddy and Lydia Petráňová, 'The diffusion of food culture', in Derek Oddy and Lydia Petráňová (eds) *The diffusion of food culture in Europe from the late 18th century to the present day* (Prague: Academia 2005), pp. 18–28.

9. John Kim, 'Nutrition and the decline of mortality', in Kenneth Kiple and Kriemchild Conée Ornelas (eds) *The Cambridge world history of food*, Vol II (Cambridge: Cambridge University Press 2000), pp. 1381–9; William Muraskin, 'Nutrition and mortality decline: Another view', Ibid., pp. 1389–97.

10. Gretel Pelto and Pertti Pelto, 'Diet and delocalization: Dietary changes since 1750', in Robert Rotberg and Theodore Rabb (eds) *Hunger and history. The impact of changing food production and consumption patterns on society* (Cambridge: Cambridge University Press 1983), pp. 309–30.

11. This comparative agenda was defined in Hans Teuteberg (ed.), *European food history. A research overview* (Leicester: Leicester University Press 1992). It characterizes, for example, John Burnett and Derek Oddy (eds), *The Origins and Development of Food Policies in Europe* (Leicester: Leicester University Press 1994); Adel P. den Hartog (ed.), *Food Technology, Science and Marketing: European Diet in the Twentieth Century* (East Linton: Tuckwell Press 1995); Peter Scholliers (ed.), *Food, drink, and identity. Cooking, eating and drinking in Europe since the middle ages* (Oxford: Berg 2001); Marc Jacobs and Peter Scholliers (eds), *Eating out in Europe. Picnics, gourmet dining and snacks since the late eighteenth century* (Oxford: Berg 2003); Carmen Sarasúa, Peter Scholliers and Leen van Molle (eds), *Land, shops and kitchens. Technology and the food chain in twentieth-century Europe* (Turnhout: Brepols 2005); and Oddy and Petráňová (eds), *The diffusion of food culture in Europe* (Prague: Academia 2005). Beyond Europe the nation-centred framework of analysis is also dominant, for example Warren Belasco and Philip Scranton (eds), *Food nations. Selling taste in consumer societies* (New York: Routledge 2002).

12. Anneke Van Otterloo, 'Fast food and slow food. The fastening food chain and recurrent countertrends in Europe and the Netherlands (1890–1990)', in Sarasúa *et al.*, *Land, shops and kitchens*, pp. 255–77, takes one single country as a model for 'Europe'. A. Lynn Martin, 'Old people, alcohol and identity in Europe 1300–1700', in Scholliers, *Food, drink and identity*, pp. 119–37, takes three countries. Adel den

Hartog, 'Technological innovations and eating out as a mass phenomenon in Europe: a preamble', in Jacobs and Scholliers, *Eating out*, pp. 265–80, makes a larger but still exclusively Western European selection.

13. For further discussion and references see Erik van der Vleuten, 'Toward a Transnational History of Technology', *Technology & Culture* 49 (2008), pp. 974–94. See also the introduction to this volume.

14. Carmen Sarasúa and Peter Scholliers, 'The rise of a food market in European history' in Sarasúa *et al.*, *Land, shops and kitchens*, pp. 13–29; Van Otterloo, 'Fast food'.

15. The concept is thus much older than often assumed: Roger Thévenot, *A history of refrigeration throughout the world* (Paris: IIR 1979), pp. 105–6.

16. Explicitly in Erik van der Vleuten, 'In search of the Networked Nation', *European Review of History* 10 (2003), pp. 59–78. Compare Barbara Orland, 'Milky ways. Dairy, landscape and nation building until 1930', in Sarasúa, Scholliers and Van Molle *Land, shops and Kitchens*, pp. 212–54; Shane Hamilton, 'Trucking country: Food politics and the transformation of rural life in postwar America', *Enterprise & Society* 7 (2006), pp. 666–74.

17. Van der Vleuten, 'In search of the Networked Nation'. Inspired by Ingo Braun, 'Geflügelte Saurier. Zur intersystemische vernetzung grosser technische Netze' in Ingo Braun and Bernward Joerges (eds) *Technik ohne Grenzen* (Frankfurt: Suhrkamp 1994), pp. 446–500.

18. 'Institutional uses' here refers to the dictionary meaning of formal, real organization structures (as opposed to informal institutions) that structure social order, possess a social purpose and permanence, and transcend the individual level. It adds to a large literature on the uses of technology that predominantly studies individual end-users and their representing organizations. Van der Vleuten, 'In Search of the Networked Nation.'

19. This form of transnational history is contrasted with other forms (cross-border studies and international organization studies) in Van der Vleuten, 'Towards a transnational history of technology.' Another example from infrastructure history is Van der Vleuten et al., 'Europe's system builders.'

20. Ezekiel (FAO) to Doré (FAO), 5 February 1948. UNECE archives (Palais des Nations, Geneva), G.IX 13/5/2 box 1337 index 3352.

21. Inland Transport Committee, 'Transport of perishable foodstuffs. Resolution No. 18' (6 February 1948, restricted document E/ECE/TRANS/64). UNECE archives, G.IX 13/5/1/1 box 1337 index 3323.

22. David Wightman, 'East-West cooperation and the United Nations Economic Commission for Europe', *International Organization* 11(1) (1957), pp. 1–12, on p. 1.

23. For a survey see David Wightman, *Economic Co-Operation in Europe. A study of the United Nations Economic Commission for Europe* (London: Stevens & Sons 1956); Jean Siotis, *ECE in the emerging European system* (New York: Carnegie endowment for international peace 1967); ECE, *ECE, The first ten years 1947–1957* (Geneva: United Nations 1957); ECE, *Fifteen years of activity of the Economic Commission for Europe 1947–1962* (New York: United Nations 1964). For a sceptical view see Brian Tew, 'Economic co-operation in Europe', *The economic journal* 67(265) (1957), pp. 110–11.

24. ECE Secretariat, 'Note on short-term problems raised by the transport of perishable foodstuffs' (20 February 1948), sent as annex to request to governments concerned. The replies were analysed in ECE Secretariat, 'Transport of perishable

foodstuffs. Note by the Secretariat' (28 April 1948, restricted document E/ECE/Trans/85). UNECE archives, GIX 13/5/1/1 box 1337 index 3323.

25. Food and Agriculture Organization, *European programmes of agricultural reconstruction and development* (Washington: FAO 1948), p. 5.
26. Ibid., annex 2, p. 2.
27. ECE Secretariat, 'Survey on transport of perishable foodstuffs', chapter II, p. 1.
28. J.M. Latsky, 'The nutritional importance of perishable foods', in ECE 'Survey on transport of perishable foodstuffs', Annex 2 B.
29. ECE Secretariat, 'Survey on transport of perishable foodstuffs', annex 2, p. 1.
30. Ibid., annex 2A.
31. Ibid., annex 2, p. 2.
32. Yves Berthelot, 'Unity and diversity of development: The regional commissions' experience' in Bethelot (ed.) *Unity and diversity in development ideas*, pp. 1–50.
33. Jean Siotis, 'The secretariat of the United Nations Economic Commission for Europe and European economic integration: the first ten years', *International Organization* 19(2) (1965), pp. 177–202.
34. Incidentally, trade made up a minor part of supply. For instance, fish trade made up some 20 per cent of fish supply. Calculated on the basis of fishing totals of 4,326 thousand metric tons in Nils Jangaard, 'Preliminary statement by FAO fisheries division regional office for Europe on European fisheries' interests in the inter-European transport question' (March 1948). UNECE archives, GIX/13/5/2 box 1337 index 3352.
35. ECE Secretariat, 'Survey on transport of perishable foodstuffs', Preface and summary, p. 3.
36. Ibid., chapters IV and V and annexes 4, 4A, 5 and 5A.
37. Ibid., Preface and summary, p. 4. For the following see particularly chapter VII.
38. 'Miscellaneous notes on the refrigerator chain', ibid., annex 7, p. 1.
39. ECE Secretariat, 'Survey on transport of perishable foodstuffs', chapter I, p. 1.
40. Historians in the UN Intellectual History Project count producing and propagating such *ideas* among the most important UN contributions to development: for example Louis Emmerij, Richard Jolly and Thomas G. Weiss, 'Economic and social thinking at the UN in historical perspective', *Development and change* 36(2) (2005), pp. 211–35.
41. Hughes, *Networks of power*.
42. Working party on the Transport of Perishable Foodstuffs, 'report by the working party on its first session' (11 June 1949. Restricted document E/ECE/Trans/WP.11/3). UNECE archives, G.IX 13/5/2/2 box 1342 index 6688.
43. Nils Jangaard (FAO), 'Statement on trade and transport of fishery products in Europe' (not dated; early 1948). UNECE archives, G.IX 13/5/2 box 1337 index 3352.
44. See session reports 1949–60 in Working Party on the Transport of Perishable Foodstuffs, UNECE archives, G.IX 13/5/2/2 box 1342 index 6688.
45. ECE Secretariat, 'Review of progress made in other studies initated by the working party or by its sub-groups' (31 May 1950, restricted document TRANS/WP11/14) and 'Review of the Working Party's programme and of the possibility of concentrating the studies at present in progress' (18 April 1951, Restricted document TRANS/WP11/32). UNECE archives, G.IX 13/5/2/2 box 1342 index 6688.
46. International Chamber of Commerce, *International transport of Perishable Foodstuffs. ICC Brochure no. 149* (Paris: ICC 1951). Thanks to Frank Schipper for providing this document.

47. 'Report by the Working party on its third (special) session' (30 June 1950, restricted document E/ECE/TRANS/225). Ibid., Index 6688. 'Elimination of, or reduction in, delays at frontiers' (5 April 1951; restricted document TRANS/WP11/28), Ibid. Index 6688. *International Convention to Facilitate the Crossing of Frontiers for Goods carried by Rail* (UNECE: Geneva 10 January 1952).
48. UNECE, *TIR Handbook* (New York/Geneva: United Nations 2002). For Conventions and signatory lists see www.unece.org/trans/conventn/legalinst.html (accessed 21 April 2007).
49. For the troubled early history of this committee see Wightman (1956), pp. 144–53. See also ECE, *Fifteen years*, pp. 40–5.
50. ECE, *Fifteen years*, p. 44.
51. For example, 'Recommendations concerning the standardization of packaging for fruits and vegetables grown in Europe…', annex to 'Report by the Working party on its fourth session' (23 May 1951, Restricted document E/ECE/TRANS/278).
52. *Agreement on the International Carriage of Perishable Foodstuffs and on the Special Equipment to be Used for such Carriage (ATP)* (New York/Geneva: United Nations 1976); *Agreement on the International Carriage of Perishable Foodstuffs and on the Special Equipment to be Used for such Carriage (ATP) as amended on 7 November 2003. ECE/TRANS/165* (New York/Geneva: United Nations 2003), pp. 73, 81.
53. 'Report of the first meeting', p. 14 ff.
54. 'Report of the Working Party on its seventh session' (2 April 1953, restricted document TRANS/WP11/84), ibid. Index 6688, p. 8.
55. *Transfrigoroute Europe* (Brochure, Basel, no date, presumably late 1950s). UNECE archives, G. IX 13/5/2/11 Box 1345 Index 13106.
56. Beatrice Rohen, *50 years of Transfrigoroute International. A retrospective of the early years and the most important developments* (Bern: 2005); *Statutes 29 June 2005*, available on www.transfrigo.com (accessed 25 February 2009).
57. Compare Van der Vleuten *et al.*, 'Europe's system builders.'
58. Myrdal, 'Twenty years', pp. 618–19.
59. For a survey see Erik van der Vleuten, 'Institutional uses of infrastructures: a research strategy for studying European food chains. TIE working document no. 19' (Eindhoven 2007), p. 11 ff. Available at www.tie-project.nl (accessed 1 August 2008).
60. For the following see the individual session reports in 'Transport of perishable foodstuffs. Working Party: Record of meetings and reports 1949–1960.' UNECE archives, G. IX 13/5/2/2/ box 1342, index 1342.
61. The contracting parties to UNECE legal instruments are listed at http://www.unece.org/trans/conventn/legalinst.html (accessed 25 February 2009).
62. *General Agreement on economic regulations for international road transport and set of rules. Protocol relating to the adoption of annex C.1: Transport of perishable foodstuffs* (Geneva, 1 July 1954). The British declined because regulation of road traffic would hamper, not stimulate, this form of transport. 'Comment of her Majesty's Government on the draft annex C.1…' (3 June 1954). UNECE archives, G.IX 13/5/2/12 Index 16031.
63. 'Report of the Working Party on its eighth session' (11 March 1954, restricted document TRANS/135). 'Draft report of the working party on its eleventh session' (14 June 1956, restricted document TRANS/WP11/Conf.Room Doc 3).
64. Czechoslovakia 1982; Poland 1983; Hungary 1987; Rumania 1999. *Agreement on the International Carriage of Perishable Foodstuffs and on the Special Equipment to be Used for such Carriage (ATP)* (New York/Geneva: United Nations 1976).

65. 'Report of the first meeting', p. 14 ff.
66. Ibid., p. 17.
67. 'Intra-European list of customs offices en route at which TRANSFRIGOROUTE requests priority clearance and frontier checking of special vehicles', annex to ECE, 'Difficulties encountered'.
68. 'Granting of facilities to "Transfrigoroute Europe" vehicles. Note by the Secretariat' (21 November 1956, restricted document W/TRANS/230). UNECE archives, 13/5/2/11 Box 1345 Index 13106.
69. Ibid., p. 3.
70. ECE, 'Difficulties encountered by "Transfrigoroute" vehicles at frontiers. Note by the Secretariat' (28 February 1957, restricted document TRANS/WP30/Conf.Room Doc. 19), p. 2; compare 'Transfrigoroute. Communication from the International Road Transport Union' (14 May 1956, restricted document W/Trans/WP11/65). UNECE archives, index 16031.
71. 'Difficulties encountered at frontiers by road vehicles transporting perishable foodstuffs' (15 October 1957, restricted document W/TRANS/WP30/82). UNECE archives, ibid.
72. ECE, *Ten years of agricultural trade in Europe 1951–1960* (United Nations: Geneva 1962). The following data are taken from this report unless otherwise noted.
73. Ibid., p. 4.
74. Ibid., p. 5.
75. Ibid., pp. 15–16.
76. Ibid., p. 13.
77. Berthelot (ed.), *Unity and diversity*; Emmerij et al., 'Economic and social thinking at the UN.'
78. For a discussion see Raymond Hopkins and Donald Puchala, 'Perspectives on the international relations of food', *International Organization* 32(3) (1978), pp. 581–616, on p. 610.

Biography 4: Mobilizing Europe's Capital

Frank Schipper

There have always been those who thought Europe would best be governed by uniting Eurocrats in splendid isolation. The correspondence of Paul Hoffman, Administrator of the Economic Cooperation Administration steering the Marshall Plan for European reconstruction, contains a letter claiming 'Europe needs a Canberra center, viz. a place where people from all states of Europe would live together all the year round in order TO STUDY how to further international connections.' A loan of 1 million dollars would allow constructing the right place; the author suggested Corsica as an adequate choice. Yet often proposals for housing Europe's decision-making institutions concerned urban settings rather than marginal outposts. Becoming the residence for such organizations had a profound impact on the fabric of urban infrastructures and simultaneously gave occasion to a discussion on connections between the would-be capital and its continental hinterland.

If people were asked to identify the capital of Europe today, it is increasingly likely they would pick Brussels as their answer. The EU's complex spatial set-up with dispersed capital functions concentrated in Luxembourg and Strasbourg and countless agencies scattered around the continent notwithstanding, the Belgian capital seems to be emerging victorious out of a hard-fought competition among several contenders. In the beauty contest among the various candidate capitals of the 1950s, being a 'node' enhanced the chances of being chosen. Maps displaying the excellent air or railway links supported the bids of Nice, Strasbourg and Stresa. The massive public works projects preparing Brussels for the Expo '58, including major road works and the improvement of Zaventem airport, supported the Belgian ambition to host the European organizations.

In many ways, Geneva was Brussels' predecessor in the period prior to the Second World War. Infrastructural connections from and to Geneva were a primary concern for the League of Nations Secretariat and its various technical committees. In November 1924 Athanase Politis, vice-chair of the subcommittee for transport by rail, reported on his participation in the European conference on timetables in Naples. The subcommittee members had condemned

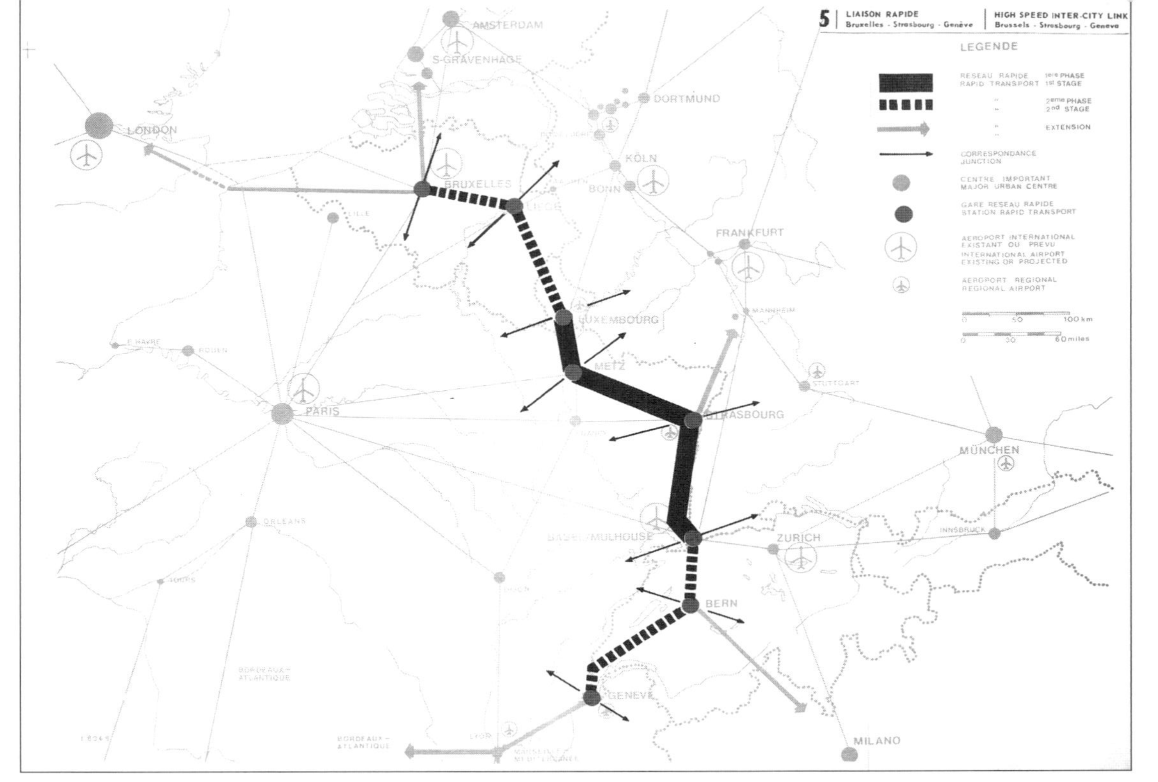

Figure B4.1 Proposed 'Eurometro' link, 1972

Source: Courtesy of the Council of Europe.

existing connections as 'inadequate' and 'inconvenient'. In Naples Politis therefore urged the delegates of the railway administrations to improve railroad services between Geneva and the 'principal capitals of Europe' to facilitate the arrival and departure of those who came to Geneva 'to place at the disposal of the world their knowledge and experience'. Although infrastructural connections gradually improved over the years, the city of peace was by no means placed 'on an entirely equal footing with the great capitals'.

The main function of the League being the maintenance of peace worldwide, communications with Geneva under exceptional circumstances in 'times of emergency' acquired special importance. In 1925 the League had expressly stated that member states were obliged 'to do all in their power to facilitate communications with the League in every form' during a crisis. The League's Committee for Communications and Transit subsequently received instructions in 1927 to examine the subject. (Radio-)telegraphic connections in particular would enable the Council, the League's supreme decision-making body, to 'collect opinions forthwith' and 'put forward suggestions'. In February 1932 the League put a wireless station into use at Prangins in the environs of Geneva. It enabled communications as far as Argentina and Australia. Next to telecommunications, transport aspects were worth considering as well. Special measures were formulated for all modes of transport. As soon as the normal diplomatic machinery of international relations broke down, road vehicles in the service of the League should bear distinctive identification marks like a flag or an S.d.N. (*Societé des Nations*) plate. All details on their itinerary should be swiftly communicated to the governments of the states to be traversed. The same applied to aircraft using the facilities of the improved aerodrome near the League's premises. Geneva's connective capabilities would thus ensure that the Secretariat would optimally keep pace with developments and allow the League to strive for a solution to any conflict that flared up.

Infrastructures even had a quality that allowed overcoming the continuing squabbles over which city to choose as a European capital. A 1972 Council of Europe report declared it would be artificial to pick a single city as a capital and warned against the 'dangerous tendency towards centralisation and concentration'. In its stead, a committee chaired by Mr Radius promoted the creation of 'Europolis', a polycentric capital for the Europe of tomorrow. A high-speed intercity link called 'Eurometro' would join Brussels, Luxembourg, Strasbourg, Basle and Geneva in a polynuclear conurbation. Eurometro's cutting-edge air cushion technology would turn the Brussels–Geneva corridor into a vanguard macropolis. At a speed of 350 kilometres per hour, the new infrastructure would shrink the overland journey to a trip of just 2 hours and 10 minutes, allowing a 2-minute stop at every station. It would finally 'put an end to the pointless disputes concerning "the Capital" of Europe'.

Literature

Carola Hein, *The Capital of Europe: Architecture and Urban Planning for the European Union* (Westport: Praeger 2004).

Consultative Assembly of the Council of Europe, Report on the Organisation of a European Network of Trunk Road Communications as a Part of European Regional Planning (Rapporteur: Mr. Radius) (Strasbourg 1972).

Jauzin to Hoffman, 26 July 1948, box 21, Paul G. Hoffman Papers, Truman Library.

League of Nations, Advisory and Technical Committee for Communications and Transit, Minutes of Seventh Session (26–9 November 1924), Ninth Session (12–17 July 1926) and Fifteenth Session (4–6 September 1930).

League of Nations, Ten Years of World Co-operation (Geneva: Secretariat of the League of Nations 1930).

League of Nations, The Aims, Methods and Activity of the League of Nations (Geneva: Secretariat LoN 1935).

6
Eurocheque: Creating a 'Common Currency' European Infrastructure for the Cashless Mass Payments System

Barbara Bonhage

Introduction

This contribution is concerned with the Eurocheque, an instrument of the European mass payments system for cashless payment that was in use during the last three decades of the twentieth century. European banks introduced the Eurocheque in the late 1960s as a national as well as an international (as the name suggests, *European*) payments instrument. During this decade many banks fostered cashless payment methods in the hope of reducing overall payment costs.

Starting in 1968, Eurocheque could be used in Austria, Belgium, Denmark, the Federal Republic of Germany, Finland, France, Great Britain, Italy, Ireland, Liechtenstein, Luxembourg, Monaco, the Netherlands, Norway, San Marino, Sweden, Switzerland and Spain. At the height of its diffusion in 1998, forty-six countries participated in the Eurocheque system – needless to say some of them were beyond the boundaries of most definitions of 'Europe', and certainly outside the European Union and its predecessors. Among participating countries, many were Eastern European, countries of the Middle East and Maghreb countries. In December 2001, thirty-three years after its introduction, the paper-based history of the Eurocheque came to an end. The cheque was no longer accepted as an international payments instrument; however, it is still used in some countries as a national cashless payments method.

The fundamental precondition for using Eurocheque was having an active bank account. Anyone who had an account could buy Eurocheques at his or her bank and exchange them against cash in a foreign country at the counter of a bank participating in the system. Thus, businesspeople as well as tourists could cover their current needs in cash during a journey in Europe without actually taking cash along. In many European countries during the 1960s banks also introduced the possibility of cashless wage and salary payment. Many salaried and waged employees subsequently disposed over a transactions account, which enabled them to carry out cashless payment, either by the means of a cheque or over the public giro system. With this development during the 1960s, many European banks entered the field of retail banking.

This chapter shows that the Eurocheque's actual success was paradoxically its demise during the 1980s and 1990s. In this phase, Eurocheque in its original paper-based form was replaced step by step by other, increasingly computer-aided payment instruments in the mass payments sector. To trace the social and technological changes connected to this development, three mutually interwoven layers of analysis will lead me through my investigations: *first*, the institutional emergence of a new payments infrastructure; *second*, the Europeanness of the system; and *third*, the role attributed to the USA as both a technological leader and a cultural challenger.

1. The payments infrastructure: We can best begin an analysis of technological change in the payments infrastructure with a brief sketch of general trends in cash-based payment systems. Since the beginning of the twentieth century, payment systems were slowly complemented by cashless payment methods. Cashless payments were at first based on paper, but from the 1970s were based more and more on electronics. Cash-based payment methods in Europe were originally effected as a public service executed in most countries by the national post, telegraph and telephone companies (PTTs). Cashless, electronic payments, by contrast, were carried out later by private companies as a private service through banks.

2. European framework and the Swiss perspective: With the name 'Eurocheque' the infrastructure considered came about in an explicitly European context. However, the term does not refer to a positively defined political, geographical, economic, cultural or other notion of Europe. Upon closer examination, the 'Euro' in 'Eurocheque' is a negative definition, which means 'not-American'. Looking at the case from the Swiss perspective demonstrates this aspect quite well: Switzerland was one of the leading countries in so far as infrastructural development is concerned, but at the same time never belonged to the EU politically, and only partially economically. The infrastructure thus developed totally decoupled from the political process of unification, but includes different aspects of social and cultural affiliation.

3. The USA as role model and object of delineation: The leading force for establishing a European cashless payments method was developments in the USA in a technological as well as a cultural dimension. The aim of the Eurocheque infrastructure was to offer a European version of cashless payment methods, which would keep mostly credit card-based American systems from entering the market. At the same time, American technological developments were thoroughly observed in order to catch any opportunity of using promising electronic technologies developed in the US. European banks were very eager to keep up with overseas developments.

Cashless payment means in Europe and in the USA

During the 1960s payment habits and payment options for the general public in Europe were quite different from those in the USA. Cashless salary payment to employees by cheque was common outside Europe, though employees did not necessarily dispose over a banking account. In most parts of Europe, the pay packet was the prevailing vessel for salary and wages payment. The cheque was known in principle, of course, long before the introduction of the Eurocheque. In France and Great Britain – the so-called cheque countries – it was actually quite common. In contrast, in Switzerland, Germany, the Netherlands and Sweden – the so-called giro countries – cheques circulated, but played a relatively minor role. Still, everywhere in Europe most people used cash almost exclusively for everyday payments. Salary and wages were paid in cash. Rents and bills were paid in at the post offices. Cashless payments only played a role in the institutional sector. They were used for transactions between banks, between the PTTs and banks or the central banks. In the mass payments sector, that is, payments for the public, cashless transactions were used rarely or – as for example in Switzerland before the 1960s – not at all.

During the 1960s, European banks began to assure themselves of the fact that cashless payments needed to be developed for the broader public as well. One by one they entered the so-called retail banking business, dealing with the smallest amounts of income and fortune. The banks hoped that this would generate an inflow of assets on their liabilities side, which certainly would be able to stimulate their credit business. All of the participating banking institutions agreed to foster cashless payments methods because they generally assumed that this would reduce overall payment costs. Investigations in Switzerland showed that during the 1970s expenses in the mass payments sector represented 1 to 2% of the gross national product.[1] On top of that, it was to be expected at the beginning of the 1980s that costs in the payments systems would rise in all European countries annually by 7 to 10%.[2] If the population could be brought to make more of their common payments on a cashless basis, they assumed, costs in the payments sector would rise much more slowly.

It is important to note that cashless payment with Eurocheque was based technologically on the exchange of records made of paper, not of information available electronically. The administration of the records required almost endless manual labour. The idea of a remotely controlled electronic data processing system for cashless payments did emerge around this time, but not in Europe. In the USA, bankers were very excited about the possibilities of electronics for the payments infrastructure. They started to imagine a payments system based principally on electronic data transfer. Even if they were still far away from implementing this kind of system, excerpts from American branch magazines show that bankers imagined that electronic funds transfer systems would soon arrive. Dale L. Reistad, for example, deputy manager of the American Bankers Association (ABA), stated in 1967 that all paper would be replaced by 'terminals, communication links, computers, and related technologies in a system based on electronic fund transfers' as early as 1980. The explicitly declared aim of the 'Chequeless Society Committee' of the ABA was the total substitution of cheques and cash by the use of new funds transfer systems, based on digital information and communication technologies.[3] The technological means would radically alter the banking business and the payment habits of the people:

> Joe Smith is travelling and needs some ready cash. He goes into a bank and presents an identification card (the only card he has to carry) to a teller, who puts the card into a terminal box. A green light appears. The teller punches a few buttons and hands Joe his money. Joe signs a receipt. Joe is not worried about the size of the balance in his bank account back home because the day before was payday, and his employer passed the funds through the wire transfer system to his bank. Joe also knows his money is 'good' money. Even if his wife has been drawing on their joint account, the bank (through a loan agreement) guarantees to place the necessary funds at his disposal. [...] Every few days Joe takes his machine-readable bills to a pay station on the corner. He calls the central computer exchange and inserts his identification card into a slot. A verification voice acknowledges him. One by one he drops in his bills, and the voice repeats instructions until the last bill has been processed.[4]

Robert Kramer and Putnam Livingston, working for Bankers Trust Company, were also convinced in the 1960s that the state of the art in technological development would allow these kinds of systems to be introduced in the financial sector. They saw questions of how to finance the systems, how to educate people to use them, and how to market them as the remaining issues to be resolved.[5] The idea of a 'paperless', 'chequeless' or 'cashless' society was ubiquitous in the USA during the 1960s. However, the transition from cash and paper-based transactions to digital data transfer of funds in the US lasted almost as long as in Europe. Only at the beginning of the 1980s did the first digital systems in customer-oriented banking services become operational.[6] Nowhere did the full substitution of cash occur, nor has it to this day.

Even if the American ideas of the 1960s were far from being realized, however, they were quite significant for the intense pressure they placed on European bankers. They felt they were in an inferior position given the technological possibilities of the time. However, European conditions differed fundamentally from the American ones. On the old continent payment infrastructures had been built up across numerous small markets with different currencies. European banks did not principally focus on electronically based systems but saw two possibilities for fostering cashless payment practices for the public: offering transaction accounts and fostering giro payment methods on the one hand and promoting cheques as a means of payment on the other. Both methods would internationalize payment methods by using already available channels for the exchange of records, above all the public postal service.

In Switzerland it was known in 1962 that banks and the PTT together handled 350 billion francs in the cashless mass payments sector. This total amount could be raised, along with the share of it going to the banks, by increasing the use of cheques. Banks hoped that the costs for the handling of cash-based payments – in particular security measurements – would thus diminish remarkably. Therefore, the Swiss Bankers Association (SBA) decided in 1963 to campaign for cheque payments.[7] A uniform national or Europe-wide cheque system was not yet agreed upon, however. Banks were simply asked to increase the number of their existing cheques that they issued. With regard to their principal aim of fostering cashless payment methods, it seems that European bankers often referred to the American practices as a role model, often without really knowing what their system was. They stated that cashless payments were quite common in the US. 'It principally is accomplished weekly and most of all by the cheque, the cashless means of payment used there almost exclusively.'[8] Despite the common use of cheques in the US, many elements of the US system differed fundamentally from the European impression of it. Indeed, it is striking how little attention the bankers gave to these discrepancies while repeatedly taking the American system as a role model. In the US, for example, an account relationship with a bank was not necessary to be able to make use of a cheque. In Europe, the promotion of cashless payment methods went hand in hand with the promotion of private bank accounts for everyone.

In Germany the promotion of cashless wage and salary payments started during the 1950s. Larger industrial companies agreed with banks upon cashless salary payment.[9] At first, banks met the industrial initiatives with scepticism. Even if they were ready to foster cashless payments, they were afraid of the surplus work of serving their new clients and dealing with the masses of records that would result from introducing transaction accounts for people with low income and savings. Nevertheless, they welcomed the surplus of money to be worked with in their credit business. At first only a few banks were ready to work together with the industries. Over the course of the 1960s, however, so many banks had dared to enter the retail banking that the rest began to fight for their share of the market.

Between 1969 and 1971 most of the banks in Switzerland introduced transaction accounts.[10] Compared with other Western European countries, this step was belated by 5 to 10 years. In any event, wages and salary payment through a bank account instead of in a pay packet grew common all over Europe within only a decade. In 1978 in Switzerland 40% of the working population got their salaries by a cashless transfer to an account.[11] Only four years later, in 1982, they were the majority.[12] It was this rise in private bank accounts that facilitated access to the Eurocheque, the new European cashless means of payment for private individuals.

As it had been in promoting cheques, America was also considered a role model with the introduction of the transaction accounts, even if, again, many things were quite different. The industries stated that, with a transactions account, 'a transfer of functions from other branches to the appropriate economic sectors, in effect the banks, occurs. [...] In the USA operational side functions have long since been factored out and made independent.'[13] The success of the American economy, which was generally explained by the reduction of industries to their core competences, played an important role in expanding cashless payment means during the 1970s in Europe.

Not only in Switzerland, but in other European countries as well, in the early 1980s bringing the masses into the banking system was achieved by widespread opening up of transfer accounts. 'In competing for deposits, the banks in all countries succeeded in greatly increasing the banking habit. In the main industrialized countries there are now only small percentages of the population who have no form of account relationship with a bank and in most cases a majority of the population now has access to and uses the non-cash payment services provided.'[14] The Eurocheque system, founded in 1968, was part of these new cashless payment methods promoted by the banks. It was subject to the same technological and social possibilities, as well as restrictions, as other cashless payment means. Critics had always warned that introducing Eurocheque would generate an overwhelming flood of paper. This Cassandra's call came all too true, as will be shown further on. Hope was placed on the American electronically supported systems, which, it was said, would run peerlessly.[15] This concept of the existence of a progressive and electronic American payments system was typical of European perceptions but did not correspond with reality. Rather, it was part of a European methodization of American developments during the 1960s and 1970s.

Eurocheque, regional mobility and credit cards

European bankers not only took American developments in the mass payments sector as a role model, they also perceived them as a threat to their own market. Many believed that American systems were further developed technologically. 'The technological backwardness of Europe reveals itself most alarmingly in the field of computers [...]. As far as computers are concerned, the state of not being able any more to catch up could be reached at any moment. [...] With the computers one can see if Europe is still alive!'[16] In the field of payments, the feeling of backwardness was expressed repeatedly, particularly in reference to the credit card. Many European banks insinuated that these systems were running on an electronic basis during the 1970s. Thus, in further developing the Eurocheque system, European bankers during the 1970s tried to protect the European market against American influences, especially credit card companies. They assumed that in Europe, as was the case in the USA, non-banks active in this field would also enter the consumer credit business.

With this in mind, European banks observed the development of American credit card systems during the 1960s carefully. To the banks, it seemed obvious that American companies would attempt to expand especially into the travel and entertainment sector. The 1960s and 1970s in Europe were marked by booming regional mobility. Not only tourism but business travelling also increased during this time of intensive economic growth. 'The object of America's interest is the change of the European market into a typical leisure time market. Travelling nowadays is a basic need; the increasing regional mobility resulting from it leads to higher travel expenses and this in turn reinforces the demand on payment services.'[17] This imagined change of everyday habits made the perception of an American threat even more justified. On top of that, the bankers knew that the revenues from the credit card business in the States had begun to stagnate. To the European banks, it seemed obvious that American companies would enlarge their radius of action to Europe to profit from further economies of scale and to diminish transaction costs. Given the American threat and the small national markets, co-operation between European countries became more and more significant. In addition, European bankers assumed that business and tourism travelling would be rather limited to the continent of Europe for the foreseeable future. A system that was applicable worldwide, or co-operation with American institutions, thus did not seem necessary.[18] At the same time, high development costs for electronic applications did demand a common European solution to get to a cross-border payments system. Several concurring systems in Europe were to be avoided at all costs.[19]

The Eurocheque system, together with the masses of transaction accounts in the hands of banks, proved to be an important milestone for further developments in a common European mass payments system. These happened in strict delineation to the concurring American credit card institutions. The European banks, therefore, agreed in 1972 to issue a standardized guarantee card for Eurocheque keepers. With this card a bank that had issued Eurocheques to a certain customer guaranteed that this client was creditworthy. Together with the guarantee card, the Eurocheque could now be used in any participating bank like a credit card.[20] It was accepted by all the banks involved in the Eurocheque system. Existing national experiences in several countries facilitated a fast introduction of the European guarantee card. Some countries already disposed of a nationally applicable guarantee card to be combined with locally used cheques. In Switzerland, for example, a uniform guarantee card of all Swiss banks had been circulating since 1969.[21] As with the European guarantee card three years later, it aimed at fostering cashless payment and at increasing acceptance of the cheque.[22]

However, not only the Eurocheque system benefited from experiences made on a national level. On the flip side, the existing national systems also profited from the standardization that occurred through the Eurocheque system. A similar Swiss guarantee card, which circulated in addition to the so-called Swiss Cheque, could now be used also in foreign countries and could be used in Switzerland instead of the Eurocheque card. All these cards could only be used with banks, and not yet at the point of sale of a retailer.[23] Over the course of the 1970s Swiss banks totally adapted their own Swiss Cheque system to the Eurocheque system. The Swiss Cheque and the Swiss guarantee card disappeared. Also in other countries national cheque systems stopped and were replaced by the internationally standardized Eurocheque system. In 1978 the community of the Eurocheque card holders all over Europe counted 28 million individuals. Meanwhile, thirty-nine European and Mediterranean countries participated in the system.

Step by step, these guarantee cards were enhanced not only organizationally but also technically. The magnetic strip added to the card, and agreements with retailers, facilitated its use also in the retail branch. Moreover, it now could be used to withdraw cash at automated teller machines (ATMs). From 1975 on, in the Benelux countries, the Federal Republic of Germany, Finland, France, Great Britain, Ireland and Switzerland, tourists could pay in many stores and hotels with Eurocheque and the guarantee card.[24] Thus, the Eurocheque system came more and more to resemble the American credit card systems. In contrast to the US system, however, it was meant to be used as a debit card. While credit cards enable cash or commodity supply over a credit system, with a debit card the needed amount is directly debited from the bank account without making any credit system effective. It was therefore the massive introduction of the transaction accounts opened up during the 1960s and 1970s that granted access to this new payments instrument to the masses of individual clients. At the same time, these accounts, combined with the Eurocheque system, helped European banks to place themselves in a more advantageous position with regard to the American credit card institutions.

Supplementary to the Eurocheque and guarantee card system, European banks co-ordinated their efforts on another payment means to foster cashless transactions: they planned to create a European credit card. Already in 1964, Eurocard International SA was founded in Brussels as a Swedish initiative. Only in the second half of the 1970s was the card issued, however. From 1978 on, more and more European banks associated themselves with the system. These banks issued national standardized credit cards to be used across the European borders. The credit card enabled cashless shopping, payment in restaurants, and cashless payment for hotels and travel.[25]

Like the guarantee card and the Eurocheque, this European credit card system remained strictly in the possession of banks. Non-banking institutions did not enter into competition in the sector: here as well, the declared aim was to block the introduction of any other payment card. Furthermore, as was underlined, the banks kept the responsibility for administration and control of cashless mass payments. Moreover, offering Eurocard and Eurocheque would continue to win clients for the bank agencies in the consumer credit sector.[26] With this as a welcome side effect, the broad network of agencies that was typical of the European banking system of this time would retain its traditional role.

With the creation of the European credit card, the demarcation against the American market was an important issue during its introduction. Many of the European bankers were convinced that American credit card companies would be tempted to take over the Eurocard companies in the European countries. They believed US companies wanted to acquire the European market, abolish the cheque card system and replace it with credit cards, controlled from the USA.[27] Dr Eckard van Hooven, president of the commission for retail banking of the German association of banks and member of the board of directors of the Deutsche Bank AG in Frankfurt, was convinced that European co-operation in the payments system for the public had to be reinforced. Only then would they be able to strengthen the debtor's side of the credit institutes, together with the whole banking system, in the long run. The American temptation 'to bias or even acquire large parts of the European consumer market' seemed to him quite threatening. Only through joint European co-operation could substantial annoyances in the market be avoided. Either European credit institutions would become agents of sales for American credit card organizations or they would succeed in implementing a specifically European solution by designing a European payments system.[28] He was convinced that 'with the acquisition of Eurocard by European credit institutes, they could confront the endeavours of the Americans in a sector for which a plastic card should be designed in Europe as well; a so-called T&E, Travel & Entertainment Card for global travelling'.[29] The bankers themselves argued constantly over whether Eurocard was indeed better able than the Eurocheque system to answer the American threat in the credit card sector – certainly coming from American Express, Diners Club or Visa.

To answer that question, representatives of the top management of European banks from Belgium, Denmark, France, Great Britain, Ireland, the Netherlands, Switzerland and the Federal Republic of Germany conjoined on 15 September 1978 into a 'European Council for Payment Systems'. Eurocard, Hooven was convinced, should become 'the core for a European credit card policy'. The Eurocheque system should be abolished step by step in favour of a European credit card. On top of that, he pleaded foresight-edly not only for European co-operation in the field of the Eurocheque and Eurocard, but also on the basis of planned ATMs.[30]

In 1978 the Federal Republic of Germany, Denmark, Switzerland, banking groups in Great Britain, France, Italy, Sweden and Spain were affiliated with the Eurocard system. The Benelux countries were preparing to take the same step. By going together in the Eurocard system, the guarantee card and the Eurocheque system cashless payments systems – which became more and more popular – these countries were increasingly safe from the grasp of American businesses.

Frustration, self-service and networking

Even if, or indeed *because*, the spread of the Eurocheque system proved quite successful, at the beginning of the 1980s, this genuinely European system, based on the transfer of paper receipts, proved unprofitable. 'Cashless transaction for banks is only profitable if the booking can be effectuated directly, which means not through paper-based intermediaries. Cheques have to be handled several times, signatures have to be checked, the post has to be bothered for transmission and other time consuming processes are repeated many times for a single transaction at different banks. And this quite often for small and smallest amounts. [...] Eurocheque for the banks is, as it is used these days, a losing deal. The propaganda through the free distribution of Eurocheque cards and set forms was a failure.'[31] Even if all commissions raised were counted, Eurocheque remained a losing deal due to the flood of paper. The bankers had not expected that the spread of the cheque would be as successful as it was. Thus, the related transaction costs had been underestimated. Another reason for financial failure was that the retailers and other companies in the service sectors quite willingly accepted Eurocheque, and thus contributed to its diffusion, but did not participate in the costs.[32]

Yet in 1978 Eckard van Hooven stated that Eurocheque was a system 'without equals in the world in terms of efficiency and cost effectiveness'.[33] By 1983 disillusion was evident, however. The Swiss National Bank referred to the cheque as the most expensive of any payment means in circulation. While they provided banks with a means to enter retail banking, cheques would not have any future as a common means of payment. A transitional solution would have to be found to reduce transaction costs.[34] The endeavours in Switzerland, as well as in other countries, aimed to stop dealing with the cheque by physically sending it around between banks, but instead to keep it at the bank where it was presented and transfer the data electronically. As stated above, such so-called cheque truncation was practised in other countries already.[35]

At the beginning of the 1980s methods of electronic data processing and transaction in the payments sector were not yet established as a matter of course. In Switzerland, in fact, the first mainframe computers had been acquired already in 1953.[36] At the end of the 1960s, when the Eurocheque system was introduced, computers managed accounts or dealt with internal administrative processes. During the 1970s computers were broadly used in banks, but their applications were quite restricted and clearly not designed for the payments sector. In this decade, transaction processes in the back offices were well automated, but they did not anticipate the capacity they would need for the flood of paper arising from the popularity of Eurocheque. Machines for booking, punch card and sorter machines were used in the records administration and thus for the transactions with Eurocheque. So it is not astonishing that the cost of a records-based transaction during the 1980s ranged between 3.5 and 7 Swiss francs, depending on the calculation.[37] For quite a long time banks could not help but regret that 'the introduction of electronic data processing had not been able to revolutionize [...] the organisation of the process of goods and services rendered in the banking business as it was the case for the conveyor belt in the industries.'[38] The technical infrastructures were in fact linked to a central computer; they did not function in a nationally networked system, however, let alone an internationally networked one. At the end of the 1970s it was thus clear that, with the technical applications then running, cashless mass payments system could not be dealt with. This was in spite of the fact that data processing technologies had experienced massive acceleration in the past. 'During the 1950s electronics, which then meant a punched card system and printer, took two weeks to sort a messy card index of a million clients, during the 1960s with magnetic plate and cathode ray tube it took two hours and during the 1980s with a laser disk and liquid crystal display it will only be two minutes,'[39] claimed the prognostics. Confronted with these problems, starting with the Eurocheque system in the 1970s, banks began to consider new forms of technical and social compatibilization. They started considering looking for ways, such as cheque truncation, for dealing with cashless payments on a paperless basis. Banks thus increasingly transferred data into a networked computer system. This was not only paralleled by a massive technological upgrade of the banks and an acceleration of transactions, but also made the tellers, employed to serve the clients, dispensable. The clients should now help to reduce costs by participating in the process, that is, by filling in the records by themselves.

Credit Swiss, for example, wrote in a strategy paper of 1971 designed to enlarge data processing at the headquarters by 1973: 'Clients should be educated as much as possible to fill in the number of their account or deposit on their orders. This surplus service of the clients will simplify the work of our controllers and relieve the computer system substantially.'[40] A similar example can be found in UBS's records, where they also saw in the contribution of the clients the potential for rationalization. 'Great efforts must be made to make the clients deliver standardized and completely filled out records easy to process. Enforcing strict rules in contact with the clients is reasonable.'[41] The idea of including clients in the data processing work pointed generally to a more rational process of records transaction.

The logic of including the clients, that is, making them participate directly in the process of data entering in the digitized systems, was part of the increasing self-service standards of the 1980s. Twenty years after having entered retail banking, banks now seemed to perceive in the paradox of approaching the clients with telecommunicative distance the key to their problem: 'The bank at home – the most extreme form of client proximity!'[42] This not only meant eventually introducing home banking, the administration of the account directly by the clients, but also cashless payment at the points of sale and future development of cash withdrawing at machines. In short: telecommunicative self-service and data entering by clients. The vision of the bankers reads: 'Cash dispensers, ATMs, post-terminals and maybe even one day the telephone at home in connection with the TV set will be the nerve-endings of an electronic transactions system, the arm of the credit business with the client prolonged in time and space.'[43] Banks soon would produce new and more efficient services by means of telecommunication technologies as an offer to the masses: this was the euphoric idea, which was very similar to the euphoria of American banks during the 1960s.

The services in electronic data processing delivered by the clients could now be linked with new telecommunication equipment of the time in the form of self-service technologies. As Hooven had already pushed for in 1978, the broader introduction of ATMs was at stake. Given the distribution of the Eurocheque card, the banks aspired to a joint European system. The banks were aware that in creating such a system they would no longer foster cashless payments but cash-based transactions. However, given the costs in the Eurocheque system, it had become clear that cashless transactions could only be profitable if they were executed paperlessly by means of electronic data processing.[44] The dream of a European cashless society still was not narrowed by taking a detour over cash-based transactions, effectuated through ATM services.

Only now, in the course of the 1980s, computers became the networked telecommunication machines of a self-serving consumer society. Eurocheque and Eurocard, given their broad distribution, had spurred this new computer-based way. With hindsight now the Eurocheque, which deemed likely drown in the paper jam of the 1970s, emerged as the adequate means to foster telecommunicative networking during the 1980s and 1990s. On the basis of the European payments system, this means that the co-operation for Eurocheque and Eurocard internationally also led to a co-operation in terms of the conditions for withdrawing cash at ATMs. In 1981 the Eurocheque assembly had decided to establish the precondition for internationally withdrawing cash with the Eurocheque card at ATMs. Border crossing pilot tests became possible from 1 June 1984. At the same time the establishment of a point-of-sales system (POS) effectuated with the Eurocheque card was envisioned. As on the national level, the establishment of these systems was slower than expected; first measurements into this direction could be effected only in 1988.[45] This meant that in the early 1980s a redefinition of what had been the Eurocheque occurred. The much too expensive cheque transactions should be substituted by a debit card system. The way to a European cashless society again seemed to lead over an internationally networked cash-based self-service system, which later, step by step, could be transformed increasingly into a cashless system.

As soon as 1999 the Eurocheque debit card was so well established that its function as a guarantee card could be stopped. 'Because of dynamically increasing electronic debit functions at the POS and ATM and the decreasing importance of paper based Eurocheques the board of directors of Europay International decided on 22. April 1999 to suspend Eurocheque guarantee at the end of 2001.' Existing cheques would count as normal cheques within the national legislation.[46] Thus, in many countries the use of cheques was theoretically possible; however, it was no longer part of the commonly used cashless payment instruments.

Conclusion

With the example of the Eurocheque, this article shows how the emergence of a specific European infrastructure in the cashless payments sector can only be understood by considering at the same time the American process of development in this field. Introducing Eurocheque in 1968, its amplification as guarantee card and later European credit card during the 1970s, always aimed at maintaining dominance of the European mass payments market by the European banks. Orientation on the American role model and delimitation against it went hand in hand. Europe felt threatened and challenged by the American system, certainly the credit card system. This counts not only for the field of payments and for the history of the Eurocheque only, but for many fields of economic development since the 1960s, as Jean-Jacques Servan-Schreiber has impressively recorded.[47] Again and again, the question of delimitation and adaptation to American systems, infrastructures and technologies was at stake. However, the need for international European co-operation, being based on the existing banking system, was never fundamentally questioned.

What role did technologies – certainly computers – play in the course of this process? During the last three decades of the twentieth century, computers effectively entered many fields of life and work. On top of this, as a matter of fact, in the form of small and smallest chips they form parts of machines at public or private disposal. Some became part of everyday life in traditional and newer devices for different forms of communication. The history of the Eurocheque has shown that the accelerated social changes of the past decades cannot be explained simply as the consequence of technological innovation. The history of the development of the information society should rather be described as a process, which was marked by an interdependent social and technological change. Concrete case stories, such as that of Eurocheque, can help to historicize the processes of this change. The information society, then, is not the result of a technological revolution, but much more the result of backlashes and meanders on a local, national, and increasingly international basis. The European dimension plays a central role in it, but not in terms of the political and economic unification process that occurred during recent decades. The European dimension, rather, facilitates the emergence of an infrastructure mirroring effective ways of human interactions, ways of business mobility or tourism, habits of payment as a self-evident part of daily life. The paper-based Eurocheque was part of establishing an electronic Europe-wide common currency.

Notes

1. Peter Bernhardt and Wolfgang Dambmann, *Elektronisches Geld. Die neuen Dienstleistungen der Banken.* (Frankfurt a. M.: Knapp 1979), p. IX; (Christoph Büchenbacher): 'Bald schon bargeldlos Benzin Tanken. PTT und Banken orientieren über die Zukunft des Zahlungsverkehrs', *Berner-Zeitung* 14 January 1983; Meyer and Werner (1983), 'Banken und PTT Arm in Arm oder: ein Traum von Bequemlichkeit', Output 2: 15–16, p. 15; 'Zahlungsverkehr im Umbruch', February 1984, p. 2. Archive SwissBanking.
2. 'Auf dem Wege zu einem gemeinsamen europäischen Konzept im Zahlungsverkehr mit Privatkunden', Vortrag von Dr. Eckart van Hooven, gehalten bei der World Convention on Payment Systems and Electronic Funds Transfer, 22. März 1979, Monte Carlo, p. 2. Archive SwissBanking, A.043.
3. Dale L. Reistad,. 'The Coming Cashless Society. Implications and benefits of a pending system'. *Business Horizons* 10(3) (1967), pp. 23–23, p. 23–32. The notion of a chequeless/cashless society is generally attributed to Dale L. Reistad (Elinor Harris Solomon (ed.) (1991), *Electronic Money Flows. The Molding of a New Financial Order* (Boston, Dordrecht, London), p. 30, Fn 1), although similar ideas date back to the mid-1950s (see citations in Robert L. Kramer and Putnam W. Livingston, 'Cashing in on the chequeless society', *Harvard Business Review* September–October 1967, p. 143.)
4. Kramer and Livingston, 'Cashing in', p. 143.
5. Ibid., p. 143f.
6. James W. Cortada, *The Digital Hand. How Computers Changed the Work of American Financial, Telecommunications, Media, and Entertainment Industries* (Oxford: Oxford UP 2006), p. 12.
7. Bargeldloser Zahlungsverkehr, März 1961-Juli 1995 Archive SwissBanking, A.036; 'Der Kartencheque ein neues Zahlungsmittel', *Schweizerische Finanz Zeitung,* 46 (November 1963), p. 14.
8. H. Schmidt, 'Die bargeldlose Gehalts- und Lohnzahlung in der Sicht der Kreditinstitute', *Monatliche und bargeldlose Lohnzahlung – ein Vorteil für alle* (Frankfurt a.M. 1961) p. 49; compare further: 'hwg', 'Bankschalter statt Lohntüte',

Der Volkswirt 2(54) (1959), p. 54; Hans von Lilienstern Rühle, 'Die teure Lohntüte', *Zeitschrift für Organisation* 5 (1957), p. 192.

9. Barbara Bonhage, 'Die Einführung der bargeldlosen Lohn- und Gehaltszahlung. Der schweizerische Zahlungsverkehr zwischen öffentlicher und privater Dienstleistung' In Laurent Tissot *et al.* (eds) *Dienstleistungen. Expansion und Transformation des 'dritten Sektors'* (Zürich: SGWSG 2007).

10. Christoph Lengwiler, *Kooperation als bankbetriebliche Strategie* (Bern und Stuttgart: Haupt 1988), p. 153.

11. Archive PTT, PC 4-21-16, Protokoll über die Konferenz der Checkamtsleiter, 19./ 20. 10. 1978.

12. Still a third of all employees, however, got their earnings in cash: of about 3 million Swiss employees, only 2 million disposed over a transactions account. Archive PTT, PC 4–21-1982, Protokoll über die Konferenz mit den Leitern der Postscheckämter, 26./ 27. 5. 1982.

13. A. Marx, K. Prucker, W. Schaefer, H. Schmidt and L. Schulze (eds) *Monatliche und bargeldlose Lohnzahlung – ein Vorteil für alle* (Frankfurt am Main: Verlag für Bürotechniek 1961), p. 20.

14. David Hopton, *Payment Systems. A Case for Consensus* (Rolling Meadows: Bank Administration Institute 1983), p. 9.

15. Compare footnote 2, p. 4.

16. Jean-Jacques Servan-Schreiber, *Die amerikanische Herausforderung* (Hamburg: Hoffmann und Campe 1968), p. 148.

17. Dr E. van Hooven, 'Grundprobleme im Zahlungsverkehr mit Privatkunden' (September 1978), p. 2. Archive SwissBanking, A.043.

18. Compare footnote 2, p. 5; investigations showed that 95 per cent of the banking customers did not travel overseas but enjoyed their vacation on the continent.

19. Compare footnote 17, p. 3.

20. The International Association of Science and Technology for Development – IASTED, Exposé of L.J. Schalm at the EFMA Congres of April 7, 1981. Archive SwissBanking, A.158.5.

21. ZFA CSG 02.102.201.302, VR-Protokolle SKA, 23. 10. 1969. Issuing banks did guarantee with it to any cheque holder the encashment of a cheque to a maximum of 300 francs per cheque.

22. Fritz Klein and Guido Palazzo, *Kulturgeschichte des Geldflusses. Die Entwicklung des Zahlungsverkehrs mit Fokus Schweiz* (Zürich: Verlag SKV 2003), p. 56.

23. ZFA CSG 02.102.201.302, VR-Protokolle SKA, 23. 10. 1969.

24. Compare footnote 17, p. 5.

25. Leo Schuster (ed.), *Revolution des Zahlungsverkehrs durch Automation* (Frauenfeld, Stuttgart: Huber 1984), p. 40.

26. Compare footnote 17, p. 6. Many European banks had a robust structure of branch offices during the 1970s. At the beginning of the 1980s, however, with the introduction of direct banking by means of self-service and telecommunication technologies, the branches became less important.

27. Compare footnote 17, p. 5.

28. Ibid., p. 10.

29. Ibid., p. 5

30. Ibid., pp. 3, 10.

31. Werner Meyer, 'Banken und PTT Arm in Arm oder: ein Traum von Bequemlichkeit', *Output* 2 (1983), pp. 15–16, p. 15.

32. Ewald Judt, 'Der eurocheque 1968–2001', *Bank-Archiv* (2000), p. 291ff.; 'Der eurocheque 1968–2001 – ein Nachtrag', *Bank-Archiv* (2003) 2, p. 136ff.

33. Compare note 17.

34. Compare footnote 2, p. 3.

35. Archive SNB, Direktoriumsprotokoll Nr. 678, Konventionsentwurf der Bankiervereinigung betreffend Check-Truncation, 15. 12. 1983, p. 1043.

36. Hans Neukom, 'Early Use of Computers in Swiss Banks', *IEEE Annals of the History of Computing* (July – September 2004), p. 52f.

37. Schuster, *Revolution des Zahlungsverkehrs*, 42; Abschlussbericht. Ist-Aufnahme über ZV-CH bei 6 repräsentativen Banken (ohne Interbank-Aspekte) im Rahmen des Projektabschnitts 2, Gesamtkonzept ZV-CH, April 1980, p. 10. Archive SwissBanking, A.043.

38. Bernhardt and Dambmann, *Elektronisches Geld*, p. 35.

39. 'Zahlungsverkehr im Umbruch' (February 1984), p. 4. Archive SwissBanking.

40. ZFA CSG 11.101.204.325, Dr. W. G., Automationsentwicklung 1980 – 1990 (different protocols) Arbeitsgruppe EDV-Planung (AEP), 'Die geplante erweiterte Datenverarbeitung am Hauptsitz per 1.1.1973' (September 197), S. 3.

41. Archive UBS, SBG, Protokoll der GDIR-Plenarsitzung vom 18./19. August 1975, Beilage 3 'Bericht über die Voruntersuchung und Schlussfolgerungen für das weitere Vorgehen bei der Neuplanung des integrierten Datenverarbeitungssystems', p. 6.

42. Bernhardt and Dambmann, *Elektronisches Geld*, p. 69.

43. Ibid., p. 39.

44. Werner, 'Banken und PTT' (1983), pp. 15–16.

45. See note 32.

46. Ibid.

47. Servan-Schreiber, *Die amerikanische Herausforderung*.

Biography 5: Georges Valensi: Europe Calling?

Leonard Laborie

Georges Valensi's important achievements in television colour coding are well recorded in textbooks dealing with the history of television technologies. By contrast, his day-to-day activities have almost been forgotten. An engineer specializing in long-distance telephony, Valensi built on his experiences, expertise and social skills to be the longtime general secretary of the International Telephone Consultative Committee (CCIF), from the creation of this intergovernmental institution in 1924 to 1956.

Born in 1889 in the French department of Algeria, Georges Valensi entered the prestigious engineering school *Ecole polytechnique* in 1908. After three years there and before finishing his studies at the *Ecole Supérieure des Postes et Télégraphes* (ESPT, where he was ranked number one), he spent a year at the *Ecole Supérieure d'Electricité*, probably attending lectures on 'radioelectricity' in a recently opened section sponsored by the Army. This complementary training allowed Valensi to be at the cutting edge of electrical science and signal transmission.

The First World War proved a decisive point in turning his career from its purely national trajectory to a more international dimension. When he graduated in 1913, Valensi joined the public administration operating the French telecommunications network (PTT) as a telephone engineer. At the outbreak of the war, with transmissions playing an unprecedented role in the battlefield, Valensi volunteered as a liaison officer to the British army. His good command of English served him further when the United States joined the Entente. A visit to the American telephone operator AT&T with some of his colleagues between May and July 1917 proved formative for the 27-year-old. AT&T's achievements and universal service philosophy came as a revelation. His mission was to observe *in situ* the implementation of electronic repeaters, which enabled transcontinental telephony – a technological and strategic breakthrough that came with the first New York–San Francisco line in 1914. Valensi's expertise with US firm Western Electric's repeaters made him one of the very few French specialists on electronic devices for long-distance telephony. Back in France he naturally became liaison officer to the American Army, enforcing his links with American engineers.

After peace returned, European countries considered long-distance telephone lines a matter of great interest, at both national and international level. The technology was available and the political agenda was geared toward strengthening national territories and reconstructing the European economy. Stimulated by Western Electric's apparent intention to operate a transnational network in Europe and also concerned with the German advances in this field, the French PTT administration took an international initiative: building on long-standing co-operation between national administrations – the International Telegraph Union dated back to 1865 – it invited its foreign counterparts in 1923 to explore ways of enhancing co-operation on long-distance telephony. Recognizing his expertise, language skills (he also had a good command of German) and previous experiences in structuring new organizations, the meeting's French president, Alfred Dennery, nominated his close associate Valensi as secretary. A 'preliminary technical committee on long distance telephone communications in Europe' was established, which a year later became the CCIF, an intergovernmental organization acting as the specialized body of the ITU for telephony, with Valensi its permanent general secretary.

Valensi's conception of the role of such a forum was clear. Like others contemplating how to build a continental network comparable to the American one, he believed that a central authority was necessary. He believed that, for political reasons, no private company would be endorsed by the European states. Because there was no 'effective' federal government in Europe, no federal administration could carry into effect a common policy. Experts' meetings that would respect national sovereignties and collegially design the network were the solution.

Like his organization itself, the secretary's position was one not of power but of influence. His statutory tasks were to support the work of the various specialized commissions, providing them with all information they could need, and to prepare the CCIF annual assembly. Valensi considered himself the 'brain' of the CCIF, explaining that a brain was both a museum and a laboratory: he stored and dispatched information, and he prepared and anticipated future needs. As official representative of the CCIF, Valensi was at the crossroads of various international technical committees that flourished during the 1920s, in particular the *Commission mixte internationale*, which gathered low and high voltage specialists to work on protecting telecommunications networks from interferences coming from electrical networks. He also had close contacts with the International Chamber of Commerce and the International Broadcasting Union, which used international telephone circuits from the second half of the 1920s on to organize such radio events as the *nuits nationales* or live 'European concerts', such as the one opening the tenth plenary assembly of the League of Nations.

Figure B5.1   George Valensi early and late in his career at the CCIF

Source: *Journal des télécommunications*, 1976.

While his work brought him close to the pan-European movements, it is not clear to what extent he can be considered part of them. In his mind, the CCIF had a strictly technical scope: standardizing the equipment and planning the expansion of the telephone network. He did publish in *L'Europe nouvelle*, a review close to the League of Nations, and meeting point for early Europeanists. Valensi's articles described how European telephony was managed and how it could be improved, notably to foster the emergence of a 'European public opinion', as he wrote in 1926. One of Valensi's preoccupations in telephony was to cope with users' needs, and for these statistics studies were necessary to establish where new traffic capacities should be installed. He argued that to have relevant statistics 'implies having an international currency unit (various European currencies backed to gold standard), stable customs agreements, and the suppression of all formalities which could prevent the circulation of people, goods and capitals'. The order of ends and means is characteristic of the engineer Valensi: the *end* was an integrated telephone network and the *means* was the lowering of economic and political barriers.

During the Second World War, the CCIF ceased activities and Valensi himself ran afoul of Vichy's racial laws in November 1940, but he was finally reintegrated into the telecommunication public administration in September 1941. As early as September 1944, he went back to Paris to reorganize the CCIF, and meetings in London and Montreux followed shortly thereafter. Valensi's post was renamed in 1947: he became 'director' of the CCIF. Two years later, the direction moved from Paris to Geneva, joining the headquarters of the ITU – now a member of the United Nations system. Between the wars, the CCIF had gradually expanded its membership to become truly pan-European. The Cold War did not alter this. While co-operation in international telephony was still strongly focused on the European area, it enlarged to include North African, Middle Eastern and Asian countries.

Valensi retired from the CCIF in 1956. Seldom visible on the world stage, the organization had built a lasting platform for co-operation; its main task at the time of Valensi's retirement was the standardization of high-speed lines (coaxial cables and hertzian beams) and of semi-automatic and fully automatic switching in international liaisons. A year before he died, Valensi received the first 'ITU Centenary Prize' (1979) intended to reward an individual or group of individuals for international activities recognized as serving to promote the development of international telecommunications.

Literature

Robert Chapuis, 'Le CCIF et le développement de la téléphonie internationale', *Journal des télécommunications* (March 1976), pp. 184–97.

Léonard Laborie, *La France, l'Europe et l'ordre international des communications* (PhD dissertation, université Paris-Sorbonne, 2006).

Jean Lalou, 'Georges Valensi', *Le Rouge et la Jaune* (Feb 1981), p. 1.

Georges Valensi, 'La téléphonie européenne', *L'Europe nouvelle* 417 (1926), pp. 204–9.

7
Off the Leash. The European Mobile Phone Standard (GSM) as a Transnational Telecommunications Infrastructure

Patrick Kammerer

Transnational telecommunications networks seem to be emerging from, as well as main driving forces behind, the processes we generally label *globalization*. There are various concepts of globalization, but they all refer in one way or another to the diminishing of borders.[1] Since structural changes in information and communications technologies (ICT) challenge or transform existing borders by generating new possibilities for transfer or transactions across them, transnational telecommunications networks such as the *Global System of Mobile Communications* (*GSM*) can be observed and described as a concrete form of globalization. Following the theoretical perspective of Marshall McLuhan, who introduced the metaphor of the Global Village, global telecommunications networks can be seen not only as bridging distance between a sender and a receiver, but also as transforming borders by enabling communication across them.[2] Historiographical approaches in economic history often stress the ambivalent dimensions of globalization concepts; they have introduced careful delineations of the term 'global' as referring to 'worldwide' rather than 'covering the total area of the globe', for example, and underlined the existence of de-globalization processes in the nineteenth and early twentieth century alongside globalization processes.[3] While the 'backronym' GSM now refers to a global or worldwide market, its original meaning in 1982 was *Groupe Spécial Mobile*, which referred to a visionary group consisting of representatives of national Public Telecommunications Operators (PTOs) in Europe within the structures of the Conférence des Administrations Européenes des Postes et Télécommunications (CEPT). How the standard went from this 'special group' to a 'global system' is the trajectory this chapter will trace.

Alongside other global telecommunications networks, such as the internet or the *Global Positioning System* (GPS), a global network for mobile telephony is being built. The telephone in its new form, wireless and mobile, was not only literally cut off its traditional 'leash'; the transformation to a wireless device soon became strongly reflected in successful trade based around the new possibilities of mobile communications. The 'constant touch'[4] or 'perpetual contact'[5] as a new pattern of personal communication does not only seem to have changed individual behaviour and affected communication culture.[6] The demand for mobile communication services also enabled an unleashing of economic development. Unexpected growth rates and immense gains by economies of scale led to a worldwide proliferation of mobile phone technology over the last two decades. Today most of the populated areas on the planet are covered by mobile phone networks and nearly a third of the worldwide population owns a mobile phone. At the moment there are about nine or ten more or less important mobile phone standards, but the GSM standard is surprisingly dominant. It was developed in Europe and introduced as mandatory during the early 1990s, and since expanded well beyond that protected market. At the beginning of 2007, when the mark of 2 billion GSM subscribers worldwide was reached, GSM covered about 80% of the worldwide cell phone technology market share.[7] The Deutsche Bank was not exaggerating when it commented that 'GSM mobile communications is, without a doubt, one of the most explosive developments ever to have taken place in the telecommunications industry.'[8]

The GSM success story becomes even more impressive by the historical fact that mobile phone technology was originally invented not in Europe but in the USA, and that the US market set the tone for research and development of analog mobile phone technology until the mid-1980s. The idea of cell-based mobile radio systems appeared at Bell Laboratories in the United States in the late 1940s.[9] However, the technical proposals for a cellular standard were not drawn up by AT&T and its Bell Labs until 1971.[10] This standard was called 'Advanced Mobile Phone System' (AMPS). During the early 1980s, analog cellular telephone systems grew rapidly in Europe, particularly in Scandinavia and the United Kingdom. Due to the dominance of the US market in analogue cell phones, AMPS remained the most common standard for mobile communications worldwide as regards the number of subscribers until the middle of the 1990s.[11]

Europe's predominant role in mobile phone technology today seems to have come along with the switch from analogue to digital mobile phone technology. Given the dominance of American and Asian industries in information technologies, consumer electronics and semiconductors in the 1980s and 1990s, the European breakthrough in mobile phone technology during the digitalization process makes for an interesting case. Such a strikingly prosperous telecommunications infrastructure development raises important questions about the relevant success factors. On one hand, some claim that the success factors lie in specific technical or standard features such as the subscriber identity module (SIM), short message service (SMS) or international roaming; some have argued, on the other hand, that the lessons learned during the analogue mobile phone standardization were crucial.[12] In addition, several actors today claim (sometimes single-handedly) to have played a key role in the process.[13] One commentator invented the concept of 'hurdles' to explain the GSM success story.[14] Most analytical papers on the subject mention the right timing; already in 1994 Gabriela Cattaneo wrote that '[t]he analysis of the GSM standard helps to highlight the mix of factors [...] and the importance of the right timing in a favorable historical context.'[15]

The analysis in the present chapter mainly focuses on the early phases of development of cell phone standardization in Europe. Starting with a structural overview over the standardization process of the American cell phone market, the focus then shifts to the development in Europe, particularly during the first phase (1982–7), when the basic parameters of the GSM system were specified. Finally, I will provide an outlook on the development towards a worldwide transnational mobile phone network. In looking toward standardization processes as an analytical category the goal is not to create another list of success factors but instead to highlight the dynamics, as well as the ranges of contingency, in the formation of the network technologies. The notion of standardization here is inspired by the approach of Bowker and Star and their theory of classification.[16] According to them, standards act as intermediary functional entities, not only by fitting one technological element to another, but also as common means of identifying and bargaining over technology in political and socioeconomic contexts. Following that, technological standards can be seen as patterns of perception and patterns of discourse. In Bowker and Star's analysis, standards can be viewed as a *process* rather than as a given factor or a structure. They have to be built up in complex classification processes. Since the complexity of a standard refers not only to a technological need but also to bureaucratic and identity-related processes, establishing standards is always connected to the development of institutions and organizational entities. Moreover, a standard like GSM could also be described as a system of standards, standard umbrella or a standard family. From a technological point of view, such a system could be described as a gateway with the capacity to link different systems on different levels of complexity.[17] Therefore a standard like GSM includes an interoperable system of phone numbers, roaming agreements, roaming billing standards, comparable licence policies, shared frequencies, similarities in the user interfaces of terminals, and so on.

The change of classifications or standards can be seen as the result of learning processes along with the development and commercialization of technology. This approach seems fruitful for a historical analysis of the GSM case because the costs of standardization were immense. As David Bach argues, these enormous costs can be seen as a problem of collective action.[18] Since co-ordination and/or co-operation are seen as genuine problems connected to the development of telecommunications infrastructure,[19] debates often follow a structure that emphasizes the distinction between monopolist and market settings, or between the state and private actors. Although the GSM mobile telephone system has already been the subject of several studies,[20] it can fruitfully add to the historians' understandings of the development of Europe-wide infrastructural systems.[21]

From unity to diversity: Cell phone standardization in the USA (1970s – 1990s)

Although the first concept of cellular radio telephony was submitted to the Federal Communications Commission (FCC) in 1947 by AT&T with a request for adequate frequency allocation in the radio spectrum, a strong lobby for television services – fearing there would be insufficient frequencies for TV broadcasting – was able to hinder the reservation of a radio frequency spectrum for mobile phones throughout the 1950s and 1960s. Early development of mobile phone technology in the USA can thus be characterized by two major structural layers: 1) the unrivalled research and development of the telephony monopolist AT&T without any direct product competition and 2) the lack of a frequency spectrum that prevented establishing a mobile phone standard until 1971.[22] Those structural layers were essential to forming expectations of the future mobile phone development: 'At the beginning of the 1970s, almost everyone assumed that AT&T would be operating a cellular network as an extension to its monopoly on the land-based connections. Moreover, only this company was considered capable of raising the enormous investments necessary.'[23]

However, the situation changed in the mid-1970s when Radio Common Carriers (RCCs) – smaller companies often serving no more than a few hundred customers with radio-related services like paging – and Motorola, which had begun the development of its own standard, took up interest in a future US mobile phone market. FCC saw itself confronted with a rapidly growing group of firms wanting to participate in a forthcoming market and ready to sue if they were excluded. The FCC's licensing and regulations procedures were significantly slowed down as questions of system interoperability and fair market entry grew more important. After the break-up of the AT&T monopoly in 1982, when the FCC started to award licences for commercial mobile phone services, far more applications were submitted than expected and far more than the FCC was ready to process.[24] By adapting the evaluation procedure FCC managed to award licences for a first group of thirty markets[25] – but many awarded licences were challenged in court by unsuccessful applicants. The award for the second group of licences attracted even more applicants and FCC had to adjust procedures again: a lottery-based procedure was adopted.[26] But the change from comparative hearings to a lottery system created both new strategic options for the applicants and some uncertainty about the interpretation of FCC licence award procedures.[27] In a retrospective report to Congress reflecting on their different licence award procedures, the FCC commented:

> Under the lottery system, the FCC sustained a flood of license applications because some lottery applicants submitted speculative entries with uncertain intent of building out a service. Many lottery winners resold their licenses in secondary markets. One speculator spent $5 million on licenses to be resold in a year and a half for $34 million without building so much as an antenna. The costs associated with these resale transactions, such as those for cellular licenses in 1991, have been estimated at $190 million.[28]

Nevertheless, the first commercial AMPS service started successfully in 1983 and only a few years later AMPS networks succeeded in some major US cities.

The complexity of the FCC's changing regulation procedures as well as the end of AT&T's monopoly resulted in the AMPS standard remaining more or less unchanged from its conception in 1971 to the first commercial launch in 1983. The absence of a dominant player in the US telephone market since 1984 also influenced the development of mobile telephony: although AMPS was refined into a digital successor named D-AMPS, the concept, at least in part, was considered outdated. The firm Qualcomm challenged the pottering AMPS standard by developing main elements of a digital cell phone standard called CDMA, based on code division multiplexing rather than time division as used in AMPS. CDMA was selected by the Telecommunication Industry Association (TIA) as a technically advanced standard alternative to AMPS.[29] When the FCC announced the auction of licences for additional mobile phone services called Personal Communications Services (PCS) in the 1900 MHz frequency spectrum, proposals from no fewer than seven mobile phone standards were submitted.[30] The auctions finally resulted in three major competing standards in the US cell phone market: AMPS, IS-95 CDMA and PCS-1900 (a GSM variant), starting their services in 1996.[31]

Looking at the characteristics of the US mobile phone standardization process in terms of learning processes by relevant actors or institutions, we notice the significant shift from one standard developed by a *de facto* monopolist (AMPS) towards a variety of at least three different major standards. While in the 1970s everyone assumed that a future cell phone system would be operated by AT&T, the splitting up of the telephone giant significantly delayed the first cell phone licence awards by the FCC and encouraged research and development by firms like Qualcomm in the late 1980s. For the second licence award the FCC changed the procedure again and held an auction that kept the market open for several standards. The rather complex change from the unrivalled AMPS standard in a monopolist setting to a multi-standard mobile phone market slowed down the American development until systems comparable to GSM started to be operational in 1996.

The beginning of mobile phone standardization in Europe

In the years before CEPT (Conférence des Administrations Européenes des Postes et Télécommunications) formally initiated the GSM standardization project in 1982, co-operation on analogue standards for mobile communications had already been attempted between France and the UK as well as between France and Germany.[32] However, simultaneous efforts by the national governments to protect their 'home' industries frequently interfered with co-operation. While France,[33] Germany,[34] Italy[35] and the UK[36] and their PTOs (Public Telecommunications Operators) each developed national cell phone standards more or less incompatible with each other to support their domestic telecommunications industries, the Scandinavian analogue standard, NMT 450, arose from a successful co-operation between Sweden, Finland, Denmark, Norway and, later on, Iceland. The idea of a common Nordic mobile telephone system dates to as far back as 1969, when a Swedish official first proposed it at a meeting of NordTel (an organization for the co-operation between telecommunications administrations of Norway, Denmark, Finland and Sweden). He 'saw the advantages of a Scandinavian system, a market with 23 million inhabitants that was big enough for the industry to consider it profitable to develop systems and mobile telephones'.[37] NordTel established the Nordic Mobile Telephone Group (NMT) and it was assigned the task of developing a common Nordic mobile telephone standard.[38] In October 1981, NMT 450 was inaugurated in Sweden, followed soon by Finland, Denmark and Norway.

Having created an integrated cellular network for Scandinavia, NMT 450 became a successful export commodity and NMT 450 standard networks were built in Saudi Arabia (as early as 1981), the Netherlands, Spain, Thailand, Algeria and Belgium. Realizing that frequency allocations in the 450 MHz band would become insufficient in the light of growing demand, the Nordic Mobile Telephone Group developed a similar system for the 900 MHz band, which was rolled out in Scandinavia in 1986. NMT 900 systems were subsequently adopted in the Netherlands, parts of France and also in Switzerland.[39]

The success of NMT 450 and NMT 900 systems in Scandinavia as well as on the international market resulted in considerable competitive advantages for Scandinavian equipment manufacturers, such as Nokia and Ericsson.[40] Already in 1985, for example, Nokia and Ericsson controlled roughly one-fifth of the world market for mobile phones, whereas all other European manufacturers held less than 10 per cent altogether.[41] While concern about their domestic industries had impeded co-operation on analogue standards among France, Germany and the UK on bilateral and multilateral levels, successful co-operation in Scandinavia through NordTel clearly strength-ened the position of Scandinavian manufacturers with regard to their inter-national competitors. The success of NMT held at least two basic lessons for equipment providers and national regulation experts. First, co-operation on a common standard opened broader markets for equipment providers across national borders. Second, the PTOs of smaller countries such as Denmark or later the Netherlands, Iceland and Switzerland saw the advantages of shar-ing development costs for a complex technology and the chance to provide mobile telephone networks at reasonable costs and in an assessable time frame. On top of that, NMT was the first standard worldwide to provide a feature called 'roaming', which enabled use of a mobile phone in foreign networks with the same (NMT) standard.

As mentioned above, the GSM standardization process was formally ini-tiated by CEPT in 1982 by establishing the so-called *Groupe Spécial Mobile* (GSM) as an institution to co-ordinate future cell phone standards of its members. It is important to note that every CEPT member nation state had the chance to participate in the *Groupe Spécial Mobile* with a PTO del-egation representing its national interests. The first meeting of this group, held in Stockholm in December 1982,[42] was the result of CEPT's decisions taken on a proposal from the Dutch PTO to reserve the 900 MHz band 'to achieve a form of harmonization in the field of the land mobile services for European purposes.'[43] In 1984, when the GSM received a letter from Bell Communications Research (BCR) 'proposing a liaison between BCR and GSM',[44] it was not only the political matter of the issue that was discussed. 'Further on, some delegates questioned both the possibility and the need for a worldwide standard.'[45]

In the beginning, the main goal of GSM was to build up efficient working procedures and decision structures. It soon became clear that it would not be possible to discuss all issues in plenary, so GSM decided to set up several working parties (WP) in order to prepare proposals for the plenary. WP1 was concerned with service facilities, WP2 with radio questions and WP3 with network aspects. In the early stages of the standardization process the GSM initiative clearly benefited from the already existing institutional framework of CEPT, which included the national PTTs on a proven basis of co-operation.[46] Furthermore, the CEPT framework allowed countries (or their PTTs) with different preferences and strategies to start co-operation. For smaller European countries such as the Netherlands or Switzerland, the GSM initiative emerged increasingly as the only roadmap to a mobile phone system at reasonable cost that would allow them participation in decisions and with international connections. Countries with major home markets and correlative telecommunications industries such as Germany, France or the UK saw the early GSM standardization by CEPT as one among many possible approaches on a bilateral or multilateral level to a transnational cell phone standard in Europe. Their strategy became obvious as soon as

France and the FRG, later on together with Italy and the UK, started to elaborate R&D programmes independent of CEPT in exclusive meetings.[47] Nevertheless, they joined the GSM group and contributed substantially to the early standardization phase, although the final success of the group was widely doubted when the GSM startup meeting was held.[48]

Standardization process in danger: The Madeira meeting

During the standardization process, the *Groupe Spécial Mobile* had to take several crucial decisions concerning the technical specifications of the main functional features of connection methods and data communications. There was mutual consent that the new system should be based on digital technology as opposed to analogue; among other reasons, the digital solution promised a high level of compatibility with the Integrated Services Digital Network (ISDN), which was being developed at that time. While most of the crucial standardization questions were 'largely solved by engineers and technocrats without significant controversy, the political battle erupted over the question whether to adopt a wide-band or narrow-band TDMA solution'.[49]

A French–German coalition supported a wide-band solution, whereas the Scandinavian countries favoured the narrow-band alternative.[50] These preferences of the PTOs/PTTs were a clear reflection of the preferences of the respective countries' domestic equipment manufacturers. After the ITT Corporation had sold the German SEL (Standard Elektronik Lorenz) – including their rights on the CD 900 speech transmission[51] – to French-based Alcatel, CD 900 was made compatible with the forthcoming GSM specifications through substantial investments.[52] The CD 900 system was a really forward-looking technology, but functionally needed a broad frequency band.[53] Due to the NMT standardization process, the Scandinavian manufacturers acquired great experience in the narrow band technology.[54] They saw no need to change their technology path.[55]

The controversy culminated at the CEPT's meeting in Madeira in February 1987, at which the basic specifications of the GSM standard were to be determined. Despite the fact that most of the CEPT members were on the side of the narrow frequency band coalition, German and French officials still had a strong counterposition. Because the decisions of the CEPT would have to be taken unanimously – following standard intergovernmental procedures – French and German officials had a *de facto* veto position.[56] The report of the Madeira meeting commented that 'the administrations of France and FRG were asked to reconsider their position for the sake of European unity and the future of the GSM project. However, no final decision on this matter could be reached during the meeting.'[57]

The whole GSM standardization process was in danger of being wedged, or even splitting, along the coalition borders. From an evolutionary point of view the GSM standardization process was in a rather 'open' situation. As the French administrator Philippe Dupuis at GSM put it:

> Those who did not believe in the success of the GSM Group had already made contingency plans. In 1986 two 900 MHz analogue cellular standards were operating successfully in Europe, TACS in the UK and NMT 900 in the Nordic countries. If the GSM Group failed to deliver a workable solution either could have been adopted as a 'Pan-European' cellular system instead. In the competition which would have been developed NMT 900 would have led.[58]

The vision of a common European market and the European Commission to break the deadlock

The deadlock situation at the Madeira meeting was easy to foresee, because of the principal interests of the main actors (governments and PTOs/PTTs) with regard to their domestic telecommunications industries.[59] It was precisely in that critical moment of the whole GSM standardization process that the EC (European Community) came into play. France and Germany encouraged the European Commission to outline the state of the GSM project to the heads of state at the European Summit in December 1986 just before the Madeira meeting. Up to then the EC had had no formal role in the GSM standardization process since they were not a corporate member of the CEPT. But from the moment France and Germany pushed it GSM standardization became to a major issue of EC activity. The GSM project seemed to fall on fertile ground at the EC. While in the middle of the 1960s the PAL-SECAM controversy[60] between France and Germany had hindered successful co-operation towards a pan-European colour television standard as a distinctive symbolic issue of nationally focused European standard politics, the political discourse about transnational infrastructure in the second half of the 1980s was shaped by the perception of the lack of Trans European Networks (TENs). A closer look at the chronology towards a common standard uncovers the step by step strategy of the French and German coalition.

At the Madeira meeting in February 1987 all the basic specifications of the GSM standard were determined by unanimous agreement – except for the crucial question of the frequency band. Directly after the Madeira meeting, the GSM activities continued on the EC level. Already in July 1987 the European Commission published two remarkable regulatory instruments: a Directive (87/372/EEC) and a Recommendation (87/371/EEC).[61] The Directive required the EC member states to reserve the 900 MHz frequency band for the forthcoming digital standard while the Recommendation advised the telecommunications administrations to 'implement detailed Recommendations concerning the coordinated introduction of public pan-European cellular digital land-based mobile communications in the

Community',[62] and further stipulated that 'the service should commence in 1991 at the latest.'[63] Since there was no other digital standard for mobile communications at that point in time, the GSM standard was the only one that would fit with the directive and the recommendation. The GSM standard thus became an unrivalled standard in all EC member states. In addition, the EC proposed the founding of a European Telecommunications Standard Institute to co-ordinate the process of building the physical GSM networks as an interface to the local PTOs, ensuring that some additional co-ordination was given.

The activities on the EC level changed the situation in significant ways. The whole (EC-)Europe was expected to become one big market for mobile communications with high barriers of entry for non-European manufacturers and good chances for economies of scale for the domestic ones. The EC could be used as a political platform to enable the shift of expectations towards a common market. Under those circumstances, France and Germany were now ready to sign a Memorandum of Understanding (MoU) to the GSM standard. This agreement was manifested on 7 September 1987 as fifteen operators (the national PTOs/PTTs of thirteen states and two independent UK operators) signed the MoU in order to complete the introduction of GSM networks by 1991. Article 1 of the MoU states: 'The purpose of this MoU is to provide a framework for all the necessary measures to be taken by the signatories together to ensure the opening of a commercial pan European public digital cellular mobile telecommunications service in their respective countries in 1991. This shall provide amongst other things an international roaming service whereby a user provided with a service in one country by one of the network operators can also gain access to the service of any of the other network operators in their respective countries.'[64]

One year after the agreement, the European Telecommunications Standard Institute (ETSI) was founded in order to ensure additional co-ordination along the implementation of the GSM standard. It is interesting to note that just before, and especially after, the formal agreement on the introduction of GSM systems in Europe the institutional and bureaucratic setting around the standard changed completely. ETSI meetings, for example, were open to manufacturers, in contrast to the earlier CEPT GSM meetings, which were exclusively open to representatives of PTOs of the CEPT members. In addition, ETSI began renaming most elements of the internal GSM structure.[65] Furthermore, ETSI took the forward-looking decision to 'rename' GSM from *Groupe Spécial Mobile* to its present meaning of Global System for Mobile Communications.

The launch of GSM networks

The launch of GSM started with a first GSM digital cellular network in Finland in 1991; an experimental network with 5,000 handsets had also been installed at the Telecom 91 exhibition in Geneva and Lausanne. In early 1992, only a few GSM networks were launched, but within seven years

GSM networks had over 50 million subscribers in Europe. Among other early countries to run GSM networks were Germany, Denmark, Portugal, Sweden, Italy and France. The first roaming agreement was signed between Telecom Finland and Vodafone in the UK on 17 June 1992; as further roaming agreements followed shortly after, a European space for mobile communications became a key feature in the mobile phone advertisement campaigns of the ational PTOs (See Figure 7.1).

By 1993 the MoU embraced seventy members from forty-eight countries and twenty-five roaming agreements. In the following year the number of operators passed 100, serving more than a million subscribers in amazingly

Figure 7.1   Europe of 'roaming coverage' 1994

Note: National borders are overlaid by the GSM coverage areas, representing a common space for mobile communications.

Source: GSM advertisement brochure of the Swiss PTT in 1994, PTT-Archive Berne.

rapidly growing European markets. Just few years after its launch, GSM had expanded beyond Europe, establishing a presence in Australia, Africa, India, Asia (except Japan) and the Arab world. The MoU was formally registered as an Association in Switzerland,[66] with 156 members serving twelve million customers in eighty-six countries, by June 1995.[67]

From a customer's point of view at that time, GSM (and its twin system called DCS 1800, operating at 1,800 MHz[68]) was probably perceived as just another system, entering the market and competing with existing mobile phone technology, such as NMT 900 or AMPS. Choices were probably based not only on technological features such as good speech quality, data transmission services or international roaming, but also on the way it was introduced and the way the cellular market across Europe was being reorganized. The national PTOs found themselves exposed to high tensions. On the one hand they had the possibility to introduce new mobile phone customer services at reasonable cost for a mass market based on the GSM standard. On the other hand they saw the liberalization of the telecommunications markets in Europe right around the corner. They had to be quick to ensure themselves a large market share. At this point in time most of Europe's public telecommunications operators were concerned about privatization and greater operational flexibility. The impact of increasing competition on a standardized transnational infrastructure helped to shift mobile communications away from the business community and into the mass market. Time was a crucial element for national PTOs' advertising campaigns, which aimed especially to attract new private customers, since business customers were the main focus of earlier advertisements for the analogue mobile phone systems. For example, the German Telekom and the Swiss PTT organized joint press events that focused on the use of roaming, which was not possible between Germany and Switzerland using analogue systems, especially for private customers. (See Figure 7.2). Hence, the number of mobile phone subscribers in Western Europe, which had grown by roughly a third in each of the two previous years, increased by almost 50 per cent in 1993 (See Figure 7.3).

Success of GSM towards a global network

GSM was already perceived as a distinctive success story by 1995.[69] While there were still more cell phone users in North America than in Europe at that time, more than half the growth in Europe derived from digital systems, opposed to the growth in the US, which still operated on analog AMPS networks. The completion of the GSM Phase II standardization made data services such as fax, video, e-mail and short messages (SMS) technically feasible. While video and data communications were functionally limited due to the (then) lack of input and output devices, SMS unexpectedly evolved into a new form of everyday communication.

Figure 7.2   Border crossing while phoning

Source: Press Photography by the German Telekom for a Joint Press Event with the Swiss PTT in 1994, PTT-Archive Berne.

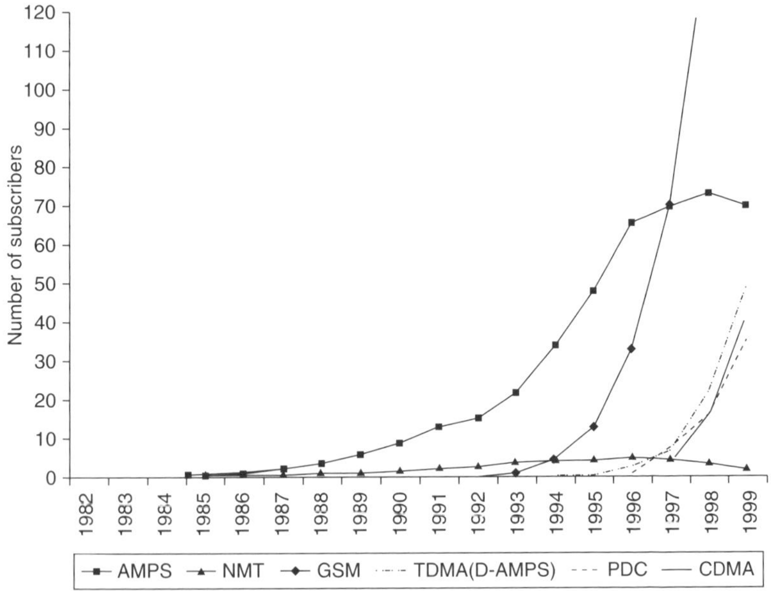

Figure 7.3   Number of worldwide subscribers per cellular standard, 1982–99

An adaptation of DCS 1800 (GSM variant at 1,800 MHz) for an even higher frequency level was produced to meet the opportunities created by the recent FCC (Federal Communications Commission) auction in the USA: PCS 1900.[70] In 1995, US cellular operators were expected to face competition from PCS companies, using high frequencies at a similar range of the spectrum to the DCS 1800 systems allocated to the UK cellular operators One-2-One, Mercury and Orange, as well as E-Plus in Germany. New PCS operators in the US recognized the advantages of an open standard in creating a global multi-vendor market for GSM products; this made network deployment more cost-effective. In May 1997, there were already fifteen PCS 1900 (now GSM 1900) networks operating and over 400,000 users.[71]

In 1997 the GSM MoU Association, the global industry body, already represented 239 international GSM network operators, regulators and administrators of 109 countries/areas. Customer totals for GSM had reached 44 million and were equivalent to 28 per cent of the world mobile wireless market. In 1998, the EU Green Paper on Convergence was written with the purpose of launching a debate on the regulatory implications of the convergence of the telecommunications, media and IT sectors, and to discuss options for future regulatory policy.[72]

As a genuine GSM standard feature, *roaming* became more and more important on a worldwide level. From the beginning roaming was conceptualized as both a 'national' and an 'international' feature, since the Scandinavian PTTs already had rich experience due to NMT-roaming in the Nordic countries. In 2007, roaming agreements among most GSM operators allowed their customers to use their mobile phones in 300 to 600 GSM networks on the planet.[73] In the early stages of roaming technology, 'straying' into other networks was still limited because handsets were limited to one radio frequency band. Already in 1997 Motorola presented the first *dual band* GSM handset, called Motorola 8900 Traveller, capable of using both the 900 MHz and the 1,800 MHz frequency band; only two years later even tri-band devices (GSM 900/1800/1900 MHz) were commercially available. Nowadays, mobile phones or so-called smart phones usually give access to other networks using quad-band technology or even combining completely different wireless network standards in one single device.[74]

Digital convergence: Standardization beyond GSM

The regional success of mobile phone networks during the second half of the 1990s in Europe, Japan and the USA, as well as the successful research programmes for broadband telecommunications, stimulated discussions about a worldwide mobile phone standard at different levels by all relevant actors.[75] As the International Telecommunications Union (ITU) relaunched the discussions about a worldwide standard by renaming their activities from FPLMTS (Future Public Land Mobile Telecommunications System) to IMT-2000 (International Mobile Telecommunications-2000), all actors undertook attempts to influence the standardization activities in their favoured direction. The main alliances were formed along two co-ordinating organizations: the 3rd Generation Partnership Project (3GPP), including several standardization bodies with interests in a further development of the GSM and its successor UMTS,[76] and the 3rd Generation Partnership Project 2 (3GPP2), representing several standardization bodies in favour of the further development of CDMA2000.[77] Moreover, a patent dispute between Qualcomm and Ericsson slowed down ITU standardizing activities. In the end, the complex matrix of interests and standardization bodies involved led to a harmonization of technology that embraced several approaches according to defined principles rather than to a single, consistent worldwide standard. For example, the air interface of IMT-2000 consists of at least four different radio interfaces based on the two access technologies CDMA and TDMA; one of the TDMA air interfaces is an enhanced variant of GSM called EDGE.[78] Nevertheless, in 2001 the first networks according to the IMT-2000 standard went live in Japan and Europe; in March 2007, about 6 or 16 per cent (depending on whether 'CDMA 1x' is counted as an IMT standard) of worldwide subscribers used standards meeting the IMT requirements. Although broadband mobile phone technology under the IMT standard UMTS or CDMA 2000 has been in commercial use since 2001, service providers have had difficulties in providing the new technology to the market at reasonable cost. But the increasing computing capacities of mobile phones and network components, enabling different yet compatible standards for air interface, network and multimedia, forced mobile phone service providers to build networks and feature roaming agreements in multi-standard settings. In a multi-standard setting with handhelds enabling different standards with different air interfaces, GSM was then perceived as a possibility for enabling compatibility in the sense of a 'minimal standard' rather than as an 'outdated technology'.[79] To emphasize the benefit of the multi-standard mobile phone network setting, 'UMTS is sometimes marketed as 3GSM, emphasizing the combination of the 3G nature of the technology and the GSM standard which it was designed to succeed.'[80]

Conclusions

Analysing mobile phone standardization in Europe as a transnational telecommunications infrastructure, we realize that GSM technology in the making is not only based on structures and actors that can be labelled as 'European' but in fact is creating new 'European' structures and actors. If we compare institutional, organizational and legal settings at the start of the process with those once the standard was adopted, we see a completely new institutional matrix. This matrix was changed by the important actors during the GSM standardization process, who also changed themselves, reinventing and reproducing 'Europe'. Observing this process shows that, while classical analytical categories such as the 'nation state', 'market regulation' or 'negotiation analysis' are fruitful for analytical purposes in the GSM case, they have to be combined with questions concerning tensions that actors were willing to sustain in co-operation with others within these various frameworks.

The Madeira meeting can be seen as a crossroads in European mobile phone standardization; policymakers realized that only the vision of a common mobile phone market could break the deadlock in the negotiations and lead to a single standard. European mobile phone standardization had become an objective of political bargaining and was closely bound to the construction of a European market, where regulations would exclude other standards. The traditional setting of the mobile phone industries in Europe – focusing on national markets – was therefore changed completely and actors had to reorientate themselves towards the new GSM setting. As German and French officials saw the inescapable outcome of the specifications negotiations either with or without Franco-German involvement, they lifted the issue onto the EC agenda, obviously for their own benefit. The French and German activities may be seen as a kind of case study for a historical approach to standard negotiations, since not only strategies, but also the institutional embedding of the actors, changed during the negotiation process. The strategies of the major national players, namely France, Germany, the UK, Italy and the Scandinavian countries, seems to reflect changing political agendas, but with consistent preferences. The role of the 'minor' actors such as the Netherlands, Switzerland, Belgium, Austria and so on seems to be quite ambiguous and needs further research.

Finally, there can be no doubt about the dramatic success of GSM, in Europe as well as worldwide. As European Industries have been outperformed by Asian and US competitors in the fields of personal computers, consumer electronics and semiconductors, digital mobile communications is a building block of information technology, in which Europe established and retained an important comparative advantage. This comparative advantage, however, is the result of a concerted European effort throughout the 1980s and 1990s to establish a single market and thus enable economies of scale in the field of mobile telecommunications. The creation of a single technical standard was a prerequisite for such a market. Especially the emergent political stage of the EC helped to break the bargaining deadlock at the Madeira meeting and – together with the member states' PTOs/PTTs – ensured stable co-ordination of the implementation process. On the level of discourse, one could argue that the shifting expectations of the main protagonists became visible at the moment the name of the *Groupe Spécial Mobile* was changed to *Global System for Mobile Communications*. In 1988 this title was far from reality, but today it has become an accurate description.

Notes

1. See, for example, D. Ruloff (ed.), *Globalisierung: Eine Standortbestimmung* (Zurich: Verlag Rüegger 1998); J.A. Frankel, 'Globalization of the Economy', NBER Working Paper No. W7858, August 2000.
2. M. McLuhan and B. Powers, *The Global Village – Transformations in World Life and Media in the 21st Century* (Oxford: Oxford University Press 1989).
3. Jeffrey G. Williamson, 'Globalization, Convergence and History', *The Journal of Economic History* 56(2) (1996), pp. 277–306; Richard Tilly, *Globalisierung aus historischer Sicht und das Lernen aus der Geschichte* (Cologne: Forschungsinstitut für Sozial- und Wirtschaftsgeschichte an der Univ. zu Köln 1999); also Frankel, 'Globalization'.
4. John Agar, *Constant Touch. A Global History of the Mobile Phone* (Cambridge: Icon Books 2004).
5. James E. Katz and Mark A. Aakhus (eds), *Perpetual Contact. Mobile Communication, Private Talk, Public Performance* (Cambridge: Cambridge University Press 2002).
6. Gerard Goggin, *Cell Phone Culture: Mobile Technology in Everyday Life* (New York: Routledge 2006), pp. 6–16.
7. See 3GSM Statistics, the GSM Association, http://www.gsmworld.com/technology/3g/statistics.shtml (accessed 23 January 2007and 3GSM World Coverage 2007, published by Europa Technologies for the GSM Association, http://www.coveragemaps.com/gsmposter_world.htm (accessed 16 February 2007).
8. G. Jenkins, 'Brilliant Past, Bright Future', GSM White paper, *Deutsche Bank Global Equity Research, Industry Focus* (London: Deutsche Bank 2004), p. 1, online at: http://www.3gamericas.org/documents/gsm_whitepaper_feb2004.pdf (accessed 16 February 2007).
9. A.C. Peterson Jr, 'Vehicle Radiotelephony Becomes a Bell System Practice', *Bell Laboratories Record* (April 1947).
10. R. Bekkers and J. Smits, *Mobile Telecommunications: Standards, Regulations and Applications* (Boston: Artech House 1999), p. 24.
11. In terms of total number of subscribers AMPS was leading the global market share with about 46 per cent, followed by GSM (Global Systems for Mobile Communications) with 20 per cent and TACS (Total Access Communications System; an AMPS-Derivant developed by British Telecom and Mercury) with 16 per cent of the global market.
12. For a list of success factors see Jenkins, 'Brilliant Past', pp. 32–5.
13. 'The GSM standard is an European success story: the technical standard itself was developed through EU research and deployment, and encouraged by European regulation of the communications industry. The resulting competition drove further development, driving hardware and call prices down in a virtuous circle from which everyone wins.' 'Europe's Information Society Thematic Portal: Mobile and Wireless Communications.' http://ec.europa.eu/information_society/industry/comms/mobile/index_en.htm (accessed 16 February 2007).
14. See Jacques Pelkmans, 'The GSM Standard. Explaining a Success Story', *Journal of European Public Policy* 8(3) (2001), pp. 432–53.
15. G. Cattaneo, 'The Making of a Pan-European Network as a Path-Dependency Process. The Case of GSM versus IBC (Integrated Broadband Communications) Network' in G. Pogorel (ed.) *Global Telecommunications Strategies and Technological Changes* (Amsterdam: Elsevier Science Publishers 1994), p. 59.

16. Geoffrey Bowker and Susan Leigh Star, *Sorting Things Out: Classification and Its Consequences* (Cambridge, MA: MIT 1999).
17. Paul N. Edwards et al., 'Understanding Infrastructure: Dynamics, Tensions, Designs. Report of a Workshop on "History & Theory of Infrastructure: Lessons for New Scientific Cyberinfrastructures"' (January 2007), pp. 15–16. Online at: http://www.si.umich.edu/InfrastructureWorkshop/documents/Understanding Infrastructure2007.pdf.
18. D. Bach, 'International Cooperation and the Logic of Networks: Europe and the Global System for Mobile Communications (GSM)', BRIE Working Paper 139 (2000), p. 2. See also S.D. Krasner, 'Global Communications and National Power: Life on the Pareto Frontier', *World Politics* 43 (1991).
19. Krasner, 'Global Communications'.
20. For an overview concerning literature and primary sources see A. Manninen, *Elaboration of NMT and GSM Standards: From Idea to Market*, PhD Dissertation (University of Jyvaskyla, Finland 2002); P. Kammerer, 'Das entfesselte Telefon: Kommunikationstechnologische Standards am Beispiel des "Global System for Mobile Communications" (GSM)', H.-J. Gilomen, M. Müller and B. Veyrassat (eds) *Globalisierung – La globalization: Die Schweiz in der Weltwirtschaft 18.–20. Jahrhundert* (Zurich: Chronos 2004), pp. 339–55.
21. T. Misa and J. Schot, 'Introduction – Inventing Europe: Technology and the Hidden Integration of Europe'; E. Van der Vleuten and A. Kaijser, 'Networking Europe', *History and Technology* 21(1) (2005), pp. 1–19 and 21–55, respectively.
22. See Bekkers and Smits, *Mobile Telecommunications*, pp. 23–4. AMPS (Advanced Mobile Phone System) was the first mobile telephony standard worldwide.
23. Ibid., p. 25.
24. SRI Policy Division (ed.), 'Science, Technology and Economic Development. The Role of NSF's support in Enabling Technological Innovation – Phase II, Chapter 4: The Cellular Telephone', pp. 9–10. FCC even had to alter the hours of operation of mobile services divisions reference rooms to manage the large number of applications submitted. Federal Communications Commission (FCC), Public Notice 5377, 18 July 1983.
25. To award licences FCC divided the US market into areas, so-called Metropolitan Statistical Areas (MSAs) and Rural Service Areas (RSAs).
26. Federal Communications Commission (FCC), Public Notice 6277, 30 August 1984.
27. Ameritech Mobile Communications Inc., for example, filed a *Petition For Declatory Ruling* [sic] with the Mobile Services Division of the Common Carrier Bureau. Federal Communications Commission (FCC), Public Notice 966, 23 November 1984.
28. Federal Communications Commission, Wireless Telecommunications Bureau, The FCC Report to Congress on Spectrum Auctions, Released on 9 October 1997, p. 22.
29. Commonly referred to as CDMA, IS-95 or IS-95 CDMA.
30. D-AMPS, IS-95/CDMA, PACS, CCT, DCT-900, W-CDMA and PCS-1900. For an overview see Bekkers and Smits, *Mobile Telecommunications*, pp. 32–7.
31. For the GSM development, see below.
32. See Annina Ruottu, *Governance within the European Television and Mobile Communications Industries: PALplus and GSM – A Case Study of Nokia*, PhD dissertation (University of Sussex 1998), pp. 250–1.
33. C-2000, with 65,000 subscribers in 1997, only used in France. See Bekkers and Smits, *Mobile Telecommunications*, p. 31.

34. C-Netz (by Siemens), with 618,000 subscribers in 1997. Also used in Portugal. See Bekkers and Smits, *Mobile Telecommunications*, p. 31.
35. In Italy the RTMS standard was developed. But just before the Football World Championships in 1990 a TACS (Total Access Communication System) network with 1.8 million subscribers was established. See Bekkers and Smits, *Mobile Telecommunications*, pp. 29–31.
36. TACS is an AMPS variant in the 900 MHz frequency band, developed in the UK. It was also used in Italy, Spain, Austria and Ireland.
37. S. Hultén and B. G. Mölleryd, 'Entrepreneurs, Innovations and Market Processes in the Evolution of the Swedish Mobile Telecommunications Industry', Paper presented at the Eighth International Joseph A. Schumpeter Society Conference, 28 June – 1 July 2000 in Manchester, p. 4.
38. Hultén and Mölleryd, 'Entrepreneurs', p. 4.
39. Ibid., pp. 7–8.
40. See also Kammerer, 'Das entfesselte Telefon', p. 346.
41. Ibid.
42. CEPT–CCH–GSM, Report from Meeting no. 1; 7–9 December 1982 in Stockholm.
43. CEPT Telecommunications Commission, Vienna, 14–25 June 1982. Public Mobile Communications Systems in the 900 MHz band. The Netherlands PTT Administration, p. 1.
44. CEPT–CCH–GSM, Report from Meeting no. 6; 12–6 November 1984 in London, p. 2.
45. Ibid.
46. CEPT already completed, for example, the standardization or the CEPT1 standard for videotext in 1974.
47. For detailed description see Philippe Dupuis, 'Section 3: The Franco-German, tripartite and quadri-partite co-operation from 1984 to 1987' in Friedhelm Hillebrand (ed.) *GSM and UMTS. The Creation of Global Mobile Communication* (West Sussex: John Wiley 2002), pp. 23–30.
48. Ibid. p. 24.
49. Bach, 'International Cooperation', p. 9.
50. Kammerer, 'Das entfesselte Telefon', pp. 346–8.
51. For more technical detail see Kammerer, 'Das entfesselte Telefon', p. 347, and Gerd Bender, 'Technologische Innovation als Form der europäischen Integration. Zur Entwicklung des europäischen Mobilfunkstandards GSM', *Zeitschrift für Soziologie* 28(2) (1999), pp. 77–92, see pp. 84–6.
52. Hultén and Mölleryd state that about $50 million were invested; 'Entrepreneurs', p. 24.
53. CEPT–CCH–GSM, Second Status Report for WP2, GSM doc 21/87, 'Solution 1: Wideband TDMA Solution: This solution is a revised version of the CD 900 concept, with a lower number of channels per carrier.' Annex 1.
54. W. Kaiser, 'Die Weiterentwicklung der Telekommunikation seit 1950' in Hans-Jürgen Teuteberg and Cornelius Neutsch (eds) *Vom Flügeltelegraphen zum Internet. Geschichte der modernen Telekommunikation* (Stuttgart: Franz Steiner Verlag 1998), p. 223.
55. The concept of 'path dependence' was introduced by Paul David; see P.A. David, 'Path–dependence. Putting the past into the future of economics, Institute for Mathematical Studies in the Social Sciences', Stanford University, Technical Report no. 533 (November) (Stanford 1988). Its evolutionary consequences are discussed in Bowker and Star, *Sorting*, pp. 13–14.

56. See also Bach, 'International Cooperation', p. 9.
57. CEPT–CCH–GSM, Report from plenary Meeting no. 13; 16–20 February 1987 in Funcal, Madeira, p. 6.
58. P. Dupuis, 'The Role of the Commission of the European Communities'. pp. 52–5, in Hillebrand (ed.) *GSM and UMTS. The Creation of Global Mobile Communication* (West Sussex: John Wiley 2002), p. 53.
59. As clearly shown by Philippe Dupuis, 'Franco-German', pp. 31–2. There was also an attempt by the Swedish delegation on the Madrid Meeting in Autumn 1986 to reach a pre-decision concerning the *Access Method* that would have strongly affected the question on the frequency band. This caused an exhaustive debate on the earlier agreed decision procedure. See CEPT–CCH–GSM, Report from Meeting No 12 (Madrid, 29 September to 3 October 1986), GSM doc 31/87, pp. 3–4. The Swedish proposal is documented in GSM doc 72/86.
60. A. Fickers, *'Politique de la grandeur' versus 'Made in Germany': Politische Kulturgeschichte der Technik am Beispiel der PAL-SECAM-Kontroverse* (Munich: Oldenbourg 2007).
61. See EU, Radio frequencies: development of mobile communications GSM – UMTS, http://europa.eu.int/scadplus/leg/en/lvb/l24128.htm (accessed 24 February 2007).
62. EU, Radio frequencies, http://europa.eu.int/scadplus/leg/en/lvb/l24128.htm (accessed 24 February 2007).
63. EU, Radio frequencies, http://europa.eu.int/scadplus/leg/en/lvb/l24128.htm (accessed 24 February 2007
64. Memorandum of Understanding on the Implementation of a Pan European 900 MHz Digital Cellular Mobile Telecommunications Service by 1991, 7 September 1987, Article 1, p. 4.
65. Thomas Haug, 'The Detailed Specification Work Leading to the GSM Phase 1 Standard used for the Opening of Service (1987–1991)' in Friedhelm Hillebrand (ed.) *GSM and UMTS. The Creation of Global Mobile Communication* (West Sussex: John Wiley 2002), pp. 57–9.
66. The status of an 'association' in Switzerland is limited to organizations that pursue non-profit objectives and engage in beneficial, scientific, cultural, political or social activities. However, some of the more important associations are formed to pursue economic goals, for instance, professional organizations and trade unions. Non-profit associations may, for the better attainment of their goals, carry on an industrial or commercial activity. Associations acquire the status of a separate legal entity as soon as the articles of association are drawn up. See: Types of Business Entities, Commercial Law Page. See http://geneva.ch/genevaguidetypesbusinessentities.htm (accessed 21 April 2002).
67. Memorandum of Understanding. The GSM Association, http://www.gsmworld.com/about/history_page14.html (accessed 23 September 2000).
68. DCS was developed in the UK to reach higher capacities in urban areas.
69. Cattaneo, 'The Making', pp. 59–62.
70. Federal Communications Commission, Auctions, see http://wireless.fcc.gov/auctions/ (accessed 12 April 2002).
71. GSM Association: Going Global, http://www.gsmworld.com/about/history_page14.html (accessed 21 April 2003).
72. See EU: Convergence of the Telecommunication, Media and Information Technology, http://ec.europa.eu/archives/ISPO/convergencegp/ (accessed 10 October 2007).
73. GSM Association: GSM Operators, Coverage Maps and Roaming Information, http://www.gsmworld.com/roaming/gsminfo/index.shtml (accessed 21 July 2007).

74. Smart phone is a term for PDA (Personal Digital Assistant) or pocket computer with included mobile phone technology.
75. For example, the RACE (Research and Development in Advanced Communications Technologies for Europe) 1988–92 and ACTS (Advanced Communications Technologies and Services) 1994–8.
76. European Telecommunications Standards Institute (ETSI), Association of Radio Industries and Businesses/Telecommunication Technology Committee (ARIB/TTC) (Japan), China Communications Standards Association [2], Alliance for Telecommunications Industry Solutions (North America) and Telecommunications Technology Association (South Korea).
77. ARIB/TTC (Japan), China Communications Standards Association, Telecommunications Industry Association (North America) and Telecommunications Technology Association (South Korea).
78. CDMA technologies are: W-CDMA (the European UMTS, Universal Mobile Telecommunications System, the variant used by *NTT DoCoMo*) and CDMA 2000 (in different variants). TDMA technologies are: UWC-136/EDGE (an enhancement for GSM-systems) and DECT (for indoor 'pico'-cells).
79. For example, Nortel, 'GSM-UMTS Network Evolution Positioning Paper' (Maidenhead: Nortel 2005) online at: http://www.ivynetwork.co.kr/sup_img/pdf_03.pdf.
80. G. Müller and S. Wohlgemuth, 'Study on Mobile Identity Management', *FIDIS Future of Identity in the Information Society, EC Contract No. 507512* (www.fidis.net) (2005), p. 82.

Part III

Europe between Projects and Projections

8
Eventing Europe: Broadcasting and the Mediated Performances of Europe

Andreas Fickers and Suzanne Lommers

Introduction

Studying the role of broadcasting in the making of Europe can help to emphasize technology's role as central actor in the story of Europe's hidden integration, and – here's the other side of the story – its fragmentation. This chapter aims to study the history of Europe by starting with the idea that broadcast communication was the most powerful and influential means for both national and transnational communication in the twentieth century. The central objective is to problematize Europe as a broadcasting space by describing and analysing European radio and television broadcasts originating from the International Broadcasting Union and the European Broadcasting Union and by questioning their specific contribution to the medial construction of European and international communication spaces in constantly changing political and cultural environments. In retracing both sound and audiovisual broadcast transmissions in the 1920s, 1930s and 1950s we will link the development of different broadcast technologies (radio and television) to visions of European broadcasting spaces and their role in the continuous reinvention of Europe or re-imagination of European identities. Starting with an *a priori* geographical definition of Europe is futile given the need to embed the discursive construction of 'Europe' into changing material, legal and institutional maps. Here again, the very nature of broadcasting as a transnational or transborder phenomenon with its inevitable spillover effects challenges the classic ways of mapping Europe.

To meet the general purpose of this book, that is, to study the nature and role of transnational infrastructures in the construction of Europe, we follow the threefold conception of infrastructures as material, institutional and symbolic interfaces laid out in the introduction. As Badenoch and Fickers describe, the discursive construction of Europe, European identities and European spaces are most visible in so called European 'events'. Until recently, events have been favoured objects of study of sociologists interested in the 'extra-ordinary', in social agency or collective activity transgressing the quotidian or routine social behaviour.[1] Generally speaking, events as social happenings are planned and organized occasions of collective participation – either mediated or proximate participation. While events originally consisted in a bodily and physical experience of an organized happening by a larger group of people (think of the Roman circus games lasting several days, a medieval conclave or a modern political event such as the Vienna congress), modern communication technologies have deeply changed both the nature and the experience of social events. The live coverage of events by various media technologies has transformed the social situation of the happening: those who bodily participate have themselves become the stage for the unknown mass of mediated participants. Together they perform what Daniel Dayan and Elihu Katz have described as 'media events'. Focusing their investigation on television, Dayan and Katz define media events as extraordinary experiences of medial participation: 'Audiences recognize them as an invitation – even a command – to stop their daily routines and join in a holiday experience. If festive viewing is to ordinary viewing what holidays are to the everyday, these events are the high holidays of mass communication.'[2] While the definition of media events by Dayan and Katz has been criticized as being too rigid in its characterization of media events as pre-planned and highly stereotyped forms of mediated social interaction,[3] media sociologist Nick Couldry has wondered whether they can be 'read' as expressions of social order at all or should instead be interpreted as medial constructions of collective identities.[4]

Without entering into the media-theoretical debate about the social or medial nature and meaning of media events, we propose to use the concept of event as an analytical tool for the study and interpretation of European radio and television broadcasts in the 1920s, 1930s and 1950s. In focusing on two IBU radio programme series, 'Nuits Nationales' and its successor 'Concerts Européens', and on early Eurovision television programmes organized by the EBU, we will try to analyse these European broadcast performances as European events. We view them as events in the sense that they can be interpreted as simultaneous enunciations of the material infrastructures necessary for the complex technical realization of these transnational transmissions, of the organizational efforts involved to co-ordinate the various experts involved in both national and international institutions, and finally of the symbolic expression and discursive construction of Europeanness in the transmitted programmes and their diverse ways of individual and collective appropriation of these codified European meanings.

Proceeding chronologically, we will first present the historical case of the IBU radio programmes called 'Nuits Nationales', which – starting in 1926 – inaugurated a series of monthly broadcast music programmes addressed to a Europe-wide audience. In 1931, this initiative was replaced by a new series called 'Concerts Européens', which was transmitted on a regular basis until 1939. While these radio programmes as serial events have contributed to the eventing of Europe in sound, the second case study will study the eventing of Europe in vision. In contrast to the serial character of the 'Nuits Nationales' or the 'Concerts Européens', early Eurovision programmes were singular and mostly live programmes, promoting the idea of television as 'window to the world' – although a world consisting of a small number of European nations participating in the early Eurovision adventures. As we will show in the conclusion, the changing programme formats and the varying solutions found to achieve the technical realization of these European broadcast events go hand in hand with new conceptions about Europe as a cultural communication space. To unpick the forces at work in such infrastructural events, we need to see the way in which the material, institutional and symbolic layers of European broadcast infrastructures work together and shape each other in a process of mutual co-construction.

Eventing Europe in sound: International radio broadcasting in the Interbellum

Throughout the 1920s and 1930s broadcasting grew enormously. Systems of wireless transmitters, as well as an international relay infrastructure of wires and cables, developed from almost nothing. While wireless communication before the Great War mainly consisted of point-to-point communication and thereby invented radio as an interactive communication medium, the post-war period saw the birth of a new concept of point-to-mass communication called broadcasting. By 1925 numerous broadcasting organizations covered and surpassed national territories with their broadcasts, which were sent by means of long and medium waves, while the first experiments with short-wave transmission to aim intentionally at foreign audiences began.[5] Often signals interfered and organizations were (un)intentionally jamming each other's broadcasts, a situation that decreased the quality of transmission. Since these signals were transnational in nature, the explosion in broadcasting activities throughout Europe became a problem beyond the control of individual nations. The problem also impacted negatively on the quality of reception: 'Reception became torture; the listener suffering constant interference between stations of different countries was the pitiable victim of these profligate signals in the form of whistling, grinding, cracking, groaning, which he remembers with horror to this day.'[6]

On the initiative of Maurice Rambert, President of the Swiss broadcasting organization, ten European broadcasting organizations from Austria, Belgium, Czechoslovakia, France, Germany, Great Britain, the Netherlands, Norway, Spain and Switzerland established the International Broadcasting Union (IBU) in 1925.[7] Initially these organizations were mostly private and regional in nature, but over the years radio became more widely considered a public utility and most of the IBU members became public organizations. Though all its founding members were European, already in its first brochure the IBU stressed: 'As the majority of these problems, whether technical, legal or artistic, are of a worldwide character, it is felt that the time has come when the benefits arriving from this Union of broadcasters should be extended to broadcasters in all countries.' The IBU thus aimed to create a transnational public sphere that was international, worldwide in scope rather than European in nature and welcomed extra-European countries into its organization. These world-encompassing desires notwithstanding, the IBU could not help but first of all focus on Europe and the considerable increase in members in the ensuing years mostly came from within the European broadcasting zone. Whereas long-distance broadcasting in the United States, for instance, could develop rather easily, in Europe it was hampered by distinctive systems of administrations and control.[8] In order to allow functional international broadcasting, and hence a high quality of transmission, these distinctive systems needed to be adapted and/or coupled by means of international agreements and co-ordination of infrastructure. IBU played a key role in this process.

Though the co-ordination of frequency allocations to bring the chaos in the European ether to a halt was of primary importance, IBU also wished to set up an intense international exchange of programmes over long distances. On the one hand, international programme exchange would promote radio with special programmes from other countries in order to seduce a group of people who until then had had no interest in radio.[9] On the other hand, programme exchange would serve the Union's ideological goal of rapprochement and mutual understanding between the peoples by means of broadcasting. Seen in the light of the international situation at the time, the Union's ideological goals perfectly matched the aims of the League of Nations.[10] The creation of mutual understanding would lead to rapprochement between the peoples in Europe and the world and, it was believed, would help to build a lasting peace.

In order to establish a satisfactory international long-distance programme exchange the Union needed to change the existing technological status quo, which did not allow any of these activities. The transmission stations in Europe simply lacked the power to allow people to listen in over long distances without being bothered by annoying background noises. The interception and relaying of programmes over long distances by wireless proved ineffective and unsatisfying. Another option, the European long-distance telephone network, which had been under construction since the early 1920s, and in some cases enabled international telephone conversations, could not transmit the broad band of frequencies that accompanied musical performances. In December 1925 the IBU turned to the International Telephone Consultative Committee (CCIF), an advisory body of the International Telegraph Union (ITU), to ask them 'for a systematic examination…of the possibility of creating an international network for telephonic circuits specially suited to the needs of broadcasting'. CCIF received the request favourably, and this turned out to be the start of continuous and long-term co-operation between the two bodies to develop a European long-distance telephone network that ensured high-quality transmission of music. In a few years' time this international circuit of mostly cables and some aerial lines carried over poles started to diffuse between the

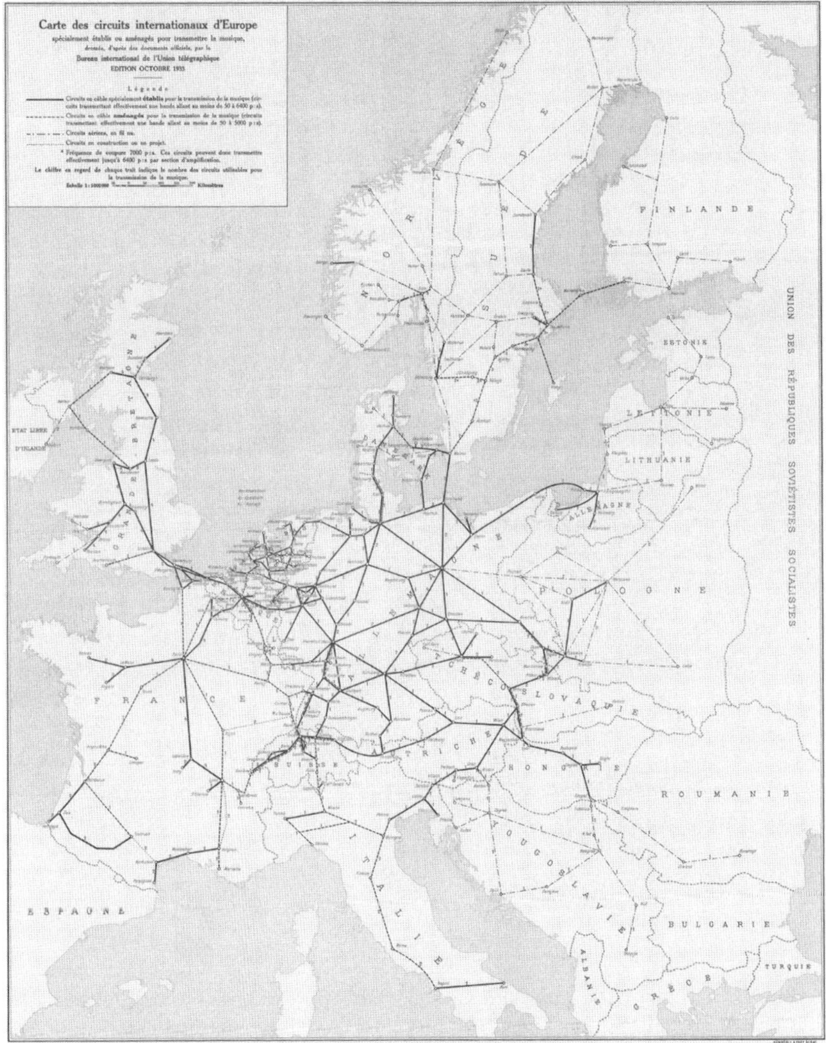

Figure 8.1   Office of the International Telegraph Union: Map of circuits specially established or available for transmitting music (ITU, Berne: October 1933)

Source: Reproduced with kind permission of the International Telecommunication Union.

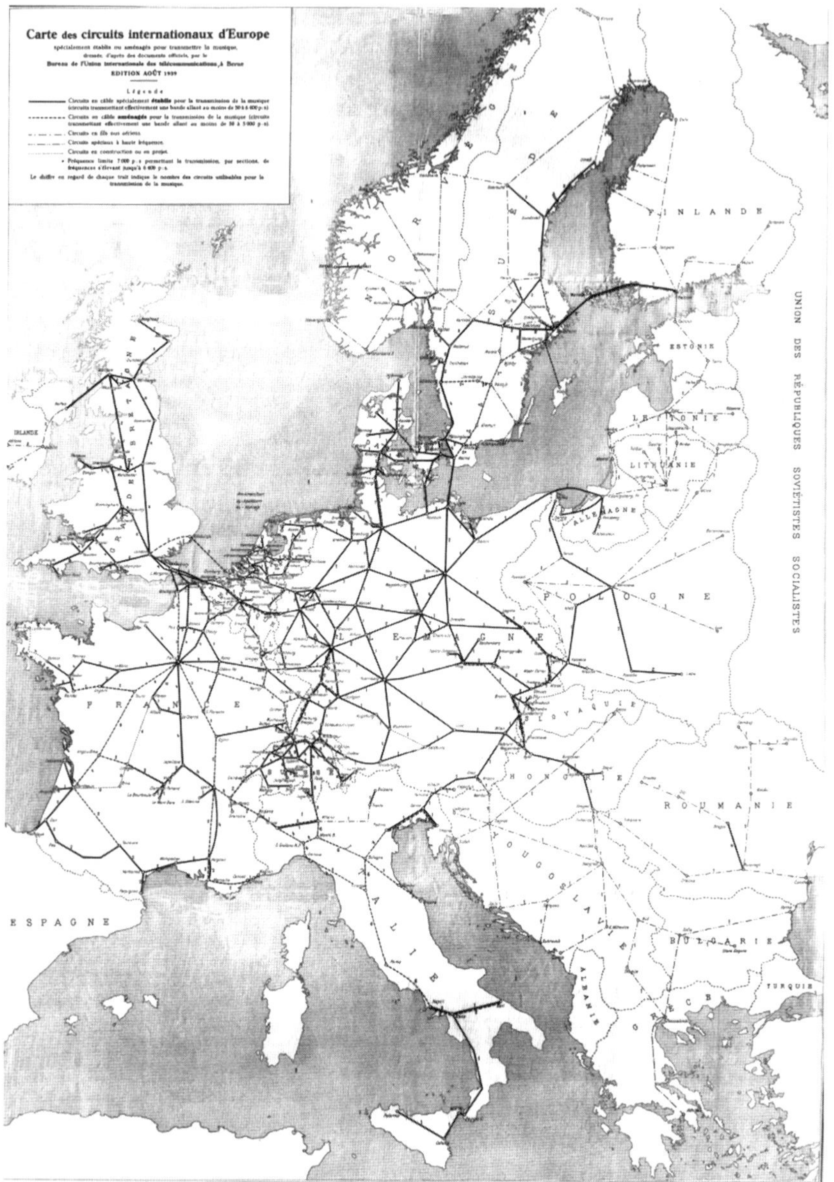

Figure 8.2   Office of the International Telegraph Union: Map of circuits specially established or available for transmitting music (ITU, Berne: August 1939)

Source: Reproduced with kind permission of the International Telecommunication Union.

various European capitals and make connections at national boundaries (see Figures 8.1 and 8.2).

National Nights: A first joint effort in international programming

As the technological situation did not allow an international exchange of programmes, the IBU, acting on a proposal from the Secretary General of the Radio Union S.A. Madrid, found a provisional solution in the form of the so called *Nuits Nationales*, the National Nights.[11] Once a month, co-ordinated by the IBU, a National Night was to be broadcast all over Europe, bringing a high variety of national music and literature from one specific European country. Broadcasting, as a result, would enable the people in Europe to get to know each other and learn about their similarities and differences. These programmes, though completely national in character, served the idea that, by stressing not only unity, but also cultural diversity, people would learn to understand each other, to stand near to each other in the hope that a peaceful Europe (and hence a peaceful world) would be one step closer.[12]

The National Nights were an improvised solution for a complete lack of technological options. There were neither satisfactory technical standards to transmit music over long distances in an acceptable quality nor harmonized recording standards. The only possible solution to enable a simultaneous transmission of the National Nights throughout the European zone was by accurately synchronizing the parallel transmission of the programme by the participating national broadcasters, who all shared the same programme script, but performed it with their in-house staff (announcers, technicians and musicians). As one can easily imagine, creating such a synchronized multi-platform performance required an immense organizational effort on a transnational level.

But what did the programmes look like? The main idea behind the National Nights was that all participating countries were given the opportunity, in rotation, to present themselves to the other nations by creating a musical programme, reflecting or representing the national spirit, tradition or culture of the 'honoured' country. The country responsible for the National Night had to develop its programme in consultation with the national PTT Administration. The final programme, including documentation for the introductory speeches and promotion material for local newspapers, had to be presented to the IBU Office in Geneva six weeks before the broadcast. The office then would translate and send the programme, the documentation and a list of all participating IBU members to the broadcasting stations who joined in the National Nights. All participating broadcasting organizations, as participation happened on a voluntary basis, had to announce the National Nights in the local press to attract a widest possible audience.

In fact, each singular National Night in reality was a series of national appropriations of the programme created by the country to be presented. All participating countries had to perform the National Night according to a script in the language of the honoured country as well as in English, French and/or German. Both the announcements and the music that national audiences could hear were performed by the national host (broadcaster) with its local artists.[13] Since every radio orchestra had its own stylistic and aesthetic tradition, their interpretations differed by definition from the performance of the original ensemble. Furthermore, each member was free to make necessary modifications to the programme to better suit local needs.[14]

Not surprisingly, one of the main discussions within the IBU centred on the question of quality. What kind of music would fit the quality standards of high culture entertainment? How often and when should the programme be broadcast in order to reach the desired audience and impact? In general the members regarded classical music or short opera pieces, as well as national folklore music, as suitable for the National Nights. Light operas, by contrast, would go against their intention of creating understanding and rapprochement, as these pieces often caricaturized specifics and habits of nations. In the view of most members, the repertoire should consist of music without too much singing in order to reach the largest audience.[15] Intentions, however, turned out to clash with reality. By the end of 1928, Secretary General Arthur Burrows presented a rather depressing summary of the first experiences with the National Nights programmes to the responsible IBU Committee on Intellectual, Artistic and Social Rapprochement. The last National Nights had attracted very little attention, he summarized: only ten member countries out of twenty had participated, coinciding with about thirty stations out of 130. The audience reached by the Nights was hence a lot smaller than expected. During the meeting, the discussion on how to improve the programmes centred on the shortening of the Nights rather than on a change of content. Furthermore, Burrows stated that not only the broadcasting countries, but also the countries that were being honoured, showed a decreasing interest in the Nights. Honoured countries provided their programmes and promotion materials too late, which led to ignorant mistakes on behalf of the broadcasting countries. Burrows gave a painful example: 'Most of the times the participating countries had to look for illustrations representing the particularities of the honoured country; as it happens, a famous journal announcing a National Night hosted by Switzerland published a photograph of the Mont Blanc [sic!]'[16].

In the light of scheduling, initially all members enthusiastically supported the idea of a monthly series of National Nights at a fixed date and time, but in reality this proved to be extremely problematic. Whereas the IBU was trying to invent a new broadcasting tradition, the broadcasting organizations feared the erosion of the established scheduling and listening routines of their national audiences. In January 1928, Oscar Czeija, head of the Committee on Intellectual, Artistic and Social Rapprochement of the IBU, addressed his own Committee to discuss the German and Austrian complaints about the fact that the National Nights schedules clashed with their own traditions. Germany claimed that the Sunday evening programmes traditionally addressed a very specific and demanding audience, and in Austria listeners had complained that they wanted their favourite local programme instead of the National Nights. Sunday evenings had already become moments in which German and Austrian families listened to popular national radio programmes and thereby had established a routinized collective radio usage.[17] Both the representatives of Germany and Austria thought that the National Nights were better to be scheduled on another evening.[18]

Despite these difficulties and declining attention to the programmes at the end of the first series in April 1929, the Committee decided to continue with a second series. Despite remaining problems with the quality of sound transmission, the programmes retained their symbolic capital, and some countries still wanted to have the honour of organizing their National Night. For the second series, the IBU decided on some organizational and practical improvements. The transmission dates had to be set far in advance and honouring countries needed to contact the principal music and literature organizations in their countries to discuss the best ways to make a programme that matched their own national spirit.[19] During the Administrative Council meeting in May 1929, the IBU stipulated that each country had to appoint a contact person who could deal with all questions regarding the organization of the National Nights.[20] The second series continued up to December 1931, when Portugal had the honour of closing the series.

European Concerts: A truly European programme?

Over the course of the two seasons of National Nights, Europe-wide broadcasting infrastructures diffused steadily on the continent, co-ordinated by the IBU. The wireless network had increased considerably throughout the second half of the 1920s, from 170 transmission stations in 1926 to 230 in 1930. After 1930, technical developments enabled the construction of high-power stations that considerably improved the quality of the transmissions but at the same time inaugurated a constant increase of transmitter power.[21] These developments in wireless radio also strengthened the IBU's intent to exchange programmes internationally and to relay specific programmes over all of Europe, enabling people to listen simultaneously to the same programme. The programmes were relayed over the European long distance telephone network, and on arrival would be coupled with the transmitting stations of the member organizations. The members would then send the broadcast over the local frequencies and enable the audience to listen to foreign programmes via their home channel. Construction of the international long-distance relay network throughout the second half of the 1920s developed steadily. By 1927, in several parts of Europe, experiments headed off with the exchange of music, especially with symphonic concerts. These joint efforts between several national broadcasting organizations and national PTT Administrations were not meant to build bilateral links, but aimed explicitly at extending the effort throughout the entire European zone.[22] Central Europe took the lead when Germany, Austria and Czechoslovakia met in 1927 on the initiative of Poland. After some initial tests, regular experimental relays started in spring 1928.[23] By 1929 Hungary and Yugoslavia had joined them.[24] In the meantime, Great Britain, Belgium and Germany took the initiative to develop international relaying in Western Europe by linking London to Berlin via Belgium. By 1928 relays from London had extended to Liège and Cologne, and no less than two years later the network had developed into the Netherlands and throughout the whole of Germany. In 1931 the network extended into France and Scandinavia, and Italy was connected to Austria.[25]

The IBU got heavily involved, either officially or unofficially, in both the Western and Central European initiatives. On the one hand, IBU representatives were present at the various meetings. On the other hand, many IBU people had hybrid identities, performing important tasks within the IBU and within their national broadcasting organization. Oscar Czeija, for instance, head of IBU's Committee on Intellectual, Artistic and Social Rapprochement, was also Director of the Austrian broadcasting organization, one of the initiators of the Central European initiative. In the end, the people who jointly constructed the European broadcasting network were a small group of people of engineers, diplomats and intellectuals, who shared similar dreams and who in their national and international functions worked to make it happen. As Léonard Laborie and Suzanne Lommers have recently put it, the European Concerts were an attempt to translate a diplomatic metaphor into a radio message.[26]

In October 1930 the programme directors of both the Western and Central European initiatives gathered for a meeting under the auspices of the International Relay Committee. Mr Chamiec, the committee's president and president of Polskie Radjo as well, headed the meeting and decided that the two initiatives should be coupled such that straightforward co-operation would lead to the complete unification of both groups. Furthermore, the programme directors agreed that a series of concerts of the highest quality should be broadcast each month at fixed dates when all participants would be able to relay the concerts. These concerts carried the name European Concerts, and were to become *'un évènement artistique d'importance européenne'* – an artistic performance of European importance and high representative value.[27]

The European Concerts were made 'with the aim of spreading the notion of radio's usefulness and making the public understand that there exist certain manifestations of art that can unite all European listeners'.[28] As with the National Nights, the Member organizations had to organize the European Concerts in rotation. Though not a legal obligation, participation in these concerts was considered a moral obligation. In those places in Europe where the international long-distance relay network fell short, short-wave broadcasting could form an important supplement to the telephone network, the council decided.[29] Countries could only participate provided their technical conditions were sufficient to allow high-quality broadcasts. Furthermore, the council observed, the interest of the audience, to a large part, depended on the programme contents. The council preferred the organizers to focus on popular oeuvres of high quality rather than on symphonic concerts of long duration. Only by attracting a large mass of people would the European Concerts be able to respond to the Union's ideal of uniting the peoples in Europe by means of music, the universal language.[30]

Despite the high symbolic capital of the project, the organization of the European Concerts encountered similar difficulties as the National Nights had faced before. First, the concerts often lasted too long and audiences lost interest. Secondly, organizers often announced their concerts too late, thus excluding some countries from participation. After the initial decision to stop the European Concerts in 1934 and replace them with a new type of European or international programme,[31] in 1935 the programme directors decided that the European Concerts in fact best represented the aims of the Union and that the problem mainly resulted from the medium and the message being out of balance.[32] They claimed that 'if radio becomes nothing but remains just a means of reproducing applied music and therefore an expression of a primitive amusement (dance, appeasing unconscious senses) it would do little justice to its high technical value'.[33] The council adopted a resolution that stated that the European Concerts should continue, but in a shortened one-hour format with a relay every six weeks. The programmes could contain both classical and modern oeuvres of all genres, as long as they were of a high quality and represented the national character of the country. Unlike the first series, IBU members were now obliged to participate.[34]

In retrospect, the European Concerts were broadcast with great regularity from 1931 until 1939, and, in total, twenty-eight European countries organized a concert.[35] Throughout the first half of the 1930s, the IBU intensely worked to establish short-wave intercontinental connections with North and South America, Japan, Australia and the various European dominions and colonies. The intention was to organize common European programmes and to enable a dialogue between personalities in the various European and non-European territories.[36] Despite all the technical difficulties and cultural challenges mentioned earlier, it seems that most of these intentions were achieved over the course of the 1930s.

The European Concerts were a unique concept enabled by the construction of an international long-distance relay network that was built in the years 1927–31 and that continuously diffused throughout Europe and the world until 1939. The European Concerts aimed to create a sense of liveness and shared immediacy amongst their audience. The concerts, though received over the audience's home stations, were explicitly announced as European broadcasts and were easily recognized as 'foreign'. They were announced in two languages, in French and in the language of the country that relayed them. Furthermore, the names of all participating countries, rather than the names of the stations, were announced.[37] These serial events shaped European experiences by creating an imagined community of listeners all over Europe and by stimulating a virtual dialogue between transmitted and received visions of a European communication space.

Eventing Europe in vision: The early days of Eurovision

Cold War politics: The foundation of OIRT and EBU

As mentioned above, the IBU was founded in 1925 in response to the explosive rise of broadcasting stations in the world.[38] Because of the unhindered radiation of radio waves, the 'chaos of the ether' became a serious problem for international broadcasting. The creation of the IBU can be interpreted as a successful example of self-regulation in international policy. In a free process of rule-making, all broadcasting nations established a kind of 'ether police', controlling the keeping of the frequency plans agreed upon.[39] The choice of Geneva as legal seat of the IBU was only one little allusion to the political self-definition of the IBU as a 'United Nations of Broadcasters'. Despite the initial success of one of the first non-governmental organizations, the close interrelation between broadcasting and politics made co-operation in times of rising political extremism more and more difficult. Like its model the League of Nations, all the good intentions of the IBU broke down during the Second World War. The German army even used the material of the technical centre of the IBU in Brussels for bugging activities. At the end of the war, the IBU was reduced to a small circle of German-friendly countries and therefore unacceptable to most of its original founders.[40]

Although the Technical Centre in Brussels took up its activities under the lead of the Belgian *Institut National de Radiodiffusion* (INR) and the BBC, a heated debate about the future of the IBU began. The driving force of this debate was the Soviet Union, which, during an informal meeting of the IBU in March 1946, surprisingly proposed the foundation of a new international broadcasting organization, in which each of its member republics would have a vote. Only a few weeks later, this proposition led to the foundation of the *Organisation Internationale de Radiodiffusion* (OIR, later OIRT including television) with legal seat in Brussels. Even though the powerful BBC and the Scandinavian countries prevented the dispersal of the IBU, the broadcasting landscape was divided *de facto*. Finally, in May 1950, after some years of bitter competition, the IBU was officially broken up. Following an initiative of the BBC, a new 'western' counterpart of the OIR was founded with the name of 'European Broadcasting Union' (EBU). As Rüdiger Zeller says in his history of the EBU, the foundation of the EBU was 'the result of the splitting of Europe in an eastern and western block'.[41] At the beginning of the television age in the early 1950s, the European television landscape offered the image of a politically divided and technically fragmented continent. Despite this sober picture of the European television landscape, some rays of hope rose up to the European television sky in the early 1950s. Under these rays of hope, the light of one star shone with great promise: the star of 'Eurovision'.

From Neuro- to Eurovision or the French–British 'entente cordiale'?

In an article of the 'Evening Standard' from 5 November 1951, the British journalist George Campey wrote down his visions about the future of television in Europe and gave them the easily remembered headline 'Eurovisions'.[42] The real father of the idea of a systematic television programme exchange on a European level, however, was the Swiss Marcel Bezençon. Already at the second meeting of the advisory board of the newly founded EBU, he presented a paper developing his thoughts about future programme exchange. As the minutes of this meeting show, some doubts were expressed about his proposal, especially from the juridical committee. They feared legal problems caused by international copyright.[43] But the technicians hurried on ahead of jurists and civil servants, and it was the Franco-British alliance of RTF and BBC officials that took the lead.

In August 1950, technicians of the British Broadcast Corporation and the Radiodiffusion & Télévision Françaises conducted the so-called 'Calais Experiment', the first ever transnational live transmission of television pictures (see Figure 8.3). On 27 August, 100 years almost to the day after the first submarine telegraph cable was laid, a one-hour variety programme called 'Calais en Fête' was carried by means of four lightweight micro-wave radio links in tandem from Calais to London.[44] While the French 'offered' Calais as a symbolic location for this bilateral endeavour,[45] the BBC and the British radio industry provided the complete technical infrastructure.[46] As an engineering press statement from the BBC stated, the broadcast was 'the culmination of much painstaking research and experiment by the BBC's engineers and the British radio manufacturers'. Especially the 65 km leap across the Channel presented special problems to the engineers, as the television signals received at Dover fluctuated with changes in the weather and the tides, and was even affected by the passage of ships through the Strait.[47]

The Calais experiment had demonstrated the technical feasibility of a trans-Channel television transmission, but the enterprise had been – at least on the technical level – a purely British one and the programme could only be watched by viewers on the Island. The next step, therefore, was to create a real transnational programme, connecting Paris and London in a two-way link. For this purpose, an 'Anglo-French Television Liaison Committee' was founded shortly after the Calais experiment, which consisted of television

Figure 8.3   Richard Dimbleby in Calais, 1 August 1950
Source: EBU Archives.

experts from both the BBC and the RTF. The main preoccupation of this Committee soon became the planning and realization of a programme that 'would be of interest to both the French and British audiences with a double commentary in French and English and equal credits to both RTF and BBC'.[48] From a technical point of view, the BBC was without doubt the senior partner in this experiment, while the development of a television infrastructure in France proved to be rather problematic.[49]

Despite this mismatch on the technological balance of power of the two nations, the 'Paris-week' of 1952 proved to be an impressive joint venture of the two public services. Between 8 and 14 July, eighteen programmes were originated in Paris and seen, simultaneously, by viewers in both France and the United Kingdom (See Figure 8.5).[50] As the map in Figure 8.4 shows, a chain of relays linked not only Paris with London, but also the British capital with British heartlands and the major Scottish cities.

The mutual praise in testimonies by RTF and BBC officials after the 1952 'Paris-week' show that both the British and the French saw themselves as the pioneering engine of a coming European television era. In a letter from the Director General of the BBC to his French counterpart, Wladimir Porché, William Haley confessed: 'I'm sure that in the years to come this

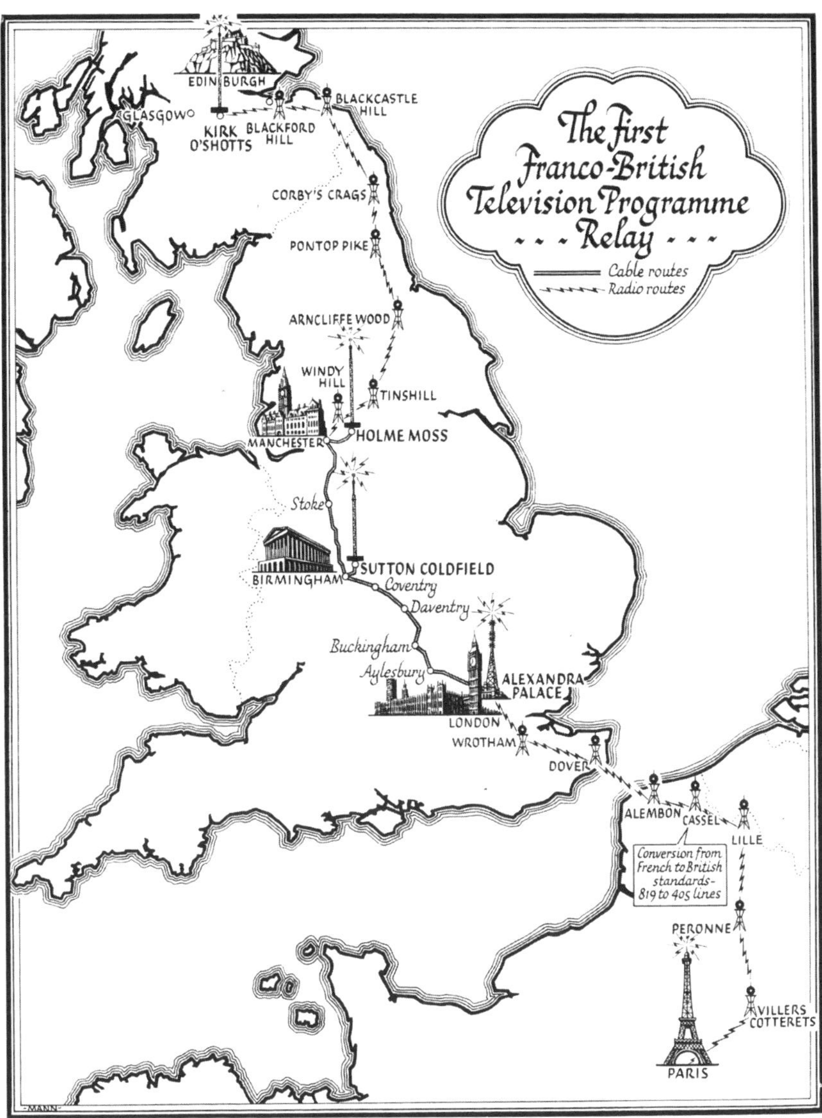

Figure 8.4   Map of the first Franco-British television relay, 1952
Source: EBU Archives.

Figure 8.5   British–French co-operation as expressed on the cover of the *Radio Times*, 6–12 July 1952

joint effort between RTF and the BBC will become an historic landmark in the progress of broadcasting, and we are pleased and proud that it should have been jointly undertaken between two such comrades in arms as the Radiodiffusion et Télévision Françaises and the BBC.'[51] In his reply two days later, Porché admitted that this performance was the most memorable and substantial ever realized by the RTF, and shared Haley's pride in France and Great Britain being the motor of European collaboration on television matters. However, technicians and programme controllers involved articulated clear doubts about the aesthetic quality of the programmes and the nature of the French–British collaboration. Cecil McGivern, controller of BBC television, noted that 'there was little of the recent Paris/London week in which we could take real pleasure,'[52] and BBC head of outside broadcasts, Peter Dimmock, sharply criticized that 'circumstances made it quite impossible for me to exercise much authority and leadership in connection with the programmes.' And with a petition for historical mercy he ended: 'All in all, it was a heartbreaking experiment but I sincerely hope that if a long term view is taken it will have been considered worthwhile.'[53] In a slightly conciliatory tone, Richard Dimbleby, who had already officiated as BBC presenter in the Calais experiment, confessed: 'I hope, next time – if there is a next time – that a great many of our initial troubles will have been righted. I think that everyone on our side worked tremendously hard under unbelievable difficulties. I was rather doubtful in the first few days whether we were straining the entente cordiale a little too far but I think that a friendly last night proved that we have made many friends among the French.'[54]

Despite these serious criticisms from the BBC staff, the 'Calais-Experiment' and the 'Paris-week' had demonstrated the feasibility of a bilateral television programme and thereby backed Bezançon's plans for a regular television programme exchange organized by the EBU. But the vision of 'Eurovision' needed another impulse to break through. This impulse was the coronation of Queen Elizabeth II in June 1953. For the first time in television history, an event was broadcast live into five countries: Great Britain, France, Germany, Denmark and the Netherlands. From a cultural history perspective, the effect of this transmission on the public cannot be overestimated. The feeling of a 'televisual participation' created by the live transmission of motion pictures undoubtedly pushed television development all over the world.[55] An unknown fascination provoked by this 'window to the world' could be measured everywhere. Although the coronation transmission had been realized by the national broadcasting institutions of the five countries involved and therefore had not been an official EBU activity, its effects on the latter were strong.[56] As Wolfgang Degenhardt and others have shown, the technical expenditure was enormous – especially the costly equipment for the line conversion – 'but the propagandistic effect of this pioneer performance can't be weighted with money'.[57] Without doubt, the coronation event shaped a new horizon of televisual expectations in a lot of European countries. At the end of July 1953, a first conference of Western European countries on international television relays was hosted at the Broadcasting House in London. Representatives of France, Great Britain, Western Germany, the Netherlands, Belgium and the European Broadcasting Union made an evaluation of the coronation experience and discussed the future of television programme exchanges in Europe.[58] While technical problems clearly dominated the debates – especially the problem of line standard conversion[59] and the possibility of permanent radio links between the different countries – the French launched a new programme exchange initiative at Christmastime 1953.[60]

But the French plan proved to be too optimistic. Due to the technical challenge of creating a two-way transmission network linking the six countries involved (the coronation was 'only' a one-way transmission from London to the other countries), the project was postponed and finally realized as the first EBU Eurovision programme exchange in the summer of 1954.[61] The first European television exchange was the biggest experiment in international television collaboration of its time. Over 4,000 kilometres of radio circuits linked forty-four relay transmitters in eight countries (Great Britain, France, Germany, Italy, Denmark, the Netherlands, Belgium and Switzerland). Again, the challenge of line standard conversion and sound transmission was enormous. In Breda (NL), a converter point was realized for the conversion from either French and Belgian 819-line or British 405-line pictures to 625 lines. The RTF team in Paris managed the conversion from either 625 or 405 lines to 819 lines, while BBC staff in Dover secured the conversion from either 625 or 819 lines to the British 405 line standard. Because no electronic converter systems existed at that time, the technical solution of this problem was to place a 405-, 625- or 819-line camera, respectively, in front of a 405-, 625- or 819-line receiver in order to re-televise the picture in the standard of the pick-up tube (camera). As BBC chief engineer Edward Pawley remembers in his 1979 retrospect headed 'Eurovision: Faith & Works', the development of standards converters became a 'conditio sine qua non' for the whole Eurovision adventure.[62]

The following description of the journey of a British 405-line picture taken in London to different countries of destination might help demonstrate the complexity of this endeavour. The programme left London and travelled in a series of hops via Wrotham and Dover across the Channel to Cassell, France, where it was taken over by the RTF and carried to Lille. Here the programme was divided: in one direction it went to Paris for conversion to 819 lines and distribution on the French network; in the other direction it went over a series of links installed in Belgium to Holland. In the Netherlands (Breda), the British 405-line picture was converted to the continental standard of 625 lines and then distributed in one direction to Belgium and in the other to the Dutch network and then onwards to Cologne over new relay stations especially installed for this purpose. Here the signals joined the

Western German TV network and were fed to all the German transmitting stations. From Hamburg, a series of special links continued the circuit as far north as Copenhagen, while from the southern end of the German network near Baden-Baden a link was established to Chasseral, Switzerland. From this point the signals travelled to Zurich for transmission on the Swiss network and also separately across Switzerland to Italy, the intermediate relay points being on the Jungfrauenjoch and Monte-Generoso before finally descending to Milan. At Milan the signals joined the Italian network and found their way as far south as Rome.[63]

But it was not only the pictures that had to travel, but sound too. For BBC controller Cecil McGivern, sound transmission was even more complicated due to the different languages involved. Because of the limited bandwidth, it was not possible to transmit the voices of commentators of all seven countries participating in parallel. At each filming location, only two or three commentators were actually on the spot presenting and steering the cameramen. For the large majority of programmes, local commentaries were added in each of the receiving countries based on the picture seen by the commentator on a monitor receiver. To assist the commentator in these cases, a 'guide' at the programme end passed on information and advice in either English or French to the commentator. This – of course – could not be heard by the viewers generally.[64]

The eight-nation Eurovision premiere started on 6 June with a live broadcast from the 'Fete des Narcisses' in Montreux and ended with the transmission of the final of the 1954 football world championship in Berne on 4 July. Over nearly a month's period, on 22 days to be exact, viewers could 'experience' – among other things – the Pope addressing them in a welcome speech, sporting events (football, Davis Cup, Wimbledon, Athletics, car race in Le Mans) or the German socialist youth dancing in Lederhosen around a camp fire, or witness the suspense of the famous horse race in Siena, the Palio.

Two months before the start of Eurovision, BBC controller television Cecil McGivern held a speech on Eurovision at the Radio Industries Club Luncheon in London. 'When we first, and extremely airily, began to talk about an exchange of European programmes,' he opened his talk, 'one of the television critics coined the word "Eurovision". The other day a colleague of mine – one of my bosses – was in my office when I was talking for quite a long time to one of the European countries who are going to give us some programmes, and when I put down the phone with a worried brow, he said: "You shouldn't call it Eurovision; you should call it Neurovision." I think he is quite correct, for at present the emphasis is much more on the nerves than on the vision.'[65]

Despite this ongoing scepticism, the vision of Eurovision had finally been realized. In November 1953, the general meeting of the EBU decided to create a regular television programme committee with Marcel Bezançon at its head. But, once established, the programme committee saw itself confronted with the question of future programme contents of international interest. On an EBU television forum held in Sandpoort in 1954, journalists of the eight European countries involved in the Eurovision project had serious problems finding subjects of common interest, which led one British journalist to suggest ironically: 'Another coronation'![66] While the technical accomplishment of Eurovision as a material performance of Europe was generally celebrated as a historic milestone in television history and European integration by both the makers and the public, the programmes themselves mainly reflected national partialities and often mirrored stereotyped images of national customs and traditions. As Cecil McGivern concluded with a hint of desperation in his speech at the Radio Industries Luncheon: 'Every country is typical – France, Versailles and the revue; Germany, the youth camp on the Rhine, etc., and it was impossible to get away from that.'[67]

In spite of the enthusiastic and slightly pathetic rhetoric of EBU officials – first and foremost of Eurovision's first programme director Marcel Bezençon and his French colleague Jean d'Arcy – who were busy in promoting the networking activities as an important tool in the construction of a European identity, the programmes themselves rather reflected the idea of a Europe characterized by cultural heterogeneity and national traditions. In 1969, Jon McLin, a member of the American Universities Field Staff Inc. (AUFS) based in Brussels to report on 'the re-emergence of Europe as a political and social entity', published a study on Eurovision with the telling subtitle 'A modest example of successful European co-operation'. After his prosaic depiction of the 'modest reality' of Eurovision 'as a set of administrative and technical arrangements' followed by a short characterization of the principal programmes handled on Eurovision (sport, news and special events), he wondered about the intercultural potential of these kinds of television programmes: 'Encouraging as this growth is to advocates of cultural interchange and the growth of a European consciousness, they are sometimes dismayed by the program content. Sports – where the participants are frequently national teams and the emphasis thus on international conflict, not co-operation – have constantly accounted for a major portion of the exchanges, a portion which has at times exceeded 60% and is now on the order of 40%.'[68] He continued by stressing that the other important programme category, the so-called 'special events', mainly consisting of coronations, royal weddings and funerals, without doubt create a sense of imagined community and shared historical experience, 'but it is pomp, excitement, and immediacy rather than Europeanness which qualifies an event for such treatment', he concluded.[69]

Conclusion

Starting with the National Nights radio broadcasts in the mid-1920s, this article has retraced the various initiatives by the International Broadcasting

Union and its post-war Western European successor, the European Broadcasting Union, to realize a technical infrastructure, create an organizational platform and function as a promoter for the exchange of radio and television programmes on a European and international level. The various case studies show an interesting relationship or interconnectivity between programme exchange initiatives that have been driven by important national actors (both individual and institutional ones) on the one hand, and explicitly international European initiatives on the other hand. The prosopographic reconstruction of the radio and television networks reveals an interesting – and, for historical understanding, important – intersection of institutional frames (national broadcast institutions were affiliated to international bodies) and overlapping of responsibilities and functions of individual actors (Sir Ian Jacob was both Director General of the BBC and Head of the EBU). The 'paramount reality' of these actors was highly fragmented: it was characterized by a continuous tension between the national and international, regional and European, collective and private nature of broadcast communication and the ambiguous relationship between circulated and appropriated meanings. Without doubt, both the radio and the television experts formed a relatively stable group of people, sharing a common set of knowledge, cultivating a specific style of intercultural communication and international co-operation.[70] Despite evident cultural and national differences of the delegates, the institutional frames of the IBU and the EBU created a laboratory for the negotiation of a transnational and pan-European communication space.

The examples of the 'National Nights', 'European Concerts', pre-Eurovision and Eurovision television exchanges have shown that the changing material performances of broadcasting technology (especially on the transmitting side) have been paralleled by changing medial dispositifs and a continuous reinvention of the European broadcast space. While the 'National Nights' – lacking technical alternatives – were nationally appropriated or interpreted performances of Europe as planned and imagined by a member country of the IBU (the honoured or represented nation), the 'European Concerts' for the first time in European history created moments of simultaneously shared listening experiences all over Europe. The 'liveness' of the 'European Concerts' (same date, same time, and same programme) had a different nature or authentic quality compared with the 'Nuits Nationales' (same date, same time, same programme script but performed by a national or regional broadcaster). Despite these differences in the 'ontological' status of the broadcasts, both programmes had an explicitly serial character, which distinguishes them from the unique televisual events in the early 1950s.[71] The 'Calais-experiment', the 'Paris week' as well as the coronation and first Eurovision television exchanges can claim the same 'ontological' status as the 'European Concerts': they were all broadcast live and thereby enabled the construction of an imagined European community. But their singular and non-regular nature made them extraordinary performances of Europe – or better: of a Europe limited to the nations participating in these experimental transnational television exchanges, but with a clear aspiration to be an instrument of European integration. As Marcel Bezençon formulated it in 1964: 'Eurovision must not be just a toy, but an instrument as well. An instrument to be used for what purpose? To build Europe, for example!'[72]

All the programme initiatives discussed above were promoted as great European ventures by IBU and EBU officials. But a closer look behind the scenes – especially at the minutes and notes of some of the technicians and engineers involved – has revealed a more nuanced and sometimes less enthusiastic image. While the pro-European rhetoric often speaks out of the official sources, the programmes themselves confront us with narratives peppered with hints of national rhetoric and cultural differences. The programmes often mirror a concept of Europe that might best be characterized as the 'diversity in unity' model. The term 'Eurovision' was for sure the most successful invention and strongest promoter of a European television space – but it conceals the tricky reality of an often fragmented European television landscape (different line standards) and the sometimes overt nationalist impregnation of the programmes. But it is exactly this tension between vision and reality, circulated and appropriated meanings, integrating and fragmenting forces that makes the study of Europe as a constantly de- and reconstructed, linked and de-linked, boosted and jammed broadcast space so worthwhile.

Notes

1. Hubert Knoblauch, 'Das strategische Ritual der kollektiven Einsamkeit. Zur Begrifflichkeit und Theorie des Events' in Winfried Gebhardt, Ronald Hitzler and Michaela Pfadenhauer (eds) *Events. Soziologie des Außergewöhnlichen* (Opladen 2000), pp. 33–50.
2. Daniel Dayan and Elihu Katz, *Media Events. The Live Broadcasting of History* (London/Cambridge: Harvard University Press 1992), p. 1.
3. Sun Wanning, 'Media events or media stories?', *International Journal of Cultural Studies* 4(1) (2001), pp. 25–44.
4. Nick Couldry, *Media Rituals. A Critical Approach* (London/New York: Routledge 2003), pp. 56–8.
5. A. Huth, *La Radiodiffusion: Puissance Mondiale* (Paris 1937), pp. 39–41; T.I. Williams, *A history of technology Vol. VII: The Twentieth Century c.1900 to c.1950 Part II* (Oxford: Oxford University Press 1978), p. 1255.
6. 'La réception devient un martyre, l'auditeur souffrant des interférences constantes entre les stations des différents pays, est la pitoyable victime de ces émissions prodigues en sifflements, grincements, craquements, gémissements, dont il conserve, aujourd'hui encore, un souvenir horrifié!' Huth, *La Radiodiffusion*, p. 46.
7. IBU, *Twenty years of activity of the International Broadcasting Union* (Geneva 1945), p. 12.
8. IBU, *The problems of broadcasting*, p. 105.

9. IBU, 85, Relais, Général III, 1929, Document: 1 Feb. 1929, Série 1237, Rapport general du secretaire a la commission des relais internationaux, p. 2; IBU, 85, Relais, Programmes Nationaux (Nuits Nationales), Général 1926–1931, Document: 22 June 1927, Série 567, Programmes Nationaux, by O. Czeija, p. 1.

10. IBU, *Union International de Radiophonie*, 15; IBU, P.V. Conseil Administrative 1925, p. 26.

11. IBU, 85, Relais, Programmes Nationaux (Nuits Nationales), Général, 1926, Document: 18 May 1926, Série 203 and also see 204. Letter from Secretary General A.R. Burrows to IBU Members.

12. A.R. Burrows, 'Les moyenes modernes de diffusion utilisés dans l'intérêt de la paix', *Radiodiffusion* 5 (November 1937), p. 83. IBU, 85, Relais, Programmes Nationaux (Nuits Nationales), Général, 1926–1931, Document: 22 June 1927, Série 576, Programmes Nationaux, by O. Czeija.

13. IBU, P.V. Conseil Administrative 1926, 58; IBU, P.V. Conseil Administrative 1927, 97, 109–10.

14. IBU, 85, Relais, Programmes Nationaux (Nuits Nationales), Général 1926–1931, Document: 18 May 1926, Série 203 and also see 204, Letter from IBU Secretary General A.R. Burrows to IBU Members, p. 1.

15. IBU, 85, Relais, Programmes Nationaux (Nuits Nationales), Général 1926–1931, Document: 22 June 1927, Série no. 576, Programmes Nationaux by O. Czeija (Director of Committee on Intellectual, Artistic and Social Rapprochement), pp. 1–2.

16. IBU, 85, Relais, Programmes Nationaux (Nuits Nationales), Général 1926–1931, Document: 4 Dec. 1928, Série 1152, Nuits Nationales, Rapporteur A.R. Burrows, Commission de Rapprochement, no. 6 de l'Ordre du Jour.

17. For a discussion of the enduring importance of Sunday radio listening traditions in Germany, see: A.W. Badenoch, 'Making Sunday what it actually should be: Sunday radio programming and the re-invention of tradition in occupied Germany, 1945–1949,' *Historical Journal of Film, Radio and Television* 25(4) (October 2005), pp. 583–6.

18. IBU, 85, Relais, Programmes Nationaux (Nuits Nationales), Général, 1926–1931, Document: 24 Jan. 1928, Série 843, Fixation des dates pour les programmes nationaux, no. 11 de l'Ordre du Jour de la Commission de Rapprochement (Série 817), Rapporteur M. O. Czeija.

19. IBU, 85, Relais, Programmes Nationaux (Nuits Nationales), Général 1926–1931, Document: 4 Dec. 1928, Série 1152, Nuits Nationales, Rapporteur A.R. Burrows, Commission de Rapprochement, no. 6 de l'Ordre du Jour.

20. IBU, 85, Relais, Programmes Nationaux (Nuits Nationales), Général 1926–1931, Document: 3 May 1929, Série 1330, Nuits Nationales.

21. Huth, *La Radiodiffusion*, pp. 39–40.

22. IBU, 85, Relais, Général I, 1927 et précédents, Document: Copy of 14–16 Oct. 1927, Procesverbal de la Conférence des délégués des Administrations Postales et Télégraphiques d'Allemagne, d'Autriche, de la Pologne et de la Tchécoslovaquie tenue à Varsovie, p. 3.

23. IBU, *Twenty years of activity of the International Broadcasting Union*, p. 32.

24. IBU, 85 Relais, Programmes Nationaux (Nuits Nationales), Général. 1926–1931, Document: 4 Nov. 1929, Série 1592, L'avenir des nuits nationales, Rapporteur H. Giesecke, Conseil, no. 4 de l'Ordre du Jour.

25. IBU, 85, Relais, Général V, 1931, Document: Second talk to be given on 13th of April (Not checked by Achkridge), Relaying from a distance, p. 5.

26. Léonard Laborie and Suzanne Lommers, 'Les concerts européens à la radio dans l'entre-deux-guerres. Mise en onde d'une métaphore diplomatique', *Le Temps des Médias* 11 (2008), pp. 110–25.

27. IBU, 85, Relais, Concerts Internationaux, 1931 à 1939, Général, Document: Budapest October 1930, Groupe des echanges de programmes de l'Europe Centrale et de l'Europe Occidentale, p. 1. / (Quote) Added to this document: Decisions taken at a meeting in Varsovie 25 to 26 Sept. 1930, p. 2.

28. *'dans le but de répandre l'idée de l'utilité de la radiodiffusion et de faire comprendre au public qu'il existe certaines manifestations de l'art qui doivent unir tous les écouteurs européens.'* IBU, 85, Relais, Concerts Européens, Général 1931 à 1939, Document: 22 July 1931, Série 2694, Concerts EUROPEENS pour la saison 1931–1932, letter from Secretary General A.R. Burrows to IBU Members.

29. IBU, P.V. Conseil Administrative 1931, p. 47.

30. IBU, P.V. Conseil Administrative 1931, pp. 77–8; IBU, 85, Relais, Concerts Européens, Général, 1931 à 1939, Document: 22 Oct. 1931, Série 2880, Concerts européens, Conseil no. 16 de l'Ordre du Jour.

31. IBU, P.V. Conseil Administrative 1934, p. 213.

32. IBU, 85, Relais, Concerts Européens, Général, 1931 à 1939, Document: 11 Feb. 1935, Série 4763, Concerts pouvant faire l'objet de Relais internationaux, Réunion des Directeurs de Programmes, no.1 de l'Ordre du Jour (Observations de M. K.B. Jirak, Directeur du Département Musical de Radiojournal, Prague, pp. 1–2).

33. *'Si la radiodiffusion ne devait rester qu'un moyen de reproduction de la musique appliquée en tant qu'expression d'un amusement brutal (danse, bercement inconscient des sens) elle serait en effet peu digne de sa haute valeur technique'*, IBU, 85, Relais, Concerts Européens, 931 à 1939, Document: 11 Feb. 1935, Série 4762, Détails d'organisation des concerts pouvant faire l'objet d'une diffusion internationale, Réunion des Directeurs des Programme no. 2 de l'Ordre du Jour (rapporteur M.K.B. Jirak, Directeur du Dep. Musical de Radiojournal Prague), p. 3.

34. IBU, P.V. Conseil Administrative 1935, pp. 259–61.

35. Algeria, Austria, Belgium, Bulgaria, Czechoslovakia, Danzig, Denmark, Egypt, Estonia, Finland, France, Germany, Great Britain, Hungary, Ireland, Latvia, Lithuania, the Netherlands, Norway, Palestine, Poland, Portugal, Rumania, Spain, Sweden, Switzerland and Yugoslavia. Turkey also had been a full IBU member during the Interbellum, but its membership was suspended exactly during the period in which the European Concerts were broadcast as a result of non-payment.

36. IBU, 85, Relais, Général IV, 1930, Document: 29 April 1930, Série 1652, Rapport General sur les progres accomplis dans le domaine des relais internationaux, rapporteur A.R. Burrows, Commission des Relais, no. 1 de l'Ordre du Jour, p. 2.

37. IBU, P.V. Conseil Administrative 1935, p. 251.

38. Rüdiger Zeller, *Die EBU – Union Européenne de Radio-Télévision (UER) – European Broadcasting Union (EBU): Internationale Rundfunkkooperation im Wandel* (Baden-Baden: Nomos 1999).

39. See George A. Codding, *The International Telecommunication Union: an Experiment in International Cooperation* (Geneva 1952) (dissertation).

40. Léo Wallenborn, 'From IBU to EBU', *EBU Review* (1987), Part I (January), pp. 25–34 and Part II (March), pp. 22–30. For the work of the technical committee of the IBU see Andreas Fickers, 'Broadcasting as critical infrastructure. A technopolitical story of European fine-tuning and national interferences', paper for the

EUROCRIT international workshop 'Transnational infrastructures: coping with scarcity and vulnerability', Stockholm, 21–24 May 2008 (www.eurocrit.eu).
41. Zeller, *EBU*, p. 38.
42. George Campey, 'How I gave birth to Eurovision', *The Listener* 1 (1975).
43. Wolfgang Degenhardt and Elisabeth Strautz, *Auf der Suche nach dem europäischen Programm. Die Eurovision 1954–1970* (Baden-Baden: Nomos 1999), p. 27.
44. The one-hour programme, presented by the two bilingual commentators Richard Dimbleby and Alan Adair from the BBC, was inaugurated with a speech of welcome by the Mayor of Calais. It than showed various features of a French town fete, including a torchlight procession, led by the Municipal Band of Calais, consisting of local inhabitants in their national costumes, a presentation of a family in the typical local dress, a short film feature demonstrating the devastations of Calais during the Second World War and shots of public dancing on the big stage in front of the Town House with a firework display as finale of the proceedings. A telerecording of this historic programme was consulted at the Audiovisual Archives of the BBC in Brentford.
45. In a BBC Television News release from 21 August 1950, Calais was announced as 'the key to France'. According to this press statement, the purpose of the programme was to 'show the lighter and brighter side of life in one of France's most important ports' and to link two nations 'separated by water and speaking different languages'. See BBC Written Archives, Caversham, signature T 14 / 214 / 2, TV OB, Calais Programme, File 1 B, August 1950–51.
46. The planning and transmission of the programme were co-ordinated by the Engineering Division of the BBC, while the equipment for linking Calais with London was supplied by four British companies: Standard Telephones and Cables Ltd, Marconi's Wireless Telegraphy Company Ltd, Pye Ltd and Mullard Electronic Products Ltd. The whole project was realized in co-operation with the General Post Office, the Mayor of Calais, the Calais Chamber of Commerce, the French Post Office and Radiodiffusion Française.
47. See 'First Television Outside Broadcasting from the Continent', BBC Engineering Statement No. 83, 15 August 1950, in BBC Written Archives, Caversham, signature T 14 / 214 / 2, TV OB, Calais Programme, File 1 B, August 1950–51.
48. See Minutes of meetings of the Anglo/French Television Liaison Committee held in London on July 3rd & 4th, 1952, in BBC Written Archives, Caversham, signature T II / 8 / 1, TV Foreign Relays, Eurovision, General, File 1 (1949–53), 5 pages, here p. 3.
49. The unclear legal statute of RTF as a public service institution entailed serious financial problems hindering a determined expansion of a nationwide television infrastructure. In comparison with other European countries, the dynamics of television development in France were significantly slower than in other television nations. See Jérome Bourdon, *Haute Fidélité. Pouvoir et television 1935–1994* (Paris 1994).
50. The programmes were controlled by the French director of programmes at RTF, Jean d'Arcy, and by the head of outside broadcasts at the BBC, Peter Dimmock. The series of programmes started on the eighth of July with an opening speech at the British Embassy in Paris followed by a long panorama shot from the Eiffel tower. In the following days, viewers in France and the United Kingdom could 'participate' – among other things – in a visit to the Louvre, a fashion show, a military tournament, a film over the Tour de France, and an impressive 'Défilé Militaire' and a glamorous 'Bal populaire' on the French national

holiday, 14 July. A telerecording of most of the programmes is conserved at the Audiovisual Archives of the BBC at Brentford.

51. Letter of William Haley to Wladimir Porché, London, 14 July 1952, in BBC Written Archives, Caversham, signature: T II / 18 / 3, Foreign TV Relays, Paris Week, General, File 3, July 1952–53.

52. Written notice of Cecil McGivern, London, 21 July 1952, ibid.

53. Peter Dimmock, 'Paris week – O.B. Report', London, 5 August 1952, ibid.

54. Letter of Richard Dimbleby, London, 24 July 1952, ibid.

55. Monika Bernold: 'Fernsehen ist gestern. Medienhistorische Transformationen und televisuelles Dabeisein nach 1945', in *Österreichische Zeitschrift für Geschichtswissenschaft* 12(4) (2001), pp. 8–29.

56. The coronation broadcast of 2 June 1952 was the last one in a series of fifteen programmes transmitted in May and June from the BBC to French viewers (ranging from newsreels and music hall to panel shows and children's television). Again, the coronation was acclaimed a milestone of French–British collaboration by Porché in a letter to Sir Ian Jacob, the new director general of the BBC: 'To come finally to the most recent relays which have taken place this year, we should remember that these were first planned by the BBC and RTF, that we formed, as it were, the common tree trunk on which were grafted the branches providing for the other continental television services; in short, we bore together, your organisation and ours, the heaviest responsibility and, again together, we took the initiative in this magnificent undertaking', in BBC Written Archives, Caversham, signature: T II / 18 / 3, Foreign TV Relays, Paris Week, General, File 3, July 1952–53.

57. Degenhardt, Strautz, *Auf der Suche*, p. 38.

58. On the sometimes problematic relationship between the EBU and Bezancon's plan of a European programme exchange and the bi- or multilateral initiatives see Degenhardt, Strautz: *Auf der Suche*, pp. 29–39.

59. For a detailed analysis of the line standard problem see Andreas Fickers, „Politique de la grandeur" versus „Made in Germany". *Die Analyse der PAL-SECAM-Farbfernsehkontroverse als Beispiel einer politischen Kulturgeschichte der Technik* (München: Oldenbourg 2007); Andreas Fickers, 'National barriers for an *imag(e)* ined European community: The technopolitical frames of post-war television development in Europe', *Northern Lights, Film and Media Studies Yearbook 2005* (Copenhagen 2006), pp. 15–36.

60. See M.J.L. Pulling (Senior Superintendent Engineer, BBC Television Broadcasting), 'Conference on International Television Relays', 2 pages, in BBC Written Archives, Caversham, signature: T II / 8 / 1, TV Foreign Relays, Eurovision, General, File 1 (1949–53).

61. For a meticulous historical reconstruction of the prehistory of Eurovision see Paul Bellac, *L'orgine de l'Eurovision* (Berne 1962). Unpublished machine-typed script of twenty-three pages with nineteen annexes of original sources, in EBU archives, signature EV 5, Geneva.

62. As Edward Pawley, BBC chief engineer of external relations, remembered in his autobiographical retrospect of the early Eurovision years in 1979, the conversion was not technically as simple as it looked. In fact, the display tube had to have an unusually long afterglow (so that the trace made by the scanning spot remained for a fraction of a second after the spot had passed) and the spot had to be widened to fill the spaces between the lines. Apparently, a French firm later developed an optical converter of this kind, used until much-improved

electronic converters were developed in 1963. See Edward Pawley, 'Eurovision: Faith & Works', seventeen machine typed pages (here p. 9), in EBU Archives, signature EV, Geneva.

63. See 'The Expansion of television', a 20-minute BBC documentary on the history of early European television development (1961), BBC Audiovisual Archives, Brentford.

64. See 'Handout for the press conference in Paris', 2 June 1954, in BBC Written Archives, Caversham, signature: T 23 / 26, TV Publicity, Eurovision, 1953–5.

65. Speech of Cecil McGivern at the Radio Industries Club Luncheon, London, 22 April 1954, in BBC Written Archives, Caversham, signature: T 23 / 26, TV Publicity, Eurovision, 1953–5.

66. *Der Spiegel*, 2 June 1954, p. 37.

67. Speech of Cecil McGivern at the Radio Industries Club Luncheon, London, 22 April 1954, in BBC Written Archives, Caversham, signature: T 23 / 26, TV Publicity, Eurovision, 1953–5.

68. Jon McLin, 'Eurovision. A modest example of successful European co-operation', *Fieldstaff Reports*, West Europe Series IV(2) (1969), p. 4.

69. Idem, p. 6.

70. Christian Henrich-Franke, 'Organisationskultur in den internationalen Beziehungen: Anknüpfungspunkt für einen interdisziplinären Dialog?', *Geschichte und Gesellschaft* 3 (2006), pp. 344–63; Léonard Laborie, *La France, l'Europe et l'ordre internationale des communications (1865–1959)*, unpublished PhD thesis, University of Paris IV (Sorbonne) (Paris 2006).

71. There were also unique radio events during the Interbellum period, such as *La Jeunesse chante au-delà des frontiers*, and Eurovision television programmes in the 1960s, that had the same organizational structure as the National Nights. A good example is the programme 'The largest theater of the world', a high-culture promotion initiative of the EBU. See Degenhardt, Strautz, *Auf der Suche*, pp. 119–31.

72. Marcel Bezençon, 'Eurovision, or the price of fame', *EBU-Review* B 85 (1964), p. 8.

Biography 6: The Radio Station Scale: A Materialized European Event

Andreas Fickers

> [...] I am down on my knees / At the wireless knobs / I am down on my knees / At those wireless knobs / Telefunken, Telefunken / And I'm searching for Luxembourg, Luxembourg, Athlone, Budapest, AFN, Hilversum, Helvetia [...]

In his song 'In the days before Rock'n Roll', the Irish songwriter Van Morrison conjures, in a slightly 'technostalgic' mood, his sensations when turning the radio dial in search of rock'n roll sounds. 'Without those wireless knobs,' he sings, 'Fats did not come in [...], Elvis did not come in [...] Nor Fats, nor Elvis / Nor Sonny, nor Lightning / Nor Muddy, nor John Lee'. Illuminated station scales have engraved themselves as imagined world maps in the collective memory of a whole radio generation. Although Van Morrison primarily reflects on the radio as an 'ear to the world' and medium of cultural modernization, the song starts with the description of the bodily interaction with the radio as an intimate companion, and – even more interesting for our purpose – he enumerates a number of radio stations listed on his radio scale. As most of the European stations in long and medium waves bore the names of the cities or places of transmission, radio station scales read like atlases of European broadcasting landscapes. Metaphorically speaking, station scales became a roadmap and timetable for the journey through the ether – each frequency point mutated into a 'station', inviting the listener to dwell for a while. Looking at the dial was an open invitation to an imagined ether voyage, where London, Paris, Oslo and Hilversum were just a little turn away from each other. Station scales evoked to the radio listener – who was a radio *watcher* too – a mental map, which could only be decoded by the listener himself. Turning the dial was an act of symbolically appropriating the world.

The development and introduction of the calibrated station scale marked an important innovation both in the technical improvement of the receiver and in radio design. While the regulation of the European broadcasting space was a crucial precondition for the development of calibrated station

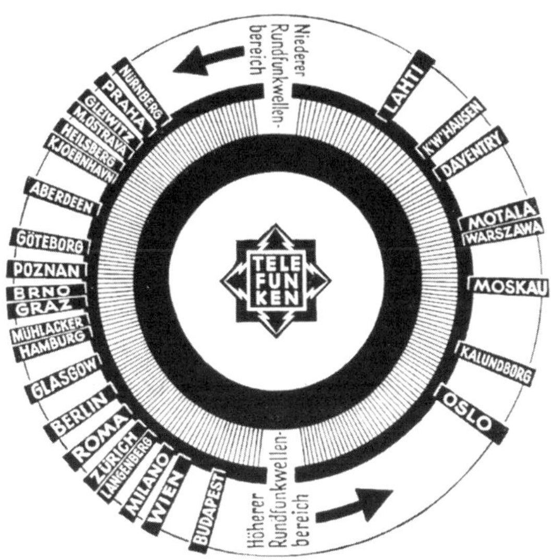

Figure B6.1 Top: Early radio station scale developed by the French inventor–entrepreneur Joseph-Louis Routin in 1929. His patents were bought in 1930 by *Telefunken*, which produced receivers based on Routin's invention under the label of 'Autoscala' from 1931 on (bottom). Both pictures originate from the archives of the Deutsches Technikmuseum in Berlin, signature: DTM, Historisches Archiv, III, 2, sog. Firmenschriften, Nr. 51641.

scales (see the chapter 'Eventing Europe' in this volume), the creation of the dial was no minor challenge for the radio industry. Because of the relative neighbourhood of a lot of stations in the narrow frequency bands, a complicated mechanical construction was necessary in order to produce the optical illusion of a scale with evenly spread stations. The conversion of a turning movement on the station selection knob into an automatic fine-tuning of the electrical circuits was a real masterpiece of electromechanical handcraft. The optical solution of this problem reminds us of the invention of non-scaled maps for the London underground railroads by the electrical engineer Henry Beck in 1933. The new underground map developed by Beck owed its success to its simplicity and clearness, constructing a symbolic proximity or connection of the suburbs with the city centre. Instead of a realistic representation of the scary immenseness of Greater London, it converted the real geographical distance into an invitation to the city.

In a very similar way, the station scale reduced the seemingly endless wideness of the ether to a recognizable topography of European cities. In a process of acoustic networking of the world, the radio set manifested itself as both a material and symbolic representation of the broadcasting space. While the visual appropriation of the broadcast landscape by the way of the station scale was the result of the abstract topographies of transmission locations on the body of the receiver, the symbolic appropriation of the broadcast reality resulted from the complex interplay of the haptic and the hearing sense, producing a feeling of both bodily and mental discovery of, and participation in, the world.

With the emergence of broadcasting, the process of spatial and communicative networking of the world acquired a new quality. While all kinds of traffic routes, electricity, telephone and telegraph cables left visible traces in the private and public spaces, wireless broadcasting heralded the age of the invisible but audible networking of the world. The radio complemented the increasing possibilities in transportation and travel and invited people to stay home and travel with their minds. As René Schikele, a German radio critic, put it in an article called 'Paneuropa der Sender' (Paneurope of transmission stations) in 1931, even the farmer in the Black Forest became connected to the world: 'Today,' he reasoned, 'you can be lonesome without losing the world.'

Literature

Andreas Fickers, 'Sichtbar hörbar! Radioapparat und Stadt – Knoten im vernetzten Kommunikationsraum' in Clemens Zimmermann (ed.) *Die Stadt als Kommunikationsraum. Medialität und Raumgefüge der Großstädte im 20. Jahrhundert* (Stuttgart: Steiner Verlag 2006), pp. 83–103.

Alexander Geppert, Uffa Jensen and Jörn Weinhold, 'Verräumlichung. Kommunikative Praktiken in historischer Perspektive (1840–1930)' in Geppert, Jensen and Weinhold (eds) *Ortsgespräche. Raum und Kommunikation im 19. und 20. Jahrhundert* (Bielefeld: Transcript Verlag 2005), pp. 15–49.

René Schickele, 'Paneuropa der Sender' in Irmela Schneider (ed.) *Radio-Kultur in der Weimarer Republik* (Tübingen 1984 [1931]), p. 141.

9
From Sea to Shining Sea. Making Ends Meet on the Rhine and the Rhone

Cornelis Disco

Nowadays, by the terms of the peace that has been made, the biggest European rivers have been internationalized, have been withdrawn from exclusive rule by single nations and been opened to ships of all flags.…The Rhine too is one of these rivers. It is the major artery connecting inner Europe to the North Sea. But by virtue of its upper reaches it also belongs to the chain of canals that might connect inner Europe to the Mediterranean and Black Seas. That is telling if we believe in a common spirit in Europe which is only waiting to take the offensive in actually realizing these possibilities, which today exist only as projects.[1]

Reclaiming the Rhine

This hopeful remark, written in 1920 by the German social critic Alfons Paquet, suggests that a 'common spirit in Europe' could 'take the offensive' in realizing waterways over both of Europe's continental divides. As a German, Paquet conceived of these as extensions of the Rhine – via watershed-spanning canals into the basins of the Rhone and of the Danube. In this chapter I want to take a closer look at this 'common spirit,' particularly at whether it was merely an ideological pose to cloak what were essentially local or national projects in transcontinental European grandeur, or whether it was in fact a material force in promoting visions of such waterways and the projects to realize them. I will address this question by considering two visions of a waterway spanning the continental divide between the Rhine and Rhone basins. The first is the actually accomplished French *Canal du Rhône au Rhin* connecting the Rhine via the so-called 'Burgundian Gate' to the Rhone basin. The second is the envisioned, but never built, German–French–Swiss *'transhelvetique'* over the *Hochrhein* via the River Aare and Geneva and on to the *Haut Rhône*. Both projects penetrate the

'European' watershed dividing the Rhine and the Rhone, which can be held to 'connect' the North and Mediterranean Seas via a trans-European waterway, and thus provide an interesting comparison (See Figure 9.1). One was accomplished as an explicitly national project (though with European overtones) while the other was steeped in transnational imaginings from the first; one was a more or less routine challenge in hydraulic and political engineering while the other was dauntingly innovative in both respects.

I will examine what motivated the actors in both cases to envision the projects they did when they did, and what stories they told themselves and others in order to realize the projects or even just to aggrandize them by

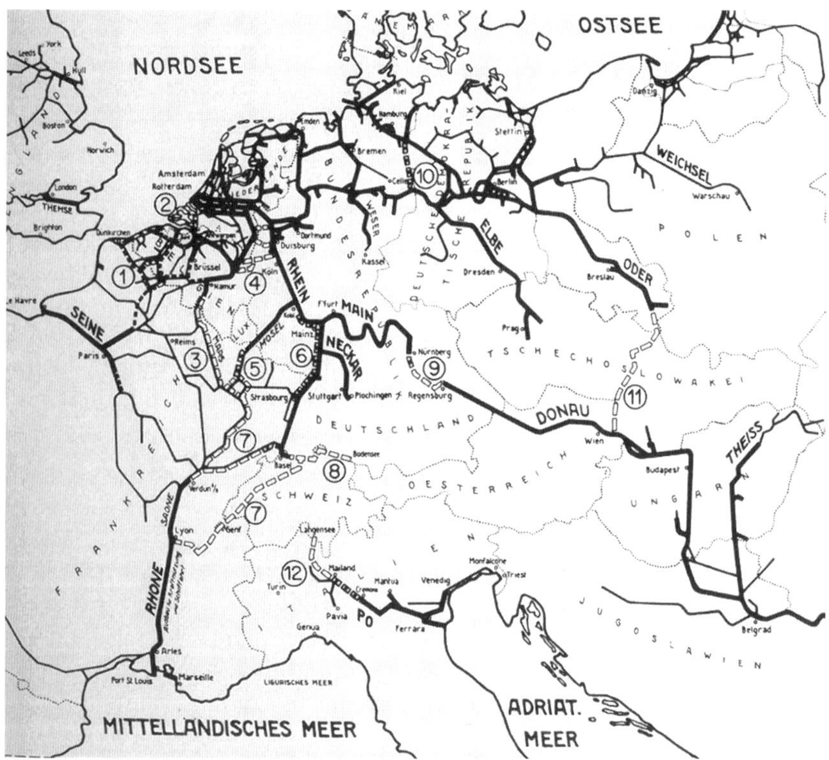

Figure 9.1 European Rivers and Waterways showing existing and projected waterways (dotted lines) as of 1975, almost all of them with the same status as in 1947

Note: The Rhine is the physically and economically central artery for east–west and north–south links, but embedded in international tensions. In 1927–9 the Rhine carried 60 million tons, the Danube 3 million tons, and the Rhone only 300,000 tons.

Source: H. Wanner, 'Bedeutung der internationalen Rheinschiffahrt und Zukunftsprobleme nach Eröffnung der Rhone-Rhein- und der Rhein-Main-Donau Verbindung', *Wasser und Energiewirtschaft, sonderheft Rhein* 67(5/6), p. 191.

framing them as part of a grander scheme. It is important to emphasize that effectively – that is, seductively – imagining a new waterway always means imagining it as an *augmentation* of an established – or presumptively established – *network* of waterways, railways and roads; which, being subject to many masters, is itself dynamic and unpredictably so. The imagined link may even anticipate the network's actual development in the sense that its proponents may simply postulate a probable future state of the network to which the new link is a sensible augmentation. But, by dint of this very imaginary making sense in a putative future network, it may paradoxically bring that network closer to realization. Other actors may see the new imaginary link as sufficient motivation to expand or upgrade portions of the existing network in 'its' direction. It is only in connection with and in relation to this existing system of links and the heterogeneous actors behind them that the new link takes on meaning and becomes a project to which more actors can commit themselves. To understand this we must make a brief detour into the 'metaphysics' of imagining (transnational) waterways across continental divides.

Envisioning waterways

In their programmatic call to study European infrastructural networks as *transnational* projects and accomplishments, Erik van der Vleuten and Arne Kaijser argue for special attention to *visionary* transnational infrastructures.[2] Though this is certainly laudable, there is an ambiguity in the idea that some projects are visions (or visionary) and others are not, perhaps depending on the level of ambition, that is, how divorced from 'reality' they are. I would, however, take Bruno Latour's point that imaginings and visions are an essential feature of any technological project, and, I would add, *a fortiori* of transnational waterways. Latour argues:

> If one thinks of a 'social network,' misinterpretation is assured inasmuch as the networks deployed by the sociologist of innovation mix many actors of which very few possess a human form. If one thinks of a 'technical network,' the misapprehension is no less great, because the configurations are again not simply the objects, *but just as much the projects, the dreams, the attempts, the societies themselves.*[3]

So, aside from characteristically encouraging us to confuse humans and non-humans in analysing technological projects, Latour is also encouraging us to confuse visions and practice. Reality emerges somewhere between dreaming and doing. But, with this said, we will also want to make some distinctions in styles of doing and styles of dreaming. In the first place we should discuss the difference between envisioning national and transnational infrastructures. In the second place, we must clarify what is entailed in imagining new inland waterways, especially ones that span watersheds.

This will put us in a position to consider how, in the case of the two Rhine–Rhone linkages, the vision of a *transnational* watershed-spanning waterway has involved different, and in fact much more heterogeneous, actors, interests, strategies and gambles than the vision of a *national* watershed-spanning waterway – despite the fact that in both cases claims were being made about bridging European and uniting seas.

Taking Latour's point about the importance of 'dreams' and 'societies' in constituting technologies, it stands to reason that if the 'society' in question (and its 'dreams') refers to a nation state the dynamics will be different than if they refer to a transnational community. To envision an improved infrastructure is to imagine new orders of economy, space, community and identity, and this involves different socio-logics according to whether these imaginings refer to reconfigurations within a nation state or within and among some community of sovereign nation states. For our purposes, perhaps the most concise way to express this difference is that it involves different orders of risk and uncertainty and hence more or less extreme gambles. Because transnational visions by definition transcend the co-ordinating powers of national governments, they acquire something of the structure of a prisoners' dilemma. From the point of view of the government of any specific nation state the question is always: what is the likelihood that other actors and nations involved in the imagined infrastructure (actors largely beyond one's control) will do their part in realizing the imagined infrastructure? In other words, what is the likelihood that one's own efforts to realize the vision will not be in vain or will not simply encourage passivity and free-riding? Michèle Merger and her co-editors hit this nail squarely on the head when they subtitled their volume on European transnational networks 'which wagers?' (*Quels Enjeux?*)[4]

The dilemma arises from the fact that national or local governments have invariably been the agents of 'transnational' projects. Hence, however extended and transnational the imagined networks may be, they have always come into being by a process of accretion of piecemeal national decisions and projects. Aligning these national actors into a single vision of a transnational network is only possible by mobilizing them on the basis of manifest self-interest, but even then the readiness to act is always contingent on expectations that other actors will in fact do their part in order to realize the full synergetic benefits of the transnational network. Building transnational infrastructures inevitably involves taking a gamble on whether others will also do their parts to realize the synergetic effects of full participation, which economists call 'network effects'.[5] Existing works on transnational infrastructures (including those assembled here) attest to this double bind, despite the co-ordinating efforts of transnational bodies such as the Central Commission for the Navigation of the Rhine, the League of Nations, the United Nations Economic Commission for Europe and the various predecessors of the present-day European Union.

In the history of European infrastructures, comprehensive European-scale visions of future transport networks, such as the project for a trans-European highway network put forth by Piero Puricelli in the late 1920s, actually appear to have been rather exceptional occurrences.[6] Imaginings – and certainly actual executions – tended more often to centre on providing 'missing links' or eliminating specific bottlenecks in existing (transnational) transport networks. These imaginings and projects at sub-European levels, indeed, sometimes even restricted to the commercial elite of a single city or region, imagined and sometimes even produced European networks despite themselves. Such dynamics underlie what Misa and Schot refer to as the 'hidden integration' of Europe.[7] It is the production of transnational transportation infrastructure as it were 'behind the backs' of the actors themselves, that is, an emergent Europe not explicitly envisioned in the imaginings and plans of network-builders – at least not as more than 'wishful thinking'.

To the extent one can speak of a continental European network of inland waterways, one must indeed conclude that it has developed in a thoroughly piecemeal fashion, albeit frequently in the context of emergent (and always tentative) national waterway plans. What exists is in any case not (yet) the outcome of any kind of transnational or European superplan.[8] That certainly holds for the Rhine–Rhone linkages, which are our present concern. However, while the literature shows that this hardly distinguishes the development of networks of inland waterways from the development of other kinds of transnational networks in continental Europe, such as those devoted to flows of energy, goods, people or information, waterways networks have certain geographic and economic peculiarities that bear mentioning here. Geographic and economic aspects are of course fused in practical visions and projects, but it is useful to distinguish them.

The essential geographical difference between waterways and overland transport rests on the fact that water is a fluid and seeks the lowest possible level, that is, it flows downhill due to gravity unless retained by sills or artificial dams. This is the origin of rivers and lakes and also the reason why it is so difficult and expensive to make navigable waterways through accidental-terrain. In their uphill reaches rivers tend to flow fast and shallow through rocky beds; building artificial waterways through hilly territory and *ipso facto* across watersheds necessitates facilities for retaining the water, while allowing ships passage, such as double-gated locks or boat-lifts. Both the poorer navigability of rivers in their upper reaches and the toil and expense of extending the navigable network into elevated regions by means of canals explains why inland navigation networks originally developed from the lower and generally more navigable reaches of rivers and only gradually moved upstream and uphill.

If indeed 'upstream the course of empire takes its way,' it does not do so of its own accord. It is the outcome of human struggles with rivers and terrain, and it is not surprising that the interests and capabilities of the actors concerned should differ according to their position along the (proposed) watercourses, primarily their relative upstream–downstream position, but also in some cases their location on right or left banks. In general, and certainly with the rivers we are dealing with here, navigability deteriorated (became less capacious, less profitable and less reliable) as one went further upstream.[9] Hence, the extension of navigability was always of interest for downstream actors, such as the Dutch on the Rhine, inasmuch as it extended their markets to new upstream hinterlands. However, particularly when different nations or states were involved, downstream actors had little or no authority to actually undertake the upstream engineering projects necessary to improve navigation. They were 'committed spectators' who had a clear and present interest, but who could only voice that interest and try to represent it as the interest of the whole or as the inevitable course of history in the hope that upstream actors would take up the challenge.

But what of these upstream actors? What, in an abstract and generic sense, was *their* interest? Inasmuch as water transport and access to seaports could cheapen essential commodities, they too would have an economic interest in joining up with mainline downstream navigation. Chambers of commerce, parliaments and trade associations would press their governments to make the necessary investments – at least insofar as the navigational state of the art or river engineering made their visions feasible.

However, in practice matters were always more complicated. 'Upstream' is always relative to some 'downstream', but it by no means precludes a yet further 'upstream'. What this boils down to is that we must conceive of the production of mainline navigability on a river – and the Rhine is almost an ideal type – as taking place at a front which moves upstream in the course of time. At any given moment there will be downstream actors, actors at the dynamic front, and actors upstream of the front. They will have different interests in relation to further progress and different capacities to realize that progress. The downstream actors are almost by definition committed to improving navigability further upstream. At the very least they are 'committed spectators' and will egg on the actors at the front to do their bit. Post-Second World War Dutch commentators like Van Looveren, who pleaded for extending the Rhine's navigability up to Lake Constance (and beyond), are typical.[10] The actors at the front and just downstream of the front, who are investing both in river engineering and in outfitting their harbours, have an ambiguous interest in maintaining the new status quo. On the one hand they can make good on their investments by establishing a monopoly position as 'head of navigation' [11]. On the other hand, their port and portion of the waterway they command only increases in value with the extension of 'normal' navigation further upstream.

Whether upstream regions can be economically serviced by the head of navigation depends on the capacity and condition of alternative modes of transport, especially railways but also including 'substandard' shipping adapted to the upstream stretches. Upstream of this active front where the head of navigation and its regional supporters are located there are also actors who have a generic interest in circumventing the monopoly position of the head of navigation and establishing direct links with mainline downstream shipping. Unfortunately, the readiness and freedom of governments to invest in the necessary river improvements seems to decrease proportionately to the increase in technical difficulties and costs as one goes further upstream. Cities and regions far from navigable waterways may well lobby against committing national tax moneys to further the particular interests of riparian port cities at the general expense, especially where alternate and more democratic means of transport like roads and railways are available.

Governments' reticence to invest in improving waterways is greatest with respect to the actors furthest upstream, those on the watershed itself. They must wait for the active front of navigational improvements to come close enough so that it even makes sense for their governments to invest in improvements to the upstream stretches under their purview. Until that time, these most upstream actors can also only be 'committed spectators', urging actors at or just upstream of the navigational front to persevere in their efforts to extend the navigational front, but formally powerless to influence progress in any material way.

While downstream 'committed spectators' can generally only wait and see, hoping that fortune will smile on them, upstream 'committed spectators' can try to influence the choice behaviour of the 'dynamic actors' at the navigational front by producing images of *shared* future prosperity thanks to the improvement of waterways. One way to do this is to create projects which rhetorically magnify the freight potential of upstream hinterlands.

Rhine–Rhone: The French connection

An important tributary of the Rhine, the Aare, originates in the high glaciers of the Swiss Alps very near the headwaters of the Rhone. It might be supposed that the Swiss would have been the first to consider uniting the two main rivers and thus creating a waterway over the continental divide. However, the continental divide between the two river basins extends into France as well. Here the distance between the two rivers is greater than in Switzerland, but the intervening terrain is far less elevated and the rivers far better navigable than they are in their upper reaches in Switzerland. This is certainly one reason why a French connection considerably pre-dated any Swiss imaginings.

There had long been visions of connecting the Mediterranean Sea with the Atlantic Ocean and the North Sea across French territory by means of its navigable rivers and an imaginary inter-basin canal system. As the French inter-basin canal system actually began to take shape in the early seventeenth century, these visions increasingly began to cohere into concrete projects.

The system originated with the joining of the basin of the Seine to that of the Loire via the pathbreaking *Canal du Briare*, the world's first watershed-spanning canal, completed under a private concession in 1642.[12] This created a continuous navigation across the agricultural and commercial heart of the nation. In the decades to follow, visions of extending this waterways network to prosperous Burgundy, proceeding both from the upper Loire and from the Yonne (a tributary of the Seine), gained ever more support, both in Paris and in Burgundy itself. The obvious juncture in Burgundy was the upper course of the Saone River (a tributary of the Rhone). Its navigability, however, left much to be desired and hence it first had to be canalized.[13] This canalization project gave new impetus to a third long-imagined inter-basin waterway over the continental divide: a canal between the Rhine and the Rhone through the so-called Burgundian Gate, along the Doubs River and thence to the Saone. By the mid-eighteenth century plans for this canal project were taking shape as the *Canal du Rhône au Rhin*. By then, construction of the other two inter-basin canals from the Saone to the Seine and the Loire, respectively, was also imminent.

This bounty of canal projects cast the canalization project of the upper Saone into the role of a trunk sprouting three branches: north to the Seine and the English Channel ports, west to the Loire and the Atlantic, and east to the Rhine and the North Sea. The Saone itself flowed into the Rhone and thence to Lyon and the Mediterranean. Burgundy was set to become the obligatory overland point of passage between the Western European seas. The *grandeur* of the notion was not lost on the Burgundian ruler, the Prince of Condé, who in 1784 ordained that with the laying of the first stone in each of the Saone locks a commemorative plaque be placed bearing the following (Latin) text: 'Both seas are here joined in a triple junction. The door is opened alike to the Loire, the Seine and the Rhine.'[14]

What the Prince was doing was redefining his humdrum local locks as elements in a grand transcontinental project, part of a *continental* trans-watershed system of waterways, even though they were wholly on (Burgundian) French soil. Nonetheless, it is difficult to assess the practical significance of the commemorative text. It cannot easily be seen as an appeal to other distant actors to do what they had to do in the hope that the Saone works would actually realize their promise of becoming a link in the North–South waterway. After all, the rest of the transcontinental waterways scheme (the canals to the Loire, the Seine and the Rhine) were already well under way, even if far from finished. We can certainly see the Prince's plaque as an attempt to aggrandize the significance of the Saone canalization and to position Burgundy at the centre of a putative French (and European) waterways system. Still, it might not be far-fetched to see the text as an *encouragement* to the other actors engaged with the three watershed canals to persevere in their efforts to ultimately realize this grand plan – to preserve the Saone canalization from irrelevance and to contribute to the greater glory and prosperity of Burgundy.

This said, the *Canal de Bourgogne* (Saone–Seine), opened in 1832, and the *Canal du Centre* (Saone–Loire), opened in 1792, were so thoroughly embedded in the French river and canal system that they were forever condemned to the latter's necessarily limited dimensions and freight capacity. While these were considerable by eighteenth-century standards, nineteenth-century industrialization rendered them increasingly obsolete from an economic point of view. System-wide upscaling to the so-called Freycinet gauge after 1879, which allowed ships of 300 to 350 tons burden, made some sense in a French domestic context, but from a European perspective with the Rhine navigation as a standard it could only be seen as a rearguard action.

The upshot was that, as the nineteenth century wore on, the tacit claims of the *Canal du Centre* and the *Canal de Bourgogne* to be part of a trans-continental north–south link between the two seas became less and less convincing – at least if *European* significance were being claimed. This was not necessarily true of the third watershed canal, the *Canal du Rhône au Rhin*, which connected two rivers that were actually or potentially capable of large-scale navigation. The only limit was the dimensions of the intercon-necting waterway itself. So by the mid-nineteenth century it was only this canal that could make a claim to inherit the Prince of Condé's grand vision of a junction of both seas and to justify his Saone canalization as part of that junction.

A vision was one thing but its realization quite another. Completing the *Canal du Rhône au Rhin* itself took another half-century. During this time its name changed repeatedly to reflect the changing visions of the builders. The French revolutionary directorate, interested in consolidating the east-ern frontiers of the new state and not particularly concerned with uniting Europe, called it the *Canal de l'Est*; under the Empire it became the *Canal Napoléon*. Only after the 'bourgeois' Restoration of 1830 did the canal again assume its original name, underscoring its commercial role in uniting major river basins.

In the early 1820s the canal had been incorporated into the ambitious *Plan Becquey*, which envisioned several thousand kilometres of new canals and standardized the measurement of locks and bridges with the aim of creating a uniform national network for inland navigation.[15] The com-pany charged with building the Rhine–Rhone Canal ran into financial difficulties shortly thereafter and the wealthy city of Strasbourg saw an opportunity to turn the proposed canal to its own advantage. Strasbourg, it turned out, had its own interpretation of the new canal. The intent, according to its active chamber of commerce, was: 'To unite Marseille, the entrepôt of the commodities of the East, with Strasbourg, to which accrues the merchandise of the North', and further to contest the 'transit from Holland and the northern portions of Germany to Switzerland and Italy' by means of land traffic (roads and railways) along the German right bank of the Rhine through Baden.[16] In the Strasbourgers' vision, the canal was to serve as a means of (re)positioning their city at a major crossroads of trade. Not the watershed, but Strasbourg as inter-basin *entrepôt*, was now the defining feature of the canal. Along with this new vision came a northward extension of the canal between Colmar, the original point of junction with the Ill, to Strasbourg. This 'northern branch' was in effect a lateral canal to the Rhine from Strasbourg to Huningue just downstream from Basel. The *Canal du Rhône au Rhin* new-style was opened for traffic in 1833. In 1835 about a thousand ships navigated the canal, a figure that had risen to 2,580 by 1846.[17]

However, shipping on the Rhine itself was revolutionized after the mid-nineteenth century by the introduction of huge barge-trains towed by paddle-wheel steamers – made possible in part by energetic Prussian efforts in the 1850s to transform the 'romantic' middle Rhine into a dependable large-scale shipping channel. The brand new *Canal du Rhône au Rhin*, built to the very modest (Becquey) dimensions of the French national network, was tiny by comparison. Some idea of what this meant can be gathered from the following figures. The 261 kilometre-long journey from Strasbourg to St Symphorien on the Saône required the passage of no less than 152 locks! It seems to have taken nearly two months to make the passage from Lyon to Strasbourg in the 1830s; by the 1870s it still took no less than 12–15 days.[18] In the end this mattered little for the Rhine–Rhone navigation because the new regime of steam navigation was also retiring Strasbourg itself from the Rhine trade. Despite – and in some cases thanks to – the extensive river corrections associated with the engineer Gottfried Tulla, the stretch of river upstream of Mannheim remained too shallow and fickle to support the new regime of large-scale steam-powered shipping.[19] Railway competition did the rest and Strasbourg ceased to be a Rhine harbour for nearly forty years after 1870. This, of course, utterly dashed its hopes of becoming an obligatory passage point in the much-vaunted link between the North Sea and the Mediterranean Sea. The final blow was dealt by the incorporation of Alsace (and Strasbourg) into the German Reich in 1871 as a prize of the Franco-Prussian war. This also moved the French–German border from the Rhine to the crest of the Vosges Mountains and consequently split the *Canal du Rhône au Rhin* into a French and German part. Though this prevented neither France nor Germany from improving the canal on its own side of the border, it long paralysed all efforts to upgrade the Rhine–Rhone canal as a watershed-spanning waterway.[20] In a report to the Chamber of Deputies, a French government engineer mused that 'assuredly, if it had not already been built, we would hesitate to build it.'[21]

However, one thing Prussian rule in Alsace did accomplish for Strasbourg was to establish political conditions for improving the navigability of the upper Rhine and thus for reinstating Strasbourg as a Rhine port. The German Reich now had an interest in promoting Strasbourg as a Rhine harbour and hence no longer blocked projects to improve the river.[22] Though it took years to reach a decision because of continued opposition by Mannheim's commercial elite, by the end of 1901 Strasbourg could envision a future as a Rhine port.[23] By 1912 the effects of the completed Rhine normalization were visible in dramatic increases in the annual tonnage processed in Strasbourg's new port facilities.

Meanwhile, the Swiss, especially Basel's commercial and engineering elite, were pondering their future on the Rhine. There had been a regular steamship line between Basel and Strasbourg in the 1840s, but it had succumbed to railway competition. In 1902 Rudolf Gelpke, a Basel engineer and representative to parliament, with the backing of the municipal gasworks director, had demonstrated that thanks to powerful new steam tugs it was possible to tow coal barges of 300 tons burden to Basel over the open Rhine. This inaugurated a spate of harbour-building in Basel, which somewhat anticipated that city's actual accession to Rhine commerce. The poor condition of the Rhine, the rapids at Istein, freezing conditions in the winter, swift currents during high water, and shoals during low water continued to make shipping to Basel over the open Rhine a chancy and economically marginal business. Clearly Basel was the next city in line to agitate for improvement to the river – but to whom could they turn as ally? This is an important issue for our topic, because Basel was the inevitable gateway from the Rhine into Switzerland and hence the starting point for all imaginings of inter-basin waterways across Swiss territory.

Extending the navigable Rhine

The First World War and after: The great Rhine robbery

The First World War once again transformed politics on the upper Rhine. After the war, France was able to achieve a commanding position thanks to certain mercenary provisions of the Versailles Treaty. Strasbourg's German-built port could now became the apple of France's eye. But there was more to be gained on the upper Rhine than better navigability. Article 358 of the Versailles Treaty granted France a monopoly on the generation of hydro-electricity on the upper Rhine. Specifically, by the terms of the treaty France was entitled to withdraw from the Rhine all water deemed necessary for the generation of electricity and could appropriate right-bank German territory for the construction of dams and power plants. This enabled France unilaterally to carry out a project that had first been proposed by Mulhouse industrialists in a more modest form in 1902. The French interpreted the Versailles accords as giving them *carte blanche* to build an enormous lateral canal between Basel and Strasbourg entirely on French soil. Measuring 80 m wide at the bottom, with a depth of 8.5 m, the proposed canal would exceed both the Suez and Panama Canals (and indeed the Rhine itself) in cross-section. The canal was to consist of eight pounds, each containing a power-generating station, movable weir and navigational lock. The anticipated power output of 5.7 billion KWh would require the extraction of some 98% of the river's flow during dry periods, reducing the river itself to a trickle.[24]

Large-scale navigation through the canal would be possible thanks to a series of double locks, of which the largest was to measure 185 m × 25 m. The generous dimensions of both the canal and the locks were crucial to the project because the canal was designed to replace the river as the navigational artery. Though France clearly had no qualms about stealing the Rhine from its German neighbours, it respected the spirit, if not the precise letter, of the 1868 Act of Mannheim, which guaranteed unobstructed rights of navigation on the Rhine to ships of all nations. Had the canal been smaller, the water flow necessary for the generators would have required prohibitively fierce currents. Likewise, more modest locks would forever have sealed the fates of both Mulhouse and Basel – and whatever might lie beyond – as Rhine ports. Though France could mobilize the Versailles Treaty against the Germans in a spirit of vengeance, it was not in a position to incur the combined wrath of the rest of the Rhine riparian states organized in the Central Commission for the Navigation of the Rhine – even if it had a motive for doing so.

While it is understandable that the Germans were dismayed by the French plans, the Swiss were equally recalcitrant. For the latter, Basel's navigational accessibility was never just a municipal or regional interest. Basel's harbour was the national beachhead on the Rhine and the key to Swiss industrial prosperity. It was also, at least for the time being, the focus and natural starting point of an imagined Swiss network of inland waterways. Under Gelpke's inspired leadership, the Swiss mounted an international campaign for the preservation of what, with a fine feeling for pathos, they rhetorically called the *Freie Rhein*.[25] Despite French assurances that from the point of view of efficient and reliable navigation they would be far better off with a *Grand Canal d'Alsace* than a normalized *Freie Rhein*, the Swiss were not happy with the idea of having to navigate a French canal to get to the sea. They insisted on their rights to free and open access as set out in the Act of Mannheim.

The Germans, for their part, were not only denied access to the hydroelectric potential of the upper Rhine, but were also threatened by desiccation due to lowering of the water table in Baden on the Rhine's right bank. The German state, however, had been all but disqualified as a bargaining partner by the terms of the Versailles Treaty and their only hope of frustrating France's new plans was to mobilize other allies. This involved framing the new canal not as a hydroelectric project, but as a French ploy to appropriate the navigable Rhine and to transform it into the first part of a new large-scale Rhine–Rhone linkage over the route of the existing *Canal du Rhône au Rhin*. This is how the German social critic, Alfons Paquet, defined the *Grand Canal*:

It stands to reason that this is an attempt to reconstruct the Rhine-Rhone Canal... The new canal between Basel and Strasbourg must, as it were, acquire the significance of a large-scale waterway. Plans are under consideration to tie it into the French canal network; it will connect the Rhine to the Mediterranean Sea...it will carry ships up to 1200 tons capacity without reloading from the lower Rhine to Lyon, to the Mediterranean. On this important canal, meanwhile, navigation will not be free, neither for Germany, nor for Switzerland, nor for other nations. The canal, as far as it accompanies the Rhine, is robbery from Germany, inasmuch as it will destroy the waterway which up to now has belonged in common to both the *allemanischen* lands facing one another on the upper reaches; for Switzerland it will be the definitive end of a free connection to the North Sea; it will transform the Rhine into a dead-end street.[26]

The rancour is understandable but, *pace* Paquet, I have come across no evidence that the *Grand Canal d'Alsace* was envisioned by the French as a part of a large-gauge replacement for the existing Rhine–Rhone canal, though it could certainly have fulfilled that purpose. It seems to have been pretty much what it appeared to be: an opportunistic grab at the upper Rhine's hydroelectric potential, designed in such a way that that potential would permanently accrue to France without in any technical sense seriously compromising Rhine navigation. The canal was as big as it was not because it was conceived as a navigational link, but because the French wanted to appropriate as much of the Rhine's water (i.e. hydroelectric potential) as they could get while the Act of Mannheim prohibited all riparian powers from compromising the Rhine's navigability. This is not to deny that the vision of a high-capacity Rhine–Rhone link through French territory (which could in part consist of a section of the *Grand Canal*) also functioned as a secondary legitimation for the *Grand Canal*. The idea of the link, as opposed to actual steps to realize it, remained a vital element of French technopolitical culture throughout the Interbellum and beyond.[27] It served as a backup legitimation, especially for work on the Rhone and as a way to link these activities to the prosperity and *grandeur* of the French nation, without actually shaping work in progress to any great degree.

Meanwhile, the all-German Rhine normalization scheme initiated in 1906 under tripartite agreement between Elsass–Lothringen (formerly French Alsace–Lorraine), Baden and Bavaria, which aimed to extend the year-round navigable channel from Mannheim to Strasbourg, had attracted a lot of attention in Basel. The Swiss were convinced that the new tactic of creating a low-water shipping channel using wing-dams could also work on the even more challenging stretch of the river between Strasbourg and Basel. At the end of November 1920 the Swiss government submitted a memorandum to the Central Commission for the Navigation of the Rhine stating that it preferred a regulated free Rhine to all other forms of navigational improvement, be it canalization or a separate lateral canal (the French option).[28] They argued that such 'free normalization' was in any case essential as a temporary measure, since the alternatives would take many years to implement and would be very costly.[29] The German government, which had assumed central management of inland waterways in August 1919, had few qualms about backing the Swiss proposal.[30]

At about the same time the French also submitted their detailed plan for the proposed *Grand Canal*. The Commission now had to take both plans into consideration. A technical subcommittee wisely chose to limit its deliberations to the most upstream of France's proposed hydroelectric plants at Kembs, which would be the first to be built. Since the Swiss normalization scheme would, in the usual fashion, proceed in the opposite direction (i.e. from downstream to upstream), the two projects would not immediately interfere with one another. Better yet, the French had planned the Kembs power plant and its shipping lock in a deviation that circumvented the rapids at Istein (the *Isteiner Klotz*). The construction of the power plant would thus already eliminate the most formidable navigational barrier to Basel's accessibility.[31]

In May 1922 the Commission presented what came to be known as the 'Strasbourg Compromise'. France was given the go-ahead for the Kembs power plant, on condition that, in order to facilitate shipping, the current in the pound above the weir to Basel be reduced from 1.2 m/s to 0.7 m/s.[32] This could be achieved by further increasing the canal's cross-section. At the same time, the Swiss government was given the go-ahead to have the Rhine normalized between Strasbourg and Basel.

For the Swiss, normalization could have been an expensive gamble. The way things looked, at some point in the future the *Grand Canal* was literally going to drain the upper Rhine dry and render the entire stretch of the river between Basel and Strasbourg useless for navigation – normalization or no normalization. The question was whether that future was far enough away for the Swiss (and Germans) to recover their investments in their normalization project. As things turned out, the upstream Kembs power plant and bypass were not completed until 1932, and the Depression and the Second World War delayed further construction to such an extent that Basel's accessibility depended heavily on the normalization until the 1950s.[33] By then the French had recommenced building new power plants, but now at a feverish pace, thanks to Marshall money and new construction technologies. By 1977, ten hydropower plants along the entire French Rhine were utilizing a total drop of some 121 m to produce 1,509 MW of electricity (Electricité de France, 1975). However, in the process the grand design of the *Grand Canal* itself had dissolved in the post-war spirit of co-operation. What remained was a series of 'diversions' from the riverbed and hence a navigational route that relied as much on the normalized river as on the French canal.[34]

Building on Basel: The Hochrhein or the Canal du Rhone au Rhin

As the above account shows, for many years a *navigable* Upper Rhine, that is, the stretch of the river between Mannheim and Basel (and forming the border between France and Germany), had been something between a vision and an expectation. In 1912, after years of dreaming and negotiation,

Strasbourg's harbour and commercial interests were re-included in the Rhine's navigational community. As Basel in its turn appeared to become ever better incorporated in the Rhine trade after Gelpke's 1904 trial and the twin projects of the 'Strasbourg compromise' after the First World War, the newly domesticated stretch of river itself became a jumping-off point for new imaginings and a stimulus to revive those that had become dormant. One set of German and Swiss imaginings extended the navigable Rhine past Basel, up the *Hochrhein* and into the Aare River and Lake Constance (Bodensee) – and thence to Austria, the Danube, Italy and the Rhone. A second set of imaginings seemed to justify Alfons Paquet's accusations that the *Grand Canal d'Alsace* was a mere first instalment in a large-scale Rhine–Rhone link over French territory. These envisioned a Rhine–Rhone route that branched off from the *Grand Canal* just below Kembs and copied the existing *Canal du Rhône au Rhin*, but this time to a much larger scale and with many fewer locks. Let us first take a closer look at the Swiss visions.

Even prior to Basel's gradual renaissance as a Rhine port after the First World War, there had been modest small-scale shipping upstream of the city on the *Hochrhein*, at least between Basel and the Rhine Falls at Schaffhausen. But after the Frankfurt Exposition of 1891, where the feasibility of long-distance transport of alternating current was first demonstrated, the *Hochrhein* quickly became targeted for hydropower development. Its swift current, steady flow and 150 m drop between Lake Constance and Basel over a distance of only 130 km made it a desirable natural resource. For our purpose the salient question is the same one that later plagued the French designers of the *Grand Canal d'Alsace*: how should hydropower development be reconciled with navigability? And who defined the level of 'navigability' that ought to be achieved?

The *Hochrhein*'s first hydroelectric power plant, a joint venture by Switzerland and Baden, was completed near Rheinfelden in 1899. River navigation was accommodated both by a 20 m wide lowered sill in the dam suitable for log rafts and by a tiny gated lock of 15 m by 3 m.[35] A second power plant at Laufenburg, 30 km upstream, was completed in 1905, and fitted with a much bigger lock of 34 m by 9 m. A third plant at Augst-Whylen, scheduled for 1907, was designed with a lock of 30 m by 8 m. What accounts for the sudden upscaling between Rheinfelden (1899) and Laufenberg (1905)? It is highly probable that visions of improved navigability *up to* Basel prompted the power plant builders to anticipate larger-scale navigation *above* Basel as well.

The difference between 1899 and 1905 was that by the latter year the *Hochrein* was no longer significant only as a source of hydropower, but also as an extension of the navigable Rhine to Lake Constance. This was again largely Gelpke's work, who understood that in order for Basel to become a major port on the *Freie Rhein* the reconstruction of the Upper Rhine between Strasbourg and Basel would have to become a *national* and not merely a municipal project. This, in turn, could only be accomplished if Basel were framed not as the new head of navigation on the Rhine, but as a way station in extending the navigable Rhine into a network of Swiss waterways (and even to Austria, via the Lake Constance port of Bregenz). The *Hochrhein* was the key artery in this concept, and from 1901 on Gelpke committed time and energy to establishing societies for the promotion of navigation on the Rhine, not only at Basel, but also at Konstanz and St Gallen around Lake Constance.[36] These booster groups successfully petitioned for the construction of a much larger lock – 90 m by 12 m – at Augst-Whylen, which would be sufficient to accommodate the large-scale shipping regime of the time. The wealthy backers of these associations put their money where their mouths were and actually paid the extra expense of the larger lock. This set the tone for the construction of the four remaining power plants constructed on the *Hochrhein* in subsequent years. Though lacking facilities for locking ships through, they were designed so as to facilitate the construction of locks should the need arise.

In 1929, with the impending completion of the dam and power plant at Kembs (first instalment of the *Grand Canal d'Alsace*), the governments of Switzerland and Baden signed a treaty proclaiming that in view of the impending improvements on the upper Rhine they would pursue the construction of a large-scale waterway from Basel to Lake Constance. The Great Depression delayed matters, but in 1941 the Swiss government submitted a detailed plan for the navigational reconstruction of the *Hochrhein* to the German government. This struck a responsive chord, for after the Austrian *Anschluss* the Nazis were anxious to integrate the new southeastern part of the Reich into the central German economy, based in part on ample supplies of Ruhr coal. An extension of the navigable Rhine to Lake Constance fitted perfectly into this imperial strategy. As with the other Austrian link via the Rhine–Main–Danube canal, however, the Nazis' tenure was simply too brief (and too filled with distractions) to actually allow their indomitable political will to materialize in the form of locks and weirs. Moreover, the powerful Swiss State Railways mobilized their considerable weight against improvements to the *Hochrhein*, contesting that transfer of railway transit freight to the proposed waterway would cost them – and the state – millions of francs in revenue.

After the Second World War, the plans lost their imperial allure and had to face the test of cold economic calculation. The first thing the Swiss did was to downscale the navigational parameters from the German pre-war standard of 1,200-ton towed barges to 600-ton self-propelled motorships. Though this made the proposed waterway considerably cheaper, it was not enough to tip the scales, despite the additional hydropower potential that could be tapped. What would make the improvement of the *Hochrhein* attractive enough to make the financial and technological risk worth taking – for both Germany and Switzerland? To start with, where was the *Hochrhein* going?

That was a bone of some contention. The German interest prior to and during the Second World War, the Austrian interest after the war, and the interest of Konstanz and St Gallen, was to establish a large-scale waterway from Basel to Lake Constance. This could transform Konstanz and the Austrian city of Bregenz on the eastern end of the lake into something like little Basels on Lake Constance. Bregenz, especially, could become a major railway terminus for Rhine shipping and a gateway for Austria to the Ruhr and the North Sea. The question was whether Germany and Switzerland (which would bear the financial burden) found this option interesting enough, given their parallel interests in roads and railways and in alternative waterways, in particular the German Rhine–Main–Danube canal.

But there was a grander conception of Lake Constance based on the ironic railway image of a *Drehscheibe* (turntable) for trade between the Rhine and Eastern Europe that might have forced the issue. This conception projected a new canal between Lake Constance and the Danube. Since 1908 a number of different plans, serving different interests, had already been put forward. It was clear that, though all the relevant powers seemed to agree on the desirability of some link between Lake Constance and the Danube, and thus supported the Swiss *Drehscheibe* concept, they each did so for their own reasons and as much as possible through their own territories, gainsaying others the rent of the transit trade. But the rub, in all cases, was that first the *Hochrhein* had to be reconstructed. Lacking this, none of the projects could be more than fantasies. The irony was that the reconstruction of the *Hochrhein* itself depended on the perceived feasibility of these fantasies, that is, on expectations that Lake Constance could lead somewhere else and, as it were, draw traffic up the *Hochrhein* by capillary action.

Up the *Hochrhein* and beyond: Swiss 'conceptions grandieuses' and images of 'travaux pharaoniques'

In regard to the *Hochrhein*, the Swiss had their own navigational dreams based on the fatal attraction of the numerous lakes and rivers criss-crossing their country. A cursory glance at the map makes clear that the chains of long and eminently navigable lakes simply begged to be connected by waterways, so that Switzerland too could share in the international bounty of inland navigation (Figure 9.2). After the turn of the twentieth century, Basel's impending navigational renaissance only added fuel to these heated imaginings.

Because access to the Rhine was essential to the economic viability of any imaginable Swiss waterway system, visions of different waterways always had a terminus in this wet highway to the sea. But, if the Rhine was the ultimate goal, the proximate goal in these imagined waterways was the town of Brugg on the River Aare, just upstream of the latter's confluence with the *Hochrhein*. The Aare was the only Rhine tributary that breached the Jura Mountains and made the *Hochrhein* accessible from the Swiss interior.

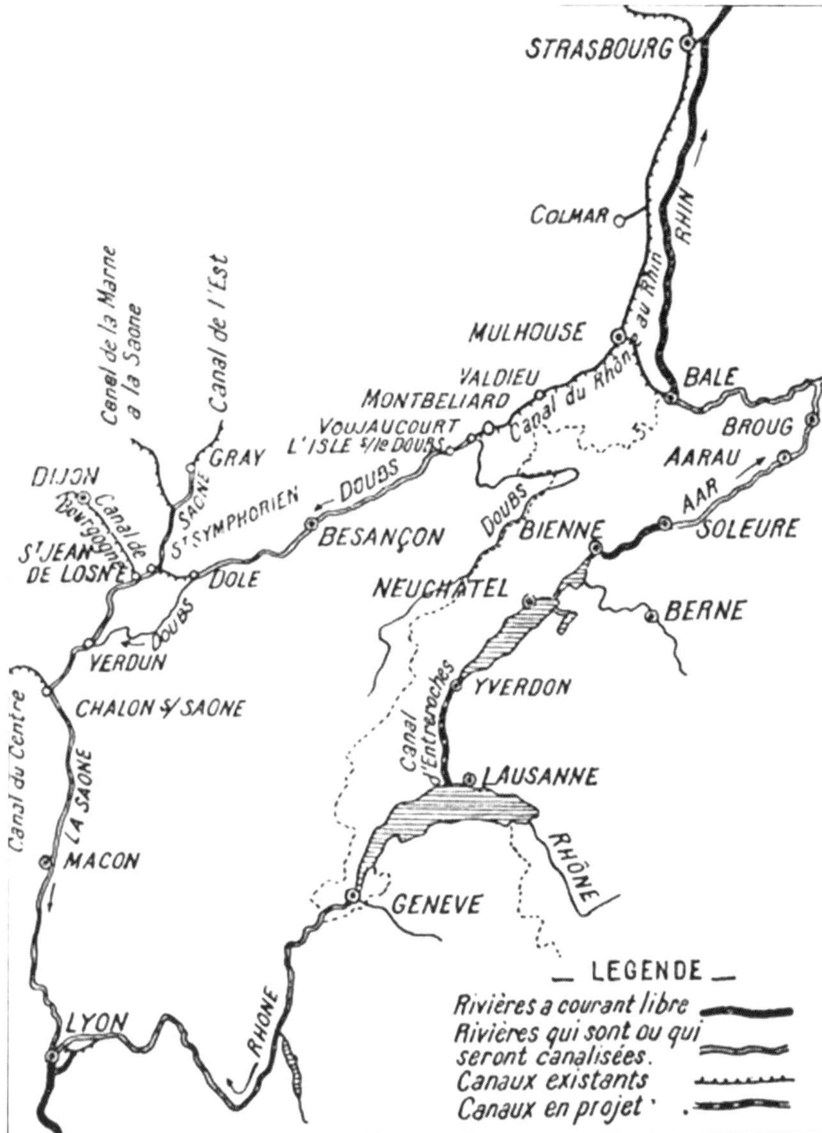

Figure 9.2   The French and the Swiss version of the *Liaison Rhône-Rhin* in 1947

Note: The Swiss link is full of promise, but the French link exists.

Source: J. Comte, *Pour une Politique Maritime et Fluviale. La Suisse, La Méditerranée, Le Rhône* (Paris: Librairie du Receuil Sirey 1947), p. 87.

In addition, its upper course took it tantalizingly close to Lake Neuchâtel, the gateway to Lake Leman and Geneva. Finally, the relatively steady and voluminous discharge, coupled with a reasonably steep slope, made the *Hochrhein* attractive as a source of hydropower – which inevitably improved the economic chances for its reconstruction as a navigable waterway.

After the Second World War not one, but three, different routes were being projected from Brugg (See Figure 9.3). Each of them had proponents in different regions and urban centres and was pursued with the intent of regional enrichment. At the same time they could also be construed as having a national and even a European component, inasmuch as their actual construction would putatively reduce freight costs both within and through Switzerland, including the rail transit traffic across the alpine passes and through France to Marseilles. This rhetorical appeal to the 'general interest' packaged in visionary Europeanism was in this case explicitly mobilized to neutralize competitors and win over potential allies. In any case, all the proposed waterways depended first and foremost on Swiss–German agreement over the reconstruction of the *Hochrhein*, while paradoxically at the same time the reconstruction of the *Hochrhein* found an important legitimation (at least on the Swiss side) in the apparent will to complete the derivative waterways. I will describe two of these waterways briefly and dwell a bit on the third. I will be drawing heavily on the accounts by Van Looveren and Merger, as I have also done in the preceding paragraphs.[37]

Brugg, the projected future 'Basel on the Aare', is situated at the confluence of three rivers, each of which presented an entry into a different region and inspired a different waterway: the Limmat to the southwest, the Reuss to the south and the Aare to the southeast. The route via the Limmat would pass through Zurich (creating yet another Basel) onward to Lake Zurich and via a reconstructed River Linth to the *Walensee*. Further imaginings projected an additional 16 km canalization of the River Seez up to the Gonzen iron-ore mining district. The waterway would be a civil engineering tour de force, especially near Zurich, where it was projected through a 4.5 km long tunnel around the city which it would share with a ring road built on pillars above the waterway. Van Looveren reports that as of 1948 in Zurich '...funds have been allocated...to study the question: "Zurich, inland harbor connected to the transport network of the Rhine," a decision which has meanwhile been met by mixed feelings on the part of the State Railways'.[38]

The second imagined waterway would utilize the Reuss to create a waterway to Luzerne, thence across the *Vierwaldstättesee,* and on to the city of Fluëlen at the head of the *Untersee.* The intent of this waterway was to cheapen north–south freight prices by substituting part of the rail passage via the St Gothard tunnel by a waterway. The Italian terminus would be Bellinzona at the head of navigation on the Ticino River, which flowed into the *Lago Maggiore* at its northern end. Not even the fevered imaginings of the period after the Second World War managed to come up with a canal project over

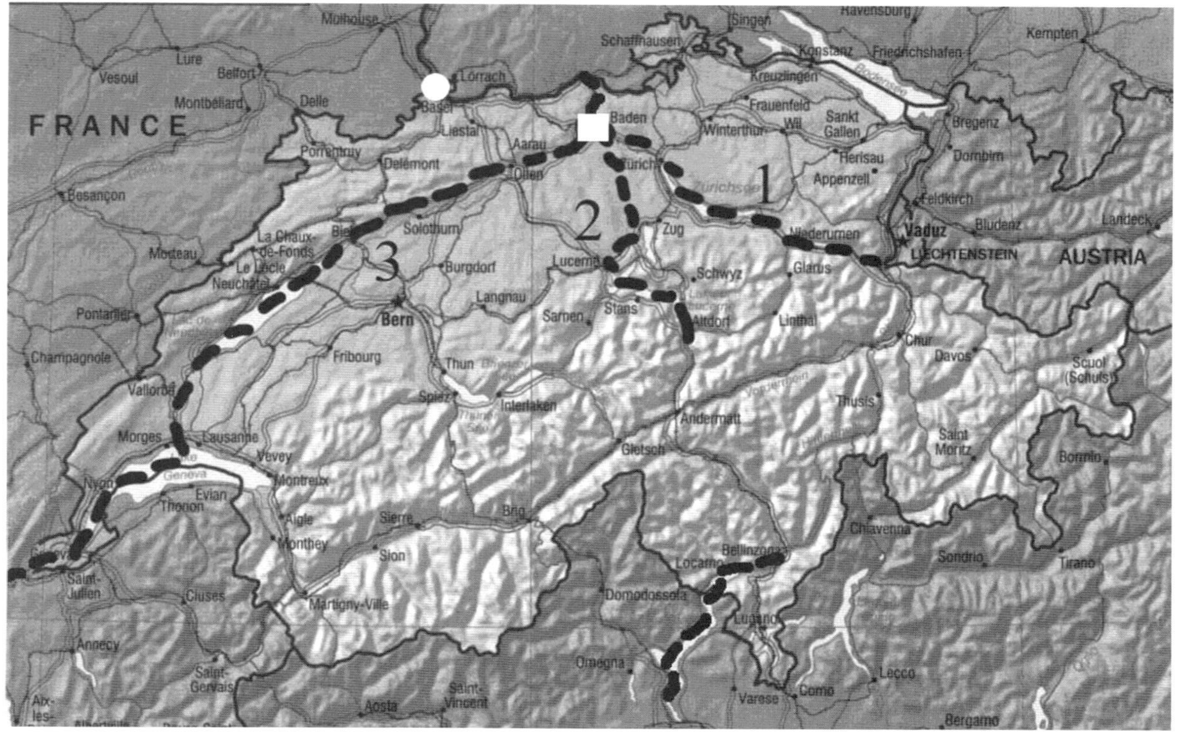

Figure 9.3   Switzerland showing three tentacles of the *Drehscheibe*

Note: 1) route via the Limmat through Zurich; 2) route via the Reuss through Luzerne and *Vierwaldstättesee* (connecting with transalpine rail link to Italy); 3) the *Transhelvetique* via the Aare and Lake Neuchâtel to Lake Leman and the *Haute Rhône*. The white circle is Basel and the white square is Brugg on the Aare.

the Alps, so the big question here was whether the cheaper waterway would compensate for the extra costs of loading ship cargoes into railway cars on one side of the Alps and loading them from railway cars into ships on the other side. Nonetheless, the volume of freight that might be expected over this link might not only justify the construction of the link itself, but could be a powerful stimulus both for shipping on the navigable Rhine and for extending navigability to the *Hochrhein* at least up to the mouth of the Aare. However, this remained a big gamble because it depended on Italy doing the homework of realizing a waterway from Lago Maggiore to the Po, homework which might or might not get done.

The final imagined waterway was perhaps the most ambitious of all. Not only did it aim to connect Geneva to the Rhine, but it also aimed to connect Geneva to the Rhone, and hence constituted an alternative to the existing French Rhine–Rhone Canal and its possible future upscaling to a *Liaison Rhin–Rhône*. The route of this so-called 'Transhelvetique' between Brugg and Geneva followed the Aare upstream to Lake Bienne, and thence to Lake Neuchâtel and Lake Leman via several interstitial canals. To realize this plan, the navigable Rhine would have to be extended from Basel upstream half-way to the falls at Schaffhausen, the Aare would have to be canalized, and, most daunting of all, the watershed separating the Rhine and Rhone basins between Lake Neuchâtel and Lake Leman would have to be conquered by a sizeable new canal. The surface of Lake Neuchâtel is 57 m higher than that of Lake Leman and the watershed lies an additional 20 m higher: the summit level would thus require locking up nearly 70 m from Lake Leman. This would require some ten sizeable locks in the 37 km length of the canal.

The idea of the *Transhelvetique* as an integral waterway had tantalized the Swiss since the accession of Basel to Rhine commerce (see note 12), but optimism after the Second World War about European co-operation and Marshall funds breathed new life into the plans. The protagonists (and chief beneficiaries) were the French-speaking cantons of Switzerland, who saw in the *Transhelvetique* their own wet highway to the sea via the Rhine. But there was also, of course, an even closer sea, the Mediterranean, which had proved its worth as a (railway) route to the world's oceans during the Second World War when traffic on the Rhine had been blocked. Hence, the imagined *Transhelvetique* also stimulated Swiss visions of a regulated upper Rhone that would link their Alpine waterways not only to the North Sea, but to the Mediterranean as well – and in the process, almost by accident, realize the long-cherished Rhine–Rhone liaison as well.

The Swiss were quite sanguine about mastering the technological challenges and about the economic potential of the proposed waterway. The Swiss political economist Jean Comte argued that 'Technically the biggest difficulty is the traverse of Geneva. The rest of the waterway offers no difficulties comparable to those of regulating the upper Rhine. To the contrary, the vast expanses of water comprising the lakes offer an ideal passage for motorships, whose engines can run at full speed, save time, and thus augment the transport capacity of the waterway.'[39] To this rosy picture was added the possibility of exploiting the Aare's hydroelectric potential, the conventional strategy for balancing the (imaginary) books in waterway construction throughout the century.

However, the *Transhelvetique* depended on a French commitment to render the upper Rhone navigable. This conflicted with the perennial French interest in a Rhine–Rhone link along the route of their existing Rhine–Rhone Canal, particularly the approach to the Rhone via the Saone, rather than the precipitous Alpine stretch below Geneva. Like the Dutch vis-à-vis the extension of Rhine navigation and the various projects for inter-basin links, the Swiss could only be 'committed spectators' of the French debates about where to connect the Rhone and the Rhine. However, like the Dutch, they could try to influence French political and navigational landscapes by their own rhetoric, imaginings and constructions. Jean Comte, for example, argued that from an economic point of view the existing Rhine–Rhone Canal could never compete with the proposed *Transhelvetique* and a canalized upper Rhone.

> 'The *Canal du Rhône au Rhin*, open to barges of 300 tons, will not be able to offer serious competition to the *Transhelvetique*. On the regulated Swiss waterway, a motor-barge leaving Marseille could navigate to Antwerp or any other northern port without having to break up the cargo at any point, while he would certainly have to do so at Lyon if he chose to take the French *Canal du Rhône au Rhin*, assuming his dimensions would permit it, where kilometer after kilometer he would be forced to run his engines at a sluggish, detrimental and costly pace.'[40]

It is clear that the French themselves were of the same opinion, as witnessed by the scheme launched in 1958 (and finally scuttled for environmental reasons in 1997) to reconstruct the entire route of the old canal into an all-French *Liaison Rhin–Rhône* suitable for ships of 4,000 tons. But, despite their differences, this *Liaison* shared a major common problem with the Swiss *Transhelvetique*, namely the poor navigability of the Rhone even downstream of Lyon, relative to that of the Rhine. Much steeper than the Rhine, less regular and burdened with several rapids, it was described by Jules Michelet as a 'furious bull that leaps from the Alps to the Sea'.[41] Clearly, if any Rhine–Rhone waterway were to prove viable it would have to be a link from sea to sea, and both the Rhine and the Rhone would have to be navigable from the junctions with the intervening canal to the sea. As we have seen, the Rhine (even the *Hochrhein*) showed every indication of meeting these criteria, but the Rhone still had a very long way to go. However, this consideration – the 'misfit' of the Rhone as part of a new Rhine–Rhone waterway – did not appear to be pre-eminent in the law enacted by French parliament in 1921, which called for the integrated hydraulic 'management' of the Rhone with a tripartite aim: hydropower, navigation and agriculture.

To effect this 'taming' of the 'wild river' a new public–private corporation was called into being, the *Compagnie National du Rhône* (CNR) (Figure 9.4). But no-one seemed in a rush, even discounting the bad economic times. It took until 1931 for the statutes to be ratified and until 1933 before the complex financing was agreed on.

One of the first three projects that the *Compagnie* started in the late 1930s was a hydroelectric power station and flood regulation dam at the town of Genissiat, just 20 km downstream from the Swiss border. Construction started in 1937, but it was 1948 before the first turbine came online. Genissiat's role in improving the navigability of the Rhone was thoroughly ambiguous, however. Though the reservoir formed by the dam created a navigable waterway for several kilometres upstream – having literally drowned several formidable obstacles – the stretches of river both upstream and downstream retained their wild Alpine character. To avoid torpedoing the perennial plans for developing the upper Rhone as a navigable waterway, provision was made for navigational locks to overcome Genissiat's 60 m drop, but, in the absence of complementary improvements on the Swiss end, and further downstream to Lyon, these were quite sensibly never completed. To this day the upper Rhone has remained primarily a source of hydropower. In regard to navigability, the impetus of the *Compagnie Nationale du Rhône* was diverted to improving the unruly river between Lyon and Marseilles. This became a brilliant example of French post-Second World War 'radiance', particularly the huge dam–lock–canalization–hydropower scheme between Donzère and Mondragon.[42] However, with navigability on the upper Rhone abandoned as a major goal, it was crystal clear that if there were to be a new Rhine–Rhone waterway it would, for the time being at least, not pass by Genissiat.

In terms of French national interest and autonomy this was understandable. A route from Lyon to the Rhine via the *Haute Rhône* would inevitably have to pass through Swiss territory and, aside from the necessity of co-operating with the Swiss to construct such an international waterway, French shipping would always remain vulnerable to Swiss navigational politics. Moreover, although such a waterway would doubtless accrue to the benefit of Lyon and Marseilles (as well as to Lausanne and Geneva), it would leave Strasbourg out of the picture. Finally, though the Swiss had worked the project of the *Transhelvetique* out in some detail, it remained essentially a paper tiger. There was absolutely no guarantee that it would actually be executed, meaning that French efforts to render the *Haute Rhône* navigable (an extraordinarily expensive project) would come to naught. Access to Geneva alone could hardly justify the investment. At the same time – and for this very reason – the Swiss had equal reason to be doubtful of French intentions to turn the *Haute Rhône* into a navigable waterway and hence equal reason to temporize the construction of the *Transhelvetique*. It was, in short, a classic transnational stalemate, and, all things considered, it made much more sense for the French to invest – at least rhetorically – in the creation of a *Liaison Rhône–Rhin* via the old route of the *Canal du Rhône au Rhin*, that is,

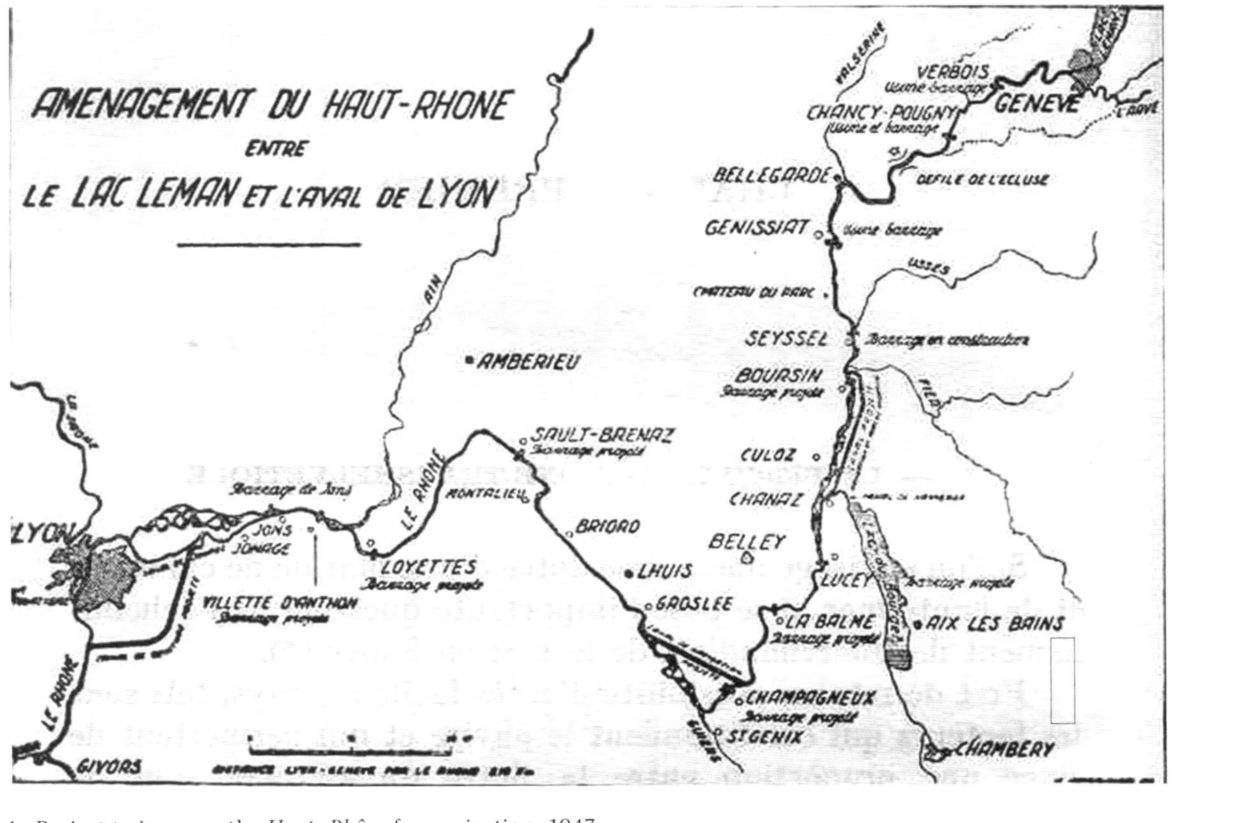

Figure 9.4 Project to improve the *Haute Rhône* for navigation, 1947

Source: J. Comte, *Pour une Politique Maritime et Fluviale. La Suisse, La Méditerranée, Le Rhône* (Paris: Librairie du Receuil Sirey 1947), p. 130.

over Colmar and via the Burgundian Gate to the Doubs and the upper Saône. This would keep the link entirely on French territory – an expensive though indisputably more glorious and perhaps more profitable option.

While the *Transhelvetique* and the other Swiss–German projects branching off the *Hochrhein* have continued to lead a ghostly life in transnational limbo, the French project to upgrade the existing Rhine–Rhone Canal has been pursued with at least rhetorical vigour since the early 1960s, both by local and regional interest groups and by the French state.[43] Since the 1970s the slow pace of negotiations about the technological and financial aspects of the French project has hardly been accelerated by mounting concerns about the ecological damage to the Doubs Valley consequent on the transformation of the old *Canal du Rhône au Rhin* into a large European-scale waterway suitable for pusher barges.

While the EU appears to agree with Michelle Merger that 'beyond a doubt this axis represents an essential element in the transportation strategy of Western Europe',[44] it lacks confidence that the French will actually want to realize this axis as a waterway. The Rhine–Rhone liaison is indeed one of the thirty major transportation axes included in the TEN-T programme, but it is now being conceived more modestly as a railway, rather than a waterway, link. In fact, of the thirty European transport axes included in TEN-T, only two are waterways: the project for a new *Canal du Nord* between Antwerp and the Seine, and the Rhine–Danube waterway, effectively accomplished with the completion of Germany's Rhine–Main–Danube Canal in 1992.

Conclusion

In considering the immensely complex histories of the two imagined and partially realized Rhine–Rhone waterways, we see similarities but also marked contrasts. They are similar in that the exigencies of carrying a canal over the continental divide demanded more than merely the construction of the canal itself. In both cases the 'approaches' to the canal, that is, the navigabilities of the river sections leading up to the canal, were at some point a major impediment to completing the watershed-spanning navigational bridge as a whole. And in both cases, at least portions of the canal itself involved a considerable hydraulic challenge. For the French canal, 'feeding' the upper pounds of the old French canal to recompense water lost during locking operations posed a major difficulty, while the section of the proposed Swiss canal between Lake Neuchâtel and Lake Leman (the old Canal des Entreroches) demanded very challenging and expensive locks to master the 80 m rise to the watershed.

This said, however, the differences are certainly more striking than the similarities. There was, in the first place, a staggering difference in the sheer complexity – technological, political, economic and rhetorical – of the two cases. The Swiss *Transhelvetique* simply involved many more technological challenges, more actors and governments, and many more complex estimates of economic risks and opportunities than the French Rhone–Rhine linkage. It was also a much trickier card to play in an ideological and rhetorical sense. For example, aligning distant but politically critical actors like Great Britain behind the scheme required complex chains of historical reasoning and highly speculative projections into a purported common future for European nations – even those nations separated from the continent by a stormy sea.[45]

These differences were partly rooted in the technical and geographical features of the respective waterways. Although the proposed Swiss waterway would have to surmount an elevation of some 450 m (the summit level of the Canal des Entreroches), compared with only 342 m for the highest pound in the French *Canal du Rhône au Rhin*, this was not the decisive issue in terms of the watershed-spanning canals themselves. The main effect of the 100 m height difference was to distance the Swiss route much further from more or less navigable portions of the Rhine and the Rhone. Hence, in addition to organizing a waterway through Swiss territory in the form of a chain of lakes and canals, the Swiss needed to ensure that the final stretches of river (up to Brugg on the Rhine side and up to Geneva on the Rhone side) were made navigable. The French canal faced similar obstacles, to be sure, but at the time of the canal's construction in the early nineteenth century 'navigability' was less of an engineering challenge than it would become in subsequent decades. The French, moreover, faced fewer constraints than the Swiss about where their inter-basin canal could join up to the river system on either side. Given the terrain's rather gentle inclination at both ends of the canal, there was a relatively simple trade-off between making the canal longer and extending the navigable portions of the Rhine and the Saone. In fact, on the Rhine side the canal was originally designed to join up with the Ill at Colmar (Alsace), a tributary of the Rhine. It was only thanks to Strasbourg's financial intercession that a branch was added up to Strasbourg, whence it finally joined the Rhine. The Swiss had far fewer options: both Brugg and Geneva were obligatory points of passage and both were far removed – certainly given the state of the art in navigation at the outset of the twentieth century – from anything resembling a navigable river.

These basic technological–geographical differences set the stage for the widely divergent political and rhetorical histories of the two Rhone–Rhine links. In this respect too, the French had a relatively easy time of it. At the time of the canal's original conception and construction, 'navigable' portions of both the Rhine and the Rhone were wholly or partially within French territory, as was the route of the canal itself. This meant that – at least to the extent that foreign powers did not prevent navigation up to Strasbourg – the French needed to deal only with themselves in negotiating the terms of the 'transcontinental' waterway. This national context, although volatile enough, provided a much more predictable future for taking waterway wagers than the transnational environment the Swiss necessarily had to operate in. Nobody in France had to be merely a 'committed spectator' rooting for congenial navigational developments but formally powerless to influence the course of events. In the context of a centralized nation state, interest groups, chambers of commerce, and provincial governments could all directly influence the future course of waterways development and place their bets accordingly. To be sure, matters became more difficult, both internally and internationally, after the mid-nineteenth-century technological revolution in fluvial navigation made the old *Canal du Rhône au Rhin* increasingly obsolete and only a major upscaling of the 'liaison' could preserve its status as a 'European' waterway. At that point not only the navigability of the Rhone, but also that of the Rhine up to and past Strasbourg, became pressing issues. As we have seen, it took the unique position of vanquisher after the First World War to force the issue and plan a first instalment of the new waterway in the form of the *Grand Canal d'Alsace*.

This was a far cry from the Swiss predicament during the same years. In order to realize their far-off vision of a *Transhelvetique*, they had first needed to ensure a window on the Rhine, that is, to create the conditions for extending large-scale navigability on the Rhine up to Basel. Even for this 'modest' first step, the post-First World War agenda, they had needed to mobilize the entire community of Rhine riparian nations, but particularly France, which had manoeuvred itself into a commanding position on the upper Rhine thanks to the Treaty of Versailles. When year-round navigational access to Basel seemed assured thanks to the parallel projects of the French *Grand Canal d'Alsace* and the Swiss–German normalization of the open river, the next hurdle was clearly enrolling Baden into the project of making the *Hochrhein* navigable up to its confluence with the Aare. This also required intensive lobbying by local chambers of commerce within Switzerland, chiefly to overcome the Swiss State Railway's active lobby against spending money on more waterways. But all this paled into insignificance in comparison with what had to be accomplished on the Rhone. As described, the section of the Rhone between Geneva and Lyon was a wild and unruly river, and bridging the 135-metre difference in height between the two cities with a proper large-scale navigational channel would have been phenomenally expensive. Why would France be interested (especially given the alternate possibility of the all-French route via the Burgundian Gate)?

Given their utter dependence on surrounding states, especially France, it is hardly surprising that the Swiss frequently invoked 'the general interest' or 'the interests of commerce' or 'Europe' to redefine their national (or even regional) interest in the *Transhelvetique* as the interest of European or even of all 'commercial' nations. And, indeed, there was never any doubt that from a gravitational standpoint Switzerland could in fact become a *Drehscheibe* (turntable) where waterways from north and south, east and west could meet. But even if the Swiss could come to internal agreement on the desirability of investing in the internal waterways, the big question was whether at various moments in time France, Baden, the other Rhine nations and even the Great Powers would be willing to invest in the waterways leading up to it.[46] In the debate about the *Grand Canal d'Alsace* after the First World War as well as in the post-Second World War period with Marshall money abroad, it made sense for the Swiss to invoke European international prosperity as the guiding principle for their route to the sea and their envisioned waterways network. The Swiss were ready to supply the bridge, but who was going to build the abutments and approaches? Burgundy had already proclaimed its 'triple junction' between 'both seas' as far back as 1784. After the Second World War the Germans revived their projects to connect the Rhine and Danube and ultimately opened the large-scale Rhine–Main–Danube Canal to traffic in 1992. This link too was always touted as a 'European' waterway and has in fact been adopted by the EU as transport corridor 7. Still, they were both, like the Swiss *Transhelvetique*, eminently *national* projects, carried out in the sheltered spaces of national economies and legal systems.

This may in fact be sealing their fates, as highly effective opposition to their expansion or reconstruction has been mobilized by ecological groups operating at regional and national levels. Plans to create a large-scale French Rhine–Rhone liaison succumbed in 1997 to environmentalist protests against despoiling the Doubs valley. German authorities' plans to canalize a final section of the Danube to remove a bottleneck in the Rhine–Main–Danube waterway have equally fallen afoul of environmentalist groups protesting the demise of the 'free river' and the despoiling of 'God's creation'.[47] And, finally, in 1993 the Swiss parliament lifted the ban on construction within a 100 metre-wide strip of land along the course of the proposed *Transhelvetique* that had been in effect since the 1960s, at a time when realization seemed, if not immanent, at least within the realm of possibility.

In sum, the history of trans-basin waterways connecting the Rhine, Rhone and Danube suggests that, to the limited extent that these links have actually been built, they do not owe their existence to the force of grand conceptions nor to the seductions of the 'common European interest', but rather to the play of mundane national and regional interests in the context of European political and diplomatic history. Nonetheless, grand conceptions did play an important role in mobilizing actors at national levels and might, in some cases, actually have been able to tip the scales by imagining profitable hinterlands and markets for large-scale waterways extending across the watersheds. The problem apparently was not and is not only the price tag, but the unpredictable and possibly threatening shifts of economic and political advantage that might result from connecting hitherto separated seas by large-scale inland waterways.

Notes

1. Alfons Paquet, *Der Rhein als Schicksal, oder das Problem der Völker* (Bonn: Verlag von Friedrich Cohen 1920), p. 17.

2. Erik van der Vleuten and Arne Kaijser (eds), *Networking Europe: Transnational Infrastructures and the Shaping of Europe, 1850–2000* (Sagamore Beach, MA: Science History Publishers 2006).

3. Bruno Latour, *Ces réseaux que la raison ignore* (Paris: l'Harmattan 1992), introduction. (Translation and emphasis CD)

4. Michèle Merger (ed.), *Les Réseaux Européens Transnationaux XIXe – XXe Siecles. Quels Enjeux?* (Bordeaux: Ouest Éditions 2005).

5. B.M. Frischmann, 'An Economic Theory of Infrastructure and Commons Management', *Minnesota Law Review* 89 (2005), pp. 917–1031.

6. See Frank Schipper, *Driving Europe: Building Europe on roads in the twentieth century* (Amsterdam: Aksant 2008), p. 104ff.

7. Tom Misa and Johan Schot, 'Introduction – Inventing Europe: Technology and the Hidden Integration of Europe', *History and Technology* 21(1), pp. 1–20.

8. Though this may change thanks to the EU's TEN-T programme, which as one of its thirty transport axes envisages a major European large-scale waterway comprising the Rhine, the Rhine–Main–Danube Canal, and the Danube; that is, an inland waterway from the North Sea to the Black Sea. Much of this is already in place thanks to prior centuries of hidden and piecemeal Europeanization, but the TEN-T programme seeks to co-ordinate (and subsidize) the elimination of a number of important bottlenecks, especially on the lower Danube in the former Warsaw Pact zone.

9. This is only a matter of general principle and is by no means uniformly true for empirical rivers. Most navigable rivers, though they *tend* to be more navigationally challenging the further upstream one goes, exhibit rough patches (rapids, sills, waterfalls), upstream of which navigational conditions may improve once again. These rough patches, like the Rhine gorge between Bonn and Bingen or the 'Isteiner Klotz' below Basel on the Rhine, the 'Iron Gate' rapids on the Danube, or the rapids at Donzère-Mondragon on the Rhone, were the 'reverse salients' in establishing uniform navigations on the rivers and have in fact been targets of major river improvements over the years.

10. Willem van Looveren, 'Een en ander over grenzen en waterscheidingen in en om het stroomgebied van de Rijn, die reeds overwonnen en nog te overwinnen zijn' in T. Ligthart (ed.) *Physisch- en Economisch-Geografische Beschouwingen over de Rijn als Europese rivier* (Rotterdam: Van Kouteren's Uitgeversbedrijf 1948), p. 186.

11. Cornelis Disco, 'Taming the Rhine. Economic Connection and Urban Competition' in M. Hård and T.J. Misa (eds) *Urban Machinery. Inside Modern European Cities* (Cambridge, MA: MIT Press 2008), pp. 23–48.

12. R.G. Geiger, *Planning the French Canals: Bureaucracy, Politics, and Enterprise under the Restoration* (Newark, Del. and Cranbury, N.J.: University of Delaware Press 1994).

13. Canalizing a river involves damming it up at intervals by means of adjustable weirs. These weirs retain the water and create a 'staircase' of relatively tranquil 'pounds' while allowing the river's discharge to pass through. In order to enable ships to navigate the difference in water level produced by the weirs, gated ships' locks are constructed that lift or lower the ships from one pound to the other.

14. Looveren, 'Een en ander', p. 186.

15. Louis Becquey was a royalist deputy to the Assembly and engineer of the *Corps des Ponts et Chaussees et des Mines*. After the restoration he became the Corps' director. In this capacity he saw his plan enacted into law. The new standards for lock dimensions were 30.4 metres by 5.20 metres. Maximum draught was 1.6 metres and headroom was 3.0 metres. These were techno-economically

progressive standards, given prevailing technologies of haulage. A number of older canals had to be thoroughly revamped. The state supervised execution of the plan, but a number of the canals, including the Rhine–Rhone Canal, were built and co-financed by private canal companies. http://fr.wikipedia.org/wiki/Louis_Becquey

16. Looveren, 'Een en ander', p. 187.
17. Looveren, 'Een en ander'.
18. Ibid.
19. M. Cioc, *The Rhine: An Eco-Biography, 1815–2000* (Seattle: University of Washington Press 2002).
20. Merger (1995), pp. 186–7.
21. J.B. Krantz, 'Rapport sur la situation des voies navigables dans le bassin du Rhone présenté à la Chambre des Députés' (23 janvier, 1874), *Journal Officie* (1874) annexe 1568, pp. 1290 ff.
22. Cornelis Disco, 'Taming the Rhine'.
23. Mannheim had flourished as *de facto* 'head of navigation' on the Rhine since the 1850s. It had been loath to surrender this lucrative position to Strasbourg, and as long as Strasbourg had been French it had enjoyed the support of the German Reich.
24. K. Spiess, 'Ausbau des Rheines vom Bodensee bis zum Main' in Wasser- und Schiffahrtsdirektion Duisburg (ed.) *Der Rhein. Ausbau, Verkehr, Verwaltung* (Duisburg: Rhein Verlagsgesellschaft mbH 1951), pp. 127–8.
25. R. Gelpke, *Free Access to the Sea for Switzerland and The Rhine a Highway of British Trade* (London: s.n. 1919).
26. Paquet, *Der Rhein*, pp. 76–7.
27. A. Giandou, *La Compagnie nationale du Rhône (1933–1998). Histoire d'un partenaire régionale de l'Etat* (Grenoble: Presses Universitaires de Grenoble 1999); Michèle Merger, 'La liaison Rhin-Rhone ou l'histoire d'un serpent de mer (1834–1991)' in M. Merger et al. (eds) *Les Réseaux Européens Transnationaux, XIXe – XXe Siècles. Quels Enjeux?* (Bordeaux: Ouest Éditions 1999), pp. 185–212; Sarah Pritchard, 'Reconstructing the Rhone: The Cultural Politics of Nature and Nation in Contemporary France, 1945–1997', *French Historical Studies* 27(4) (2004), pp. 765–99.
28. The Central Commission for the Navigation of the Rhine, established by the Congress of Vienna in 1815, ensured enforcement of the various Rhine Treaties pertaining to free navigation on the river – culminating in the Act of Mannheim (1867). All projects for modifications to the river bed that affected navigation had to be submitted to the commission for its approval. All riparian states had seats on the commission, but after the First World War, by virtue of stipulations in the Treaty of Versailles, England, Italy, Belgium and Switzerland were added and France stacked the Central Commission in its favour by claiming more than its fair share of representatives and monopolizing the chairmanship. Despite this 'political' imbalance, indications are that the requirement of unanimous voting (i.e. *de facto* veto for all members), the importance of technical subcommittees in framing decisions, and of course the danger of delegitimizing itself as a constructive member of the international community, restrained France's hand and maintained the Central Commission's equanimity; J.P. Chamberlain, *The Regime of the International Rivers: Danube and Rhine* (Washington: Columbia University 1923), W.J.M.v. Eysinga, *La Commission Centrale pour la Navigation du Rhin* (Leiden: A.W. Sijthoff 1935).

29. 'Normalization' refers to a form of river regulation whereby the aim is to achieve a navigational channel of uniform depth and breadth along the entire course of the river. This is usually effected by a combination of dredging and the strategic placement of wing dams (perpendicular to the current) and sometimes longitudinal dams.
30. Spiess, 'Ausbau', p. 127.
31. Looveren, 'Een en ander'.
32. C. Béliard, *Le Grand Canal d'Alsace. Voie Navigable. Source d'Énergie* (Paris: Berger-Levrault 1926).
33. É.É.d. Rhin, *L'usine hydroélectrique de Kembs: premier échelon du Grand Canal d'Alsace* (Mulhouse-Dornach: Braun & Cie 1932).
34. Cioc, *The Rhine* (2002).
35. Looveren, 'Een en ander', 132.
36. The French-speaking portions of Switzerland (Suisse Romande), particularly Geneva, also soon felt the attraction of Basel as an emergent Rhine port. In 1909 the newly founded *Association Romande pour la Navigation Interieure* (strategically renamed the *Association Suisse pour la Navigation du Rhône au Rhin* in 1910) appointed a committee to study a waterway from the Rhine to the Rhone via Lake Leman, Lake Neuchatel and Geneva. A detailed project was presented at the Third National Congress for Inland Navigation at Lyon, France in 1911. While the *Association Suisse* was a useful forum to promote Geneva's civic and business elites' interests in a waterway to the Rhine, they also had a specific interest in a waterway to Lyon and beyond to Marseilles. To this end, in 1911 the Genevan chamber of commerce organized other chambers of commerce (French and Swiss) along the upper Rhone valley into a *'Comité franco-suisse du Haute-Rhône'*. The project soon fell afoul of the French Corps des Ponts et Chaussees, which saw no French interest in it and pursued its own hydroelectric projects on the High Rhone; Merger, 'La liaison Rhin-Rhone'.
37. Looveren, 'Een en ander'; Merger, 'La liaison Rhin-Rhone'.
38. Looveren 'Een en ander', 148.
39. Jean Comte, *Pour une politique maritime et fluviale: La Suisse, la Méditerranée, le Rhône* (Luzern: J. Stocker 1947), p. 154.
40. Ibid., p. 158.
41. Quoted in Pritchard, 'Reconstructing', p. 773.
42. Pritchard, 'Reconstructing'.
43. The project to create a Rhine–Rhone link via the 'Transhelvetique' was officially torpedoed by Swiss Parliament on 10 May 2006. This was despite the fact that since the 1950s a stroke of land 100 metres wide had been reserved along the entire route of the proposed waterway and that all new highway and railway bridges had been constructed with sufficient headroom for the future canal. In a sense the waterway has been imprinted on the landscape, despite its never having been realized. See Merger, 'La liaison Rhin-Rhone', p. 198ff.
44. Merger, 'La liaison Rhin-Rhone', p. 204.
45. R. Gelpke, *A Water-way from London to Basle* (Basel: Frobenius Ltd 1919).
46. J.-L. Piveteau, 'Le Transhelvétique: Vitalité d'un Vieux Projet', *Geocarrefour* 40(2) (1965), pp. 175–85.
47. http://www.danubecampaign.org/the_problem/fiting_river/germany/ and http://www.schiffahrtsverein.de/doni2.htm

Biography 7: Peaceful Atom: The Brief Career of a Symbol of Co-operation and Prosperity

Dick van Lente

Between April and October 1958, 42 million people visited *Expo 58* in Brussels, the first post-war world exhibition. Its main attraction was the Atomium, a 102-metre high building consisting of nine aluminium-clad spheres connected by tubes containing elevators to transport visitors from one sphere to the next. The structure represented an iron crystal magnified 165 billion times. At night, lights on the spheres represented the electrons circling the nuclei. Designed by an engineer from an association of metal-producing firms, the Atomium advertised the capabilities of Belgian iron industries, but its main purpose was to celebrate the coming of the atomic age. Inside the spheres, under the motto 'Atom = Hope', the American Westinghouse Electric Company and firms from Belgium, Italy and Germany showed their achievements and plans in nuclear technology. Elsewhere at the exhibition, Britain, the United States and the Soviet Union presented their nuclear reactors and all kinds of peaceful applications of atomic energy, as well as a whole array of other technological wonders. Nuclear energy was but one of many innovations exhibited at Expo 58, whose central message was that science, technology, modern design and international co-operation would create a better and brighter world. The famous biologist Julian Huxley conferred his scientific and moral authority on this optimism in a series of well-attended lectures on 'the fate of mankind at the threshold of the atomic age'.

Several other, smaller exhibitions held in Western Europe in the second half of the 1950s were exclusively dedicated to the peaceful applications of nuclear fission. Their message, echoed in popular books, illustrated magazines and films, was always the same: nuclear power, associated in the public mind with the mushroom clouds of Hiroshima and increasingly awesome nuclear tests, could also be harnessed for peaceful purposes, such as irrigating deserts and making arctic regions inhabitable. Numerous applications in medicine, agriculture and industrial research were possible. Most important, however, was that nuclear energy had arrived 'just in time', because the fabulous growth of the European economy was leading to rapid depletion of fossil fuels. All this amounted to a new industrial revolution, more ground-breaking than the first one.

The development of peaceful uses of atomic energy also seemed pre-eminently suited for international co-operation: it was a new field, research was very expensive, and raw materials hard to come by. This was the goal of EURATOM, founded in Rome, together with the European Economic Community, in March 1957 by the six countries that already co-operated in the European Coal and Steel Community (ECSC). But EURATOM failed because, as John Krige has shown, nationalism always prevailed in strategic technological projects. Among the wider public, the moment of atomic euphoria had also passed by the early 1960s, as confrontations between the superpowers around Berlin and Cuba rekindled the always present fears of a nuclear showdown. From the late 1960s, public opinion also turned against nuclear power.

The brief phase of atomic euphoria may be understood as the result of propaganda by the Western powers on the one hand and an intense need

Figure B7.1   The Atomium by night in 1958

Source: © ASBL (Atomium Brussel) c/o Pictoright Amsterdam 2009.

for happy news on the other. Propaganda for the 'peaceful atom' came from various quarters. Nuclear scientists applying for funds emphasized the economic necessity of nuclear energy and the manifold possible applications of the atom, and warned politicians not to miss out on the next industrial revolution. Eisenhower launched his 'Atoms for peace' initiative – the controlled sharing of fissionable material – in December 1953 because he believed that international co-operation was the best way to maintain American nuclear superiority, and because he needed a counter-image to the aggressive nuclear strategy ('New Look') he had announced about a month earlier. Monnet and other pioneers of European integration believed that a supranational organization similar to the ECSC would help 'relaunch' the European project, which had stalled. These common political needs were contradicted by divergent national interests. While the rhetoric strictly separated peaceful from military uses, the two were in fact closely related. The Americans stimulated European economic and military integration but feared an independent European nuclear force. France refused to renounce the option to develop its own nuclear weapons, while denying this to Germany. The Germans disliked Monnet's supranationalism and preferred an open European market, which the French feared. The breakthrough in Rome in March 1957 probably owed much to the Suez crisis, a few months earlier, which confronted Western Europe with its dependence on both Middle Eastern oil and American world politics. But this moment of common need soon passed.

Spencer Weart has explained the apparently very positive public response to atomic propaganda as a reaction to widespread, deep and largely repressed fears of atomic power. The public had every reason to be scared. During the 1950s, the United States and the Soviet Union built up huge arsenals of nuclear weapons. Newspapers and magazines reported on the increasing destructive power of nuclear tests, the worldwide spread of fall-out, failing nuclear reactors (Chalk River, Canada in 1952; Windscale, England, in 1957) and people dying of radiation sickness. Famous men like Einstein, Russell and Schweitzer issued apocalyptic warnings. One might expect that talk of the 'peaceful atom' would be dismissed by a public grown cynical by long years of war and Cold War propaganda. But the message carried conviction: it was supported and popularized by well-known scientists, the advances of nuclear medicine were real, and the threat of fuel scarcity seemed very credible after the Suez crisis. As Disney's very popular animation 'Our friend the Atom' put it, atomic energy is like the genie escaped from the bottle in the famous fairy tale: a giant that could be both immensely dangerous and immensely helpful in solving the common problems of humanity. For a few years, the giant had shown its friendly face and the public embraced it.

Literature

J. Gillingham, *European integration 1950–2003. Superstate or new market economy?* (Cambridge: CUP 2003).

J. Kint, *Expo 58 als belichaming van het humanistisch modernisme* (Rotterdam: uitgeverij 010 2001).

J. Krige, 'Atoms for peace, scientific internationalism, and scientific intelligence' in J. Krige and K.-H. Barth (eds) *Global power knowledge. Science and technology in international affairs* (Osiris 21 2006), pp. 161–81.

J. Krige, 'The politics of European scientific collaboration' in J. Krige and D. Pestre (eds) *Science in the twentieth century* (A'dam: Overseas Publishers = Harwood Academic Publishers 1997), pp. 897–918.

G. Skogmar, *The United States and the nuclear dimension of European integration* (Basingstoke: Palgrave Macmillan 2004).

S.R. Weart, *Nuclear fear. A history of images* (Cambridge, Mass: Harvard UP 1988).

10
European Civil Aviation in an Era of Hegemonic Nationalism: Infrastructure, Air Mobility, and European Identity Formation, 1919–1933

Eda Kranakis

Introduction

Modern transportation technologies have conflicting political potentials: regarded as tools of nation-building,[1] they are also depicted as engines of transnational integration, weakening national control over borders and identities.[2] How these opposing potentials play out depends on national geographies, regulatory structures, and political, technological and economic criteria. Post-1918 Europe presents a unique case for study in this regard. Nowhere else do so many states exist within such a small area; the nationalist and integrationist aspects of transport development have therefore often conflicted. Europe is also significant because the integration process that emerged after the Second World War begs the question of what role transport played in this shift. If transportation is an engine of integration, then evidence supporting this view should be visible within the European context.

This chapter examines the growth of civil aviation in interwar Europe – from the establishment of the first wave of commercial airlines immediately following the First World War up to the mid-1930s – to determine whether this new mode of transport altered identities and weakened control of national borders, or consolidated nation-state power. Was civil aviation an early, 'hidden' agent of European integration,[3] or did it serve mainly to reinforce existing boundaries of state and imperial authority? More generally, how did the prerogatives of state control and national interest interact with the transnational possibilities of air travel? Did the experience of air travel make people feel more European? And how did the creators, managers, regulators and users of civil aviation in Europe view its prospects and impact during this period?

Aviation technology posed a radically new set of challenges to European states. It not only developed more rapidly than previous forms of transport, but the speed and directness of air travel, using a new travel space far above the ground, made the confrontation with nation-state boundaries strong and immediate. Flying reduced international travel times within Europe from days to hours and easily connected locations separated by rough terrain that had previously hindered overland travel. The first commercial airlines in Europe included international routes, such as the service between London and Paris inaugurated in 1919. The London–Paris service transformed a land and sea journey that had required at least twelve hours in good weather into a two-hour jaunt.[4] It did not take much imagination to envision a network of air routes crisscrossing Europe and linking it to areas beyond. Yet European governments also saw aviation as a bulwark of national power and sovereignty, and they sought to control both the technology and the new realm of national airspace through legislation, diplomacy, organizations, control of information, and economic incentives and prohibitions.

The integrative and transformative potential of an aviation network depends on the technical characteristics of its aircraft as well as its organizational structure – which 'nodes' are included or left out, how they are interconnected and how the network is regulated. These factors must also be considered within an economic context. The unit cost of creating, maintaining and using a network shapes its role in society. Following this logic, the characteristics of Europe's early civil aviation network are analysed, taking into account the aircraft, development of routes and airlines, and also regulatory systems affecting both airlines and network. This aspect of the inquiry shows how aviation spaces in Europe were structured and linked (or fragmented), and how the network balanced nationalist and integrationist tendencies in practical terms.

Since air networks may be used or adapted for diverse purposes, this study also examines patterns and ideologies of air mobility. Partly this means analysing who flew where, and why; but it also means understanding how key actors thought the network should be organized and used. Diverse actors projected contrasting political, social and cultural visions onto this network, or evolved new visions in response to it. To uncover them, we must explore the symbolic and discursive worlds surrounding European civil aviation, embodied in posters and advertisements, speeches, memoirs and aeronautical industry literature. Visions shape practice. Implementing particular visions affected an airline network's development, use, and user identities. This aspect of the inquiry is necessary to determine the extent to which the network, the visions projected onto it, and new patterns of air mobility had a 'European' content, understood both geographically and in the sense of building a new identity and conceptual space – a new 'imagined community'.

The terms 'Europe' and 'European' have two interlinked senses within this study: one geographical, the other conceptual/ideological. The geographical sense follows popular usage for the time in relation to aviation: it includes continental Western and Central Europe, the latter comprising Poland, Czechoslovakia and Hungary, and the western part of the USSR (to Moscow and Leningrad). It also includes Britain, the Nordic countries, the Baltic countries (Lithuania, Latvia, Estonia), the Balkans and the region of Istanbul and the Dardanelles, but not eastern Turkey. The conceptual/ideological sense of the terms 'Europe' and 'European' embodies the notion of Europe as a *cohesive* space, integrated either through affection (as in European identity and patriotism), through network structures (as in a unified European civil aviation network) or through conceptual comparison with other spaces, notably the United States. In what follows, the term is used alternately in each of these senses. My aim is not to impose any predetermined geographical, conceptual or ideological meaning onto the data, but rather to reveal and replicate the complex dimensions of the term 'Europe' and 'European' as they were used and understood at that time, in relation to civil aviation.

The argument and evidence for this essay are presented in six sections. Following the introduction, the first section introduces the concept of hegemonic nationalism to characterize the style of nationalism, linked to imperialism, that prevailed in Europe from the late nineteenth century through the interwar period. Hegemonic nationalism shaped the framework of national and international regulation of civil aviation during this period. The second section surveys the nationalist, imperialist and integrationist tendencies in the network's development, showing how they interacted and conflicted. The third section analyses the resulting spatial characteristics of the air network relative to the limits of aviation technology and the politics of route development. The fourth section considers the experience of flying and time–space compression in this early period, showing how pilots, passengers and others responded to and conceptualized this new form of transport, and its implications for identity. The fifth section explores efforts to promote air travel as a new form of tourism, arguing that travel promotion shifted the cultural meaning of nationalism toward a softer view of nations as desirable consumer goods. This view, in turn, provided a foundation for a wider sense of European community that embraced national cultural differences. The final section draws up a balance sheet for aviation in the interwar period, arguing that the system's integrationist tendencies remained hidden and irrelevant for the vast majority of Europeans. On balance, civil aviation in this period functioned primarily as a tool to support and consolidate nation-state power.

Hegemonic nationalism and the growth of European civil aviation

Analysis of interwar European civil aviation must take into account the peculiarities of international and state relations from the 'new nationalism'[5] and 'new imperialism' of the 1870s to the rapid decolonization follow-ing the Second World War. This period was unique in the way imperi-alist agendas and a competitive, aggressive form of nationalism became entwined within a global political system dominated by 'Great Powers'. As a convenient shorthand, we may characterize this as an era of hegemonic nationalism. The term 'imperialism', apart from the fact that it has come to embrace so many competing theories,[6] does not adequately express the symbiosis that emerged between the 'new nationalism' and the 'new impe-rialism'. Paul Kennedy has captured the essence of the new form of nation-alism, pointing also to its tie to imperialism: 'there existed in governing elites, military circles, and imperialist organizations a prevailing view of the world order which stressed struggle, change, competition, the use of force, and the organization of national resources to enhance state power.'[7] Hobsbawm likewise observed in *The Age of Empire* that the new form of nationalism was 'built on chauvinism, xenophobia and, increasingly, the idealization of national expansion, conquest and the very act of war.'[8] Scholars, starting with J.A. Hobson, have argued that this new nationalism was a cornerstone of the renewed imperialist surge that began in the late nineteenth century.[9]

Hegemonic nationalism permeated the structure and discourse of inter-state relations during this era. Even small, neutral or poorer European states could not ignore or bypass the model; rather, they developed strategies of coexistence (Switzerland), emulation (Italy) or careful opposition to it (Czechoslovakia).[10] Hegemonic nationalism provided both a stimulus and a justification for militant imperialism and colonialism, since it assumed the existence of a hierarchy of dominance among states and regions. Colonies – seen as regions that could not achieve or maintain sovereign independence – provided unsettling examples of the consequences of lack of national autonomy and failure to keep up. Imperial powers used the latest techno-logical and organizational means at their disposal to maintain control of their colonial empires, in brutal fashion if necessary. The discourse of impe-rial domination spoke of 'punishment' to overcome 'insubordination' and to insure that lessons were 'properly learnt' by 'rebellious villages.'[11]

Aviation became a key agent in these efforts. Theorists of the period touted aviation as a cheap and efficient means to subjugate unruly territories. Throughout the 1920s and 1930s, imperial powers carried out numerous air attacks in their imperial domains. The RAF used bombing raids to quell unrest in Somaliland, India, Iraq, Aden, Sudan, Transjordan and Palestine. In Iraq, the RAF bombed tribes and villages that sought to evade taxation, citing the need to thwart such serious acts of defiance against British author-ity. In Palestine, the RAF commander's preferred policy of exerting control was to drop 'one 250-pound or 500-pound bomb in each village that speaks out of turn ... The only thing the Arab understands is the heavy hand, and sooner or later it will have to be applied.'[12] The hegemonic role of British aviation was also displayed back home, in the yearly air pageant at Hendon, 'which often culminated in displays of bomb attacks on model "Arab" or "African" villages.'[13] The French, ostensibly even more ruthless than the British, bombed tribes and villages in various parts of their empire, including Indochina, North Africa and Syria. Mussolini's bombing of Ethiopia is also well known. The point of this digression is simply to emphasize that European civil aviation grew up in an environment that vaunted hegemony, and that made technology and nationalism tools of survival, status and control within the international political system.

Hegemonic nationalism influenced critical international diplomatic negotiations and their outcome. For all the talk of national self-determination at the 1919 Paris Peace Conference, the result of the negotiations was to enhance the reach of British and French imperial dominance (through the mandate system), to finalize the destruction of the Austro-Hungarian and Ottoman empires, emasculate their resultant states (Austria, Hungary and Turkey) and, finally, to emasculate Germany by diminishing both its formal power and symbolic status. Among other things, Germany was stripped of its colonies, which represented an actual loss of imperial power as well as a potent symbol of international humiliation and loss of prestige.

The impact of hegemonic nationalism at the Paris Peace Conference also extended to aviation, including the regulatory structure of civil aviation. Aviation was held to be so important for military power that restrictions were placed on the defeated powers in this domain. They were prohibited from developing military aviation or establishing air ministries or academies, and their airspace rights were curtailed (for example, airspace above Istanbul, the Bosporus and the Dardanelles was declared to be off-limits to the defeated powers). Their civil aviation was also curbed. The defeated nations could develop civil aviation only within their own national borders, and restrictions were placed on aircraft that could be deployed. Germany's restrictions included a permanent prohibition of military aviation, and a six-month ban on civil aircraft construction starting in 1920, subsequently extended to May 1922. In 1919, and again in 1921, all German airplanes were confiscated. Further, Germany could only establish a domestic civil aviation system; it could not import or export aircraft; and it had to give the Allied and Associated Powers free access to its airspace until 1 January 1923. The Rhineland continued to be banned to all German aircraft even after 1923, while its airspace remained open to the allies. These controls were supplemented by further technical restrictions on the commercial aircraft that could be built (speed, size, engine horsepower, maximum altitude, etc.). Aviation industry observers agreed that the restrictions made it virtually impossible for German manufacturers to export, or for German airlines to establish safe and economically viable services. Only in mid-1926 were these rules lifted.[14]

The international regulatory regime for civil aviation that emerged after the First World War also reflected nationalist concerns. An Aeronautical

Commission established at the Paris Peace Conference drafted a 'Convention relating to the Regulation of Aerial Navigation' (known as the Paris Convention). Although recognizing the need for each signatory state 'in time of peace to accord freedom of innocent passage above its territory to the aircraft of the other contracting States,'[15] the treaty formalized national sovereignty over airspace. A British White Paper of 1944 explained that the Paris Convention 'embodied the doctrine of the national sovereignty of the air.'[16] Two lawyers involved in international air law were even more forceful: 'international aviation exists at present only by concession, not at all by right. The sovereignty of each nation of the globe over its own air space is absolute.'[17]

In the years following the Versailles conference, the reach of hegemonic aviation nationalism expanded, appearing in everything from speeches, memoirs, celebratory volumes and newspaper articles to aviation journals, bureaucratic memos and reports, scholarly writings and children's books.[18] Aerial triumphs were represented as feats of the nation, while successes of rival nations were treated as threats to be equalled and bettered. The Chairman of Britain's Parliamentary Air Committee, for example, saw aviation as 'the new foundation of Britain's supremacy as a world power', warning that 'with foreign aviation centres so active, it is essential that we should consider what steps are to be taken to maintain this supremacy.'[19]

States saw civil aviation as a cornerstone of military power because it promoted the growth and stability of an aeronautical industry. Leading European commercial airlines were tied to nationally based aircraft firms.[20] For example, British national policy required Imperial Airways to buy from national suppliers, and all Europe's Great Powers encouraged local suppliers. National boosters, taking this idea to its logical conclusion, touted autarky in aviation technology and criticized international licensing agreements as dangerous and unpatriotic. A 1925 editorial in a French aviation journal argued that building an aircraft engine in France under British licence would have 'a disastrous propaganda effect on foreigners', would 'unjustly' place French firms in competition with foreigners, and would tend to make the French dependent on foreigners (*'tributaires de l'étranger'*).[21]

Civil aviation also fostered complementary systems needed for military aviation, such as airfields, flying schools and meteorology, while helping to maintain a force of trained pilots who could be transferred to military duty if needed. Flying for civil airlines would also make these pilots familiar with their national airspace and that of other countries over which they flew. A pilot affiliated with the British Royal Institute of International Affairs reported that authorities in France, Italy and Spain told him they did not like him flying over their airspace because 'when you come again you will know the country.'[22] All European nations in this era were alert to the military benefits of civil aviation. Indeed, civil aviation in interwar Europe must be seen as an integral part of the system of hegemonic nationalism.[23]

The interaction of national and international aspects of civil aviation in Europe

Yet civil aviation in Europe could not achieve much within strictly national confines. The altered map following the First World War showed small new states, and aviation further reduced their effective size. Airplanes travelled as the crow flies, and even ordinary passenger planes in the 1920s travelled at 80–100 miles per hour. Further, since commercial air routes linked major urban centres, a flight of several hours between two large European cities usually meant crossing borders. The high cost of air travel in the 1920s relative to railway travel also meant that aviation could only compete against railways over long distances, such as the route between Paris and Istanbul, where planes substantially decreased travel times.[24] A private French company, CIDNA, built up the Paris–Istanbul route over the first half of the 1920s, in competition with the famed Orient Express railway.[25] In 1927, the trip by air took almost three full days (one day less than the train trip), but by 1930 the air travel time was reduced to a day, significantly enhancing the airline's competitive position.

In addition to conditions favouring international air routes *within* Europe, imperial aims of some nations also mandated an international role for aviation *beyond* Europe. Commercial aviation had a prominent imperial role because it helped move the mail, people and goods needed to maintain an empire and open new colonial areas to development. In the 1920s, European imperialist states often gave preference to air routes that established colonial connections, according domestic and inter-European routes secondary importance. From this perspective, Europe was merely a space that had to be crossed to reach the colonies. The air routes developed by Britain, France, the Netherlands and Belgium were all primarily aimed at establishing colonial connections.[26]

According to R.E.G. Davies, Britain 'showed a complete lack of interest in Europe' in the sphere of civil aviation in the 1920s and 1930s.[27] In 1924, the British government engineered a merger of several private lines to create a single, national, subsidized airline called Imperial Airways. The name summed up the airline's principal mission: to connect Britain to its colonies and dependencies. In a 1920 talk on 'Imperial Air Routes', Britain's Controller-General of Civil Aviation, Frederick Sykes, set down what he saw as 'the requirements of aviation on an Empire basis.'[28] Egypt would be the centre of his imagined space, serving as 'the "hub" or...the Clapham Junction of the India, Australia, and Cape routes, and the heart of the whole system of their expansion'. The first link in this imperial system, completed by early 1927, was a service from this hub – Egypt – to Karachi. The formation of Imperial Airways actually led to a decrease in the route mileage flown within Europe: the company's European services were limited to a few cities for most of the 1920s. In 1925, they only included flights from

London to Paris, Zurich, Ostend (for summer holidays) and Cologne (and thence to Berlin via a German airline).[29] Interior, domestic lines were likewise ignored. Only in September 1930 did Imperial Airways begin an experimental service from London to Birmingham, Manchester and Liverpool.[30]

In France, domestic routes were maintained only when they were components of colonial and other key international routes. A retrospective on the first 25 years of French aviation noted that routes such as Paris–Marseilles were only kept in service when they served as links 'with other lines, notably, with respect to Marseille, toward Algeria, Tunisia, Morocco, Syria, India, and Indochina'.[31] France devoted much effort to opening up air routes to North Africa. Casablanca was a key junction within French imperial space; it was linked by an air service to Toulouse (over 1,100 miles) before Paris was linked to Lyon and Marseilles.[32] By 1925 it was possible to fly from Toulouse to Casablanca (Morocco) and Oran (Algeria), and from Rabat to Fez in Morocco. By 1930, Toulouse was linked by air to Dakar (Senegal). Flying reduced the travel time for this journey from eight days to thirty hours.[33]

Imperialist states focused not only on gaining access to their colonies through commercial air routes (if sometimes only through the medium of airmail), but also on building air routes within their colonies as tools of economic development and political control. The Belgian national airline SABENA established a 1,422-mile route within the Congo in the first half of the 1920s, serving Boma, Leopoldville and Elizabethville.[34] The cost of establishing such routes impeded the growth of inter-European air routes and traffic.

Hegemonic nationalist thinking also created political frictions that hindered route and traffic development. European nations jealously guarded their airspace sovereignty, using it in every imaginable way to thwart enemies, to gain extra benefits from friends, or as a bargaining chip in aeronautical and other diplomatic negotiations. From 1923 to 1926, Germany repeatedly used its (partial) air sovereignty as a weapon against France in its struggle to be freed of Allied restrictions on its civil aviation. French commercial pilots bound for Prague who were forced to land in Germany (not unusual in this era of temperamental aircraft) were jailed, treated with brutality, and their planes confiscated.[35] Italy refused to allow British planes to use Italian airspace for most of the 1920s, making it impossible for Imperial Airways to establish a full air route through Europe to reach its colonies. A portion of the trip had to be done by rail. Italy's hope, according to an Italian journalist, was to use its growing strength in aviation – its 'new authority' – to control the Mediterranean region and impede Britain's imperial agenda.[36] When the Italian government did finally give Britain access to its airspace, Britain had to agree to subsidize an unprofitable Italian air route by sharing the income of the Imperial Airways routes that used Italian airspace. Foreign airlines wanting to use Greek national airspace had to land in Athens and 'coordinate their schedules with those of the domestic Greek air services.'[37] Governments also charged various fees to foreign airlines – mooring fees, commissions on passenger bookings, extra duties on fuel, and so on.[38] National sovereignty over airspace meant that negotiations for long transnational routes took years and required direct government-to-government negotiations. Airlines could not hope to develop international links without unremitting support from their national governments.

Nationalism also paradoxically fostered international co-operation in European civil aviation, however. Inter-European commercial air travel required agreement and co-operation (e.g. in meteorological data) from every country on a route. The limited range of 1920s aircraft meant that flying from, say, Britain to Switzerland required several stops in different countries. Multilateral co-operation was required not only to access airspace, airports and safety and meteorological systems along a route, but also to regulate such issues as pilot and aircraft credentials, customs procedures, baggage handling, airmail, liability in cases of death, injury or loss of goods, ticketing, co-ordination of timetables, co-ordination of passenger flows over multiple carriers, maintenance and repair services, and so on.

Ironically, the leader in organizing international co-operation in civil aviation in the early 1920s was none other than Germany, guided by nationalistic motives rooted in the severity of the Allied controls over German aviation. Germany spent the first half of the1920s evading these restrictions in clever ways. British Brigadier-General P.R.C. Groves commented that a history of Germany's efforts in this regard '…would run into several large volumes, each of which could serve as a work of reference on the kindred arts of evasion and subterfuge. The clauses were contested paragraph by paragraph, phrase by phrase, and aircraft material was constantly hidden, manufactured, and exported.'[39] Since military aviation was prohibited, Germany concentrated on civil aviation to maintain strong capabilities for a subsequent return to military flying. It evaded Allied restrictions by participating in multinational pools, by setting up aircraft factories beyond its borders and by establishing airlines in other countries that could, in turn, organize flights into and out of Germany.

The results of Germany's international efforts in aviation were so impressive that it became the leader in expanding Europe's air network. The *Deutsche Luft Reederei* (an airline company established under the auspices of A.E.G., Zeppelin and the Hamburg-Amerika shipping line) began organizing co-operative pools in 1919, followed by the Aero-Lloyd Company.[40] The Junkers firm also fostered international co-operation. It helped establish airlines in Switzerland, Poland, Estonia, Latvia, Lithuania, Sweden, Finland, Norway, the Netherlands, Hungary, Albania, the USSR and Austria. Many later grew into national airlines (e.g. Swissair, Finnair, Lot). Junkers' method to evade restrictions was to provide planes free of charge in return for shares in the new airline companies. Junkers also established factories abroad where commercial aircraft could be built or assembled without restriction, and it organized airline groupings that shared routes, advertising, costs and revenues, began standardizing equipment and co-operated in repair and maintenance. These networks included the Ost-Europa Union (later renamed Nordeuropa Union), which served the Baltic area, and the Transeuropa Union, which served the Alps area. In 1925 these two unions were merged to form Europa Union. The latter was dissolved in January 1926, when Allied restrictions on German civil aviation ended and Deutsche Lufthansa was established.[41]

Germany also helped establish the organization that became the main international forum for airline companies worldwide, the International Air Traffic Association. It began in 1919 as a co-operative effort by airlines from Germany, Britain, Denmark, the Netherlands and Sweden. In September 1919, plans were publicized for a German air postal service that would include a route from Berlin to Copenhagen. A year later, in September 1920, a multilateral arrangement was made for the Dutch airline KLM, the Danish airline DDL and the German airline DLR to establish an international air route linking Rotterdam to Copenhagen, through Amsterdam and Hamburg, the 'world's first airline pool service.' By February 1922, plans were being made to include London and Stockholm on the route, and eventually it extended from Malmoe (Sweden) to London, via Copenhagen, Hamburg, Bremen and Amsterdam. IATA continued to attract new members in the 1920s and beyond, including French, British and Belgian airlines, and the pools it helped organize became a dominant model for European international routes.[42]

Pools could be uneconomic, however. With income shared on jointly operated lines, most airlines could not make a profit. Beyond pooling, national strategic and prestige considerations also resulted in expensive route duplication. French and British airlines both served the London–Paris route, eventually leading the British companies operating the route to bankruptcy (probably because they were not subsidized as heavily as their French counterparts), after which the French and British governments agreed each to subsidize a single, national carrier for the route. Maintaining the route with separate French and British carriers became a matter of pride for the two countries.

By the mid-1930s, European civil aviation had become a culture of national airlines. Although the first European airlines arose as competitive private enterprises, most required subsidies to stay afloat. Ultimately all European states subsidized their airlines, whether as a matter of imperial policy, to maintain a state airline and prestigious international routes in situations where national pride overruled the verdict of economics,[43] or to create and maintain a military capability in aviation. The trend in European civil aviation was toward a national, subsidized airline for each state: KLM for the Netherlands (1919), Sabena for Belgium (1923), Imperial Airways for Britain (1924), Deutsche Lufthansa for Germany (1926), Lot for Poland (1929), Swissair for Switzerland (1931), Air France (1933), and so on.[44]

Spatial structure of the civil aviation network in Europe

Given the tensions within European civil aviation, what can be concluded about the spatial structure of the network that emerged in the 1920s, considering also the technical characteristics of the aircraft used? Several key points emerge. First, the network was 'self-organizing' in the sense that it did not follow any master plan and was not fully or uniformly regulated under any international body. The national sovereignty principle meant that routes evolved on the basis of bilateral agreements between governments. IATA and ICAN (the International Commission on Aerial Navigation established by the Paris Convention) served as forums for multilateral co-operation on route development and technical, legal and safety issues, but these bodies did not override national interests. International route development was still highly politicized.

Second, the unique character of the German network stands out. Deprived of colonies and of the right to develop military aviation, it alone began seriously developing domestic and inter-European air networks. Germany's domestic network grew into a hub and feeder system, with the main hub at Berlin and secondary hubs at cities close to the border (Hamburg, Munich, Frankfurt). In 1934, German commercial aircraft transported nearly 166,000 passengers, three times the number carried by British, French or Dutch airlines, and in September 1934 Deutsche Lufthansa carried its millionth passenger. Germany's domestic air system was also connected to international routes. The initial technique of achieving these connections was mutual benefit, since Germany, with no imperial advantages and limited aviation rights before mid-1926, had little political leverage. Yet mutual benefit produced results. Some cities outside Germany contributed financially to the Nord-Europa and Trans-Europa Unions in return for being included in the network. By the end of 1933, airlines had been established in all the states surrounding Germany, and a series of international networks radiated out from Germany to many areas of Europe, to the Soviet Union and to South America (on a route that came to be pooled with Air France).[45]

Third, the German case shows what European aviation was not: a coherent, integrated, *European* system. The network structure that emerged in the 1920s and 1930s was mainly a series of imperial access routes linked by interconnections between major European cities. Some areas were left out of the system entirely, while others, like Athens and Istanbul, were overserved for political reasons. Istanbul was a convenient stop on imperial and international routes because it was a free airspace. Many airlines stopped in Athens because no commercial service was allowed to fly over Greece without a local stop. However, countries like Ireland and Portugal were not linked to the European network, nor were regional cities like Manchester and Bordeaux.[46] In short, the system's spatial organization mainly followed geographies of empire and political influence in the interwar period (see Figures 10.1 and 10.2.).

Figure 10.1   Map of European air routes, 1922

Source: This map first appeared in *The Times* (London), 'World Air Routes', 22 August 1923, p. 10, Col. A.

© The Times/nisyndication.com.

Fourth, despite national sovereignty over airspace and the growing dominance of subsidized national airlines, civil aviation in interwar Europe was nevertheless a transnational project in which international routes were often pooled. Yet the pools and other forms of aviation co-operation were largely invisible to the general public. Such co-operation amounted to a form of hidden integration.[47] The pools depended on previous government agreements establishing criteria for the use of airspace, airports, and provision of lighting, communication and meteorological information, without which commercial flying was impossible. IATA, building on these political accords, also helped co-ordinate international routes and foster co-operation in areas such as ticketing, baggage and liability.[48] The extent of European international co-operation in civil aviation during this period had no parallel elsewhere in the world. ICAN was dominated by European states, and until

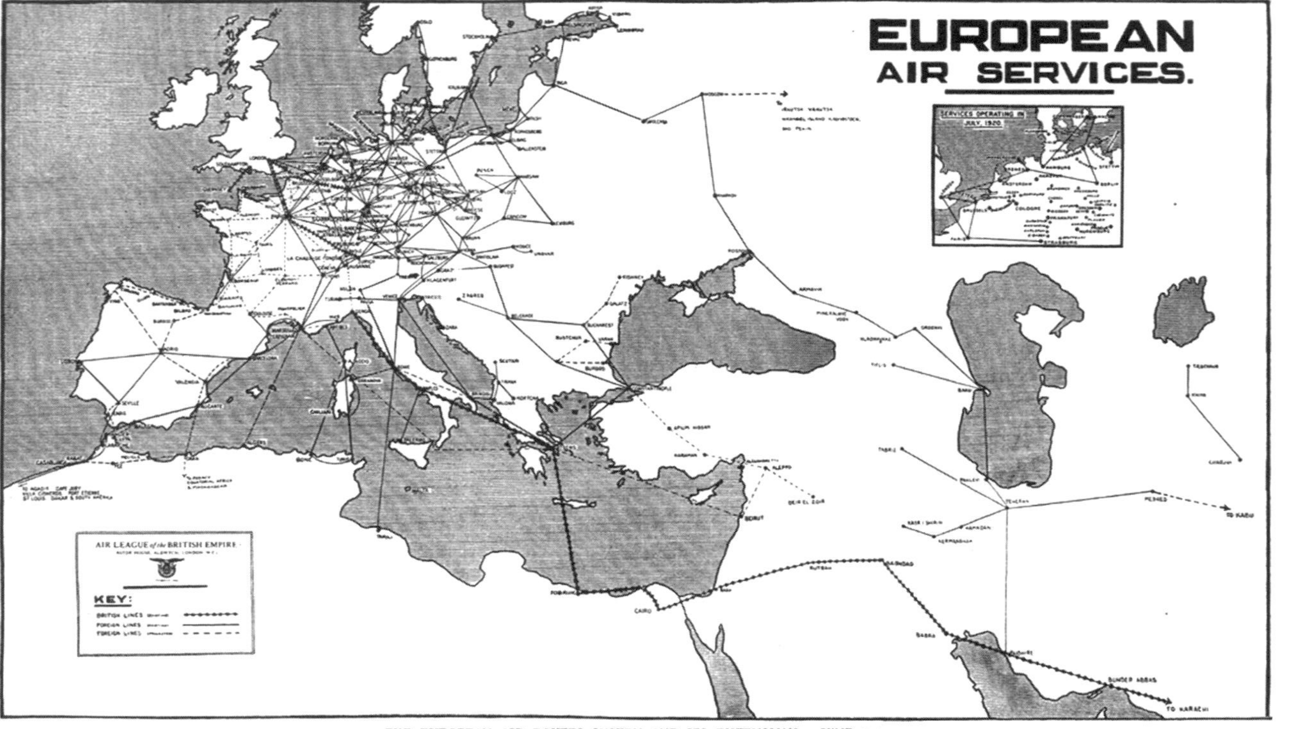

Figure 10.2 Map of European air routes, 1929

Source: This map first appeared in the article by P.R.C. Groves, 'Influence of Aviation on World Affairs', *International Affairs* (London) 8(4) (July 1929), and is reproduced with permission.

1938 IATA was strictly a European organization and had no counterpart elsewhere in the world.[49]

Technological characteristics of civil aircraft in the 1920s – low flying speeds and limited range – also shaped the network, necessitating a multilateral system of co-operation. Various types of aircraft operated on Europe's commercial lines, including a range of flying boats. France, for example, had more than half a dozen aircraft manufacturers that produced aircraft used by commercial airlines. Yet the planes of European commercial airlines all operated within a fairly restricted range of technological capabilities. Aircraft cruising speeds rose from 130–160 km/h in the early 1920s to 200–210 km/h in the late 1920s. The planes flew at low altitudes, initially around 600 m, with cruising altitudes reaching around 1500 m later in the decade (and maximum altitudes around 4,900 m). Their maximum ranges varied from roughly 400 km in the early 1920s up to 950–1200 km in the early 1930s. Payloads were small, and extra pounds so strongly affected aircraft performance that passengers and luggage had to be weighed before boarding.[50]

Junkers aircraft, widely used in the 1920s and 1930s, exemplify the capabilities of European commercial carriers of the era. The Junkers F13 series, in service from the early 1920s up to the mid-1930s, was the most widely used European commercial aircraft of its time: over 320 were sold in thirty countries. It was produced in several variations, but on average, as built in the early 1920s, it could carry four passengers plus two pilots 400 to 650 km at a cruising speed of 135 km/h. By the late 1920s and early 1930s, a new generation Junkers G23/24 could carry nine passengers over 1300 km at around 182 km/h. The speed and distance limits of the early planes meant that a long international route was really a series of short hops. Also, given the low flying altitudes of 1920s, flying over mountains was difficult or impossible. While these conditions might seem to favour development of national, domestic airline networks, competition with automobiles and cheap railway travel inhibited such a trend.[51]

Finally, the European air network – comprising many airlines, complex pooling arrangements, and routes and service shaped by political considerations – was not economically viable without national subsidies. Pooled international routes were run at a loss because the volume of traffic was not sufficient to cover the costs of maintaining multiple airlines. The emphasis on imperial access routes raised costs because a premium had to be paid to access the airspace of nations over which they flew, and because traffic volumes were low. By the early 1930s, the inefficiency of the European system – a host of national airlines serving a space smaller than the United States – was recognized and understood. An Italian engineer, reflecting in 1935 on the causes for the 'stagnation' of European aviation relative to the United States, explained that the European network followed fantasy rather than economic logic, and had accumulated 'a puzzle of small lines', all organized and equipped differently: 'In Europe, aviation is still a political affair.' He concluded that 'Europe and the European network are what they are: the United States of Europe does not yet exist.'[52]

Flying: Transcendence, time–space compression and European identity

Despite its idiosyncrasies, the early civil aviation network in Europe contributed to the formation of European identities, both through the challenges of its construction and through the new and imagined experiences of air mobility it fostered. Air travel had two characteristics that distinguished it from other types of commercial transportation. First, it was transcendent – air travellers literally flew above the Earth; and second, it was extremely fast compared with other forms of transport. Both characteristics transformed experience and contributed to the growth of imagined communities beyond the nation state.

Aviation posters in the 1920s and early 1930s often emphasized the theme of transcendence. They depicted airplanes surrounded by space and clouds, or soaring into the sun; airplanes above expansive vistas of land, sea and mountains; larger than life airplanes with tiny human settlements or buildings below. They portrayed airplanes flying over continents and between continents, with the continents appearing flat, or following the curvature of the earth, like a map or globe stretched out far below the travelling plane, often with the route drawn in (Figure 10.3).

Seeing the world from a plane gave a unique perspective on human society. Looking down from an altitude of thousands of feet, the power of nature seemed large, and the lives of humans seemed small. The incredible geographical reach of aviation – the ability to soar over seas and continents – further heightened this experience. By making human settlements seem less imposing, and by connecting them more frequently over much larger areas, civil aviation promoted a more global and less conflictive view of society, raised questions about the foundations of nations and nationalism, and suggested the need for a wider sense of community.

Aviation had this effect on Antoine de Saint-Exupéry, the famed French pilot–philosopher who worked for the French commercial airline, Aéropostale, in the 1920s. This company opened up the route that extended from Toulouse to Casablanca, Dakar, across the Atlantic Ocean to Brazil, and then across the Andes to Santiago de Chile. Saint-Exupéry thus owed his early career to French imperialism, yet he rejected its hegemonic mindset. For Saint-Exupéry, aviation was above all a tool of understanding, revealing the unity of mankind. When he and other pioneer aviators flew over vast swathes of uncharted territory to explore new routes, they gazed down upon a visibly powerful natural world that displayed no borders. And they saw tiny people whose similarities seemed more pronounced

Figure 10.3   Transcendent aviation (1919, Latécoère line to North Africa)

Source: Reproduced with permission from the Air France Museum Collection.

than their differences when viewed from a height of several thousand feet. Over multiple continents, wherever nature allowed, they saw small towns and houses and families, each with its lives and loves. In 'The Plane and Planet', a chapter from *Terre des hommes*, Saint-Exupéry noted that human settlements seemed, from a plane, like fragile bits of life that had managed to take hold in 'the fundament of rock and sand and salt':

> The airplane has unveiled for us the true face of the earth. … [From] the height of our rectilinear trajectories … we discover the essential foundation … [in which] life, like a little moss in the crevices of ruins, has risked its precarious existence. We … have now been transformed into physicists, biologists, students of the civilizations that … bloom like gardens where the climate allows. We are able to judge man in cosmic terms, scrutinize him through our portholes as through instruments of the laboratory.[53]

For Saint-Exupéry, the implication of seeing man 'in cosmic terms' was to underscore the unity of mankind and the absurdity of rivalry and war:

> Why should we hate one another? We are together [*solidaire*], borne through life on the same planet, we form the crew of the same ship. Civilizations may, indeed, compete to bring forth new syntheses, but it is monstrous that they should devour one another. To set man free it is enough that we help one another to realize that there does exist a goal towards which all mankind is striving. Why should we not strive toward that goal together, since it is what unites us all?[54]

Saint-Exupéry's globalist vision found a wide audience in the interwar period. By 1934, his first novel, *Vol de nuit* (1931), based on his experience at Aéropostale, had been made into a movie. The book articulated the experience of seeing global humanity in miniature from a plane in flight. And his later book, *Terre des hommes* (quoted above), became a bestseller when released in the United States in 1939.[55] In recounting the meaning that Saint-Exupéry derived from his knowledge of aviation, I am not trying to suggest that air travel alone created a vision of global humanity, for such thinking has a long tradition in religious, philosophical and humanistic thought.[56] But the unique experience of transcendence that aviation provided meshed with such views and gave them a new concreteness and legitimacy.

The other distinctive characteristic of air travel was speed, which permitted new and enlarged mobilities. Already in 1920, flying from Paris to Prague took only six hours, dramatically shortening a 32-hour train ride. Professionals began travelling by air within and beyond Europe because of this time advantage. A woman magazine editor, asked in 1926 why she chose to fly, responded: 'The goal I pursue? Speed!'[57] Airline travel posters also emphasized this theme. An Imperial Airways poster from the 1920s invited readers to 'Fly between Cairo, Bagdad [sic] and Basra, and save time.' A French poster of the same period showed 'Father Time' rushing through space, accompanied by an airplane, with the earth below. Its caption: 'Time is money; Wings save time' (see Figure 10.4). A 1931 poster for the French airline CIDNA featured a giant speed arrow stretching through a sky at dusk, alongside a plane in flight. The poster's text read: 'Paris-Istanbul in the same day.'[58]

The dramatically increased speed of air travel over ever-longer routes produced time–space compression. The first generation of European air travellers began using this phenomenon to manage wider social networks and to compress more work and experience into a day, a week, and ultimately into the fixed time span of their lives. Telecommunications also compressed time and space, but aviation was different. It could move *people* through space, not just voices or messages. Aviation produced a more palpable form of time–space compression, one that could be directly lived and felt. Transcendent speed leading to time–space compression was aviation's unique contribution to modernity (and post-modernity). One European businessman who took advantage of time–space compression explained, 'You can go from Budapest to Vienna and back in a day, after having devoted eight hours in Vienna to business.' Another, who worked in Casablanca, commented that he was able to 'leave from Casablanca on a Thursday, handle an affair in Paris…and come back to Casablanca on Sunday.' Colonial officials used air travel to reconnect more frequently with home and family, instead of spending years away without a trip home. A professor from Luxembourg explained that flying enabled him to condense three separate trips into one eight-day break during Pentecost: 'I had to make three visits that would have been impossible under ordinary conditions of travel. I had to travel successively to Paris, to Graz (in Styria) and to Prague, where I was invited by Director Stoklasa, the renowned professor of the young republic of Czechoslovakia.'[59] A European aviation convert in the field of cinematography explained that air travel enabled him to overtake his competitors while keeping to the deadlines that were so crucial in his profession. He also explained that flying made him feel superhuman relative to the 'ant-people' who stayed below, implying not just that they appeared small when viewed from far above, but that the content of their lives was more limited without the advantages of transcendent time–space compression.[60]

Time–space compression through aviation made it possible to contemplate tourism in a new way, as a kind of brief immersion into an alternate world. Already in 1920, a German aviation enthusiast envisioned this kind of 'instant' cultural and environmental transplantation through aviation. He mused that, as soon as even slightly improved aircraft were available,

A veritable Wonderland will then lie before us. We shall be able to take breakfast at 7 a.m. in Berlin, to get into a comfortable airplane cabin at…8 a.m. and sit there in a luxurious club chair, smoking a cigar and

Figure 10.4   Rapid air travel (French air poster, 'Time is Money', 1920s)
Source: Reproduced with permission from the Air France Museum Collection.

reading the morning paper while we glance from time to time at the world below us as we fleet by at the rate of 300 km. p.h.…and the clock will barely have struck two before we shall be sitting at lunch at Tunis, under the burning sun of Africa.[61]

Significantly, the *travel* portion of this imagined trip was a form of non-travel: the passenger merely sat comfortably, read a newspaper and smoked a cigar until lunchtime. He might have been in a gentleman's club in the city. Yet when the passenger arose for lunch, he found himself in a totally different environment. This was a new world of exotic culture for quick consumption. By the end of the 1920s, we begin to see the concept of the two-week vacation to distant lands for busy urbanites made possible by rapid air travel. In an article on 'touristic aviation', a French baron commented: 'in two weeks of vacation, it is possible to reach Lake Chad, visit English Nigeria, hunt elephants there, and get back to your office in Paris.'[62]

Among those who depicted the phenomenon of space–time compression most clearly during our period was the Spanish philosopher Ortega y Gasset, in his iconic work, *Revolt of the Masses*, published in 1930. He observed that compression of space and time was bringing about a greater density of life experiences and a juxtaposition of cultures that was unimaginable in an earlier era:

> This nearness of the far-off, this presence of the absent, has extended…the horizon of each individual existence.…[There is reason for the] worship of mere speed which is at present being indulged in by our contemporaries. Speed…made up of space and time…serves to nullify them.…By annulling them we give them life, we make them serve vital purposes, we can *be* in more places than we could before, enjoy more comings and goings, consume more cosmic time in less vital time.[63]

Ortega y Gasset saw the space–time shift of life and the expansion of its reach as a global trend, with specific implications for European nations, making them increasingly small and provincial.[64] Observing that 'the new methods of transport' had 'nullified' the role of national borders as 'natural frontiers', he argued that Europe's kaleidoscope of borders and nations could no longer be a viable foundation for European politics, intellectual creativity or economic development. The reason was not only that creative projects in this new era could easily extend beyond old borders, but also that they increasingly needed to do so:

> For the first time, the European, checked in his projects, economic, political, intellectual, by the limits of his own country, feels that those projects…are out of proportion to the size of the collective body in which he is enclosed. And so he has discovered that to be English, German, or

French is to be provincial. He has found out that he is 'less' than he was before, for previously the Englishman, the Frenchman, and the German believed, each for himself, that he was the universe.[65]

Europeans, he continued, could no longer 'breathe the air' of their nations because it was 'a confined air', and 'what was before a nation open to all the winds of heaven' was now 'turned into something provincial, an enclosed space.' He concluded that the only way to move beyond this impasse was to construct a larger European nation, and he believed that the 'psychological architecture' needed for this transformation already existed: 'we are more influenced by what is European in us than by what is special to us as Frenchmen, Spaniards, and so on[66].

In calling attention to the disconnect between the small scale of European nations compared with the growing reach of Europeans' creative endeavours, Ortega y Gasset could have pointed to civil aviation as a telling example. So pronounced was the gap between nationalist strategies and the transnational reach and mission of civil aviation that key actors engaged in building Europe's aviation network in the 1920s also developed an integrationist outlook, similar to that of Ortega y Gasset. Jean Brun, who helped to establish a pool among six European airlines (French, German, Dutch, Belgian, Danish and Swedish) in the 1920s, gave a speech in 1928 calling attention to the transnational character of civil aviation and its potential to unite Europe:

> In a few hours aviation overflows frontiers, suppresses national barriers, intensifies people-to-people exchanges, thus revealing itself as the marvelous tool to employ to construct the United States of Europe and this permanent cooperation that we so ardently desire.[67]

Others, focusing on barriers to the development of civil aviation, expressed frustration at Europe's many borders and at petty nationalism that politicized route development and obstructed full implementation of this creative project. In a 1935 talk, Imperial Airways' general manager Harold Burchall asserted that it was

> …probably not too much to say that the future of civilization depends upon moderation of the purely national spirit and upon the development of closer understanding between peoples and races. The essential link in such a bond of understanding is rapid transport. The greater the development of transport, particularly in speed and frequency, the more justified and stronger become such links. Unfortunately, during the last ten years…there has been evidence, in Europe and elsewhere, of extreme nationalism, which has hindered the full development of this new means of transport…and unless this effect of extreme nationalism is moderated,

air transport will become so hampered that the advantages of international air services will be largely discounted.[68]

In the discussion following the talk, one commentator suggested 'taking away the sovereignty of the air from the nations' and 'Europeanising civil aviation' in order to achieve 'the kind of freedom for air transport that was desired'.[69]

A sub-theme that entered Europeanist discourse during these years was the challenge posed by America. Europe's fragmentation and rival nationalisms were felt to be unworkable not only because of the possibilities created by new technology but also because they put it at a disadvantage relative to the United States: a Europe whose projects were always constrained by national jealousies would not be able to keep pace in the world. This concern with the competitive impact of America's large, integrated market was widely discussed within European business, government and intellectual circles in the 1920s and early 1930s. Ortega y Gasset took up the question as well. He argued that if Americans seemed to do more than Europeans and develop new ideas faster, it was only because they did not have to contend with a fragmented space.[70]

Within the world of civil aviation, researchers showed numerically where Europe stood relative to the United States. Enrico Venturini, an Italian engineer working in the area of air traffic management for the airline Società Aerea Mediterranea, presented data in 1936 showing that the average cost to operate a commercial airline in Europe was eighteen francs per kilometre, whereas American airlines cost, on average, less than five francs per kilometre, a three-fold difference. Venturini analysed the reasons for higher European costs: duplication of routes, lack of standardization, inefficiency of the overall network architecture, and lower passenger numbers. What is noteworthy about Venturini's analysis is not only its *European* conceptual framework, but also its concreteness. It attempted to show, directly and numerically, just how much European projects were hindered by unfettered nationalism. The answer came in at thirteen francs per kilometre, making European airline routes 260% more expensive to operate per kilometre than their American counterparts. Analyses like these reinforced a growing view that national rivalries were detrimental to the larger public good of Europeans and ultimately self-destructive.[71]

Air travel, tourism and identity

While many observers complained about the negative consequences of European nationalism for aviation, airlines began to alter the meaning of nationalism and to enlarge identities by promoting air travel – and its destinations – as consumer goods. In doing so, airlines built upon a tradition that linked transportation to a concept of pleasurable mobility.[72] People travel for diverse reasons, many far from pleasant. To promote voluntary travel for non-economic reasons, the travel experience had to be presented as something enjoyable. In the case of air travel, which was still quite expensive in the 1920s, the promotion of air tourism was directed at elites who had other options, since they could travel by car, ship or train, or simply stay home.

Airlines encouraged tourism in part through the propagation of luxury travel standards. Interwar airline posters convey themes of comfort, status and opulence, extending a practice that had evolved since the nineteenth century to promote travel by ships and railways. The great, spacious ocean liners of the 1920s and early 1930s were the undisputed leaders of this trend. They had ballrooms, theatres, swimming pools and luxury suites, and offered elite passengers fine dining and top-flight professional entertainment and music. Railways had much less room to work with, but still created a luxury environment for elite passengers. The various Orient Express services had elegant dining cars with uniformed stewards, smoking cars, and elegantly appointed sleeping cars featuring such touches as wood panelling with intricate marquetry depicting exotic birds and flowers.[73]

Airplanes were at a clear disadvantage relative to ships and railways in their ability to create luxury environments. Early air travel was cramped, noisy, sometimes bumpy and cold, and passengers had to be weighed. Yet airlines attempted to reproduce the standards of first class railway travel as closely as possible. On the Paris–London route, they imitated the standard of service provided by the competing cross-channel train service. In 1923, the French airline serving this route, Air Union, began offering its passengers a 'five course champagne lunch.'[74] In 1927, Air Union and Imperial Airways, the French and British lines that divided this route, introduced competing luxury services named, respectively, the 'Golden Ray' and the 'Silver Wing' service. The latter included a silver-painted plane with matching interior (silver and grey), and special seats with 'comfortable cushions and shoulder and head rests'. Passengers were treated to a buffet lunch with spirits, served by a uniformed steward.[75] A similar luxury service can be seen in a Deutsche Lufthansa postcard from the same period (see Figure 10.5).

Airlines also encouraged tourism by portraying other nations and cultures as desirable, intriguing – worth visiting. Statistically, tourists are strongly deterred by environments known to be dangerous or unpleasant.[76] Most prefer to go where they know they will be able to relax, have fun, see interesting and attractive sights, and get away from the problems, frustrations or dull routine of their lives. Even those who seek new adventures generally want them controlled enough to guarantee pleasure and relaxation. Airline promoters were attuned to tourists' desires. They took pains to portray their destinations in a positive light. Nowhere do cultures and places seem more beckoning, romantic, magical, fun or exotic than on travel posters, and, when linked with depictions of the transcendence of air travel, the results were captivating. With more destinations added to the roster of possible

Figure 10.5   Luxury Service, Deutsche Luft Hansa, Junkers Ju.31, ca. 1928
Source: Reproduced with permission from Lufthansa.

routes over the course of the 1920s, there was a growing marketplace of intriguing, welcoming destinations to be experienced through travel.

The conceptual influence of this kind of travel promotion was to soften nationalism and undermine belief in the moral legitimacy of hegemony, a crucial foundation of imperialism. Travel posters opened up a consumers' view of nations by presenting them not as rivals, enemies or inferiors, but rather as desirable 'others' to be consumed and enjoyed. People moreover began internalizing the messages conveyed by such images. Sociologist John Urry has argued that international tourism fostered 'cosmopolitanism', which he defines as 'an intellectual and aesthetic stance of openness toward divergent experiences from *different* national cultures. There is a search for and delight in contrasts between societies rather than a longing for uniformity or superiority.'[77] Urry sees the emergence of cosmopolitanism – via new forms of transport and the new mobilities they produced – as a defining feature of modernity: 'a modern person is one who...conceives of him or herself as a consumer of other cultures and places.'[78]

Yet tourism was not a ticket to Utopia. Air travel posters and other travel promotion media proffer fantasies; behind their optimistic stereotypes and gloss, international and human relations, and travel itself, are more complex and problematic. Tourism was often used as a tool to reinforce and validate hegemony and imperialism.[79] Showing elite citizens their empire through travel could enhance their sense of cultural superiority and 'ownership'. Tourism could also be used as a licence for excess, to escape moral codes.[80] The dissolute and insensitive tourist, and the rich, pompous, patronizing tourist, are enduring images. On the other side of the coin, however, 'locals' had many ways to take advantage of tourists, make fun of them, express hostility, or otherwise make them feel excluded and unwelcome. The actual experience of travel could also prove disappointing compared with the glossy images, and this was particularly true of air travel in its initial decades. British documentary filmmaker Paul Rotha was miserable after a twelve-week air trip between Karachi and Cape Town in 1932 to make a promotional film about imperial aviation. The film was supposed to 'tell of British civil aviation "Blazing New Highways Between Sun and Earth, Making Fresh Contact Between the Nations and the Empire"', but Rotha

> ...hated the flying. He admired neither the aircraft nor the airline [Imperial Airways], which he was supposed to be showing in a good light. He had to contend with uncomfortable seating and cabin vibration... Time was wasted at customs posts, film was confiscated, hours were frittered away ('a typical Imperials Airways day') waiting for aircraft repairs.... Aircraft shortages obliged overland travel on several occasions... [and] the flora, fauna and landscape of Empire appealed to him more than its people and settlements: he found Baghdad charmless, decaying and dirty; Johannesburg was a gimcrack, exploitative hell-hole.[81]

Tourism has always embodied contradictions, ambiguities and shattered images. Yet acknowledgement of this fact should not lead us to underestimate the discordance between the *utopian* portrayal of nations and cultures that tourism fostered, and the *dystopic* portrayals of other cultures that emanated from European hegemonic ideology. European imperialism destroyed cultures, ignored them as if they did not exist, or perpetuated negative, dehumanizing discourses about them to justify and prolong control. An intimate sense of this discordance can be understood by considering a photograph published in 1920 by Britain's Controller-General of Civil Aviation, Frederick Sykes, to accompany his article on 'Imperial Air Routes' (see Figure 10.6). The illustration, 'Weeding the Aerodrome', shows ten Africans squatting, weeding an airfield, watched by a white colonial overseer. The picture was probably posed (at least the stiff posture of the overseer suggests this), which means that there was intent to show the group in a context of work and submission. Neither the overseer, nor the photographer, nor the aviation bureaucrat appears to care much about the lives or cultural heritage of the weeders; we do not get the impression that their culture would be allowed to interfere with the work of empire. The picture also shows aviation as something imposed on the Africans, with no intent to serve

Figure 10.6   Africans weeding airfield, with overseer, 1920

Source: This image first appeared in Frederick H. Sykes, 'Imperial Air Routes', *Geographical Journal* 55(4) (Apr 1920), and is reproduced with permission.

them. Rather, they are made to serve its needs, as defined by the overseer. Whereas travel literature promoting empire touted *benefits* of imperialism for the peoples it colonized (such as maintaining peace and order, beautifying colonial cities or restoring ancient cultural monuments), this photo conveys a different message, telling us visually that the purpose of empire is not to help the people it colonizes, but to control and exploit them. It is a dehumanizing, arrogant image, far removed from the world of the travel posters. It is true that travel publicity propagated simplified cultural stereotypes, but their subjects were not represented in a way that denied them any culture or that was dehumanizingly negative. In the simplified emotional world of good and bad, travel posters sought to portray other cultures as 'good'.

Beyond the softer, more positive view of cultural diversity that tourism encouraged, new patterns of tourist travel also reshaped perspectives on nationalism and promoted a wider sense of community. To explain this point, it is helpful to draw a parallel with Benedict Anderson's analysis in *Imagined Communities*. Exploring links between mobility and ideas of community, Anderson observed that the patterns of religious pilgrims' movements delineated the geographical extent of their community. He posited a link between the mobility patterns of colonial bureaucrats as they were dispatched and reassigned from place to place over the course of their careers, and the growth of a sense of community and nationalism among them, as their paths crossed and re-crossed over the years.[82] A similar idea can be applied to tourist mobilities. The expansion of inter-European tourism by air, railway, ship and automobile, and the growing association of tourism with positive images of cultural diversity, supported integrationist thinking. Visiting one another's home territories with growing frequency made European nations seem more closely linked, compatible and co-operative.

Count Richard Coudenhove-Kalergi, doyen of interwar promoters of European integration, embraced a Europeanist identity rooted in travel. His memoirs link pleasurable mobility with a sense of community, imagining a new and more expansive European nation. A wealthy, humanist aristocrat, Coudenhove-Kalergi spent a good portion of his time in the 1920s and early 1930s – some four months a year – travelling around Europe, 'generally within the large triangle contained between Stockholm, Constantinople and Cadiz'.[83] 'Avoiding the main roads', he 'gradually and without any set plan' became 'familiar with the lesser-known parts of Europe':

> There, off the beaten track, we talked to ordinary men of no set political views. Invariably we came to speak of Pan-Europe, a Europe as peaceful as Switzerland and as wealthy as the United States.[84]

Coudenhove-Kalergi described himself as 'a European patriot' who was 'filled with a boundless love for this great continent and determined to fight to the end for its ... unification'.[85]

European aviation, nationalism and identity: The balance in 1933

The creators, regulators, users, propagandists and theorists of civil aviation in interwar Europe linked it to competing national and international visions. Agents of hegemonic nationalism wanted civil aviation to support national interests and enhance colonial access and control. Imperialists like Sykes, who saw Egypt as the 'Clapham Junction' of the British Empire's air network, were not interested in integrating Europe through civil aviation. Yet some believed this technology should be used to build a more cohesive European space. Aviation professionals like Burchall (Imperial Airways), Brun (IATA) and Venturini (Società Aerea Mediterranea) championed this goal in speeches, reports and statistics, and adopted practical measures to work toward it. At the same time, transport publicity created alluring visions of European and world cultures to promote pleasurable travel, and leisure mobility in turn fostered transnational, cosmopolitan identities, whether

European or global. Coudenhove-Kalergi's travels throughout Europe made him feel more European.

The immediate experience of air travel also had the potential to reshape identity. Aviation network users – pilots and passengers – felt transformed by the time–space compression that this new technology made possible. For some professionals and business people, air travel allowed them to become more European *in practice*, through altered mobility patterns. Although most of these users did not leave records that would enable us to know if their new mobility made them feel more European, theorists of the period, like Ortega y Gasset, argued that this was happening. He believed faster travel contributed to a growing view of European nation states as provincial confines rather than as the quintessence of human culture and affinity, and he argued that the foundations of a European identity already existed. Altered mobility could promote global more than European identity, as with Saint-Exupéry. Yet what is most important about interwar civil aviation is not the final tally of identity changes, but rather the way diverse actors began discussing the themes of mobility and time–space compression in relation to identity, nationalism, and European and global integration.

On balance, however, civil aviation's nationalist foundations remained dominant throughout this era. The new networks and mobilities that civil aviation fostered did not negate or fundamentally transform the influence of hegemonic nationalism in European politics and international affairs. Nation states impeded the growth of a cohesive European network by spending enormous sums on colonial routes and by political obstructionism that hindered European air network development. The regime of national sovereignty over airspace meant that international air routes in Europe emerged ad hoc, with no overarching plan or system of regulation. The resulting network did not provide cohesive, balanced coverage and service throughout Europe. Only Germany, within the context of the Allied prohibition on its military aviation, began seriously developing a domestic air network with an associated set of inter-European connections.

Apart from the power of nation states to control use of their airspace and regulate civil aviation, there were two other main reasons for the comparative weakness of Europeanism and co-operative transnationalism in interwar aviation. First, few Europeans travelled by air. The number of passengers carried annually on French airlines grew from under 10,000 in the early 1920s to around 37,000 in 1932.[86] Given the population of France (around 40 million in 1926), this meant a ratio of air travellers to population of less than 0.1%. To gain some perspective on this figure, it is worth noting that, in 2004, more than 75 million air travellers passed through the two main Parisian airports, Charles de Gaulle and Orly, giving a ratio of air travellers to population in the order of 125%[87]. Of course these travellers were not all French, either in 2004 or in the 1920s, but the statistical comparison does show the enormous increase in air mobility that has occurred since the interwar years. And since Europeans in the 1920s by and large did not travel by air, the altered space and time barriers that aviation permitted did not affect them. For most Europeans, transnational perspectives or the possibility of time–space compression through rapid travel could not have had much relevance for their daily lives. And with so few people travelling by air, there was no popular political pressure to change the existing regime of airspace governance and network development.

The other reason why Europeanism in aviation remained muted in this period is because the integration that did occur remained largely invisible to the public. Organizations like IATA did their work behind the scenes – it was known within the aviation community but was not vaunted widely in the public sphere through newspapers, books and so on. The aeronautical industry was also international behind the scenes. Aircraft builders and aeronautical engineers understood the international character of scientific and technological development in their field, but this reality was not readily visible to a general public who saw Handley-Page aircraft in England, Fokker in the Netherlands, Junkers in Germany, Potez in France or Savoia Marchetti in Italy.[88] And second-tier nations in Europe who could not produce their own aircraft were not obliged to advertise the fact. Governments, despite continual international negotiations to establish international and imperial air routes, often downplayed the transnational content of this work, or newspapers spun it to emphasize national accomplishments or impediments thereto. Integration also remained hidden because some of the specific forms it took – such as the use of air travel to develop and maintain transnational European business networks – were not immediately perceived to be part of an integration process.

In contrast to the muted and limited impact of transnationalism and Europeanism, nationalism formed a powerful, highly visible bond with civil aviation that grew in strength during this era. First, there was a movement in the 1920s and early 1930s toward the establishment of visibly national airlines. The development of Air France provides a case in point. It was formed during the depths of the Depression from five airlines that previously had non-nationalistic names and images: Air Union, Aéropostale, Air Orient, CIDNA, and Lignes Farman (Société Générale de Transports Aériens). With the growing world economic crisis of the early 1930s, these airlines found it difficult or impossible to survive, even with government subsidies. Aéropostale, the famous line on which Saint-Exupéry worked, had already filed for bankruptcy before the Air France merger was arranged. With the merger, the new airline took a national name, and the state became a stakeholder with a 25% share in the company. The inauguration of Air France was a highly publicized national affair presided over in a ceremony at Le Bourget airport in Paris by the French Minister of Aviation, Pierre Cot.[89]

Everywhere in Europe, nationalist forces appropriated aviation as a unifying national symbol. Mussolini and his followers encouraged a veritable cult of aviation nationalism.[90] In France, beyond the creation of Air France, even Saint-Exupéry was treated as a national hero, his successes in writing and aviation portrayed as examples of national spirit and greatness, even though the message he sought to convey was a plea for global humanism. In Germany, although transnationalism was employed as a strategy to build civil aviation in the early 1920s, when the country was a pariah state under the restrictions of Versailles, the domestic airline network that resulted further integrated the *national* economy. In the words of a British observer of the period, 'Every increase in the speed of transport amounts to a reduction in distance, therefore in a sense [Germany] has shrunk to a fraction of its original size; administration has been facilitated, and there has been a general speeding up in internal commercial intercourse.'[91] In the 1930s, Hitler and the Nazi party used this domestic airline network as a tool of political mobilization. Hitler made extensive use of air travel in the election campaign of 1932, in which the Nazis became the single largest party in the Reichstag. And after the Nazis took power, tailfins on Lufthansa's aircraft were painted with swastikas. The Nazi regime likewise transformed Berlin's airport, Tempelhof, 'from a symbol of efficiency in air transport...to a symbol of Nazi grandeur'.[92] Such symbolism is caught forever in the opening scene of Leni Riefenstahl's propaganda film, *Triumph of the Will*, which shows an airplane carrying Hitler descending from the clouds over Nuremburg.

In the 1920s and 1930s, European governments simply held the best cards when it came to aviation. They alone could approve the terms and limits of national airspace and foreign use of that airspace, they alone had the funds to keep civil airlines afloat, they (through subsidies and legislation) ultimately determined the balance between imperial, domestic and European airline network development, and they also controlled the whole of military aviation and the balance between civil and military aviation. The technical limits of commercial aviation in this period did not permit the formation of a counterweight to aviation nationalism, because they restricted air travel to a tiny minority of Europeans. Air tourism (and international tourism generally) remained little more than a dream in the 1920s for most Europeans. International organizations like the League of Nations lacked an effective power base in the day-to-day world of international affairs, as did integrationist groups like Coudenhove-Kalergi's Pan-Europa movement, which appealed to a minority of elites and intellectuals. International European organizations like IATA had a more practical role in the 1920s. IATA had the backing of powerful groups in society (notably businessmen and engineers). And, while such groups saw in aviation (and other technologies) a vehicle to build a European community beyond the nation state, the conditions for such a transformation did not exist. Their organizations had less political strength and fewer resources than the numerous and diverse institutions supporting nationalist priorities. In 1933, hegemonic nationalism was still king, and in some ways civil aviation had made it stronger.

Notes

I am grateful to the Social Sciences and Humanities Research Council of Canada for supporting the research for this paper.

1. The nation-building aspect of transport technology has been explored notably in relation to railways and aviation. See, for example, Eugen Weber, *Peasants into Frenchmen: The Modernization of Rural France* (Stanford University Press 1976); Pierre Berton, *The National Dream: The Great Railway, 1871–1881* (Toronto: McClelland and Stewart 1970); Rudolph Daniels, *Trains Across the Continent* (Indiana University Press 2000); Peter Fritzsche, *A Nation of Fliers: German Aviation and the Popular Imagination* (Cambridge: Harvard University Press 2002); Guillaume de Syon, *Zeppelin! Germany and the Airship, 1900–1939* (Baltimore and London: Johns Hopkins 2002); Bernhard Rieger, *Technology and the Culture of Modernity in Britain and Germany* (Cambridge: Cambridge University Press 2005).

2. See, for example, Debra Johnson and Colin Turner, *Trans-European Networks: The Political Economy of Integrating Europe's Infrastructure* (Macmillan 1997), which asserts transportation systems to be a crucial tool of European integration. The theme of transportation technology as an engine of integration is also a pervasive theme in the burgeoning literature on globalization. See, for example, Bruce Mazlish and Akira Iriye (eds), *The Global History Reader* (New York and London: Routledge 2005); David Held *et al.*, *Global Transformation: Politics, Economics and Culture* (Stanford: Stanford University Press 1999); Jeffrey A. Frieden, *Global Capitalism: Its Fall and Rise in the Twentieth Century* (New York and London: W.W. Norton 2006); Frank J. Lechner and John Boli (eds), *The Globalization Reader*, 2nd edn (Oxford: Blackwell Publishing 2004).

3. On the concept of hidden integration, see Thomas J. Misa and Johan Schot, 'Inventing Europe: Technology and the Hidden Integration of Europe', *History and Technology* 21(1) (2005), pp. 1–19.

4. Geza Szurovy, *The Art of the Airways* (St Paul, Minnesota: Zenith Press 2002), p. 28.

5. The term comes from E. J. Hobsbawm, *Nations and Nationalism since 1780: Programme, Myth, Reality* (Cambridge: Cambridge University Press 1990), p. 122.

6. On theories of imperialism see Wolfgang J. Mommsen, *Theories of Imperialism*, trans. P. S. Falla (Chicago: University of Chicago Press 1977); Harrison M. Wright (ed.) *The 'New Imperialism': Analysis of Late Nineteenth-Century Expansion*, 2nd edn (Lexington, Massachussets: D.C. Heath 1976); Robin W. Winks (ed.), *British Imperialism: Gold, God, Glory* (New York: Holt, Rinehart and Winston 1963).

7. Paul Kennedy, *The Rise and Fall of the Great Powers* (1987; rpt. New York: Vintage Books 1989), p. 196.

8. E. J. Hobsbawm, *The Age of Empire: 1875 and 1914* (London: Weidenfeld and Nicolson 1987), p. 160; see also *Nations and Nationalism since 1780*, pp. 121–2, 141–3.

9. Hobson explained that the 'debasement of this genuine nationalism, by attempts to overflow its natural banks and absorb the near or distant territory of reluctant and unassimilable peoples,...marks the passage from nationalism to a spurious colonialism on the one hand, Imperialism on the other', J.A. Hobson, *Imperialism: A Study* (1938; rpt. Ann Arbor: University of Michigan Press 1967), p. 6. Interestingly, although Hobson is usually credited solely with an economic theory of imperialism, he discussed the interaction between imperialism and nationalism in the book's opening chapter, the latter appropriately entitled 'Nationalism and Imperialism' (pp. 3–13). For other scholars who have explored this connection, see Mommsen, *Theories of Imperialism* and Wright, *The 'New Imperialism.'*

10. An insightful case study that traces the interaction between nationalism and imperialism in late nineteenth-century Italy is Giuseppe Finaldi, 'Culture and Imperialism in a "Backward" Nation? The Prima Guerra d'Africa (1885–96) in Italian Primary Schools', *Journal of Modern Italian Studies* 8(3) (2003), pp. 374–90.

11. Quoted from J.S. Corum, 'The Myth of Air Control: Reassessing the History', *Aerospace Power Journal* 14(4) (2000), pp. 61–77.

12. Ibid.

13. Bernhard Rieger, *Technology and the Culture of Modernity in Britain and Germany, 1890–1945* (Cambridge: Cambridge University Press 2005), p. 233. Rieger's study offers a brilliant comparative analysis of aviation nationalism in Britain and Germany.

14. The story of the restrictions on German airspace and aviation is unfortunately not discussed in Margaret MacMillan, *Paris 1919* (New York: Random House 2001). It can be traced through articles in the *Times* (London). Some information is also provided in S.W. Buxton, 'Freedom of Transit in the Air: The Present Position and How It Has Been Reached', *Economica* 16 (March 1926), pp. 49–57.

15. H. Burchall, 'The Politics of International Air Routes', *International Affairs* 14(1) (1936), p. 91. See also the discussion in Buxton, 'Freedom of Transit'.

16. 'Text of a White Paper Presented by the Secretary of State for Air to Parliament, October, 1944', PICAO (Provisional International Civil Aviation Organization) Air Transport Committee, 1945–47, Box 1, Documents, Minutes, etc., First Session, 1945, ICAO (International Civil Aviation Organization) Archives, Montreal, Canada.

17. Erwin Seago and Victor E. Furman, 'Internal Consequences of International Air Regulations', *University of Chicago Law Review* 12(4) (June 1945), p. 334. Although these Chicago lawyers were discussing the 1944 Chicago Convention on International Civil Aviation, they explained that the later convention 'continued' the regime of absolute airspace sovereignty, and did not change the existing system codified in the Paris Convention.

18. Peter Fritzsche, *A Nation of Fliers: German Aviation and the Popular Imagination* (Cambridge, Mass.: Harvard University Press 1992) examines the link between aviation and nationalism in Germany in some depth. Another important work that addresses this topic is Robert Wohl, *The Spectacle of Flight: Aviation and the Western Imagination, 1920–1950* (New Haven: Yale University Press 2005).

19. W. Joynson-Hicks, 'Development of Flying', *The Times* (1 February 1919), p. 6.

20. For the period under consideration, 1919–33, information on the aircraft used by each airline can be traced annually through successive editions of *Jane's All the World's Aircraft*.

21. Jacques Mortane, 'Le patriotisme des moteurs', *L'Air* 7(127) (15 February 1925).

22. Discussion on the paper of H. Burchall, 'The Politics of International Air Routes', *International Affairs* 14(1) (1935), pp. 106.

23. The symbiosis between civil and military aviation and aviation's tie to militant nationalism in Britain are explored in two books by David Edgerton: *England and the Aeroplane: An Essay on a Militant and Technological Nation* (Houndmills, Basingstoke, Hampshire: Macmillan 1991); and *Warfare State: Britain 1920–1970* (Cambridge: Cambridge University Press 2006).

24. Ministère de l'Air, *L'Aéronautique militaire, maritime, coloniale et marchande* (Paris: M. & J. de Brunoff, 1931), pp. 164–5. Istanbul was still frequently called Constantinople during the interwar period.

25. The early history of CIDNA is recounted in Alexandre Herlea, 'The First Transcontinental airline: Franco-Roumaine, 1920–1925' in William F. Trimble (ed.) *From Airships to Airbus: The History of Civil and Commercial Aviation*, Vol. 2 (Washington, DC: Smithsonian Institution Press 1995), pp. 53–64. CIDNA was one of six private French airline companies that merged under government auspices in 1933 to form Air France.

26. The theme of aviation as a tool of empire and colonial management was extensively developed in this period. See Robert McCormack, 'Airlines and Empires: Great Britain and the "Scramble for Africa," 1919–1939', *Canadian Journal of African Studies* 10(1) (1976), pp. 87–105. See also H. Burchall, 'Air Services in Africa', *Journal of the Royal African Society* 32(126) (January 1933), pp. 55–73; P.R.C. Groves, 'The Influence of Aviation on International Relations', *Journal of the Royal Institute of International Affairs* 6(3) (May 1927), pp. 133–52; P.R.C. Groves, 'The Influence of Aviation on International Affairs', *Journal of the Royal Institute of International Affairs* 8(4) (July 1929), pp. 289–317. Burchall was a managing director of Imperial Airways. Groves, retired from the RAF in 1922 (rank: Brigadier General), was editor of *Air* (1927–9). He was also Associate Fellow Royal Aeronautical Society and Honorary Secretary General of the Air League of the British Empire.

27. R.E.G. Davies, *A History of the World's Airlines* (London: Oxford University Press 1964), pp. 59–60. This remains the best general history of European airlines for this period.

28. Frederick H. Sykes, 'Imperial Air Routes', *The Geographical Journal* 55(4) (April 1920), p. 262.

29. *Jane's All the World's Aircraft* (London: Sampson Low, Marston and Co. 1925), p. 98a.

30. Davies, *History of the World's Airlines*, p. 60.

31. Lucien Marchis (ed.), *Vingt cinq ans d'aéronautique française*, Vol. 2 (Paris: Chambre syndicale des industries aéronautiques 1934), p. 1,085.

32. 'World Air Routes. Future of Civil Flying. Competition Among the Nations', *Times (London)* 22 August 1923, pp. 9–10.

33. Marchis, *Vingt cinq ans d'aéronautique française*, Vol. 2, p. 1,088.

34. Davies, *History of the World's Airlines*, pp. 72–3.

35. 'L'Aéronautique au Parlement: M. Raymond Poincaré s'explique à la Chambre sur les incidents franco-allemands', *L'Air* 5(98) (1 December 1923), pp. 15–16; 'La question du survol de l'Allemagne', *L'Air* 5(99) (15 December 1923), pp. 13–14; M. Oger, 'Les relations franco-allemandes', *L'Air* 7(126) (1 February 1925), p. 12

36. 'Signor Mussolini's Air Plans: Italian Dreams', *The Times* (26 January 1923), p. 9.

37. Christer Johsson, 'Sphere of Flying: The Politics of International Aviation', *International Organization* 35(2) (Spring 1981), p. 279.

38. Burchall, 'Politics of International Air Routes', p. 103.

39. P.R.C. Groves, 'Our Future in the Air. The Danger from Germany', *Times (London)* (22 March 1922), p. 13.

40. 'German Air "Combine." Austrian and Danish Companies Included', *Times (London)* (6 October 1920), p. 11.

41. In fact the downfall of Junkers was orchestrated by the German government in the wake of the Locarno agreements that halted the political exclusion of Germany and that led Germany to withdraw from its co-operative relationship with the USSR. Junkers was a victim of this shift because he was technically the owner of an aircraft factory in the USSR that had been built with loans provided

by the German government, and Germany suddenly demanded payment of the loans from the company.

42. On IATA, see Ralph S. Cohen, *IATA: The First Three Decades* (Montréal: IATA 1949). Information on routes operated as pools is widely scattered, in part because airlines were reluctant to publicize this information. Interwar political scientist Laurence C. Tombs commented in *International Organization in European Air Transport* (New York: Columbia University Press 1936) that 'not even a list of the existing pools has been published by governments, by the International Air Traffic Association, or by the individual companies with are parties to the pools' (p. 35). Also, airlines preferred not to reveal the precise content of pooling arrangements when the Communications and Transit Organization of the League of Nations requested such information in 1933. A full pool involved operating an international route jointly, regulating the number of flights and ticket charges over the route, and sharing revenues from it, based on shares of passenger-miles and cargo-miles flown. There were also partial pools and more limited forms of co-operation. For example, the London–Paris route does not appear to have been pooled, but passenger fares and schedules were agreed to in common by the French and British airlines provided service on the route for at least part of the interwar period. Tombs compiled a list of twenty-nine European airline routes that operated as full pools, all involving IATA members. *Jane's All the World's Aircraft* (1926), p. 52a reports that Lufthansa planned that year to operate a number of lines 'on the pool system'. Further information on international pools and co-operation can be found in newspaper articles in the *Times (London)*, particularly in the years 1925–8. See also *Summary and Background Material on International Ownership and Operation of World Air Transport Services, Compiled by John Cooper*, Edwin G. Baetjer II Memorial Conference, Princeton, New Jersey, 23–24 October 1948 (available at the library of the Smithsonian Institution's National Air and Space Museum), and the *Aircraft Year Book* for the years 1923, pp. 185–6; 1924, pp. 182–3, 195, 197; *1925*, pp. 140–2, 144–5, 166; *1926*, pp. 137–8, 158–9; *1927*, p. 168; *1928*, pp. 201, 214–15; *1930*, p. 275; *1931*, p. 248. Information is also provided in Marchis, *Vingt cinq ans d'aéronautique française*, Vol. 2, passim.

43. For example, Germany, France, Britain, Holland, Denmark, Switzerland, Austria, Italy, Belgium and Czechoslovakia all subsidized civil aviation in this period.

44. Davies.

45. Junkers also established an airline in Persia in the late 1920s, but it ceased operation in 1932, while Deutsche Lufthansa established an airline network in China in the 1930s that it hoped to link it to Germany. See Davies, p. 118.

46. *Jane's All the World's Aircraft* lists all scheduled, commercial flights, yearly, throughout the 1920s, but no links with Portugal, Ireland, Manchester or Bordeaux are indicated. I also found no evidence for such links through analysis of aviation journals of the period. Airline network maps of the period also reveal no links with these destinations. Further study may reveal that some links existed, but these evidently did not take the form of regularly scheduled, commercial airline flights.

47. Thomas J. Misa and Johan Schot, 'Inventing Europe: Technology and the Hidden Integration of Europe', *History and Technology* 21(1) (2005), pp. 1–19.

48. Ralph S. Cohen, *IATA: The First Three Decades* (Montréal: IATA 1949).

49. Ibid., 'The Ins and Outs of IATA: Improving the Role of the United States in the Regulation of International Air Fares', *Yale Law Journal* 81(6) (May 1972),

pp. 1105–13. In 1938, Pan American – the only international airline that operated in the United States – joined IATA as its first non-European member.

50. The average cruising altitudes of commercial aircraft in the 1920s (600–1500 m) were of course far below the altitude records set during this era. For example, in 1923, an altitude record of 8,200 m was achieved with the French-built SPAD 56. See http://www.centennialofflight.gov/essay/Aerospace/Bleriot/Aero47.htm. (accessed 11 March 2006). Aircraft capabilities can be traced most comprehensively through the yearly editions of *Jane's All the World's Aircraft* for the 1920s.

51. Characteristics of Junkers planes are described in R.E.G. Davies, *Lufthansa: An Airline and Its Aircraft* (New York: Orion Books 1991). See also Horst Zoeller's 'Hugo Junkers Homepage', which has very detailed information on Junkers aircraft: http://hugojunkers.pytalhost.com/ju_home.htm (accessed 11 March 2006). See also *Jane's All the World's Aircraft* for the 1920s.

52. Enrico Venturini, 'Théorie et réalité en Europe et en Amérique', *Revue aéronautique internationale* (18) (December 1935), p. 434.

53. Antoine de Saint-Exupéry, *Wind, Sand, and Stars*, trans. Lewis Galantière (New York: Reynal & Hitchcock 1939), pp. 97–9. A review of St-Exupéry's life story shows that he lived his vision – a transnational, global life that brought him a wife from South America, and work and travel all over the world.

54. Ibid., pp. 294–5.

55. Antoine de Saint-Exupéry, *Oeuvres complèts*, Vol. I (Paris: Gallimard 1994), pp. lxxxvii, 113–15.

56. Heinhard Steiger, 'From the International Law of Christianity to the International Law of the World Citizen – Reflections on the Formation of the Epochs of the History of International Law', *Journal of the History of International Law* 3 (2001), pp. 180–93. See also Jo-Anne Pemberton, 'New Worlds for Old: the League of Nations in the Age of Electricity', *Review of International Studies* 28 (2002), pp. 311–36.

57. 'L'Aviation commerciale jugée par les principaux intéressés: les voyageurs', *L'Air*, Special Issue, L'aéronautique française en 1926.

58. Henry Serrano Villard and Willis M. Allen, Jr., *Looping the Loop: Posters of Flight* (San Diego: Kales Press 2000); Geza Szurovy, *The Art of the Airways*.

59. Refer note 57

60. Ibid.

61. W. Wronsky, 'Commercial Aviation in Germany: Past and Future', trans. by the National Advisory Committee for Aeronautics from *Der Luftweg* 50–1 (February 1921), pp. 6–9, p. 4 of translation.

62. Baron de Foucaucourt, 'L'Aviation touristique', *La Belle France*, numéro hors série – special, 'Ailes françaises,' (8 Novembre 1936), n.p.

63. José Ortega y Gasset, *The Revolt of the Masses* (1930; New York: W.W. Norton, 1932, 1960), pp. 38–9.

64. Gasset, *The Revolt of the Masses*, pp. 38–9.

65. Gasset, *The Revolt of the Masses*, p. 149.

66. Gasset, *The Revolt of the Masses*, p. 180.

67. *Icare: revue de l'aviation française*, 82, 'Les Lignes Farman', p. 54.

68. Burchall, 'The Politics of International Air Routes', p. 89.

69. Ibid., p. 104.

70. Ortega y Gasset, *Revolt of the Masses*, pp. 149–50.

71. Enrico Venturini, 'Théorie et réalité en Europe et en Amérique', pp. 431–2.

72. See John Urry, *Consuming Places* (London and New York: Routledge 1995).

73. Melvin Maddocks, *The Great Liners*, Vol. 4 of *The Seafarers* (Alexandria: Time-Life Books 1978); Jean Des Cars and Jean-Paul Caracalla, *The Orient Express: A Century of Railway Adventures*, trans. George Behrend (London: Bloomsbury Books 1988); Szurovy, *The Art of the Airways*; Villard and Allen, *Looping the Loop: Posters of Flight*.
74. Szurovy, *The Art of the Airways*.
75. '"Silver Wing" Air Travel. New Service of Imperial Airways', *Times (London)* (18 April 1927), p. 7.
76. See, for example, Eric Neumayer, 'The Impact of Political Violence on Tourism Dynamic Cross-National Estimation', *Journal of Conflict Resolution* 48(2) (2004), pp. 259–81; M.A. Clements and A. Georgiou, 'The Impact of Political Instability on a Fragile Tourism Product', *Tourism Management* 19(3) (1998), pp. 283–8.
77. Urry, *Consuming Places*, p. 167.
78. Urry, p. 165.
79. How Europeans developed and controlled the portrayals of the cultures they colonized – how they used discourse as a tool of hegemony – is the central theme, of course, of Edward Said's *Orientalism* (New York: Vintage Books 1979). See also his later work, *Culture and Imperialism* (New York: Vintage Books 1993).
80. Furlough, *'Une leçon des choses'*. A unique and fascinating portrayal of the undersides of the cross-cultural history of European tourism to Egypt is Fayza Hassan, 'A Betrayal of History', *Al-Ahram Weekly Online* 462 (30 December 1999 – 5 January 2000), available at http://weekly.ahram.org.eg/1999/462/fayza.htm (accessed 11 March 2006).
81. Gordon H. Pirie, 'Cinema and British Imperial Civil Aviation, 1919–1939', *Historical Journal of Film* 23(2) (2003), p. 123.
82. Anderson, *Imagined Communities: Reflections on the Origin and Spread of Nationalism*, rev. edn (London and New York: Verso 1983), pp. 53–6.
83. Richard Coudenhove-Kalergi, *An Idea Conquers the World* (London: Hutchinson 1953), p. 134. Coudenhove-Kalergi apparently did not like to travel by plane during the interwar period. He mainly discusses travel by train, ship and automobile. However, he was sensitive to the ways in which aviation was reshaping Europe. For example, he wrote in 1939 that Britain was 'obliged to stick to Europe because history forces her to do so as the result of a new technical development'. This was the airplane, and, according to Coudenhove-Kalergi, 'by the invention of the aeroplane, England ceased to be an island from the strategic point of view.' He also believed that aviation and long-distance communication required a worldwide system of standard time, and he thought about how such a system should be designed. See his article 'Europe To-Morrow', *International Affairs* 18(5) (1939), p. 623; and *An Idea Conquers the World*, pp. 235–6.
84. *An Idea Conquers the World*, pp. 139–40.
85. Ibid., p. 122.
86. Lucien Marchis (ed.), *Vingt cinq ans d'aéronautique française*, Vol. 2, plates.
87. Aéroports de Paris, *Rapport annuel 2004*, p. 11.
88. For example, the British aircraft designer Handley Page criticized a speech by British Secretary of State for Air Guest, saying that he disapproved of Guest's 'belittling of foreign designs and activities'. See *Times (London*, (9 February 1922), p. 5.
89. The best general source for the history of French civil aviation is the historical review *Icare*, which has published volumes (sometimes multiple volumes) on each of the early airlines as well as Air France. They are profusely illustrated, with much useful information.

90. See the revealing analysis of Robert Wohl in *The Spectacle of Flight: Aviation and the Western Imagination, 1920–1950* (New Haven: Yale University Press 2005), pp. 49–107.
91. P.R.C. Groves, 'The Influence of Aviation on International Relations', *Journal of the Royal Institute of International Affairs* 6(3) (May 1927), p. 138.
92. Hans-Joachim Braun, 'The Airport as Symbol: Air Transport and Politics at Berlin-Tempelhof, 1923–1948' in William M. Leary (ed.) *From Airships to Airbus: The History of Civil and Commercial Aviation*, Vol. 1 (Washington, DC: Smithsonian Institution Press 1995), pp. 45, 50.

Index